COMRADES MARATHON
The Ultimate Human Race

To Diana
Best wishes
[signature]
27.5.11

Best wishes
Tony Malone

COMRADES MARATHON
The Ultimate Human Race

John Cameron-Dow

PENGUIN BOOKS

PENGUIN BOOKS

Published by the Penguin Group
Penguin Books (South Africa) (Pty) Ltd, 24 Sturdee Avenue,
Rosebank, Johannesburg 2196, South Africa
Penguin Group (USA) Inc, 375 Hudson Street, New York, New York 10014, USA
Penguin Group (Canada), 90 Eglinton Avenue East, Suite 700, Toronto,
Ontario, Canada M4P 2Y3 (a division of Pearson Penguin Canada Inc)
Penguin Books Ltd, 80 Strand, London WC2R 0RL, England
Penguin Ireland, 25 St Stephen's Green, Dublin 2, Ireland (a division of Penguin Books Ltd)
Penguin Group (Australia), 250 Camberwell Road, Camberwell, Victoria 3124,
Australia (a division of Pearson Australia Group Pty Ltd)
Penguin Books India Pvt Ltd, 11 Community Centre,
Panchsheel Park, New Delhi – 110 017, India
Penguin Group (NZ), 67 Apollo Drive, Rosedale, Auckland 0632,
New Zealand (a division of Pearson New Zealand Ltd)

Penguin Books (South Africa) (Pty) Ltd, Registered Offices:
24 Sturdee Avenue, Rosebank, Johannesburg 2196, South Africa

www.penguinbooks.co.za

First published by Penguin Books (South Africa) (Pty) Ltd 2011

ISBN 978-0-14-352792-3

Typeset by Nix Design in Adove Garamond
Cover by Publicide
Printed and bound by CTP Printers, Cape Town

The use of the official Comrades logo with kind permission
from the Comrades Marathon Association

In Memory of Gavin Rennie

CONTENTS

Acknowledgements

On 26 April 2003, I was asked by the CEO of the Comrades Marathon Association to write the official history of the world's greatest road race. What an honour! What a responsibility! I wish to express my heartfelt gratitude to the CMA for the mandate and for the confidence they placed in me.

Taking over the role as Comrades historian from Morris Alexander was a daunting task. In true Comrades style, Morris did his utmost to assist me and I thank him for graciously inviting me to utilise his superb book *The Comrades Marathon Story* as my primary reference work. A visit to the home of Morris and his charming wife Huibrecht provided one of my personal highlights in 2010.

Virtually from its inception, Comrades has been well served by those who appreciate the importance of historical records. Vernon Jones played a major role in earlier days. Barry Varty has been a most able successor and has been a tremendous help to me. Mick and Cheryl Winn, telephonically, by e-mail and at a little tête-à-tête we enjoyed at the Cape Town Waterfront, emphasised the importance of preserving the unique culture of the event, which owes much to their inspirational leadership during the race's most expansive period.

So many people have provided material, insight, encouragement, even opportunity. It would be impossible to faithfully record all contributions.

Instead, I endeavor to mention as many as possible of those who have given valuable assistance (in no particular order): Mike Bath, Richard Santrucek, Dave Jack, Tommy Malone, Jackie and Margie Mekler, Alan Robb, Bruce Fordyce, Barbara Puttick, Andy McKissock, Jonathan Basckin, Dr David Basckin, Prof. Tim Noakes, Harold Berman, Katia Jones, Chet Sainsbury, Dave Dixon, Clive Crawley, Peter Proctor, Chris Middlebrook, Gary Boshoff and Sian Theron. Special gratitude is expressed to Bruce Fordyce for his generous foreword; to Mr and Mrs Eric Clapham for providing fresh insight into the founding role of Eric's father Vic; and to Billy McNeil and Jock Stein for making 1967 a memorable year for a fallen Comrade.

The Comrades Marathon rightfully enjoys support from all sections of the media: radio, television, national and regional press, magazines etc. Without singling out any contributor, I thank all for their coverage of the great race and for the material made available through their activities.

An eight-year-long enterprise demands a great deal of administrative and secretarial support. I thank Rosemary, Christopher and Catherine Cameron-Dow for their long hours and sterling efforts.

Publication of a book of this nature requires the highest level of professionalism. Working with Penguin Books has been an absolute joy. I express my sincere appreciation to Alison Lowry, Lisa Treffry-Goatley, Reneé Naudé, Amelia de Vaal, Ziel Bergh, Gillian Spain, Candice Wiggett and Kelly Cowan. In addition, I wish to pay special tribute to Paul Wise and Sean Falconer for the microscopic attention to detail and noteworthy sensitivity with which they edited the manuscript.

To those whose names have been inadvertently omitted, I offer my sincere apology and assure you that your contribution is greatly appreciated.

John Cameron-Dow

Foreword

Why another book on the Comrades Marathon?

In my opinion there could never be enough books written on this extraordinary event. It can inspire ordinary people to do extraordinary things, and it brings out the best in all of us. I had a girlfriend who teased me with the suggestion that I run Comrades every year because I am not particularly fond of myself. Once a year, however, the 90-kilometre pilgrimage restores my self-esteem. She may or may not have been correct in her informal psychological assessment, but she was absolutely right to believe that this race has a power to transform, to inspire and to motivate unlike any other. What other event so inspires ordinary people to become athletes for a day and compete against themselves to conquer themselves and a brutal course?

To the dispassionate observer, however, this may seem a reasonable question, given that several books and many articles have been written over the years on this unique event. Most notable have been Morris Alexander's two updated editions of his 1966 classic, *The Comrades Marathon Story*.

The obvious answer is that 25 years have now passed since Alexander's book was last published, and it is time for an update and a fresh look at the race. And this race of ours has become so woven into the rich tapestry of the history of this country and into the collective consciousness of all South Africans over the past 25 years that it needed someone in harmony with the transformation of the country to cope with the task. So someone had to be approached to provide a comprehensive and accurate record of the Comrades Marathon, and in so doing take over the position of historical authority from Morris Alexander. In addition, the author would have to be sensitive enough to inspire all those who have been touched by the Comrades Marathon.

My friend John Cameron-Dow is eminently qualified on all counts. He is a successful best-selling author of several books, most notably an outstanding history of the Two Oceans Marathon, in which he brilliantly wove together the history of the race with that of South Africa and of the city of Cape Town.

He is a Comrades green-number holder (3155), and a battling one at that, having fought a crippling knee injury to complete his tenth run. So committed is he to the race that on several occasions he has quietly travelled to Durban to watch, to help, and to absorb the atmosphere of the race even though he has been injured and unable to race. John is as important a member of the Comrades family as any trustee, sponsor or past winner.

In this fresh look at Comrades, John has followed the chronological history of the race, dealing with its birth and subsequent growth, but it is his understanding of the race's link to the history and transformation of South Africa that makes it such an inspirational read and him such a suitable author.

In the early days of Comrades the race leader carried the mayoral baton until he was passed. He would then hand the baton to the new leader. For obvious reasons this became too impractical. (I cannot imagine meekly handing Alan Robb any baton; he'd have to tear it from my grasp.) However, in the true spirit of Comrades and on the strength of this book, I know that Morris Alexander would be more than happy to hand the baton of Comrades author and historian to John Cameron-Dow.

Bruce Fordyce

Introduction

Many, if not most, future Comrades runners become attracted to the sport of road-running when they see family members or friends, people they regard as normal, tackle and overcome this apparently supernormal challenge. Before long, the next step: struggling around the block, then pushing yourself to five kilometres, then ten, followed by 15. Now it's time to join a club and run that first half-marathon. After a few months, a standard marathon has been accomplished. Increasingly, club conversation turns to the 'big one', South African road-running's Mount Everest, the Comrades Marathon. 'That's only for the ultra-tough,' you think. Yet a tiny seed that cannot be denied has been planted in your mind.

So it was that I flew from Cape Town to Durban on the morning of 30 May 1984. Next to me sat a friendly chap wearing a Comrades blazer. We started talking. He had five Comrades finishes to his credit. I was totally awestruck. I was hoping desperately that I might earn just one precious medal; five would be utterly unbelievable.

Durban was an eye-opener. Everyone wore tracksuits. Everyone ate pasta. I was one of them, even though I knew I didn't really belong in such an elite gathering.

The next day, 31 May 1984, was one of the most incredible experiences of my life. Memories are still vivid: *Chariots of Fire* music and the cockcrow at the freezing start, the couple cheering us on from their bed out in the open at the foot of Polly Shortts, the chap who fell heavily on the Inchanga descent, whom nobody passed until he had received proper treatment (that Comrades spirit), the young girl sitting on a pavement in Pinetown waving me on with the stump of an arm, the realisation after Cowies that I was going to make it, the gentleman on Tollgate Bridge who greeted me with the words, 'Just call me Wally' – four years before his remarkable comeback – the bemused look from friends at Kingsmead when they saw that I, of all people, had completed the Comrades Marathon.

I was well and truly hooked. I still am. I fell into trap after trap, willingly. As many have found out, the triumph of a first success soon becomes, 'I've only run a down. Next year, we're back to complete the double.' Then, 'That second run wasn't a happy one. We'll have to go back and make amends.' All manner of lures draw us back until we find that we've managed seven or eight. Now our minds focus on the green number, awarded for a tenth finish.

I earned my ninth medal in 1997. Thank goodness, I thought, now for the big one. It didn't quite turn out as I planned. Over the next six years, I underwent three operations. On one occasion, I flew back to Cape Town from Durban two days before the race for emergency internal surgery. Every year, that tenth medal seemed to recede just a little further from my grasp. Every year, I'd wander around the expo, pass the green-number area and turn the appropriate colour with envy.

When I was told in 2003 by a running member of the medical profession that I didn't have a hope of finishing another Comrades, I was determined to make one last attempt. At the same time, I felt I needed to justify the trip to my family. It was, I thought, time to write another book. Why not make it a book about the Comrades? While in Durban, I broached the subject with the Comrades Marathon Association. They had something else in mind. They wanted someone to take over from Morris Alexander as the official historian of the Comrades Marathon, and they asked me to fill the position.

What an honour! I doubt if there has been a finer book in the broad field of South African sport than Morris Alexander's *The Comrades Marathon Story*. In my annual build-up to the race, I would always read the book and be inspired by it. All those who have run the great race talk about the legendary Comrades spirit, and Morris Alexander captured it perfectly. In fact, he went further: he enhanced it. With all the skill of a greatly gifted author and the understanding of a pioneer runner and devoted administrator, Morris provided a living record that will always remain an integral part of Comrades culture. Taking over his mantle was indeed a humbling responsibility.

My 2003 Comrades adventure turned out to be a great deal more fruitful than I'd envisaged. The eight years of my life since then have been devoted to producing what I hope will come to be regarded as an adequate successor to *The Comrades Marathon Story*. Furthermore, that journey to Durban was special for another reason. Contrary to the expectation of my family, clubmates and doctor, I returned with my proudest possession: my very own green number.

1

HOW IT ALL BEGAN

Of all regular sporting events, South Africa's famous Comrades Marathon is probably the one whose name most aptly describes its culture. It owes its origin, its title and its unique ethos to a South African Railways engine driver named Vic Clapham who was so inspired by the dedication, stamina and bravery of his colleagues in the First World War that he decided to inaugurate an annual event to commemorate fallen colleagues and to express his gratitude to one special wartime comrade who had saved his life.

Returning soldiers formed the League of Comrades of the Great War. Clapham approached the organisation at the end of 1918 with his idea, a road race between Pietermaritzburg and Durban. Derision was the unwelcome response. In 1919 and 1920, his further efforts met further rebuffs. Displaying the type of spirit that would become the hallmark of his race, Clapham doggedly persisted until he had worn away all opposition.

In 1921, Clapham's resolve was finally rewarded. He was given permission to stage his event. He was also lent the princely sum of one pound sterling in order to have the race take place under the auspices of the league. He was expressly informed that the grant would have to be returned. Immune to such indignities, Clapham happily went ahead and organised a 'Comrades Marathon go-as-you-please' between Pietermaritzburg and Durban on 24 May 1921.

Who was this man, Vic Clapham, whose legacy to his country is an annual spectacle that draws over 10 000 hardy competitors and attracts one of the largest television audiences? Born in London in 1886, Clapham emigrated to South Africa as a young lad with his family. He grew up in Cape Town. Perhaps the first seeds of Comrades were sown in his youthful mind when he walked approximately eight kilometres per day from the Clapham family home in Observatory to Wynberg Boys' School.

His son Eric, recalling family legend in an interview in 2001, spoke about his father's childhood: 'He was given a "tickey" a day to catch the train home so he could help in his father's grocery shop in Main Road, Observatory. On one occasion, he spent the tickey on sweets and walked back from school, but received such a beating from my grandmother, the misdemeanour was never repeated.'

Long distances became a way of life for Vic Clapham during the First World War. As a volunteer, he took part in the East African Campaign and witnessed the horrors of war at first hand, including the ultimate irony: although the violence claimed many victims, the major loss of life appeared to come from tropical diseases. Clapham contracted blackwater fever, dysentery and malaria and nearly died.

Eric Clapham described his father's most difficult ordeal: 'One day, he collapsed, unable to carry on. A comrade, Ernest Freemantle, carried him across sand, over rock, up hills and through bush for more than 50 kilometres of the most awful terrain in terrible heat of over 40 degrees.'

Eric continued his account of his father's wartime experiences: 'When my dad was well enough, he travelled home to Maritzburg via Mombasa by wagon and then hospital ship. He was boarded from the army as medically unfit in 1917. He worked as a fireman for what used to be the Natal Government Railway and enrolled for a course of study, which won him top marks and an impressive oak desk.'

The oak desk was central to the establishment of the Comrades Marathon. It became the drawing-board that witnessed the planning and organising of the Comrades Marathon. In the early days, Clapham was more or less chairman, secretary, publicist, arranger and ultimately slave of the race. Eric recalled his father's devotion: 'He personally organised the race for 17 years, working long hours at his prized oak desk, until his job as a train driver took him to Ladysmith.'

What is the secret of the success of the Comrades Marathon? Most who have succumbed to the beguiling appeal of an event that seduces and tortures more or less simultaneously would simply trot out the famous phrase, 'the spirit of Comrades'. Of course, they'd be quite correct. The race has a unique culture that is totally South African and yet irresistibly attractive to visitors from all parts of the world, super-athletes and backmarkers alike. But why?

Perhaps the most crucial component of this culture was the utter selflessness of Vic Clapham. His entire record is one of perseverance and dedication to the race and all those who became part of it and helped it grow. Clapham was a humble man who didn't for a moment entertain the possibility of personal gain as he established an event that would greatly enrich thousands of lives long after his death.

Then there is the uniqueness of the Comrades challenge. In other parts of the world, many thousands of runners take part in events such as the London Marathon and the New York Marathon: events run over the standard marathon distance of 42.195 kilometres (26 miles 385 yards) on courses that are mostly flat. The Comrades Marathon distance varies from year to year, according to roadworks and occasional detours, from 86 kilometres to 93 kilometres, but it is generally considered to be a 90-kilometre event: twice the standard marathon distance, and then some, over a course that is arguably more mountainous than hilly. Comrades provides a significant athletic contest for the world's top ultra-distance athletes and challenges the average man or woman to complete the event between dawn and dusk, just about the very limit of most runners' capability.

The race, in an important sense, belongs to the people of KwaZulu-Natal. Right from the first race in 1921, the local population have made it their event. Lining the route in their thousands, they are just as much part of Comrades as the athletes. The interaction between runner and spectator is the very essence of the race. It's that camaraderie that enables ordinary mortals to overcome human frailty and perform beyond their wildest expectations – and inspired visiting superstars like Alberto Salazar and Charly Doll to proclaim emotionally that they had never before experienced anything resembling the Comrades spirit.

The race has always attracted a great deal of media interest, starting from incredulous coverage of the inaugural event right up to the mass-media coverage that has helped make Comrades the extravaganza it is today. Admiring columnists have penned wonderful articles about the race and its participants. KwaZulu-Natal cartoonist Jock Leyden was drawn into the culture and, in turn, drew the atmosphere for others to follow. When television was introduced in the mid-seventies, just as international isolation was about to remove the country from world sporting competition, the Comrades Marathon was one of a handful of local events that filled our screens. Its celebrity status continued in the post-isolation era.

The race's unique spirit has produced unique gestures from its champions. Arthur Newton, 1922 race winner and the first multiple champion, inadvertently set a precedent by ceding his winner's prizes to the runners-up. Newton realised that, in the Comrades Marathon, the achievement of the last finisher can be just as meritorious as that of the winner. Hardy Ballington, Wally Hayward, Jackie Mekler, Alan Robb and Bruce Fordyce, among others, have displayed a similar feeling for the symbiotic relationship between the head and tail of the field. Backmarkers are often referred to as the 'real Comrades runners'. They have the great champions to thank for such status.

2

THE COMRADES
MARATHON COURSE

One of Vic Clapham's most significant contributions to the race that he founded was the incomparably beautiful and fiercely demanding course over which it is run, between capital and seaport in annually alternating directions. The distance and terrain are such as to take the average person to the very limit of human ability in the quest to cover the distance on foot within 12 hours. Nowhere else in the world is there any race quite like it.

Which is the easier, the 'up' or the 'down'? Many experts will tell you quite categorically that the 'up' is easier. Just as many will confidently proclaim the opposite. What is the truth, then? Frankly, there is no definitive answer. There are so many variables, including one's state of fitness, one's natural ability and conditions on the day in the two very different climates of Durban and Pietermaritzburg. Two general observations can be made: the 'down' run is, for most, slightly faster than the 'up', and the 'up' run, it would seem, produces a little less discomfort the following day. The difference is marginal.

The Comrades route is not just about distance, demanding gradients and time constraints. The road between Pietermaritzburg and Durban is a succession of obstacles, big and small, steep and (occasionally) flat. It is also a part of South Africa that is rich in history, much of it brought to mind annually by the landmarks and vantage points featured on race day.

The first race, in 1921, started in Pietermaritzburg. Consequently, with but a few exceptions caused by historical considerations, 'down' runs have been held in odd-numbered years and 'up' runs in even-numbered years. The route has remained more or less constant although conditions have changed dramatically. In the early years, tarred roads were just a dream. Today, those runners with nostalgic inclinations can look up at some of the hills and see evidence of paths that formed part of the original course. Morris Alexander's history, *The Comrades Marathon Story*, mentions water crossings, an ordeal that moderns thankfully do not have to face.

It's easy to say, as old-timers love to do, that modern runners have it easy, that the pioneers of the race faced hardships of which modern 'softies' are totally unaware. Such views may be exaggerated, yet they are based on truth. Even those who first ran Comrades as recently as the 1970s and 1980s will acknowledge that the course has become a little easier since then. Nevertheless, it remains one of the most difficult challenges in ultra-distance running in the world.

Let's go through the entire route, starting, as was the case in 1921, in the capital city of the province, Pietermaritzburg, and savour the atmosphere of the start. The build-up can take anything up to six months, depending on the experience, expectation and emotions of runners. The final three days, much of it spent at the Comrades Experience, or 'Expo', ensure that Comrades is all that occupies the minds of those who dare to meet the challenge of the great race. Late on the eve of the event, exhibitors pack up their goods and depart, their job completed. Runners, assailed by pre-race butterflies, go to their hotel rooms, the homes of their hosts or wherever they are to spend the night. After one last meal, the lonely vigil commences.

'Make sure you get a good night's sleep two nights before the event,' many are told. Why? 'You're unlikely to sleep at all the night before.' Earnest novices tend to put their heads on pillows as early as possible and then battle to sleep, their minds occupied with the task ahead. More experienced runners have learnt to stay up until tiredness sets in. There is no perfect way.

Early-morning alarm clocks bring harsh reality, no matter how long (or how little) you have slept. It's Comrades day. Everything is pre-organised, except that final toilet visit. Coffee or tea, toast and honey, banana bread, one final carbo-drink: all sorts of concoctions are consumed in the hope that breakfast will provide the all-important energy supply. Every now and then, a visit to the toilet attempts to ensure personal comfort en route.

Before long, it's time to join the conveyor belt. The lucky ones are dropped near the start. The very lucky ones stroll there from their perfectly positioned hotel rooms. The not so lucky, lost in a strange city, battle to find parking. Tog bags are exchanged for tickets (which will identify them at the finish), supporters go to their designated areas and runners take position according to their qualification times.

With approximately 15 minutes to go, Vangelis's famous title theme from the movie *Chariots of Fire* is played. The music accentuates the almost tangible mood of expectation. Pietermaritzburg, founded in 1838, was named after Voortrekker leaders Pieter Retief and Gerrit Maritz. It has been the capital of the region (first a Boer republic, then a British colony, now the Province of KwaZulu-Natal) since 1857. Television lights set off Maritzburg's redbrick city hall against the pre-dawn darkness as over 10 000 pairs of eyes look up, anxiously awaiting the moment that has dominated their thoughts for months. Eventually the music fades out, a cockcrow is heard and the gun goes off. Thousands of stopwatches click into action and another Comrades Marathon is under way.

The start determines the result. This is a truism which many have proved to their cost, and some have exploited. Arthur Newton advised in the mid-1930s: 'Don't go streaking off after the majority of the field. Keep your wits about you.' Half a century later, Bruce Fordyce echoed Newton's thoughts: 'A runner cannot have enough caution at the start of the Comrades.'

After about eight kilometres of careful running, the field arrives at the most famous of all Comrades landmarks, the notorious Polly Shortts. Fortunately, it's all downhill in the 'down' run, and the only real concern is the need to keep on exercising caution. Actually, despite its fearsome reputation, Polly Shortts is a welcome respite for all but the most determined of racers, even in the 'up' run. The majority of 'up' runners will have made allowances for the fearsome hill: if their race has gone according to plan, they will simply stroll up it and shuffle to the finish. On the 'down' run, however, we wish only to conserve our energy at this point.

For many years, the name Polly Shortts was misspelt. In August 1961, the *Natal Mercury* published a report that traced the name of this most recognisable Comrades landmark. As with most good stories, the legend is all about a man and a pub.

In the 19th century, the British government sent a Scottish doctor to examine Napoleon Bonaparte, who was in exile on St Helena. During the trip, the doctor's wife produced twins. She and one of the children perished in childbirth. The surviving baby, Portland Bentinck Shortts (known as Polly) went back to Britain with his father but returned to South Africa in 1840.

Polly Shortts settled outside Pietermaritzburg on a farm he called Shortts' Retreat, about a mile away from the Star and Garter, a popular watering hole. Very shrewdly, the pub had been built 25 yards outside the Pietermaritzburg borough boundary, and was therefore allowed to sell liquor on Sundays. Polly Shortts was an eccentric character and a regular visitor to the pub with an insatiable thirst, mainly for whisky, and a fiery temper. He was not averse to aiming his shotgun at those who annoyed him as he sat on the stoep of his favourite inn. There are no records of anyone being shot by him, but numerous accounts of hapless runners who suffered intolerable marathon-related agonies on the hill named after him.

Once they reach the bottom of Polly Shortts, runners face a relatively gentle climb of two kilometres to Ashburton. Known to regulars as Little Pollys, largely because of its proximity to the final obstacle of the 'up' run, Ashburton derives its name from the home town in Dorset of Englishman William Ellis, who settled in the area after making his fortune in the Australian gold rush.

A few kilometres down the road, the sign 'Lion Park' indicates the whereabouts of South Africa's first such park, established by Dick Chipperfield of Chipperfields Circus. Our next target is the highest point of the race, at Umlaas Road. The altitude here of 823.8 metres, when compared with the 650 metres of Pietermaritzburg and the 755.2 metres of Polly Shortts, shows just how tough the first 20 kilometres of the 'down' Comrades is.

From here until the foot of Inchanga, the course remains undulating, but without the extremes of the initial section.

Our next landmark is Camperdown, after about 25 kilometres. A huge and enthusiastic crowd, along with the inviting smell of numerous braais, tells us that this is an area that we might occupy as supporters when our own running days are over. Camperdown was the home of wealthy British immigrant John Vanderplank, who introduced black wattle, acquired from his brother Charles in Australia, into the area.

With roughly one-third of the race behind us, we come to the railway junction of Cato Ridge, named after George C. Cato, a landowner in the early days of Durban. Experienced runners will be aware that a short tunnel, followed by a right turn, introduces the back-breaking part of the 'down' run. Harrison Flats is anything but flat; it is also possibly the least inspiring section of the entire route.

The mission station on the left tells us that we are about to reach a new challenge. Scores of young children line the road with hands outstretched, eager to be touched. Immediately thereafter, on the right, is the Sports Trust's Nondlini facility for underprivileged people living in the area. The name Nondlini (literally 'the cow that has the best milk') tells us that this is a place of nurturing. It is fitting that the facility was established under the chairmanship of Bruce Fordyce, a man whose athletic career was cemented in the Comrades Marathon and who has used his success as a platform for improving the circumstances of the least fortunate of those living alongside the famous course.

We are now on Inchanga hill, a climb of about 140 metres over 2.5 kilometres that commences after almost 40 kilometres on the road. Some will be cruelly misled when they see what they think is the top of the hill, shortly before they discover a second section beyond. The crest does come as a welcome relief, although a marker board shortly after reminds us that we still have more than a standard marathon ahead of us.

The lure of halfway and a comfortable downhill tempt the impatient and the inexperienced to sprint down into Drummond, the halfway point. If you succumb, you are likely to pay the penalty later. Those who take their time will be rewarded, shortly before Drummond, if they take their minds off their ordeal for a few moments to savour the incomparable view of the Valley of a Thousand Hills to their left.

Flat sections in an ultramarathon are not quite as comfortable as the uninitiated might imagine. The short distance from the bottom of Inchanga through Drummond and on to the start of Botha's Hill is fine for the top runners, but disconcertingly trying for those at the back. Drummond was named after Sir F. C. Drummond, an immigration official in the latter half of the 19th century.

Leaving Drummond and starting the ascent of Botha's Hill, the first step is a steep one. So is the second. And most of the rest. Whether running the 'up' or the 'down' Comrades, the first hill after halfway is crucial. It is often here that the battle for first place is won or lost, this test that decides who wins the range of accolades for those who complete the race in under 12 hours – the silver and bronze medals, and those named after Wally Hayward, Bill Rowan and Vic Clapham.

The ascent of Botha's Hill includes a couple of significant milestones. Firstly, there is Arthur's Seat. According to the story, the great Arthur Newton, a five-time winner, would take a breather there. Legend has it that those who pause, greet the old champion respectfully and deposit a flower in his honour, will be rewarded with successful finishes. Those who employ such tactics as a means of overcoming lack of training and limited ability generally reject the notion. It's a nice story, anyway!

Not far from Arthur's Seat is the Wall of Honour. Originally thought of as a means of financing Comrades House, the wall, approximately a hundred metres long and ten high, includes bricks purchased by Comrades finishers which reflect their names, race numbers and any little quirks they may wish to add. Those who have earned permanent green numbers are recognised in suitable fashion.

The ascent of the hill is a succession of 'ups' and 'downs', the 'ups' being more frequent and generally longer. Alverstone Tower, on the right, will be passed along the way. It is generally recognised that Kearsney College marks the top of the hill. In the 1980s, famous author Alan Paton would often be seen at the roadside. While other claims have been made, it appears likely that Botha's Hill Village was named after Cornelis Botha, owner of an inn named Botha's Halfway House.

The descent of Botha's Hill is steep and is followed by a relatively sharp, but quite short, climb to Hillcrest. At this stage, many are becoming aware that breakfast was some hours ago. Fortunately, baked potatoes, bananas and chocolate are usually on offer here.

The gently undulating and slightly downhill stretch from Hillcrest to Kloof holds the key to a successful 'down' run. Top runners can increase their tempo without having to worry too much about overexertion, while backmarkers need only keep up a gentle shuffle, resisting the temptation to walk.

The Field family's names are enshrined in several of the towns and villages in this area. William Swann Field, Durban's first magistrate, was given a farm named Richmond by the British government in 1851. In 1867, he relinquished ownership to his brother, John, after whom Field's Hill was named. John Field's son-in-law, William Gillit (another landmark name), named his farm Emberton, a portion of which became known as Hill Crest. It's small wonder that the Comrades Marathon has something of a family nature.

Field's Hill is the longest, steepest and most damaging part of the course. Bruce Fordyce and Alan Robb, who unforgettably raced each other down the hill in 1982, are unlikely to disagree. At the bottom of Field's Hill lies an industrial and residential area that owes its existence to an inn. The Wayside Hotel was established in 1849 as a place where stagecoaches could change horses while travellers enjoyed welcome refreshments. The following year, a town was built and named Pinetown after the Governor of Natal, Sir Benjamin Pine. For Comrades runners, Pinetown offers two major attractions: huge crowd support and a marker board that tells us we have just 20 kilometres to go.

From this marker board to the start of Cowies Hill is about one and a half kilometres. It's an opportunity for those at the back to make up some time. Cowies will be partially walked by most of those who prop up the back of the field. In the 'up' run, Cowies is just about the most friendly uphill in South African road-running. The 'down' run is different but does give those who reach the top the welcome feeling that there are only about 17 kilometres to go. William Cowie, after whom the hill is named, was an English farmer who joined forces with the Voortrekkers in their advance into Natal in 1837.

If the relationship between Cowiesand the Voortrekkers seems surprising, the origin of the residential area of Westville is even more so. In 1847, two Germans, H. Jaraal and P. Jung, purchased property in the vicinity of Durban. They named the farm Westville after Martin West, the local British governor. The following year, a British merchant named Jonas Bergtheil brought a group of German farmers and their families to build up the area.

After passing Westville, the 'down' run nears its close. Two minor hills remain. Firstly, 45th Cutting, named after a British infantry regiment, the 45th Regiment of Foot (or Sherwood Forresters), presents a reasonably difficult challenge. Then the short but steep ascent of Tollgate deposits runners on the final six kilometres to Kingsmead (the home of cricket in Durban) and, hopefully, personal satisfaction. Ninety kilometres have been covered over the most trying terrain imaginable. Celebrations are in order, for those few who still have the energy to take part.

3

THE EARLY DAYS

Once Vic Clapham had persuaded the League of Comrades to grant him permission to stage his dream event, he faced two even greater challenges. Firstly, he had to organise, virtually on his own, a 56-mile road race between the cities of Pietermaritzburg and Durban, the like of which had never been attempted before. Secondly, he had to make the inaugural event so successful that it would become an annual happening.

True-blue amateurism was what sport was all about in the 1920s. The veterans of the First World War, and others of their generation, cherished the virtues of selflessness and service. 'Gallantry' and 'chivalry' were words that epitomised the ideals associated with the noble conduct of friendly competition: the terms were used to describe the nature of most, if not all, sporting codes.

Vic Clapham, in nature and in deed, was always true to the spirit of comradeship which had sustained him through his wartime experiences and which he strove to instil in his life's ambition, his Comrades Marathon. While Clapham demanded much of himself, he didn't spare his family either. His son Eric recalled the busiest day in the family's year:

'Runners would descend on our home at 31 Greyling Street before the race. My dad, an arch-scrounger, got donations of tea, milk and biscuits for all. I would have to give up my bed and sleep on the floor so a runner could have a comfortable night's rest.

'On the morning of the race, my brother Douglas would have to cycle around Maritzburg at 4.30 a.m. in the freezing air with notebook and pencil to rouse the local runners. Each had to sign he'd been wakened.

'My mother would fry thick steaks on the coal stove in the kitchen. Each runner would get a massive steak topped with a couple of eggs for breakfast. Both my parents believed protein produced energy.

'My five brothers and I had a special job. The runners brought their toiletries and clean clothes in small suitcases. We took these on a truck, which my dad had scrounged, and accompanied the athletes. If we saw a runner sitting at the roadside in pain, we'd massage his muscles with Ellerman's liniment.

'Every now and again, we'd see a guy pooped out and ready to pack up and we would find his suitcase and wait while he quickly dressed and climbed on to the truck with us, before we pulled off looking for someone else who needed a drink of water, a rub-down, a word of encouragement or, finally, a suitcase full of warm clothes.

'Much has changed since the time of tackies tackling what was then a gravel road without lines of volunteers. Runners would invade any farm that had a water tap in sight to slake their thirst.'

Clearly, it would take more than wishful thinking to establish the Comrades Marathon as South Africa's pre-eminent annual sporting happening. Vic Clapham had wonderful powers of persuasion. The media, the public, sponsors and runners all responded to his infectious enthusiasm. Yet that wasn't enough: the race needed something to ignite it.

That something came in the person of Arthur Newton. Already 39 years old when he ran his first Comrades in 1922, Newton captured the attention of the public by using his race debut as a means of airing his grievances against government apathy towards his problems as a farmer. He emphasised his protest by winning the race – and repeated the achievement four times.

Newton's legacy was multidimensional. He had a scientific approach to running and wrote several books which can be regarded as the basis of the science of long-distance running. He was also a formidable athlete. On the way to his record-breaking 6.24.45 in 1925, Newton passed through Drummond at 2.55. This was just five minutes slower than the halfway time of Bruce Fordyce in his record-breaking run 59 years later in 1984.

Perhaps Newton's greatest contribution, however, was his particular brand of sportsmanship. A man of great humility, he is looked upon by Comrades aficionados as one who played a crucial role in fostering the unique Comrades spirit. In this, Arthur Newton and Vic Clapham were soulmates.

1921 COMRADES MARATHON
BILL ROWAN'S DAY

On 24 May 1921, just a week short of the 11th birthday of the fledgling Union of South Africa, Vic Clapham's dream became a reality. Initially a memorial to those who had lost their lives during the Great War of 1914 to 1918, the Comrades Marathon would become an annual expression of the pioneering spirit of all South Africans, encompassing the hopes, fears, aspirations and doubts of a divided population who would take another 73 years to reach their true nationhood.

Such thoughts were far from the minds of those who were mad enough, brave enough and prepared enough to face the starter on this auspicious occasion. For them, this was a once-only gesture of togetherness in adversity. There was no 'up' Comrades, no 'down' Comrades, no next year's Comrades. This was their Comrades, an occasion on which they would give their all, mindful of the scepticism of those who considered the venture an impossible mission and determined to be true to their wartime heritage: steadfast to the end, whatever that might mean.

As is so often the case in this, the most hospitable climate imaginable, weather conditions for the first Comrades Marathon were perfect: a cool start followed by a relatively warm day. Of the 48 entrants, 34 lined up for the start. Perhaps one or two of the 14 non-starters woke in time, but felt the early morning chill and returned to bed, unaware of the fact that they were missing out on an opportunity to be part of history.

Race strategy was an unknown concept. The most scientific theory in vogue suggested that it might be a reasonable idea to start off fairly slowly in order to conserve one's energy. This contrasted with the view that the advantage, in any sporting contest, lay with the early leader, who would stamp his authority on proceedings and dictate the course of the race. In 1921, there were no sports scientists. *The Natal Advertiser* of 24 May 1921 described the event as a 'go-as-you-please marathon' from Pietermaritzburg to Durban, organised by the League of Comrades.

True to the informality of the occasion, the first Comrades Marathon was started by Councillor D. Sanders, mayor of Pietermaritzburg, at 7.10 a.m., ten minutes late. The Greytown entrant A. C. Purcell, who would finish in fifth place, became the first runner to be recorded as a leader of a Comrades Marathon. His main rivals in the first half were H. J. Phillips of Maritzburg and a farmer from Koster in the Transvaal by the name of Bill Rowan.

The halfway mark at Drummond proved to be the turning point. The 26-year-old Rowan had paced his race sensibly and had a distinct strength advantage as the field embarked on the formidable second half of this double marathon, moving into previously uncharted athletic terrain. Rowan's lead swiftly grew and soon became unassailable, barring mishap. With two-thirds of the route behind him, he was two miles ahead of second man Phillips. An unidentified passing motorist described the leader's progress: 'Rowan's a marvel. He was running splendidly when I saw him, and if he had been extended, he would have got into Durban before 4 p.m.'

A troop of boy scouts were camping on the side of the main road in Pinelands on race day. Unaware of the race, they were surprised to see a convoy of motor vehicles approaching, a somewhat unusual spectacle in those days. One of the scouts was a 12-year-old lad named Vernon Jones, destined to become arguably the most significant recorder of Comrades history. Many years later, Jones shared his memory of the occasion with another major Comrades historian, Barry Varty: 'As the cars approached, I was able to make out the figure of a bedraggled runner, caked with sand.' The athlete's sweat, the motor cars and the untarred roads all conspired to create a peculiar spectacle.

That runner was the winner of the first Comrades Marathon, Bill Rowan, at that stage 13 miles short of the finish. Jones didn't ever meet Rowan, but did meet every subsequent Comrades champion, right up to and including Bruce Fordyce. It is unlikely that Rowan noticed the wide-eyed boy scout as he passed by. Yet that moment when their paths crossed could justifiably be regarded as the birth of the relationship between those who made Comrades history and those who recorded it.

Rowan had predicted a finishing time of nine hours. He was spot on. In fact, he finished one minute ahead of schedule and 41 minutes ahead of second man H. J. Phillips.

Rowan's mark on the race was largely forgotten for many years, as attention focused on his immediate successor. Thankfully, this anomaly has been redressed and the legend of Bill Rowan continues to grow as befits the first Comrades champion. Nowadays, all successful Comraders who finish short of a silver medal (below seven and a half hours) but within the nine-hour target identified and achieved by Rowan receive the highly prized Bill Rowan medal.

1921 COMRADES MARATHON RESULTS

1. W. Rowan		8.59
2. H. J. Phillips		9.40
3. J. A. Annan		10.10
4. R. S. Skinner		10.27
5. A. C. Purcell		10.37
6. R. L. Mare		10.44
7. A. M. Marie		11.04
8. L. Mitcalfe		11.06
9. J. Moran, G. A. Imray		11.13
11. G. E. W. Palmer		11.20
11. I. Hirschfield		11.20
11. R. Goodricke		11.20
14. C. E. Atkinson		11.26
15. B. B. Freeman		11.27
16. F. K. Wade		11.31

It is noticeable that of the 16 finishers, two shared ninth place and three 11th place. The camaraderie of Comrades existed from day one. A special bronze medal was awarded to L. E. W. Pearson, who finished in 12.20, outside the official limit of 12 hours.

1922 COMRADES MARATHON
ARTHUR NEWTON:
THE FIRST COMRADES GREAT

Traditionally, an 'up' Comrades has a somewhat smaller field than a 'down' run. There is a logical reason for this. Although most experienced runners will claim that the 'down' run is more painful, it is the faster of the two and therefore provides a likelier opportunity to attain a successful medal-earning finish.

The first 'up' run in 1922 was, of course, an exception. In 1921, just 34 out of 48 entrants made it to the starting line, but on Wednesday, 24 May 1922, 89 runners started out of 114 who had entered: proof that the Comrades Marathon had arrived. The success of the inaugural race had caught the imagination of dreamers and adventurers, romantics and daredevils.

Yet this excitement was no guarantee of future success. More than doubling the numbers might seem impressive, but fewer than a hundred contestants hardly constituted a national endorsement of a 'day of madness'. Some extra impetus would surely be needed to boost the prestige of the race.

That impetus arrived in a form that would be repeated at crucial times in the race's future. Essentially, the Comrades Marathon is all about people, be they runners, spectators, organisers or supporters. Comradeship on its own is not enough; people need heroes, those rare individuals who are looked up to by ordinary mortals. While long-distance running is, in the words of Professor Tim Noakes, 'the most egalitarian of all sports', it still depends on exceptional characters and champions to fire the imagination.

The second Comrades Marathon introduced a real character, a champion athlete and an intelligent student of long-distance running – all in the person of Arthur Newton. He would be recognised as one of the true greats of the Comrades Marathon and as a pioneer in the science of the sport.

Newton's theories of the demands of the ultramarathon, his views on training methods and his approach to race strategy and dietary needs form the basis of the modern understanding of the sport. He could well be regarded as the father of the science of ultramarathon running. He certainly became the first cult figure to attract broader attention to the Comrades Marathon and to focus minds on the allure of world endurance records. 'Greatheart' Newton was to become the first of the Comrades greats.

Born in Somerset, England, in 1883, Newton had been a member of an English athletics club without producing any performances of note before emigrating to South Africa. There are records of his having competed in a couple of sub-marathon races without distinguishing himself in his early days in South Africa. Then came the Comrades Marathon.

A year short of his 40th birthday, Newton started his relationship with the great race for what would appear to have been somewhat selfish motives. Newton was the first runner to use the Comrades Marathon as a vehicle for a political demonstration. A farmer in the then Province of Natal, he had suffered significant financial setbacks, for which he largely blamed the local labour force. Newton was aggrieved at a perceived lack of government sympathy and decided to use the new, and highly celebrated, marathon between Durban and Pietermaritzburg as the stage on which to publicise his message.

Along with many others who were to follow him, Newton discovered that preparation for the race was possibly even more of a challenge than the race itself. His initial training runs produced pain, fatigue and the frustrating necessity of a recovery period. Eschewing the popular view that attaining success in an extreme sport required extreme but irregular dedication, Newton, without too much time available, adopted a common-sense approach. He was possibly the first long-distance athlete to recognise the need to 'listen to one's body'. His understanding of the demands of ultramarathon running is compatible with the latest developments in sports science.

The interest in the second Comrades Marathon, generated by the first, suggested that the race would soon become accepted as an annual event. The winner's trophy for the 1922 race was donated by the Natal Turf Clubs:

Durban, Pietermaritzburg and Clairwood. It was agreed that the 12-hour time limit for finishing, which had applied in the inaugural race, would be retained. The news that Bill Rowan would come down from the Belgian Congo to defend his title heightened the general anticipation.

Precision of timing was not yet a Comrades tradition. The 1922 race commenced seven minutes late, an improvement of three minutes over the previous year. The Ladysmith runner E. W. Williams took an early lead, going through Hillcrest at 2.27, four minutes ahead of second man A. C. Purcell. Bill Rowan was in the following pack, but Newton appeared out of contention, far behind the front-runners.

Newton knew precisely what he was doing, however, conserving his energy for the second half. Williams was an early casualty, dropping out before halfway. Purcell was first through Drummond. He was followed by Phillips, with Imray third. Newton's strategy was working perfectly. He now shared fourth place with Rowan, but not for long. Soon he was third, then second with only Purcell ahead. Just before Camperdown, Newton took the lead for the first time. As would so often be the case, the pursuer was stronger, both physically and mentally, than the prey. Devastated, Purcell pulled out of the race. Newton was now on his own. With a lead of fully 30 minutes, he enjoyed a half-tot of brandy.

Arthur Newton became the first runner to face the most famous of all Comrades obstacles, Polly Shortts. His comments afterwards have been echoed a thousand times, although perhaps not quite as eloquently.

'It was an enormous relief to get to the long downhill stretch after Camperdown, and I seemed almost to coast along for mile after mile. But I knew what was waiting at the bottom and wasn't looking forward to it at all. A three-quarter-mile incline followed by Polly Shortts cutting had to be climbed, and the latter was a considerable hill of some 500 feet, with just over a mile to do it in. Well, for the moment there was only one serious thing to be considered in all the world, and that was Polly Shortts. I reduced my stride as I had long since learnt to, and gently, ever so gently, crept up the long rise. Great James! It was terrible work! It might have been nothing desperate for a man who was quite fresh, but when you had already run a much longer distance than you had ever tackled before in your life, the thing became a sheer nightmare.

'Up I went, and still up, but I began to feel that it was impossible to keep going. It got so bad that when it came to the steepest part, I stopped dead in a single stride, convinced at the moment that it was absolute idiocy to attempt to carry on. Two seconds' consideration, however, told me that it was probably as bad for those behind me: also that as I had already stuck so much, it didn't make much odds if a trifle more were added. Without stopping to debate the point, I shoved one foot in front of the other and continued the climb. I have often since wondered what those in the cars nearby thought of my momentary stop.

'Even your worst time is left behind sooner or later, and when I was wondering whether I should be able to keep going on my legs at all, I reached the top and saw the city of Pietermaritzburg in the valley four miles away.'

Newton's post-Comrades introspection identified the principles that would sustain future generations in the heat of personal battle. First, when you are really struggling and despair threatens, realise that others are in the same boat. Second, when you feel that you are falling apart, don't give up: you're simply experiencing a 'bad patch'.

Newton also became the first Comrades runner to fallaciously announce his probable retirement. 'I rather think that this will be my last appearance on the road,' said the man who was to become the race's first five-time winner. Since then, countless novices have proclaimed, 'Never again!' before going on to earn permanent green numbers after ten successful finishes.

Spurred on by a convoy of cyclists, Newton reached the Royal Show Grounds finish comfortably ahead of his rivals and was given an enthusiastic reception by a crowd of approximately 3 000. He was the first winner of an 'up' Comrades and his political demonstration had been noted.

Over the years, followers of the Comrades Marathon have witnessed achievements by those who were not athletically gifted, but whose personalities would be engraved in Comrades folklore. The second running of the race produced one of its legendary figures, C. 'Big Bill' Payn. In those early days, pre-qualification was not required, and Payn, a Natal cricketer and Springbok rugby player, was persuaded by a pre-race guest, none other than Arthur Newton, to enter at the last moment.

If the story is to be believed, Payn's Comrades was an extraordinary event. He ran in rugby boots, enjoyed a breakfast of eggs at Hillcrest and stopped at Botha's Hill to share a meal of curried chicken with his friend and fellow runner, 'Zulu' Wade. After the two had each downed a beer at Drummond, Payn left his friend behind and reputedly consumed 'about 36 oranges, water, tea and even a glass of home-made peach brandy' en route to an eighth-place finish in 10.56. The following weekend, according to legend, he played rugby barefoot as he was unable to put boots on his blistered and aching feet.

Newton himself gave credence to the tale, saying, 'Bill Payn was an unusual specimen of healthy manhood, and I can vouch for every detail of the story, as I knew him well and was behind him until a third of the journey had been covered.'

One achievement that remains unique was that of 16-year-old Marist Brothers College pupil L. H. Templeton, who finished in 11.40 in 19th place. Horrified officials thereafter set a minimum age of 18. This is still in place, so Templeton is likely to remain the youngest ever recipient of a Comrades medal.

Most importantly, the 1922 Comrades Marathon proved that the 'up' run was within normal human capability between dusk and dawn. Its success established Comrades as an annual event and made the tradition of 'up' and 'down' runs in alternate years a reality. Furthermore, Polly Shortts had assumed a formidable place in road-running lore.

1922 COMRADES MARATHON RESULTS

1. A. F. H. Newton	8.40
2. H. J. Phillips	9.09
3. W. Rowan	9.13
4. J. A. Annan	10.11
5. P. Fouche	10.18
6. O. J. Lazenby	10.48
7. G. W. Taylor	10.53
8. C. Payn	10.56
9. C. Cullingworth / R. A. St George	11.02

1923 COMRADES MARATHON
A WOMAN? SURELY NOT!

The third running of the Comrades Marathon brought a clear message to Vic Clapham and his supporters: the future of the race had not yet been secured. In the inaugural race, 34 runners faced the starters. The following year, 89 were there. This year, 68 presented themselves outside the Pietermaritzburg City Hall. Although this was precisely twice the number of starters in the inaugural Comrades, the drop in numbers from 1922 was cause for concern.

Had the novelty worn off? Would the League of Comrades fade away as South Africa and the world put the horror of the First World War behind them? Was there any long-term future for an ultramarathon of a nature never before contemplated, never mind established, anywhere in the world?

Only the future could tell. For the moment, there was a gimmick to attract attention. A woman was going to attempt the race – unofficially, of course. What a horror story! No woman was capable of anything approaching the demands of the Comrades course. Such, at least, was the opinion not just of the organisers of the Comrades Marathon, but of medical science worldwide.

This was a traditional view. Women had been excluded from the ancient Olympic Games, and when the modern games were introduced, 'gender equality' was an unknown term. But male chauvinism was not entirely to blame. In the 1928 Olympic Games, an 800-metre race was held for women and turned out to be a shambles. Undertrained female athletes, with negative self-images, dropped out of the race like flies. It was widely held that participation in physically demanding sports – of which long-distance running could be regarded as the most arduous – would jeopardise women's primary function, namely child-bearing.

Miss Frances Hayward of Durban was unconcerned about her perceived gender limitations when she lined up, albeit unofficially, alongside the official all-male competitors in the 1923 Comrades Marathon. Sadly, there is no record of her views on participating in the event, but her extraordinary fortitude and determination cannot be denied.

Arthur Newton was determined to produce a better effort than his debut the previous year: his target was a course record. One could make fun of this ambition, noting that this was only the second 'down' run, the first having been a tentative journey into the unknown. Such cynicism notwithstanding, Newton's performance on the day would astound sceptics and introduce a new dimension to the Comrades Marathon. His 1923 effort would cause commentators of the day to accept that the event was not only a severe test of stamina, but also a serious athletic contest.

Race organisation was fast becoming rigorous. The third race set off on a bitterly cold Pietermaritzburg morning at 6.02 a.m., only two minutes late. Although Newton used the same 'come from behind' tactics he had employed the previous year, his superiority was so marked that he had the race virtually wrapped up before halfway.

W. N. Wratten of Durban took the early lead with Phillips, Newton, Purcell, Nel and Wolvaardt (who had a short stint at the front) in pursuit. The pace was significantly faster than that of two years before. One by one, the front-runners faltered. Shortly before Inchanga, Newton took the lead and reached the halfway mark in 3.04, not far behind the times that would be set in the great record-producing decade of the eighties.

Newton strode confidently through the second half, causing a local newspaper reporter to comment admiringly: 'He still maintained the same steady trot, appearing wonderfully fresh and well, though smothered in dust from head to foot. The road was clouded with cars and motorcycles.'

The effect of accompanying vehicles was severe, so much so that their short-lived relationship with running was recorded with the words: 'Every mortal thing was blotted out, including speech, for you daren't open your mouth. Even the side of the road disappeared'.

Old-timers happily remind today's youngsters of the realities of those early days: no modern shoes, no carbohydrates, no scientific training and, above all, no tarred roads for their tackie-clad feet to enjoy.

Whatever the complications of yesteryear, Newton clearly had all the answers. Keeping up a steady pace, which his successors would recognise as a fundamental element of Comrades strategy, he strode away from his rivals and established a lead that could not have been anticipated. As the *Natal Mercury* reported, 'It was apparent that the sports meeting at Lords Ground, which was to witness the close of the race, would not have been begun by the time this extraordinary runner got home.'

One man who was very nearly caught out by Newton's phenomenal run was Harry Hotchin, president of the Natal Amateur Athletic and Cycling Association. Walking to the Lords Ground in order to initiate proceedings for the day's sports meeting, he was astonished to witness the approach of Comrades winner apparent Arthur Newton. Suddenly, Hotchin was caught in a race of his own. He managed to dash through a hole in the fence and swiftly arranged a suitable welcome for the Harding farmer, who crossed the line in 6.56.07, 52 minutes ahead of his nearest rival, N. J. Nel of Boscombe, and more than two hours faster than winner Rowan two years previously.

In a gesture that would be recognised in later years as part of his contribution to the spirit of Comrades, Newton declined first prize on the grounds that he had an unfair advantage over his rivals because of the spare time he enjoyed as a farmer! Significantly, each of the great Comrades champions would, over the years, add to Newton's legacy of humility.

Four and a half hours after Newton's triumph, a large crowd was still in attendance to witness the race's other personality, Miss Frances Hayward, cross the line in 11.35 to a tremendous ovation. Rather ironically, in view of her own breakthrough and those by women in the latter half of the century, she commented, 'Now that I have done it, I think it is too much for women. I think it is the last ten miles that kill!' This must have disappointed many of her female admirers.

One runner who thought about being killed was 18-year-old J. J. Copley, who entered the race under the pseudonym of A. W. Harrison in order to escape the anger of his over-protective parents. Not having made any accommodation arrangements, he spent the night before the race in a field. But his ordeal was not in vain. He finished 29th in 11.39.00 and later disclosed the circumstances of his finish:

'Someone, I don't know who, poured two four-gallon tins of warm water over me. I then went home by tram car to explain to a wrathful father and worried mother where I had been and what I had been up to. Next day, stiff and with blistered feet, I went back to work at the Standard Bank. My father phoned Vic Clapham, there was an awful rumpus, the name of Harrison was summarily deleted from the records but my [real] name wasn't substituted. Race official Harold Sulin returned the silver medal to Maritzburg. I was permitted to wear the Comrades lapel badge. And some years later, I received a small medal in my correct name, J. J. Copley!'

The 1923 race was indeed a significant one. The first multiple champion had stamped his authority on proceedings, individual efforts at also-ran levels were regarded as significant and crucial to the event, and the Comrades spirit was emerging. Also, and unknown to the rest of the sporting world, women were alive and ready to make their mark, even if nobody was honest enough to say so.

1923 COMRADES MARATHON RESULTS

1. A. F. H. Newton   6.56.07
2. N. J. Nel   7.48.24
3. A. L. Purcell   8.17.03
4. W. N. Wratten   8.23.02
5. H. H. Tomlinson   8.28.21
6. J. A. Annan   8.49.17
7. G. P. Shackleford   9.02.29
8. G. A. Imray   9.30.32
9. A. M. Marie   9.30.37
10. L. G. Cary-Smith   9.33.40

1924 COMRADES MARATHON
THE FIRST HAT-TRICK

If Vic Clapham and his colleagues had been worried about the low turn-out for the 1923 Comrades Marathon, they had even more reason to be concerned the following year. Just 38 entries were received, a third of the 114 who had announced their intention to take part in the first 'up' Comrades two years previously. The survival of the race was anything but assured.

At the same time, the event was gaining a new dimension. Initially a memorial to fallen wartime comrades and in danger of becoming regarded as a gathering of freaks, the Comrades Marathon was coming to be recognised as a serious athletic contest, thanks to one man. In June of 1923, Arthur Newton had set a new world best time for 50 miles of 5.53.30 on the Comrades course, running from Pietermaritzburg to Inchanga and back. The British media were sceptical about the veracity of his claim to this achievement, particularly in view of the formidable course. The main effect of this suspicion was a new focus on the 1924 Comrades Marathon and, in particular, the performance of defending champion Arthur Newton.

The field was small, but its quality was undeniable, including the first nine finishers of the 1923 race. Brothers Winston and Ronnie Sutton, who would make their mark on the race later, were among the novices. But this would be Newton's race. The first great champion had attracted international interest and was aiming for the first ever hat-trick of Comrades wins.

Marketing an event is not a 21st-century occupation. Those who saw some benefit in an association with the race were eager to promote their involvement. Runners were advised to purchase the *Natal Witness* on 19 May 'as the final selections will be there'. It was also announced that 'Mr A. S. Brass of Drummond Hotel would give prizes for the first two competitors to reach Drummond'.

The start of the race was organised with an efficiency that had not hitherto been achieved. The *Natal Mercury* confirmed this: 'As the Post Office clock struck six o'clock, the "off" was given, and the men started on their tedious journey to the accompaniment of cheers and expressions of good luck and success from friends and relatives.' The temperature was a cool 15°C, made chillier by an unpleasant wind. Road conditions were also harsh. The tarred road ended at Mayville, less than ten miles into the race, and Field's Hill was covered with dust, which hid many sharp stones beneath.

It was on Field's Hill that Newton took the lead from Nel. With only a third of the race completed, the result, barring any unexpected mishap, was a foregone conclusion. Running easily, Newton arrived at Drummond 18 minutes ahead of second-placed Nel. On leaving the halfway mark, he immediately showed the benefit of his experience two years previously. Having great respect for the formidable obstacle of Inchanga, he reduced speed and eased his way up the bank. He later quipped, 'Unlike the bank in Monte Carlo, Inchanga was more apt to break the man!'

Unchallenged, Newton continued to dominate, despite losing part of a shoe to a distinctly unfriendly canine spectator. Reaching the final hill, Polly Shortts, he stopped for a cup of tea before attempting the testing climb. As he had done on Inchanga, he throttled back and gently shuffled up the hill, joking afterwards, 'I knew the brute. I'd been there before. It was misnamed.

It ought to be called "Jolly Longs".'

Way ahead of the field, Newton finished in 6.58.22, becoming the first man to achieve a hat-trick of wins. He was also the first to break seven hours in both 'up' and 'down' runs. Second-placed G. P. Shackleford crossed the line in 8.13.00.

The *Witness* recognised Newton's phenomenal achievement: 'All that remains to be said is that Newton is a positive marvel and probably the greatest long-distance marathon runner the world has yet seen. The truth of this will be admitted if ordinary people can grasp what the everlasting climb in 54 miles means.

'As may be truly said, even an engine must stop for water – but not Newton. If ever a man deserved well of South Africa it is Newton, and it will be a disgrace if South Africa does not do something princely on his behalf – sportsmen owe him a duty.'

Wonderful though Newton's performance may have been, it was not his main contribution to the event. The spirit of the Comrades Marathon is recognised throughout the sporting world as quite unique. As the great five-time winner Jackie Mekler would comment more than 80 years later, 'It all started with Arthur Newton.'

Newton was awarded first prize, a silver tea service. Believing that he, as a farmer, had had more time to train and consequently an unfair advantage over his rivals, Newton (as he had done the previous two years) declined the award in favour of the runner-up. A local newspaper commented: 'One cannot but admire this spirit of running for the honour of winning and not for the prize attached thereto.'

1924 COMRADES MARATHON RESULTS

1. A. F. H. Newton	6.58.22
2. G. P. Shackleford	8.13.00
3. C. E. Strassburg	8.48.23
4. J. A. Annan	9.01.25
5. C. R. Long	9.16.13
6. E. F. Williams	9.21.03
7. C. Cullingworth	9.35.05

8. A. Cary-Smith	9.40.10
9. R. T. Long	9.41.35
10. H. S. Sowden	9.45.49

1925 COMRADES MARATHON
AN UNBELIEVABLE RECORD

Prior to the 1924 Comrades Marathon, doubts had been expressed in Britain as to the authenticity of Arthur Newton's reported world record 50-mile run on the Comrades course. Following his Comrades hat-trick that year, he endeavoured to establish his credentials in the most telling way possible. He travelled to England and set a new record of 5.53.48 in the London-to-Brighton race, throwing in a world record of 5.48.42 for 50 miles for good measure. There was now no doubting his pre-eminence in ultra-distance running.

Newton or not, the number of entrants continued to be cause for concern. The 1925 Comrades field of 41 may have been three more than that of the previous year, but it was 17 short of the 68 who had started the previous 'down' run. Dwindling numbers suggested a bright but short-lived existence for the Comrades Marathon. It would take half a century before James Fixx (author of *The Complete Book of Running*, the global best-seller of 1977) and others convinced the world of the health benefits of a physically active lifestyle. Long-distance running in the mid-1920s was a spectator sport whose participants were accorded the sort of admiration and disbelief that the citizens of ancient Rome might have accorded gladiators. It was not an activity that appealed to the ordinary man or woman in the street. Those who did participate might well have been admired, but not as healthy, active, normal human beings. Instead they were venerated as superhuman or dismissed as freaks.

Not only were the benefits of long-distance running as yet unrecognised: there were also serious doubts about health hazards. 'Don't drink water on a run: avoid it if possible,' was an admonition designed to protect runners from heart attacks. A slightly moderated warning advised, 'Never drink a lot at a time.' It would be more than half a century before Professor Tim Noakes enlightened athletes on the truth about running and drinking.

Race founder and 1925 organiser Vic Clapham demonstrated his innovative thinking by inviting a local farmer, George Robertson, to race the runners on horseback. While this sideshow was largely ignored by the public, it's worth recalling the name of the horse, 'Why Not?' It brings to mind the motto of the 2003 Comrades Marathon 78 years later: 'Because we can!'

The oldest competitor was 67-year-old A. W. Browne. Strange, in retrospect, that women were not permitted to take part in arduous physical events because of their perceived frailty, and distance athletes were warned about the dangers of drinking water, yet someone not far short of his 'three score years and ten' was allowed to face the challenge of the Comrades Marathon.

At the last stroke of 6 a.m., the mayor of Pietermaritzburg, Councillor D. Sanders, sent the runners on their way. Local runner Harry Phillips, second in both of the first two Comrades Marathons, took the early lead, determined to steal a march on his main rival, Arthur Newton. At Umlaas Road, Phillips was four minutes ahead of Newton. By Cato Ridge, after one-third of the race, his lead was up to five minutes.

Sadly for the slightly built Phillips and his supporters, this was not going to be his day, although he reached Drummond in a record time for halfway of 2.51.45. Newton, slightly less than three minutes behind, was clearly stronger. Phillips took a break, but Newton, moving effortlessly, did not. The lead was diminished.

On the climb up Alverstone Hill towards Botha's Hill, Phillips stopped for attention to a stiffening leg muscle. Before he resumed, Newton went past. The defending champion, experienced in the demands of the race and demonstrably superior to his challengers, simply strode away, moving smoothly.

At Hillcrest, his lead over Phillips was 12 minutes. At Gillits, only a few miles down the road, and approximately two-thirds of the way, the margin was 28 minutes. Once again, Arthur Newton was in total command of a Comrades Marathon.

At Kloof, the runners at last enjoyed the sanctuary of tarred road. Newton reached Pinetown 34 minutes ahead of the second man, still Phillips.

Once over the last of the 'Big Five' hills, Cowies, Newton's victory was assured. The only question remaining was whether he would manage to break the record for the 'down' run. He had a few obstacles to overcome: deviations added more than a mile to the total distance, with the finish moved back to the city hall, and the dust churned up by supporters in motor vehicles cut visibility to little more than ten yards at times.

Undeterred by these distractions and the acclaim of excited spectators, Newton serenely continued on his way, putting in a little sprint over the final 100 yards. His time of 6.24.45 was more than half an hour better than his own record, set two years previously. He was undoubtedly the finest long-distance runner of his era.

Harry Phillips manfully clung to second place, ahead of Maritzburg's Shackleford. Perhaps the second most meritorious performance, after Newton, was that of 67-year-old Browne. Although 40 minutes too late to claim a medal, he kept going until the end. *The Times of Natal* acknowledged the emerging spirit of Comrades:

'His performance was no mean one and his grit an example of that displayed by every competitor, even those who by retiring showed a discretion that could well be copied by many whose zeal outran their ability.'

The horse 'Why Not?' finished ahead of Newton, but its feat has not been officially recognised. One can only ask, 'Why not?'

1925 COMRADES MARATHON RESULTS

1. A. F. H. Newton	6.24.45
2. H. J. Phillips	7.05.30
3. G. P. Shackleford	7.17.22
4. H. C. Briggs	8.04.10
5. W. A. Sutton	8.14.45
6. F. M. Henriksen	8.15.00
7. C. E. Vahl	8.35.00
8. C. E. Strassburg	8.56.15
8. R. Hulley	8.56.15
10. A. Cary-Smith	9.04.00

1926 COMRADES MARATHON
NEWTON BEATEN

The race of Vic Clapham's dreams, the Comrades Marathon, seemed to be on a downhill spiral as the sixth running approached. Media interest was minimal. Frustrated followers of the event blamed the organisers for failing to involve the press. Personalities were lacking: the legendary Arthur Newton had moved to Bulawayo and was not expected to take part.

Last-minute pressure resulted in Newton submitting an entry with less than a week to go. There wasn't much time. The train journey from Bulawayo to Durban took four days, and Newton caught the last train to reach Durban in time. Already undertrained and lacking proper mental build-up, he could hardly have relished four days in a train immediately before the race. Nevertheless, the news that he was willing to undertake the journey added a certain amount of anticipation to the event.

Although Newton's entry had boosted interest, only 24 runners faced the starter, the smallest field in the race's history. Harry Phillips, second in the first two Comrades Marathons and again in 1925, was determined to take advantage of Newton's lack of preparation. While there was no doubt that Newton was the class athlete in the field, Phillips realised that this was his one real opportunity to be a Comrades winner.

From the start, Phillips made his intentions clear. Before Tollgate, he was in the lead. Newton, looking smooth and comfortable, moved into second place, some time behind the leader. Running like a man possessed, Phillips reached halfway at Drummond in a time of 3.14. Newton was more than ten minutes behind him, with Ronnie Sutton in third place.

The formidable climb up Inchanga was and remains the scourge of front-runners. It is on this monster of a hill that early leaders have hit the proverbial 'wall' and been swallowed up by their pursuers. Not so in 1926. Phillips confidently crested the hill and cruised through Harrison Flats, marginally increasing his lead as he approached Cato Ridge.

On the equally demanding stretch from Cato Ridge to Camperdown, Phillips's early pace started to tell. His speed dropped slightly. He looked tired. Newton, on the other hand, seemed to be gaining in strength. At Camperdown, Phillips's lead was eight minutes. Newton had gained two minutes since Drummond. His supporters, including most spectators, were convinced that yet another victory was on the cards as their man steadily reeled in the leader. Phillips disagreed. Although he was clearly feeling the effects of his early efforts, his determination and confidence were undiminished. After a thigh muscle massage in Camperdown, he proclaimed, 'Newton will never catch me now!'

Although narrowing the gap perceptibly, Newton was having problems of his own. He, too, was tiring. At Little Pollys, the lead was down to seven minutes. Pursuer and prey were both struggling, and only Polly Shortts loomed ahead. First to the top would surely hold a decisive advantage. Phillips had a significant lead when he reached the treasured landmark, and victory seemed assured. He must have thought so, too: in the last few miles into the capital city he smilingly exchanged remarks with enthusiastic bystanders.

Newton, meanwhile, continued to close the gap, but it was to no avail. Phillips, three times a runner-up, set a new 'up' record of 6.57.46 that would survive ten years. His victory, after so many disappointments, was well received. Having finally achieved his ambition of winning a Comrades Marathon, he soon announced his retirement from the great race.

Newton claimed second place, just over four minutes behind Phillips. He was no longer an unbeaten Comrades champion. His winning streak of four consecutive years had failed to become five. His preparation had undoubtedly been inadequate, but he explained his defeat in true Comrades fashion: 'If ever a man had deserved a victory, I think Phillips did.'

1926 COMRADES MARATHON RESULTS

1. H. J. Phillips	6.57.46
2. A. F. H. Newton	7.02.00
3. R. A. Sutton	8.09.00
4. F. M. Henriksen	8.13.05
5. W. A. Sutton	8.17.00
6. R. N. Wratten	8.24.30
7. H. S. Sowden	9.08.20
8. T. L. Warwick	9.52.00
9. C. F. Munnery	10.07.30
10. W. G. P. Coulson	10.25.08

1927 COMRADES MARATHON
NEWTON'S LEGACY

The seventh running of the Comrades Marathon saw the final performance of the race's first multiple champion. Arthur Newton's journey from Bulawayo to Durban to take part in the event had surprised many in 1926, but his intentions were clear this time. He announced his challenge timeously and, furthermore, brought two of his Bulawayo Harriers clubmates to broaden, in effect, the southern African participation. Newton, knowing that he was not getting any younger, wanted to make a final assault on the course that had brought him fame, well aware that his exploits had similarly publicised the Comrades Marathon, at home and abroad.

On Empire Day, 24 May, a field of 41 (precisely the same number as had entered the 1925 race) faced the starter outside the Pietermaritzburg City Hall. By now, Comrades starts were being organised with clockwork precision and the city hall clock dispatched the runners at 6 a.m. on the dot.

At the top of Polly Shortts, Newton was already in the lead – not the ideal strategy so early in the race, but a circumstance reflecting his superiority over his rivals and his determination to finish his Comrades career with a flourish.

Although conditions were not unpleasant, there had been some rain in the days building up to the race. Furthermore, the 'roads' in 1927 were still paths rather than paved highways, and the routes over the major hills rather more direct and therefore steeper than those of today. Indeed, modern-day entrants might feel humbled by a comment in a newspaper report of the 1927 race: 'At Mpushini, Newton crossed without a falter, but the third man R. A. Sutton stumbled slightly at the water jump!'

Newton went through Camperdown in 1.03, just 30 seconds ahead of 1926 South African Marathon champion Willie Steytler, who had been recruited to act as pace-setter before retiring halfway. Third-placed Ronnie Sutton was nearly ten minutes behind Steytler. Had the two front-runners gone out too quickly? The following section of the race would tend to support such a view.

At Cato Ridge, Newton was clearly in trouble. Despite being in the lead, his normally effortless style started to look laboured. He paused in order to be doused with water. The *Natal Mercury* recognised his distress:

'Though this was his usual custom, from this point until beyond Drummond, Newton was in trouble. He lost a lot of his easy action and seemed worried and strained as just on leaving Cato Ridge, Steytler passed him in great style. Newton fell away badly and appeared to be absolutely beaten.'

Newton was experiencing a 'bad patch', a phenomenon that countless other Comrades runners would come to recognise over the years. His response, the only sensible one, was to soldier on, keep moving at a reduced pace and realise that bad patches are temporary, can be overcome and can also afflict those ahead.

This is precisely what happened, although Newton was to suffer a further blow before recovering. Shortly after Drummond, Ron Sutton passed him. Now he was third, and seemed to be slipping back. Not for long, however. Steytler was in pain and retired at the top of Botha's Hill. Sutton, the new leader, was experiencing cramp in his calf muscles. In desperation, he stopped three times to have his aching legs massaged.

On the crucial stretch between Hillcrest and Kloof, Newton swept past Sutton and resumed the lead that most regarded as his right. Now fully recovered, he confidently waved to spectators as he gradually increased his advantage. There was no stopping him now. Although his bad patch had put paid to any thought of a record, Newton serenely strode to the finish, winning the event by a margin of 35 minutes from Frank Sutton (second), Bill Sutton (third) and Ron Sutton (fourth). It was obvious that a certain family intended to make their presence felt in future. They would do so.

Arthur Newton's active participation in the Comrades Marathon had come to an end, but his influence on the race continues today. Newton was the first person in the world to critically analyse the stresses, demands and realities of ultra-distance running. He wrote several books which today are recognised as significant contributions to the burgeoning field of sports science. His sportsmanship, both as a Comrades runner and later as a senior statesman helping others surpass his own achievements, was instrumental in raising the noble camaraderie of the Comrades Marathon to a level unique among sporting events. When asked about the phenomenal Comrades spirit at the finish of the 2005 Comrades Marathon, race legend Jackie Mekler said simply, 'It all started with Arthur Newton.'

1927 COMRADES MARATHON RESULTS

1. A. F. H. Newton   6.40.56
2. F. Sutton   7.15.55
3. W. A. Sutton   7.52.06
4. R. A. Sutton   8.13.32
5. N. H. Walker   8.30.18
6. C. C. Erwin   8.45.05
7. F. W. Hayes   8.45.26
8. F. C. M. Watkins   9.18.00
9. W. J. Marlow   9.58.53
10. W. G. P. Coulson   10.00.00

4

STAYING ALIVE
(1928 to 1932)

Vic Clapham's dream race had survived its first seven years, but only just. In 1921, 16 out of 34 starters had completed the event. In 1927, 41 had taken part, of whom 21 had lasted the distance. This hardly constituted unqualified acceptance of a race that demanded more of its participants than any other sporting contest and offered very little in return, other than the realisation, even in its infancy, that it united those who embraced it with a feeling of togetherness that was unparalleled in sport.

The early years had been dominated by post-war nostalgia and a special allegiance felt by those who had been part of the war effort. Would this comradeship fade away as the demands of peacetime, including a shaky world economy, came to dominate everyday living? A pioneering spirit had ignited interest in the extraordinary challenge of Comrades. Would the novelty wear off? Arthur Newton, the great athlete and character, had retired. He had been the ultimate drawcard. Could he possibly be replaced?

One person who had no doubt about the future of the Comrades Marathon was its irrepressible founder, Vic Clapham. Clapham regularly came up with enterprising ideas to keep the race in the minds of people, as his son Eric recalled: 'To advertise the race, my dad got a local runner, red-haired Bill Rufus, to jog around Maritzburg wearing a purple mask, purple shorts and a purple vest with huge question marks printed on the front and back.'

Clapham's dedication and attention to detail led to a nasty accident on one occasion. Eric explained: 'One year my dad wanted to measure the exact distance of the race. He got hold of a pedometer and some runners took turns to push it from Maritzburg to Durban.

'On the way back, the car slid into a ditch. My father fell, breaking his jaw in two places, and almost all his teeth broke off at the gums. However, he always thought of others first. He ripped off his shirt, tearing it into bandages, to save the life of a runner who had severed an artery in his arm. My dad arrived home drenched. My mother made him change into dry clothes, but he had to support his jaw by tying a towel around it and holding the ends above his head. There were no taxis in those days, so I had to run to call a rickshaw to take him to Old Grey's Hospital.'

Clapham's efforts, along with the enthusiasm of a small nucleus of determined athletes, managed to keep the race alive. But only just. In the five years from 1928 to 1932, the numbers of finishers were 13, 19, 29, 29 and 24 respectively. These were the days of the Great Depression. A sombre mood pervaded life at this bleak time, as an article in the *Cape Times* during August of 1931 indicated:

'The number of starving poor grows week by week. The public has responded most generously to the appeals which have appeared from time to time in the press, and the example set by the three daily newspapers in Cape Town, who are organising a monthly collection among their staffs, has found an echo in a number of city firms.'

It was difficult enough for people to survive, never mind take interest in a crazy annual adventure for a minority who were regarded by many as somewhat abnormal. The long-term health benefits of a physically active lifestyle had yet to be identified. In fact, it was widely held that strenuous exercise was foolhardy, entailing a risk of sudden death.

Clapham realised that his race needed some sort of extra appeal, hence his innovative approach. In particular, a replacement for Arthur Newton, someone who would capture the public's imagination, was needed. In 1930, it seemed as if this might be happening when a youthful Wally Hayward made his Comrades debut. Unfortunately, his initial relationship with the great race was short-lived.

Nevertheless, enough happened to maintain the faithful following of early Comrades supporters despite the fact that both 'up' and 'down' records remained intact throughout this period. Two sets of brothers, the Suttons and the Savages, introduced a family interest, the Gunga Din Trophy for the winning team was introduced, Hayward's appearance sparked a good deal of interest, and Phil Masterton-Smith and Noel Burree provided 1931 spectators with a thrilling sprint to the finish, only two seconds separating them as they crossed the line.

1928 COMRADES MARATHON
A FAMILY AFFAIR

This year's Comrades Marathon was organised by the Maritzburg United Athletic and Cycling Club, incorporating the old Comrades Club. Times were changing. Comrades founder and inaugural chairman-secretary-dogsbody Vic Clapham was no longer around. It would be up to others to continue his great dream, or so it seemed at the time. Despite the organisational change, Clapham would remain the driving force for another decade.

Other realities had to be faced. The race's first great multiple champion, five-time winner Arthur Newton, had retired. Nobody is indispensable, we're told, though it didn't seem that way in the build-up to the 1928 Comrades Marathon. But the show had to go on. Without a defending champion, interest focused on the experienced and highly competitive Sutton family, who had finished second, third and fourth behind Newton the previous year. If they worked as a team (unheard of in those days), one of them should surely prevail.

The year saw a couple of significant changes. In the first place, the time limit for silver medals – race finishers, that is – was reduced from 12 to 11 hours. This made life significantly more challenging for the tail-enders.

The other change, which would have far-reaching effects in later years, concerned race numbers. Certain runners asked to compete in the same numbers that they had worn previously. This was some time before the allocation of permanent numbers in acknowledgement of certain criteria, such as ten finishes, five golds or three wins, as is the norm nowadays. What is worth noting is the fact that, as long ago as 1928, there were runners who wanted to retain their number from year to year. This tradition continues today. In certain other major races, runners wear different numbers every year and those earning permanent numbers simply acquire such numbers in sequential order of achievement. Those earning Comrades permanent numbers keep their original numbers, provided that they do not miss too many events en route to the attainment of their 'in perpetuity' award. Over the years, this has become a highly prized incentive and achievement for regular Comrades entrants. Morris Alexander, who passed on his race number 1 to Clive Crawley, formalised this special Comrades tradition.

Modern-day runners are often advised by their more experienced colleagues to 'drive' the course before race day in order to familiarise themselves with the route and also to 'frighten themselves'. Bruce Fordyce is a strong advocate of the practice. In 1928 Frank Sutton covered the course on a Dunelt motorcycle in just over an hour. This provides an interesting opportunity to comment on his performance on race day.

The 1928 Comrades was not the most impressive athletic contest in the race's history. Newton's departure left a significant athletic void. There was no one approaching his stature in the field. Yet there was one promising feature: a good percentage of the 34 starters were young and would hopefully continue their relationship with the race. The Comrades Marathon would never be an exclusive race about elite athletes, even though its champions would certainly take their place in the top echelon of international athletes. The Comrades Marathon would be true to its name and origin. Its members, super-athletes and backmarkers alike, would make up a close-knit family in which all of them were important.

On a cool morning, 34 runners responded to the official starter, Durban's mayor, Councillor Buzzard, and set off on the eighth Comrades Marathon at 6 a.m. on Thursday 24 May. Durban runner Fred Cole, a standard marathon specialist, took the early lead with Ron Sutton in second place. Shortly after Hillcrest, Sutton passed Cole, who was looking uncomfortable. Cole, however, seemed to have a 'second wind' and was back in front at the top of Botha's Hill. Seemingly well recovered, Cole reached halfway five and a half minutes ahead of Ron Sutton, whose brother Frank was two minutes further back in third place.

Inchanga, as so often, proved to be the turning point. In intense heat, both Cole and Ron Sutton were overtaken by Frank Sutton, who built up a four-minute lead over his brother by the time they reached Camperdown. Among the front-runners, it was now a survival battle more than a race. Leader Frank Sutton gasped out the familiar Comrades refrain, 'I'll never do it again.'

Cole didn't make the finish, but later expressed his strong positive feeling for the event. 'The marathon, with its glamour of achievement, gives running its necessary purpose and incentive. For most of those who ran each year, there was no chance of winning. Not theirs the glory, but nonetheless they gain for their own personal satisfaction.'

Up front, it was a family affair. With both brothers exhausted, Ron made a valiant attempt to catch Frank, coming within 90 seconds of him at one stage. Frank, however, was the first to crest Polly Shortts. Sniffing victory, he pulled away and breasted the tape in 7.49.07, eight minutes ahead of Ron. Strong-finishing Felix Henriksen of Bulawayo Harriers took third place in 8.19.12.

1928 COMRADES MARATHON RESULTS

1. F. Sutton	7.49.07
2. R. A. Sutton	7.57.17
3. F. M. Henriksen	8.19.12
4. C. F. Munnery	8.39.46

5. L. G. Cary-Smith	9.03.13
6. F. W. Hayes	9.16.00
7. H. Triegaardt	9.58.10
8. A. Cary-Smith	10.25.18
9. N. Nightscales	10.37.23
10. R. Shapiro	10.41.18

1929 COMRADES MARATHON
DALE'S DAY

This race cannot be regarded as a pinnacle of Comrades Marathon history. The field was weak, the organisation lacking the zeal of earlier days. Astonishingly, no timekeeper was appointed. This awful situation was resolved at the last moment when the sports editor of the *Natal Mercury*, Les Cox, sportingly provided his own stopwatch.

Only 29 runners faced the starter. No one in the field had previously managed a top-three Comrades finish, so this was a novices' race with no clear favourites. The Sutton brothers, following their triumph the previous year, had jointly opted for early retirement. Somewhat fortuitously, another set of brothers entered the Comrades arena – the Savages.

The first four miles of this 'down' run were relatively comfortable. They featured tarred roads. From then onward, almost to the end, the runners had to negotiate steep, sandy hills (far more arduous than those of today) in their effort to reach Durban victoriously (for some) or timeously (for most).

Archie Cary-Smith, a regular Comrades entrant, was the early leader. First through Camperdown in 1.53.00, he retained his lead at the halfway mark, which he reached in 3.19.45, approximately seven minutes ahead of second-placed Albert Marie, with 20-year-old Darrell Dale a further three minutes back in third position.

Despite his youth, Dale was well prepared for the race. He was also ready to challenge medical advice that had curtailed his sporting activities during his schooldays. Diagnosed as suffering from a heart complaint, he was not allowed to take part in normal sporting activities. Now, working as a bank clerk, he was no longer subject to the stifling conservatism of those who wished to wrap the frail young man in cotton wool. Instead, he took guidance from the Sutton family, who had dominated the 1928 Comrades Marathon.

On the long climb of Botha's Hill, Albert Marie struggled with cramp. Dale shot past him and set his sights on leader Archie Cary-Smith. At Hillcrest, the leader showed his first sign of vulnerability. When he paused for attention at Gillits, Dale strode past. In his very first Comrades Marathon, Darrell Dale found himself in the lead with just over one-third of the race ahead of him.

Young and strong, Dale confidently stepped up his pace. At Kloof, he was 13 minutes ahead of a well-beaten Cary-Smith and 19 minutes ahead of third-placed Fred Wallace. In Pinetown, Dale's lead was still 13 minutes, but Wallace, looking fresh, had ousted Cary-Smith from second spot.

Inevitably, as the race moved into the closing stages, Dale, lacking the strength and stamina that only come with maturity, started to wilt. Nevertheless, he pressed ahead, somewhat gingerly but fully aware of the fact that his lead was significant and the finish was beckoning. The previous year's winner, Frank Sutton, was seconding Dale. Understanding only too well the pain of the closing stages of the 'down' run and aware of the intense heat, Sutton gently sustained the leader with tea and regular sponging.

When he realised that the result was assured, a relieved Dale allowed himself the luxury of a slowish walk. There was no longer a need to push. Dale completed the race in 7.52.01, approximately 18 minutes ahead of Wallace. Although he enjoyed the distinction of being the only runner that day to finish in under eight hours, his time remains the second-slowest winning time for the 'down' run. Only Bill Rowan, winning the very first Comrades Marathon in 1921, posted a slower time.

1929 COMRADES MARATHON RESULTS

1. D. E. C. Dale	7.52.01
2. W. F. O. Wallace	8.10.17
3. A. M. Marie	8.17.31
4. W. R. du Bois	8.19.26

5. F. J. Steytler	8.39.51
6. A. Cary-Smith	8.53.12
7. J. W. W. Savage	8.53.55
8. N. H. Walker	8.54.59
9. W. E. R. Savage	9.00.30
10. J. P. van Rooyen	9.40.49

1930 COMRADES MARATHON
A YOUNGSTER NAMED HAYWARD

The tenth running of the Comrades Marathon will forever be remembered for the debut of 21-year-old Wally Hayward. Having recently won the South African ten-mile track championship, he was regarded as a promising young middle-distance athlete. Knowledgeable observers saw his participation in Comrades as an expression of the uninhibited enthusiasm of youth. Nobody could have foreseen his astounding performance in the race, his remarkable and victorious comeback in the 1950s and his near-miraculous return towards the end of the 1980s as an octogenarian.

Hayward's participation would forever enrich the memory of the 1930 Comrades Marathon. Yet there were other notable novices who would play significant roles as the race developed. Future winners Bill Cochrane and Phil Masterton-Smith both made their debuts, as did Noel Burree (a future runner-up) and Vernon Jones, the Boy Scout who had witnessed Bill Rowan's triumphant charge through Pinetown in 1921 and would become a notable Comrades historian.

Wallace Henry (Wally) Hayward, born in Durban on 10 July 1908, joined the Wanderers Club in Johannesburg in 1929. During that year, he saw a pamphlet advertising a challenge with a rather romantic name: the Comrades Marathon, details obtainable from a Mr Vic Clapham in Pietermaritzburg. Intrigued, Hayward wrote to Clapham and discovered that the distance of the race was 56 miles, far more than double anything he had attempted in his young life. Youth held the key, and Hayward posted his entry form, together with the entry fee of five shillings, to Clapham.

In his later years, Hayward remembered the excitement of the occasion. Having left Durban at the age of 18 months when his parents moved to the Rand, this would be his first encounter with the sea. Travelling by train, he was introduced to card playing by his travelling companions.

Obeying Clapham's advice, Hayward went to the start wearing two pairs of socks coated with boracic powder inside his tackies. Lacking an appreciation of the demands of ultra-distance running, he passed Frank Hayes just after Tollgate and moved into the lead. Seemingly intent on destroying his opposition as quickly as possible, he reached halfway 16 minutes ahead of second-placed Frank Munnery. At Drummond, he stopped for a rub and changed his socks, his feet already blistering.

Vic Clapham, who had been specially invited by the Maritzburg United Athletic and Cycling Club to organise the race, was following the leaders in a vehicle. Alarmed by Hayward's pace, he warned the youngster of the danger of 'hitting the wall' if he didn't slow down. Hayward, however, was unable to contain his determination and Clapham's prediction proved correct. For the leader, much of the second half was a painful battle for survival.

On Harrison Flats, Hayward began to falter, cramp attacking his right leg. At Cato Ridge, the two-thirds mark, he stopped for a second rub. The same thing happened at Camperdown. He was clearly in trouble. By Camperdown, Munnery had cut his lead to 11 minutes, and there were others closing in on Munnery. Jack Savage and Phil Masterton-Smith both looked threatening.

Munnery was the first to crack, being passed by Savage and joined by Masterton-Smith. Hayward by now had discovered a Comrades reality that would be learnt by countless others after him. He was able to keep going on the downhills, but his tank seemed to be empty on the uphills.

As the leaders approached Pietermaritzburg, it became clear that Masterton-Smith was the strongest of the line contenders. Having overtaken Savage and Munnery, he was just eight minutes behind Hayward at Little Pollys. On the descent to Pollys itself, the lead was cut to six minutes. By now, however, the pace was telling on Masterton-Smith, who had taken 16 minutes out of Hayward's lead since Drummond. It was a straight race to the finish between two exhausted men.

As they approached the stadium, Masterton-Smith was visibly eating into

Hayward's lead. It was a question of whether or not his challenge was too late. Hayward was first onto the track, soon followed by Masterton-Smith. Although Hayward stumbled momentarily, he kept his balance and his composure and crossed the line 37 seconds ahead of his pursuer. Munnery hung on gamely to claim third place.

Of the 55 starters, 29 managed to complete the race, the backmarkers having to deal with rain and hail in the closing stages. The Comrades Marathon had survived its first decade. Interestingly, John Annan's seven finishes made him the most experienced Comrades runner to date. He was followed by Arthur Newton and Rubin Shapiro with six medals each and Walter Coulson and Archie Cary-Smith with five.

Hayward's prize was a Kienzle grandfather clock. It became his proudest possession and was introduced to all visitors to his home as if it were a member of his family. For years, he would use it to time his training runs. He promised his daughter Gwen that it would become hers when he moved on to the next world. The clock has confirmed that she had a very long wait.

1930 COMRADES MARATHON RESULTS

1. W. H. Hayward	7.27.26
2. H. P. Masterton-Smith	7.28.03
3. C. F. Munnery	7.39.30
4. J. W. W. Savage	7.44.31
5. W. F. O. Wallace	7.55.24
6. J. P. van Rooyen	8.15.02
7. W. J. Cochrane	8.20.21
8. A. Marie	8.20.50
9. R. Shapiro	8.27.14
10. W. E. R. Savage	8.29.42

1931 COMRADES MARATHON
ALMOST A PHOTO FINISH

Following his 1930 Comrades victory, young Wally Hayward was heard to utter two famous Comrades words, 'Never again!' Like most others who have expressed similar sentiments, he changed his mind. He had fallen in love with Comrades, and Comrades followers had fallen in love with him. Hayward was fully committed to an attempt at a second straight win. Alas, it was not to be. On a training run in the gathering dark, he made contact with a stone and broke a bone in a foot. He was ruled out of the 1931 Comrades and would not return to the great race until 1950.

Hayward's withdrawal meant that the 1931 event would not feature a single past winner. Darrell Dale, the 1929 champion, was also excluded through injury. Nevertheless, the race was eagerly awaited, for a variety of reasons. The field of 65, the second-strongest entry to date, reflected a new-found enthusiasm for Comrades. Excitement created by Hayward's 1930 performance was a major factor. For the second time, there was a female attraction, schoolteacher Geraldine Watson aiming to emulate the achievement of Frances Hayward in 1923. The route had been made significantly easier: for the first time, the entire road was fully tarred. It seemed almost a sacrilege to those who had overcome the inaugural challenge ten years previously. Modern runners have little understanding of the hardships faced by the Comrades pioneers of the 1920s.

Of far-reaching consequence was the introduction of a floating trophy for the first team to finish. The design of the award was fully in keeping with race founder Vic Clapham's original intention, consisting of a military tin helmet mounted on a wooden base. It was donated by the Gunga Din Shellhole. The Gunga Din Trophy for the winning team remains one of the most coveted awards of the Comrades Marathon.

It is generally recognised that a calm, relaxed frame of mind is required as one goes to the start. A breakdown in travel arrangements on the morning of the race is just about the worst possible thing that could happen, and this is precisely what happened to Colenso runner Noel Burree. Having travelled to Pietermaritzburg on the eve of the race, he spent the night in the suburb of Scottsville. Cutting things rather fine, he arranged to be picked up by a taxi 20 minutes before the start. When it became clear that he was being let down, he hastily borrowed a child's bicycle, only to find that it had a puncture. He quickly repaired this and rode off frantically, arriving at the start just as the race was commencing. Shouting out his name in order not to be recorded as absent at roll call, he dashed off and swiftly caught up with the others. When the race had been won and lost later in the day, he would have every reason to rue his early morning drama.

Regular Comrades runner Albert Marie and miler George Steere were the early leaders and maintained their advantage until Cato Ridge. As usual, the massive hill of Inchanga brought about a reshuffling of the pack. Steere managed to reach Drummond first, with the strong-running Bill Savage close behind and looking threatening. The previous year's runner-up, Phil Masterton-Smith, was playing a waiting game. Looking comfortable, he went through halfway 12 minutes behind Steere. In the second half, the lead changed hands a few times. Strydom went ahead on Botha's Hill and was passed by Van Rooyen at Hillcrest. Meanwhile, Masterton-Smith's strategy appeared to be working, and he moved up into contention. Going down Field's Hill, he went ahead for the first time and began to pull away, the race now looking sewn up.

Noel Burree had looked uncomfortable throughout the morning, running with a slight limp (possibly as a result of his unscheduled bicycle ride). Nevertheless, he kept going and stayed in range of the leaders. On the flattish section through Pinetown, he took second place and began to close the gap on Masterton-Smith. It was now a two-horse race.

At Tollgate (the last of the hills), Burree was just 40 yards behind the leader, who was visibly tiring. Through the streets of Durban, the two exhausted men fought a ding-dong battle. With about 700 yards to go, Burree moved ahead. Excited motorists, following their progress, impeded them in the closing stages. Both were baulked, Burree perhaps more seriously.

Masterton-Smith was first onto the track, Burree ten yards behind. With the crowd screaming hysterically, Burree gradually closed the gap as they ran their final lap. For a brief moment, Burree was in front. Then Masterton-Smith put in a surge and crossed the line just two seconds ahead. Was the race decided in those final moments, or was Burree's dash to the start the crucial factor? Masterton-Smith summed up the situation in the Comrades spirit, shaking Burree's hand and telling him, 'It was a great race, our race.

Not a first and second – the margin was too narrow.'

The first five runners came from different parts of Natal: Masterton-Smith (Maritzburg), Burree (Colenso), Strydom (Greytown), Van Rooyen (Weenen) and Wallace (Durban). The first recipient of the Gunga Din team award was the host club: the Maritzburg United Athletic and Cycling Club 'A' team.

Running unofficially, Geraldine Watson completed the journey in a little over 11 hours, admitting afterwards, 'I had thought of giving up at Kloof.' Vic Clapham Junior fared somewhat worse, pulling out with cramp early in the second half. Sadly, no member of the Clapham family has yet completed a Comrades Marathon.

1931 COMRADES MARATHON RESULTS

1. H. P. Masterton-Smith	7.16.30
2. N. C. Burree	7.16.32
3. W. M. L. Strydom	7.32.20
4. J. P. van Rooyen	8.01.50
5. W. F. O. Wallace	8.04.10
6. A. E. Taylor	8.23.02
7. T. C. Pieterse	8.31.40
8. E. F. B. Schutze	8.37.47
9. N. H. Walker	8.48.38
10. K. O. Dubber	8.52.05

1932 COMRADES MARATHON
DURBAN'S HOPES MATERIALISE

The day of the Comrades Marathon was by now recognised as an annual occasion in which some hardy South Africans would deny themselves the normal comforts of life, take in minimal sustenance and strive to survive a challenge of their own choosing to the applause of thousands of supporters.

In 1932, ordinary South Africans were largely uninterested in such seemingly mindless masochism. The realities of day-to-day life posed enough problems. The Great Depression, as it has come to be known, affected everyone's existence. Life was tough. Luxuries were forgotten, normally accepted necessities were in short supply and soup kitchens were introduced to keep the unemployed alive. Britain had gone off the gold standard on 21 September 1931, and South Africa would follow suit over a year later.

It was in the midst of such suffering that the 1932 Comrades Marathon took place. Economic considerations suggested that no awards would be available for the successful athletes this time, but last-minute intervention ensured that there would be prizes for the first few finishers. The Durban Turf Club played a positive role. The main consideration was the fact that the Comrades Marathon would go ahead.

At precisely 6 a.m., a field of 65 left the city hall in Durban on their ambitious journey. The weather was perfect for the start, which wasn't good news for the latter part of the day. It was going to get hot, said the forecasters, and they were right. 'Do not drink!' was the advice given to runners, in accordance with prevailing medical wisdom. Such opinion would change drastically, in various ways, over the next 70 years and more.

H. A. Ward of Mafikeng, running his first Comrades, took the early lead. He would become recognised as a regular front-runner over the next few years. At Pinetown, he was three and a half minutes ahead of his pursuers despite being four minutes slower than Hayward had been at this point in his victorious run two years previously.

Over the years, various strategies have been touted as to the best way of attempting the formidable race. Some have advocated an early move to the front, in the hope that leading the event would provide motivation in itself while others might burn themselves out trying to play catch-up. The most widely accepted tactic nowadays is the 'come from behind' approach incorporating a gentle, cautious first half leading to a well-timed assault in the closing stages.

In 1932 there appeared to be no discernible pattern. The lead changed hands several times. Early front-runners fell off the pace – some into oblivion, others coming back with renewed spirit and determination. All had to face the oppressive heat, which gathered intensity throughout the day. It seemed unlikely that the previous year's battle between Masterton-Smith and Burree would be repeated. Masterton-Smith did employ a cautious approach but didn't appear to be really in contention. Burree was not properly prepared and looked unlikely to threaten the leaders.

Ward led the field over Botha's Hill. The three Savage brothers (Jack, Bill and Percy) had enjoyed each other's company for the first third of the race, but as the heat took its toll, they parted company. Jack, looking the strongest at this stage, set off in pursuit of Ward. He caught his man on the descent to Drummond and began pulling away. Ward, exhausted by his early efforts and disheartened at surrendering the lead, pulled out of the race.

Jack Savage was first through halfway, more than seven minutes ahead of his brother Bill, with novice Hardy Ballington a further two minutes behind in third place. Masterton-Smith and Bill Cochrane were 15 minutes off the pace. Noel Burree was a further eight minutes behind, too far back to have any real chance of victory.

On Inchanga, Bill Savage dropped back, looking like an also-ran. Jack Savage, still ahead, was followed by Ballington and Cochrane. By the time Camperdown had been reached, defending champion Masterton-Smith was second. Soon, he was in front and reached Umlaas Road five minutes before Ballington and Jack Savage, now running together. The race seemed over, but not for long. Masterton-Smith stopped for a massage and was clearly in trouble, as was Jack Savage. Novice Ballington now appeared to have the whip hand – but not for long.

Bill Savage had looked virtually dead and buried on Inchanga. Almost miraculously, he recovered and began to overtake those ahead. Polly Shortts provided the crucial change. Ascending the formidable hill confidently, Savage passed Ballington and Masterton-Smith and reached the top comfortably in front. He went on to win in 7.41.58, which remains the third slowest winning time for an 'up' run. Bill Savage became Durban's first Comrades champion.

Masterton-Smith and Ballington, having succumbed to Savage's challenge on Polly Shortts, lost spirit and fell back in the field, Ballington finishing fourth and the defending champion sixth. Lionel Knight took second place with future winner Bill Cochrane third.

A group of four Durban runners, including legends-to-be Vernon Jones and Allen Boyce, acknowledged the intense heat by walking together all the way from Camperdown to the end. They even stopped for a cup of tea along the way.

Geraldine Watson, albeit unofficially, became the first woman to complete both an 'up' and a 'down' run, finishing in 11.56.00.

1932 COMRADES MARATHON RESULTS

1. W. E. R. Savage		7,41.58
2. L. H. Knight		7.50.54
3. W. Cochrane		7.57.46
4. H. R. Ballington		8.01.14
5. J. W. W. Savage		8.12.45
6. H. P. Masterton-Smith		8.35.09
7. D. Terblanche		8.50.43
8. A. M. Marie		8.51.10
9. W. F. O. Wallace		8.51.10
10. J. I. Luke		8.56.21

5

BALLINGTON
SHOWS THE WAY
(1933 to 1938)

During the 1930s, small fields continued to frustrate those who were hoping to see the race grow. Yet there was an underlying strength that would sustain Comrades even when only 19, the smallest field on record, turned up to take part in the 1936 race.

This was the period in which founder Vic Clapham made his final contribution as race organiser – and his enthusiasm and ingenuity were sorely needed. Clapham's son Eric spoke years later of some of his famous father's original ideas:

'In the 1930s, my father asked the mayor of Maritzburg to write a letter to the mayor of Durban. This was folded into a tube and, after the start of the race, Dad drove down the road and handed it to the first runner. The tradition of passing the baton to the lead runner had begun. The winner would hand the letter to Durban's mayor. It was a wonderful way to promote inter-city friendship.'

Two runners who would become Comrades legends, Liege Boulle and Max Trimborn, both ran their debut races in 1933. Eric recalled an incident that would become immortalised in Comrades starting procedure:

'One year, Max Trimborn crowed like a cock just before the first chime of the clock, when the starter's gun was fired. This, too, became a Comrades tradition, and now a recorded version is broadcast through loudspeakers.'

On one occasion, the usually reliable Vic Clapham was horrified to discover that his memory had failed him and he'd left the starter's pistol at home. In desperation, he turned to a local policeman and managed to persuade him to part, very briefly, with his service revolver. Son Eric spoke of his father's further forgetfulness:

'Dad promised the policeman he would have the cartridge case chrome-plated and mounted on a plaque as a souvenir. He duly forgot the incident but kept that *doppie* in his desk drawer during all his moves to Ladysmith, Queenstown, Hibberdene, Warner Beach and, finally, Durban.

'Shortly before his death in 1962, my dad recognised the then-retired policeman in West Street, Durban, remembered his promise, commissioned a jeweller to chrome-plate and mount the *doppie*, and sent it to the ex-cop.'

The records suggest that Vic Clapham kept his promises, even overcoming the odd memory lapse. He certainly did not let down the Comrades community. He also realised his hope of finding a replacement for the race's first superstar, Arthur Newton. He would not claim credit for this, nor did he have a right to do so.

Vernon Jones, whose running career was drawing to a close, was out on a training run one day when he spotted a young man with huge calf muscles who was similarly engaged, but shuffling along bent over in a most awkward-looking fashion. 'Young man, you ought to take part in the Comrades Marathon,' was Jones's comment, little knowing that his new friend's strange running style was caused by his urgent need for an appendectomy.

When the operation had been successfully accomplished, the young man, Hardy Ballington, heeded the advice of Vernon Jones and focused his attention on the Comrades Marathon. He would become one of the greatest of all Comrades champions. In fact, he would, at his peak, become renowned as the world's finest ultra-distance runner.

Of more importance, perhaps, in the evolution of the Comrades Marathon, was Ballington's exemplary adoption, and enhancement, of that almost tangible ethos, the spirit of Comrades, at the most character-challenging moment of his career, his 1935 disappointment.

The Comrades Marathon might not have grown spectacularly in numbers during the 1930s, but it did experience an increasing realisation of its unique culture. Quantity might have been lacking; quality most certainly was not!

1933 COMRADES MARATHON
BALLINGTON ARRIVES

Right from day one, the Comrades Marathon has been an ultra-distance event between Durban and Pietermaritzburg, traditionally 'down' in odd number years and 'up' in even. Over time, start and finish points have been changed, routes altered, detours introduced. As a consequence the demands of the course have differed from era to era and year to year. Furthermore, the length of the race has never been constant. It is in the vicinity of 90 kilometres but has ranged between 86 and 93 kilometres over the years. Most habitués think of the distance as 90 kilometres. For some strange reason, the South African edition of the Trivial Pursuit board game categorically proclaims 89 as the actual figure.

The year 1933 saw the 13th running of the Comrades Marathon. The event, in these early years, was very much a Natal affair: approximately 90 per cent of runners hailed from the host province. This was understandable. Globalisation was more than half a century away. Travel was expensive, slow and not particularly safe. Conditions of employment favoured employer rather than employee: it wasn't easy for someone working in Port Elizabeth, Bloemfontein or Cape Town to say to his boss, 'I want to take three days off work in order to run from Pietermaritzburg to Durban.' The prestige that now accompanies participation in the great race did not exist in 1933. The assumption was that you had to be superhuman – or mad – even to think of such an adventure.

Fortunately, there were sufficient lunatics to keep the Comrades dream alive. The 85 athletes this year made up the second-largest field to date, just four fewer than the 89 who had started in 1922. Among the novices were Liege Boulle, who would become known as 'Mr Comrades' for his regular participation over four decades, and Max Trimborn, whose famous cockcrow, now in recorded form, heralds the start of every Comrades Marathon. Prevailing circumstances remained difficult. The effects of the Depression were still there, and the nation was in the grip of a severe drought, but, as ever, hope was in the hearts of the optimists who answered the call of Maritzburg mayor, Councillor P. H. Taylor.

Optimism was an absolute essential, as were fortitude and resolution. As is often the case in a 'down' run, bitterly cold weather dominated the early stages. After an hour and a half, rain set in, accompanied by a freezing wind. It was not pleasant. Some, however, seemed at home in the adverse conditions. As he had done the previous year, H. A. Ward took the early lead in the coldest, wettest and windiest Comrades yet.

Was this to be Ward's year? It seemed likely when he reached halfway almost six minutes ahead of second man Jimmy Sandison, with Bill Cochrane and Hardy Ballington running together, nearly four minutes adrift of Sandison. Suddenly, it all changed. Ward inexplicably lost five minutes as he stopped at Drummond. Sandison took over, but not for long. He was in trouble. Cochrane took charge as Ballington changed shoes. Leadership was almost as topsy-turvy as the previous year.

Finally, a decisive move was made, when 20-year-old Ballington, obviously happy with his new tackies, passed both Cochrane and Sandison on the ascent of Botha's Hill. Running strongly, he went through Hillcrest seven minutes ahead of Sandison, who, presumably feeling similar discomfort to Ballington's, had discarded his shoes but, unlike Ballington, not replaced them. Running in his socks, he looked rather disconsolate and out of contention.

It was now Ballington's race. He reached Pinetown 12 minutes ahead of second-placed Bill Cochrane. Wearing a sweater as protection against the rain and cold, Ballington forged ahead in the closing stages. There was no stopping him. Comrades had a new, great champion. The Ballington era had begun. Finishing in 6.50.37, he became the second runner after Newton to break the seven-hour barrier in a 'down' run. Excellent as his achievement appeared to be, and was, every 'down' run since then has been won in a faster time.

This should not detract from the significance of Ballington's 1933 effort. As all athletics champions will agree, you can only beat the challengers of your era, not those of subsequent years. Ballington's winning time was, anyway, the fastest 'down' time for six years. Over the next few years, Hardy Ballington would become known as the world's foremost long-distance athlete.

Ballington's youth, along with that of his predecessors, suggested that ultra-distance road-running suited the younger runner. Phil Masterton-Smith, aged 19 in 1931, remains the youngest Comrades champion. Other winners of the past – Darrell Dale (20), Wally Hayward (21) and Bill Savage (22) – seemed to provide evidence supporting the view that this is a young person's challenge. Modern results, though, notably the victories of old man Vladimir Kotov, suggest otherwise.

The phenomenal call of Comrades and the reality of economic depression were perhaps best illustrated by the participation of 1931 champion Phil Masterton-Smith. In order to take part, he cycled from Cape Town to Pietermaritzburg, hardly the best way to prepare for the Comrades Marathon. He finished tenth.

A noteworthy finisher was Geraldine Watson, for the third successive year. Her time of 9.31.25 was highly creditable for another 'unofficial' run.

1933 COMRADES MARATHON RESULTS

1. H. R. Ballington	6.50.37
2. W. J. Cochrane	7.11.21
3. L. H. Knight	7.16.00
4. D. J. Quigley	7.32.30
5. J. B. Sandison	7.36.28
6. W. F. O. Wallace	7.43.38
7. J. I. Luke	7.51.18
8. A. Marie	7.54.34
9. W. E. R. Savage	7.54.54
10. H. P. Masterton-Smith	8.00.10

1934 COMRADES MARATHON
A SECOND WIN FOR BALLINGTON

Participants in the Comrades Marathon were regarded, at this stage of the race's development, as 'freaks', as fringe members of normal society, punishing themselves in a bizarre masochistic ritual. Everest had yet to be climbed, and attempts to reach the summit of Earth were seen as suicidal. Those who were mad enough to try to run from Durban to Pietermaritzburg, or vice versa, were indulging in a similar form of self-flagellation.

One man tried to alter such perceptions. Violinist Stirling Robins was the leader of the Durban City Orchestra. He was a particularly well-known and popular member of Durban's cultural elite. In the minds of many, there could hardly have been a greater contrast in lifestyle than that of orchestral musician vis-à-vis ultramarathon runner. When it became known that Stirling Robins had entered the 1934 Comrades Marathon, the race drew special interest from a previously untapped section of the community.

Despite this extra attention, a disappointingly small field of 40 faced the starter, Mayor Percy Osborn, outside the Durban City Hall. Conditions were far from ideal. It was bitterly cold and rain appeared inevitable. A brave crowd of about 500 congregated to send the even braver athletes on their daunting journey.

The uninitiated believe that rain and cold provide ideal conditions for athletes as they travel on their sweaty way. Nothing could be further from the truth. When the road signs indicate that there are 75 kilometres ahead and the body feels nothing but numbing cold, the mind starts to take in the prospect of hours and hours of abject misery. By the time Westville has been reached, cold muscles are beginning to cramp. When the help of race followers is most needed, the elements do their best to deter spectators from their annual roadside pilgrimage. Nevertheless, Comrades supporters, along with the runners, are hardy individuals and the turn-out in 1934 was quite remarkable.

The Mafikeng athlete H. A. Ward was becoming almost a traditional pace-setter. At Westville, he was five minutes ahead of Knight and Sandison. Noel Burree, who had finished the 1931 race just two seconds behind winner Phil Masterton-Smith, was up with the leaders and determined to make amends for his previous disappointment. His strategy seemed sound as the previous year's winner and runner-up, Ballington and Cochrane, were just behind him.

The two big hills on either side of Drummond sorted out the true race order. On Botha's, Ward and Knight dropped back. Sandison went to the front, followed by Luke and Rufus. At halfway, Cochrane and Ballington, running together, were just over six minutes behind the leader. On Inchanga, Sandison maintained his lead but was clearly uncomfortable. Cochrane, now in second place, looked the strongest of all and seemed a likely winner.

Ballington, meanwhile, was going through a bad patch and dropped back, apparently out of contention. On the descent of Inchanga, he stopped for a drink and overheard a spectator saying that his previous year's win was a fluke. Stung by the comment, he resolved to prove his detractor wrong. He later recalled the moment: 'Little did that man realise what his remark meant to me. I was determined to win at all costs, and the further I went, the better I felt. What a thrill it was to pass all those ahead of me!'

Shortly after Cato Ridge, Cochrane wrested the lead from Sandison and now had only his close friend Ballington to trouble him. The defending champion stalked his prey relentlessly, passing him shortly before Umlaas Road. As a contest, the race was over. Ballington pulled away rapidly and became the second runner to win more than one Comrades Marathon, Newton having been the first. Cochrane, in second place, was more than 15 minutes behind the winner, with Luke coming in third.

The day's slow movement was provided by orchestral violinist Stirling Robins, who was the 24th and final finisher in 10.47.51. His andante effort was acknowledged by a crescendo of applause from the appreciative audience.

1934 COMRADES MARATHON RESULTS

1. H. R. Ballington	7.09.03
2. W. J. Cochrane	7.24.41
3. J. I. Luke	7.44.39
4. W. F. O. Wallace	7.57.13

5. J. B. Sandison	7.59.57
6. O. S. Matterson	8.26.50
7. L. H. Knight	8.29.51
8. L. L. Boulle	8.32.47
9. N. C. Burree	8.46.20
10. G. V. Jones	8.49.53

1935 COMRADES MARATHON
THE COMRADES SPIRIT ENHANCED

In the build-up towards the 1935 race, one thing appeared virtually certain: Durban would produce the winner. The seaport city provided the three most likely candidates. Hardy Ballington was going for a third consecutive victory. The previous year's runner-up, Bill Cochrane, was determined to go one better. Standard marathon specialist Johannes Coleman appeared capable of upsetting both of them.

The realisation that three top runners, all of them in peak condition, were likely to contest line honours offered Comrades followers the prospect of a new record for the 'down' run. After all, Newton's record of 6.24.45, now ten years old, had been set in only the third 'down' run. Surely one of these fine athletes would be able to show that performances were improving over the years.

Following two wet years, it was a relief for the athletes to enjoy dry conditions. Nevertheless, it was dark and cold when the 48 starters set off on their journey to the coast. First to show was H. A. Ward, followed by a bunch of enthusiastic and relatively inexperienced runners. Those in the know, who had been there before, were content to bide their time. The trio of favourites (Cochrane, Coleman and Ballington) stayed close to the action, while careful not to overextend themselves in the early stages.

By the time the leaders reached Camperdown, it was clear that pre-race expectations of an exciting event were likely to be realised. Ward was still in front, just ahead of Luke. The three favourites, Ballington, Cochrane and

Coleman, were handily placed, just over a minute behind the leader. At Cato Ridge, the status quo remained unchanged.

On the undulating stretch from Cato Ridge to Inchanga, the race started to develop. Ballington, Coleman, Cochrane and Pretorius, running together, swept past the early leaders. On the ascent of Inchanga, Bill Cochrane made his move. His timing was perfect as defending champion Ballington was struggling with an upset stomach. Running strongly, Cochrane was first through Drummond in 3.04.15. Ballington and Coleman, running in tandem, were two minutes behind the leader. Newton's 'down' record appeared to be under threat.

Over Botha's Hill, through Hillcrest and all the way to Kloof, Cochrane increased his lead. At Kloof, he held an eight-minute advantage over Coleman, with Ballington a further minute behind in third place. Cochrane looked totally in control as he eased down Field's Hill and confidently strode through Pinetown, his lead seemingly unassailable. Although the coastal region provided a new challenge in the shape of an oppressively hot wind, Cochrane was well in front at Westville, and a new record appeared to be within his grasp.

Hardy Ballington was not at his best, but he was every inch a fighter. He was also aiming at a hat-trick of wins, something only Arthur Newton had previously achieved. After a quick massage in Pinetown, he set his sights on the leader. Now fully recovered from his earlier travails, he started to make ground on Cochrane. Cochrane, meanwhile, was beginning to feel the effects of his mid-race surge. Unable to maintain the pace that had propelled him to the front, he was forced to walk on some of the hills. Before long, his lead had been reduced to half a mile.

Chasing the leader in the closing stages of a 'down' Comrades is no easy matter. Ballington, too, began to flag. Two thoroughly exhausted men approached the finish at the Alexandra Park Track Ground, still locked in combat while barely able to move their weary limbs. Any thought of Newton's record being broken had vanished by now.

Cochrane reached the stadium with his lead still intact and relatively secure. Ballington had not yet given up, however, and was already on the track when Cochrane crossed the line. The race had lived up to expectations, with the favourites claiming the first three places. Bill Cochrane was the 1935 Comrades Marathon champion with Ballington second and Coleman third.

Ballington must have been devastated. Did stomach trouble cost him his hat-trick? Or did he mount his final challenge too late? One could have forgiven him, having lost the race by less than two minutes, if he'd returned home in a huff and taken out his frustration on his family. His post-race behaviour was, however, somewhat different. After taking a rest, he was driven back to Westville, from where he jogged back gently to the finish, encouraging backmarkers to achieve their goals. Hardy Ballington's understanding of the Comrades spirit was quite remarkable.

The spirit of the organisers and local municipal officials was also evident in the participation of Robert Mtshali, a young black runner. Although legislation dictated that his effort would not be properly recognised, the crowd warmly applauded him as he finished in 9.30 and received a special presentation from Councillor V. L. Shearer.

Two athletes, R. Beisner and M. E. Trimborn, had the misfortune to be knocked over by motor vehicles during the race. Thankfully, neither was seriously injured and both completed the event. Max Trimborn was to become one of the great characters of the race.

1935 COMRADES MARATHON RESULTS

1. W. J. Cochrane	6.30.05
2. H. R. Ballington	6.31.56
3. J. L. Coleman	6.55.20
4. A. J. Reeve	7.36.20
5. S. Pretorius	7.39.27
6. J. I. Luke	7.46.19
7. L L. Boulle	7.49.29
8. J. B. Sandison	8.11.55
9. A. K. Boyce	8.13.15
10. M. E. Trimborn	8.21.13

1936 COMRADES MARATHON
IS COMRADES COMING TO AN END?

The Berlin Olympic Games dominated the international athletics stage in 1936. This was going to be Adolf Hitler's opportunity to demonstrate the superiority of his 'master race', but not everyone fell in with his plans. A black American, Jesse Owens, demonstrated his own supremacy by winning four gold medals.

Meanwhile, South Africa had its own special event, the Comrades Marathon. Early in the year, it was clear that the great race had problems. The Olympic Games claimed Johannes Coleman, third in 1935, to represent his country in the standard marathon. (He came sixth.) The reigning Comrades champion, Bill Cochrane, had announced his retirement. Thankfully, Hardy Ballington, second in 1935 and winner of the previous two races, was back. The sporting manner in which he had accepted narrow defeat in 1935, along with his phenomenal prowess as a runner, had endeared him to Comrades followers.

But not even the great Ballington, now approaching his athletic peak, could fire enthusiasm among potential Comrades runners. This year 19 hardy souls, constituting the smallest field on record, presented themselves at the starting line. The organisers were understandably downhearted. The future of the race was by no means secure. Organising secretary and Comrades founder Vic Clapham was desperate, so much so that he persuaded the untrained Vernon Jones and Harry Wilkinson to run the initial section to Tollgate, simply in order to boost numbers.

The event took place on Monday, 25 May. As if there weren't enough problems already, the usually reliable early-winter Natal weather decided to be both unreliable and unfriendly. Sunday was wet, and race day started off the same way. Five minutes before the start, the heavens opened. Nineteen miserable, bedraggled athletes answered the starter's call and set out for Pietermaritzburg unaware of what the elements had in store for them. There would be no more rain, but an unpleasantly cold wind regularly reminded participants that ultramarathon running was not for the faint-hearted.

A. J. Reeve, fourth in 1935, took the early lead, followed by Ballington, Sandison and Parr. Liege Boulle was well placed. Perhaps the cold weather had something to do with the fast pace that was being set. When the leaders passed through Hillcrest it appeared as though an attempt might be made on the record.

At halfway, this seemed even more likely. Reeve went through Drummond in 3.23.15, 13 minutes faster than the halfway leader two years previously, Fred Ward. Ballington, the winner on that occasion, was 18 minutes ahead of his own 1934 time. Now in second place, he was less than a minute behind Reeve.

The ascent of Inchanga brought about its traditional change of fortunes. Reeve, suffering from a stitch, was temporarily reduced to a walk. Ballington seized the opportunity and sailed past. He was now in full control. Without anyone ahead to worry about, he could focus his mind fully on his own plan and the record. He was feeling so strong that he adjusted his time target to smash the record by an even greater margin.

Ballington was perfectly prepared. A Durban-based man, he was on home territory. As defending 'up' run champion, he knew what it took to win the Comrades Marathon. He had trained assiduously for the event, having clocked up 1 700 miles in the preceding four and a half months. Seconding him as usual was his twin brother Stanley, who kept him well supplied with his favourite energy supplements, sugared Orangeade and beef tea.

Not as well looked after was tough little Liege Boulle. Running without a personal attendant, he was sadly in need of sustenance. A spectator, recognising his plight, offered him a cup of tea. Boulle readily accepted the offer. The spectator went off, never to return. There is no record of how much time Boulle lost, but one can safely assume that his thoughts were anything but complimentary.

Ballington, meanwhile, was in a class of his own. At Cato Ridge, he was nine minutes ahead of second-placed Reeve. At Camperdown, the lead was 25 minutes. By Umlaas Road, the margin had increased to 38 minutes, with Wallace and Boulle a further ten minutes behind Reeve.

Arriving at Polly Shortts, Ballington showed a moment's discomfort, slowing slightly and then stopping for a brief massage. He was soon on his way again and comfortably overcame his last big obstacle. The record was now a formality. Ballington's time of 6.46.14 took 11 minutes 32 seconds off the ten-year-old time of Harry Phillips. His third victory was so comprehensive that Comrades followers began to draw comparisons with the great Arthur Newton.

Early leader Reeve tenaciously clung to second spot, which he claimed in 7.50.53, over an hour behind Ballington. To his credit, he wearily overcame a last-ditch assault from Boulle, who finished a mere 25 seconds behind him. It was a best ever performance by Liege Boulle, who might have been runner-up had he not delayed his final effort until too late. Future winner Allen Boyce took fifth place, while Max Trimborn, of cockcrow fame, came in tenth.

The final gold medal was decided in the true spirit of Comrades. At this stage in Comrades history, gold medals were awarded to the first six finishers. This year, prospective finishers number 6 and 7 were making their mandatory circuit of the track, apparently intending a personal dead heat, when an official approached them and informed them that only one of the two could claim the final gold.

A. T. Sherriffs was the elder of the two. His companion, 'Ginger' Pretorius, visibly the stronger, held back and gestured to Sherriffs to move ahead and claim the last gold. This Sherriffs did, but with obvious reluctance. Pretorius's sportsmanship was rewarded when he was presented with a prize for being the first newcomer to finish. The Hardy Ballington Trophy for the first novice would only be introduced in 1969.

1936 COMRADES MARATHON RESULTS

1. H. R. Ballington	6.46.14
2. A. J. Reeve	7.50.53
3. L. L. Boulle	7.51.08
4. W. F. O. Wallace	7.53.41
5. A. K. Boyce	8.23.51
6. W. S. Sherriffs	8.30.07
7. J. L. Pretorius	8.30.20
8. D. R. Smith	8.44.35
9. R. A. Sandison	9.18.16
10. M. E. Trimborn	9.26.00

1937 COMRADES MARATHON
A CONTROVERSIAL WINNER

The 1936 Olympic Games marathon was contested on 9 August. As normal, it took place in the afternoon, starting at 3 p.m. in favourable conditions. Japanese runner Kitei Son (actually a Korean named Kee-Chung Sohn, who changed his name in order to participate as Korea was occupied by Japan at the time) won the event in a new Olympic record time of 2.29.19. Of interest to South African followers was the performance of Johannes Coleman, who took sixth place in a time of 2.36.17. When the South African entered the stadium, he triumphantly raised his arm. Germans in the stand immediately got to their feet and gave the 'Heil Hitler' salute. Coleman later claimed that he had merely been waving to his South African teammates, but he was suspected of being a Nazi sympathiser and his explanation was not widely accepted.

The selfsame Coleman, a railways employee, went to the start of the 1937 Comrades Marathon as outright favourite. The foremost Comrades runner of the era, Hardy Ballington, had forsaken this year's race in his successful quest to break Arthur Newton's world long-distance 50-mile and 100-mile records in England. Pre-race speculation suggested that Coleman, third in the 1935 'down' run in 6.55.20, would be too strong and was likely to have a fairly easy ride.

The entry for the race, held on 24 May, was once again disappointingly small. The absence of Ballington was certainly felt. Rugby cannot be blamed. The Springboks would this year beat the All Blacks 2–1 in New Zealand and become recognised as unofficial world champions, but that would only take place between July and September. Thankfully, 30 runners responded to the 6 a.m. send-off from Maritzburg mayor Councillor F. J. Lewis.

As he had done the previous year, A. J. Reeve soon went to the front and set the early pace. He was first through Umlaas Road, five minutes ahead of Coleman. Running together in third spot were Beisner and Pivalizza. Pivalizza's effort was noteworthy: it was rare to have a Capetonian so well placed. At Cato Ridge, one-third of the distance, the lead was unchanged.

On the difficult section through Harrison Flats leading up to Inchanga, Coleman started to take charge. Moving up to within a few yards of the leader, he stayed there for a while, biding his time, quite content to let Reeve do all the work. Once on Inchanga, however, Coleman made his move and swept past. He went through Drummond in a fast 2.57, a minute ahead of Reeve.

When Coleman confidently crested Botha's Hill, it was clear that the race was his. At Hillcrest, he was a full mile ahead of second-placed Reeve. Of more significance was the fact that his time of 3.45.15 was nearly five minutes faster than that of Arthur Newton at this point in his record-breaking run of 1925. From now on, it was a race against time rather than a contest for first place.

At Pinetown, Coleman's time was marginally faster than that of Newton. He had slipped somewhat and looked uncomfortable over Cowie's Hill and through Westville. The strain of his mid-race effort was telling. Newton, however, had also struggled at this stage and all was not lost. Racing in the pain-wracked final section of a 'down' Comrades is never easy.

Coleman was well aware of the prospect of a new record and determined to achieve his goal. Cheered on by a large crowd of supporters, he kept his weary body going. When he entered the stadium, the record seemed assured, even though he was unable to muster a finishing burst. His time of 6.23.11 was 1 minute 34 seconds inside the old time. For a second successive year a new record was set and Arthur Newton was no longer a record holder.

Lying on the turf afterwards, Coleman was quick to recover his strength. As he contemplated the scale of his achievement, he reflected rather oddly, 'If it had only been one second, it would have satisfied me. Please take off my shoes and socks.' The winner's prize was a cutlery service worth £10.

Seventeen minutes after Coleman, Allen Boyce arrived to claim second place, three positions better than he'd managed the previous year. He was to prove one of the most consistent runners of his era. The Cape Town entrant, Pivalizza, finished eighth and was awarded a gold medal for being the first novice home. Rather ruefully, he commented, 'I like Natal, but not its hills.'

Max Trimborn finished tenth in 8.22.45, while Comrades historian Vernon Jones claimed his seventh medal in 9.34.45. After the race, Jones announced his retirement from ultra-distance running but remained one of the greatest Comrades supporters for the rest of his life.

1937 COMRADES MARATHON RESULTS

1. J. L. Coleman	6.23.11
2. A. K. Boyce	6.40.19
3. W. F. O. Wallace	6.41.47
4. R. A. Sandison	7.34.05
5. D. J. Crafford	7.49.46
6. P. H. Beisner	7.56.25
7. L. L. Boulle	7.56.31
8. D. Pivalizza	8.04.15
9. W. S. Sherriffs	8.11.42
10. M. E. Trimborn	8.22.45

1938 COMRADES MARATHON
CLAPHAM AND BALLINGTON

The most significant contributor to the success of the world's number one ultramarathon, the Comrades Marathon, is Vic Clapham. It was Clapham whose vision inspired the event in the first place. It was Clapham who chose the course that would cause him to be loved and hated by those who struggled to meet its challenges. It was Clapham who defied legislation and the medical wisdom of the day by quietly encouraging people of colour and women to take part, albeit unofficially. It was Clapham who, year after year, welcomed new participants with a letter addressed, not very subtly, to 'Dear Lunatic'!

Ever since his little baby had first seen the light of day, Vic Clapham had nurtured the event, built his life around it and even dragged his entire family into the annual task of getting as many as possible to the starting line. Whatever titles others might have held, Clapham had, from the beginning, been the real chairman and secretary. This, the 18th running of the Comrades Marathon, would be the last to be organised by its founder. His employers, the South African Railways, had decided to relocate him to Ladysmith.

We will never know how much of a dreamer Clapham was. He must have been one, or his race would never have materialised. But how did he see it growing? He could hardly have imagined that the race would draw a field well in excess of 20 000 in the year 2000. Nevertheless, when he witnessed 20 runners standing outside the Durban City Hall in 1938, he must have remembered the 34 pioneers who went to the start of the inaugural event in 1921. Comrades wasn't progressing. Would it survive? What were Clapham's thoughts at this vulnerable time? We don't know for sure, but photographs and the memories of old-timers depict a phlegmatic pragmatist rather than a passionate idealist. Despite everything, Vic Clapham's Comrades Marathon was destined to survive.

In retrospect, the lack of interest in 1938 is difficult to understand. Comrades had a real champion, a great athlete who had demonstrated his phenomenal ability in the international arena during the previous year. Hardy Ballington missed the 1937 Comrades Marathon because he had other dragons to slay. In April 1937, Ballington travelled to England to mount an assault on the world 50-mile and 100-mile records, both held by none other than his great Comrades predecessor, Arthur Newton. He succeeded in both attempts and, in each case, was seconded by the defending record holder, Arthur Newton himself. The Comrades spirit was alive and well demonstrated in the London-to-Brighton and Great West Road events in the United Kingdom.

Now a champion of international repute, Ballington drew crowds but, alas, not too many challengers. A big disappointment was the non-appearance of Johannes Coleman, recent winner of the Empire Games marathon. Thankfully, 1937 runner-up Allen Boyce was in the field along with Comrades regulars Roy Sandison, Max Trimborn, Edgar Marie, Fred Morrison and ever-reliable Liege Boulle. One newcomer who had a special reason to match his prowess against the outright favourite was John Ballington, his younger brother.

Allen Boyce, usually a conservative starter, took the early lead. Hardy Ballington, on his heels in the early stages, was biding his time. He didn't wait long. He had a plan and was determined to stick to it. Boyce's pace didn't quite measure up to his strategy, so he took the only course possible and moved to the front shortly after Westville. Generally speaking, it is considered inadvisable for a potential winner to take such an early lead, but a field of 20 hardly suggests a tactical battle.

Nevertheless, the pressure was all on Ballington. Would he be able to control both the race and himself for all those hours ahead? At Pinetown, he was a minute and a half inside his time at the same stage in his record-breaking run two years previously. That seemed fine. At Gillits, one-third into the race, he was five minutes ahead of his 1936 time. Now there were doubts. Had he set off too quickly?

These doubts grew when Ballington made heavy weather of Botha's Hill. Now there was concern. He appeared to be struggling. His stride had lost its jauntiness. It looked for all the world as if early enthusiasm would prove to be his undoing. Evidence of his travails on Botha's Hill was his halfway time. Now he was only two minutes ahead of his 1936 time. He was slipping back and seemed vulnerable, although second-placed Boyce was a full seven minutes behind him.

Inchanga, the mighty hill that welcomes 'up' runners to the second half, is notorious for destroying the hopes of those who have unwisely pushed too hard before Drummond. This was testing time for Ballington. His response was unexpectedly sure and strong. He had been going through a 'bad patch' but had come through it successfully. Now it was the turn of others to falter. Boyce looked in trouble as he started the ascent of Inchanga. He was still in second place. Although grimly determined to hang on, he was no longer having fun.

On the descent of Inchanga, Ballington seemed well recovered. The clock provided further evidence. At Camperdown, he was nearly eight minutes ahead of his 1936 time. It all looked rosy for the flying leader. With a lead of more than 14 minutes over second-placed Boyce, he could focus his full attention on the record that was surely well within his grasp. Despite a second bad patch shortly after Umlaas Road, he reached the top of Polly Shortts approximately 12 minutes inside record pace.

A new record was now a foregone conclusion, and so it turned out. For a while, there was a suspicion that he might become the first sub-6.30 finisher in Comrades history. That didn't quite happen but his time of 6.32.26 did break the previous record (held by himself) by 13 minutes and 48 seconds. It was a wonderful performance, even more appreciated when it became known that he had steadfastly kept to the left-hand side of the road for the entire journey. Taking the shortest line through corners was not the Ballington way.

Although he had struggled through two bad patches, Ballington finished strongly and expressed his satisfaction. 'It was one of the best runs I have had, and perhaps the fact that I felt it was my last Comrades accounted for this.' He seemed determined to announce his retirement. 'I've had enough. I have got to get on with my work now and I can't manage work and marathon running.' Nine years later, he would demonstrate just how difficult it is to leave the Comrades Marathon.

1938 COMRADES MARATHON RESULTS

1. H. R. Ballington	6.32.26
2. A. K. Boyce	7.03.05
3. F. J. Morrison	7.38.57
4. R. A. Sandison	8.02.20
5. D. A. MacKrory	8.10.02
6. J. R. Ballington	8.25.35
7. D. R. Smith	9.15.15
8. M. E. Trimborn	9.20.24
9. E. Marie	9.23.37
10. L. L. Boulle	9.44.27

6

SURVIVING A WORLD WAR
(1939 and 1940,1946 to 1949)

Adolf Hitler never ran the Comrades Marathon. How would history have changed if he had? Would he have discovered a world of sharing, of helping others in challenging circumstances, of striving with others to achieve a meaningful goal? Probably not. Hitler's madness was evil, not the noble kind that draws otherwise sane and sensible individuals to a day of self-inflicted torture once a year.

So why mention Hitler in a book about the Comrades Marathon? Because, unfortunately, he had a major effect on its history. The 2010 Comrades Marathon should have been the 90th running of the great event. Instead, it was the 85th.

The 1939 Comrades Marathon took place at a time of escalating tension in Europe, when Germany had already invaded Czechoslovakia. The 1940

Comrades Marathon was a subdued occastion, and very nearly did not take place at all. There were absentees: some were already in action, others undergoing military training and unable to prepare adequately for an ultramarathon. On race day, Allied forces were being repelled in the direction of Dunkirk. Those who did take part in Comrades noticed fewer supporters along the roadside.

As one might have expected, there was no 1941 Comrades Marathon – nor was there another race until 1946, as the war effort took precedence over all else. South Africans, among them Comrades runners, served with great distinction. One who deserves special mention is Wally Hayward, who was awarded the British Empire Medal for exceptional bravery at El Alamein.

A good few men who had graced the road between Durban and Pietermaritzburg on Comrades day lost their lives in the war, among them two former winners, Frank Sutton and Phil Masterton-Smith. When hostilities ended, there was a new generation of fallen comrades: all the more reason to revive the Comrades Marathon. But would it happen? Vic Clapham was no longer available to lead the way.

The legendary spirit of Comrades made the continuation of the race imperative, even though circumstances dictated that numbers would be down. In the aftermath of war, there were those who would never come back, those who were physically and mentally damaged and those who had not yet been demobilised. Fortunately, however, there were enough to warrant a race.

Furthermore, there were people who were willing and able to do the job of administering the event, none more so than Morris Alexander. He was a top-notch athlete who completed seven Comrades Marathons, winning three gold and four silver medals from 1939 to 1952. His best year was 1949, when he finished fourth in a time of 7.18.06. He was every inch a team man, who played a significant role in the success of his club, Collegians Harriers, in winning the Gunga Din Trophy. Alexander ran in the very special number 1, a privilege that he passed on in 1957 to Clive Crawley, who in turn has worn the number with great distinction.

Morris Alexander was probably the most suitable person to take over Vic Clapham's dream. He had the same innovative approach. Remembering the early Comrades tradition of keeping the same race number from year to year, and surely conscious of his own very unique number, Alexander can rightly be credited with the marvellous idea of awarding 'in perpetuity' numbers to those who satisfied certain criteria, namely three wins, five gold medals or ten successful finishes. He is the author of *The Comrades Marathon Story*, the first generally recognised history of the great race.

This era featured not only the post-war re-establishment of the race, but also the realisation of the underlying relevance of the event in the nation's calendar. Allen Boyce won by a margin that will probably be a record for all time. Hardy Ballington became the second five-time winner. Above all, the stature of Comrades remained as high as ever.

1939 COMRADES MARATHON
ANOTHER RECORD BROKEN

The 1939 Comrades Marathon took place in an almost surreal atmosphere. Comrades is all about hope, about committed people overcoming adversity in the finest traditions of the human spirit. In 1939, despair was descending on nations throughout the world as the prospect of a second world war became ever more likely.

The invasion of Poland by Germany on 1 September is often regarded as the start of the war. For others in Europe, the war had already begun. The significance of the Polish invasion was largely the response of Britain and her allies. In March 1939, the relatively new nation of Czechoslovakia (comprising Bohemia, Slovakia and Moravia) was taken over by German forces. Within a year, 300 000 members of Czech labour unions were relocated to Germany, effectively as slaves. Over 50 000 were detained in concentration camps at the mercy (or lack thereof) of the Gestapo, the German Secret Police.

Against this background, the 1939 Comrades Marathon was held in depressing circumstances of a somewhat lesser nature. It was one of those very few Comrades days when the weather was awful: cold, wet conditions in which cold limbs stiffen up and become more vulnerable to injury, bringing numbing discomfort and the fear of long hours of misery. A bitterly cold wind, with intermittent drizzle, dominated Wednesday, 24 May 1939.

An interesting innovation was the decision of organiser 'Skilly' du Bois to hand out race numbers in alphabetical order. Morris Alexander, later to introduce the concept of 'in perpetuity' numbers, had the honour of wearing race number 1. He wore the number with distinction, as did his successor Clive Crawley. Liege Boulle was given number 8, while the controversial number 13 went to controversial runner Johannes Coleman.

Right from the start, Coleman demonstrated his total disdain for superstition, taking the lead from 1938 runner-up Allen Boyce. Comrades followers were hoping for a battle royal between the pair, and their hopes were realised. Following his sixth place in the 1936 Olympic marathon, Coleman had further proved his international credentials. On 7 February 1938, he won the British Empire Marathon in 2.30.49, his fastest time ever for the standard distance. His training had gone well and he was ready for a showdown with Boyce.

Boyce, on the other hand, was not nearly as versatile. He was a pure Comrades specialist and adopted an approach rather similar to that of Bruce Fordyce nearly half a century later. Boyce would train for six months, run Comrades and then rest for another six months, before resuming preparation for the following year. He, too, was in fine form.

The race became a classic contest between a strong front-runner and a tactician biding his time. At Umlaas Road, Coleman was two minutes ahead of Boyce, who was a further minute in front of the chasing pack. For the entire first half, Coleman sought to establish an unassailable lead. He more or less succeeded. Going through halfway in the fast time of 2.56.35, he was now more than nine minutes ahead of second-placed Boyce, who was wearing a sweater to protect himself from the cold.

At Hillcrest, the first two were more than 15 minutes apart. Coleman's strategy was working. He was far ahead and was steadily increasing the gap. Boyce, however, had not given up. He maintained a consistent stride that quickened perceptibly as Coleman started to slow. Suddenly, there was a reversal. The gap began to narrow.

Throughout, this had been a fascinating tussle between two great athletes of contrasting strengths and weaknesses. Early on, front-runner Coleman had pulled ahead of patient strategist Boyce. Now, Boyce, stronger on the hills, was making his final effort to try to haul in downhill specialist Coleman, who was reduced to walking on the uphill sections.

In the end, Coleman's early advantage proved decisive. When he crested Tollgate and saw nothing but downhill ahead, his victory was assured. This he achieved in a new record time of 6.22.05, beating his own previous best in 1937 by 1 minute 6 seconds. Afterwards, he paid tribute to his wife, who had nursed him through a knee injury that nearly put him out of the race, and stated: 'It would have been a great disappointment if I had not run after having covered 1 700 miles in training since 5 January.'

Coleman was warm in praising the effort of runner-up Boyce: 'I feel sorry he did not win – no man could have trained more thoroughly than he did.' The final margin of victory was 4 minutes 29 seconds. While this might seem a comfortable cushion, Boyce had established a new stage record from Drummond to Durban in 3.20.44. In the stretch from Hillcrest to Durban, he had run 11 minutes faster than the winner. It was the third year in succession that Boyce had finished as runner-up. He was worthy of a better result and would prove his prowess the following year.

After the race, Coleman announced his retirement, stating, 'I want to concentrate on the 26 miles – I should like to be chosen again for the Olympic Games in Finland next year.' Thanks to Adolf Hitler, the Helsinki Olympics did not take place until 1952, but Coleman would take fourth place in the London Olympic Marathon of 1948 in a time of 2.36.06. Fellow South African Syd Luyt finished sixth in 2.38.11.

1939 COMRADES MARATHON RESULTS

1. J. L. Coleman	6.22.05
2. A. K. Boyce	6.26.34
3. J. Ballington	7.28.01
4. W. D. Parr	7.58.12
5. J. L. Pretorius	7.59.52
6. F. J. Morrison	8.09.20
7. L. L. Boulle	8.10.34
8. W. Amron	8.22.59
9. M. B. Alexander	8.26.22
10. M. E. Trimborn	8.53.11

1940 COMRADES MARATHON
THE GREATEST VICTORY MARGIN

The most suprising thing about the 1940 Comrades Marathon is that it actually took place. The world was at war, and South Africans were involved. On Sunday, 3 September 1939, British Prime Minister Neville Chamberlain had committed Britain and the Commonwealth, of which South Africa was a member, to the conflict.

Several would-be Comrades entrants were unavailable to take part in this year's race, because of active duty or military training. In the end, determination to keep the race going won the day but with significantly less enthusiasm than normal. Roadside support was noticeably lacking.

The apathy was understandable. On race day – Friday, 24 May, Empire Day – Allied forces were being driven back to Dunkirk on the coast of France. From 26 May to 3 June, the greatest evacuation of beleaguered forces in history took place, an event that British Prime Minister Winston Churchill called 'a miracle of deliverance achieved by valour, by perfect discipline, by dauntless service, by resource, by skill'.

It was understandable that 1940 Comrades runners played second fiddle to events in Europe – and that consciences were troubled as athletes went to the start, aware that some of their fellow runners were elsewhere engaged. It wasn't an easy moment.

Nevertheless, the show had to go on. The Comrades Marathon, inspired originally by combatants in the First World War, responded to the call of Councillor Rupert Ellis Brown, mayor of Durban, and set off down West Street on their march to the province's capital some 56 miles away.

Legendary Liege Boulle was at the front as the field left Durban. His lead was short-lived, however. Race favourite Allen Boyce was determined to establish his authority early on. By Pinetown, his advantage was already considerable, and his time suggested that a record might be on the cards. In his wake, Liege Boulle, Max Trimborn, Edgar Marie and Gordon Morrison were doing their best to challenge him. All were superb runners, but none in the same class as the flying Boyce.

Boyce went through Drummond in 3.20.40, more than 29 minutes ahead of Parr, with Trimborn a long way behind in third place. The field, even at halfway, was so stretched out that only an unexpected mishap could possibly deny Boyce victory. Liege Boulle, perhaps acknowledging the hopelessness of his challenge, dropped out. His retirement, not a major disappointment at the time, has subsequently assumed a rather sad aspect. He was eventually to complete 39 Comrades Marathons, Finishing the race in 1940, when he was still young and strong, could have given him 40.

Allen Boyce forged ahead and the 'up' record seemed in trouble. But two factors contrived to thwart his ambition. In the first place, he discovered the severe pressure that leading this most demanding of all events (particularly from a relatively early stage) entails. Secondly, he encountered, all on his own, the disconcertingly demanding stretch from Cato Ridge to Camperdown. It was on this part of the course that his hitherto relentless pace started to wilt. He acknowledged his discomfort after the race: 'I kept to my schedule till Cato Ridge, but after that my legs became tired and slowed me up. It was pretty tough going.'

Boyce may have been struggling, but his travails were minor compared with those of his long-distant pursuers. When he reached the last major obstacle, Polly Shortts, second-placed Parr was as far back as Umlaas Road. As he crested the hill, Boyce knew that the race was his even though the record was now beyond his reach. He crossed the finish line at Alexandra Park in 6.39.23, not quite seven minutes outside the record. He did, however, set a record of another kind, one that may never be beaten. Boyce's margin of victory over second-placed Parr was 1.50.28. Although he acknowledged having been through three bad patches, he did not walk at all. Considering the fact that he ran virtually the whole race unchallenged, with minimal crowd support, his win in such a fast time was one of the great Comrades achievements.

For the next six years, Adolf Hitler would dominate the attention of the world. The Comrades Marathon, along with most regular sporting occasions, would be in limbo.

1940 COMRADES MARATHON RESULTS

1. A. K. Boyce	6.39.23
2. W. D. Parr	8.29.51

3. G. G. Morrison	8.55.21
4. M. E. Trimborn	9.03.28
5. E. Marie	9.06.07
6. P. L. Christie	10.12.35
7. W. Amron	10.19.45
8. P. Freedman	10.38.04
9. H. McIntosh	10.55.23
10. T. D. Stobie	10.59.18

1946 COMRADES MARATHON
MOTIVATED BY ANOTHER WORLD WAR

When the war ended, the world had to pick up the pieces, adjust to a peaceful way of life and resume those normal activities that sanity requires. South Africa was no exception. Twenty Comrades Marathons between the two wars had established the race as an integral part of the nation's sporting culture, so the desire to re-establish the event was strong. There was also a renewal of the original motivation. Vic Clapham's dream had been of a memorial to those who perished in the 1914–1918 war. Now another generation had been through a similar nightmare, in which Comrades runners, including past champions Frank Sutton and Phil Masterton-Smith, had lost their lives.

While a return to the great race was not in doubt, assembling a field was a complicated exercise. Apart from those forever lost to the race, there were servicemen still awaiting demobilisation and some recovering from wartime injuries. Others were simply unfit, mentally and physically, to contemplate an ultramarathon.

On Friday, 24 May, 22 runners faced the starter outside the Durban City Hall. Some were returning, others novices. Adding to the traditional Comrades spirit, excitement at the resumption of the race after a six-year gap was palpable. The pioneers of the mid-1940s were mindful of those of the early 1920s. Durban mayor Senator S. J. Smith sent the runners on their way and re-established normality.

W. A. C. Rufus of Durban became the first Comrades leader in six years. At Westville, he was five minutes ahead of Parr and six minutes in front of a trio comprising Cochrane, Vorster and Pretorius. Cochrane was regarded by many as a likely winner, having won the race before, in 1935. After that victory, he had stated categorically that he would never again attempt Comrades. The war had changed his mind.

In the build-up to the race, pundits had predicted a battle royal between Cochrane and four-times winner Hardy Ballington. Sadly, Ballington suffered an ankle injury in pre-race training and pulled out. Cochrane, denied the opportunity of a shoot-out with a fellow former champion, had to endure the pressure of expectation all on his own. He was ready, and capable.

At Gillits, with just over a third of the race behind him, Rufus was still in front, with Cochrane about five minutes adrift in second place. From Hillcrest and over Botha's Hill, the gap between the two leaders closed perceptibly. On the descent to Drummond, Cochrane went ahead and was seven seconds ahead of Rufus at halfway. Parr was in third place, three minutes behind.

The experience of a previous win told as Cochrane steadily increased his advantage over Inchanga and down through Harrison Flats. At Cato Ridge, with two-thirds already negotiated, Cochrane was 28 minutes ahead of second-placed Parr. Christie, Rufus and Alexander completed the first five at this stage.

Almost inevitably, leader Cochrane experienced one of the marathon's notorious 'bad patches'. These episodes strike suddenly. One moment, an athlete may be waving confidently to cheering crowds, enjoying the spring in his legs and mentally composing his victory speech. Suddenly, his legs turn leaden, he longingly contemplates a quiet nap on a grassy embankment – and those he'd left in his wake start streaming past. Fortunately for Cochrane, his bad patch occurred when his lead was already virtually insurmountable.

Parr did manage to close the gap slightly, but it was not enough. Maritzburg was drawing closer and Cochrane, buoyed by the realisation that a second Comrades victory was distinctly attainable, put negative thoughts behind him. Once he had crested Polly Shortts (the final major hill) with a comfortable lead, the result was assured.

On the run-in to the finish, the triumphant Cochrane, who had spent a large part of the war as a prisoner of war, was forcibly reminded of his wartime horrors. Running through Oribi Flats, he passed a local POW camp housing Italian prisoners. Seeing these men at the camp fence enviously witnessing his confident exhibition of freedom was a surreal experience. Perhaps no other Comrades leader has felt as joyful a surge of celebration in the final stages as Cochrane did then.

As he entered the Alexandra Park Track Ground, car horns sounded the letter V in Morse code: the universal 'V for victory', still vivid in the minds of all. Cochrane's triumph was warmly applauded, coming as it did 11 years after his only other win. Three other pre-war champions would return and post further victories as the Comrades Marathon reclaimed its rightful place in the nation's sporting calendar, but today was Cochrane's day.

Although the race was proclaimed a resounding success, its future was even more insecure than two decades before. In 1946, there were only eight finishers, the lowest number in history.

1946 COMRADES MARATHON RESULTS

1. W. J. Cochrane	7.02.40
2. W. D. Parr	8.00.27
3. W. A. C. Rufus	8.27.06
4. P. L. Christie	8.54.35
5. R. E. Allison	8.55.33
6. M. B. Alexander	9.01.30
7. L. L. Boulle	10.04.04
8. E. Marie	10.59.58

1947 COMRADES MARATHON
BALLINGTON'S FIFTH VICTORY

The second post-war Comrades, a 'down' run, featured an attempt by Hardy Ballington to record a fifth victory, thereby equalling the record of 'Greatheart' Arthur Newton. He was regarded as such a strong favourite that few doubted the outcome.

Safety being an increasingly important consideration, participants were advised to run on the right-hand side of the road and to wear white. While facing approaching traffic continues to make sense, the wearing of white is no longer recommended: orange, yellow and red are the colours now believed to be most easily visible to motorists.

Typical 'down' conditions greeted the runners as they went to the start early on Saturday, 24 May. It was cold, but this was not unexpected, and 47 athletes set off, hoping for a happy intervention by the sun. As usual, this materialised and the 1947 marathon was run, as is more often than not the case, in near-perfect conditions.

First to show was Liege Boulle. In second place was race favourite Hardy Ballington. Ballington soon made his intentions clear. He desperately wanted a fifth win. As holder of the 'up' record, he was determined to balance that with a 'down' record as well. As early as Umlaas Road, he was in the lead. His was now a race against the clock, not a wise strategy in this extraordinarily testing event.

All seemed to be going well as Ballington strode through Cato Ridge, comfortably ahead of second-placed Reg Allison. After confidently cresting Inchanga, he passed through Drummond five minutes ahead of Allison. Ballington's halfway time of 3.04.07 (his fastest) suggested that a 'down' record was on the cards. He was known to have the ability to run faster in the second half than in the first.

But nothing can be taken for granted in an event as gruelling as the Comrades Marathon. A solo attempt at a record asks for trouble. Somewhere along the way, the marathon will invariably show the overambitious just how hard it is to keep the momentum going over the entire course. This is not to suggest that Ballington was guilty of overextending himself. He was just so much more accomplished a Comrades runner than any other in the field. There was no one else who could challenge him, put in little surges, let him know that he was in a real race.

Shortly after cresting Botha's Hill, Ballington slowed down. He was going through a bad patch, yet his advantage over the field was such that he remained in control. At Pinetown, his lead over second-placed Allison was 20 minutes, a safe margin unless he suffered a major problem. Instead, he seemed to experience a second wind and confidently maintained a

Comrades founder, Vic Clapham

Official World War I badge presented to Private Vic Clapham in 1918

G. R.

No. 2088

War Badge awarded to... *Pte. V. Clapham.*
(Name)

late No. 487 8th S.A.I.
(Regimental No. and Unit)

for "Services Rendered" in H.M.'s Military Forces since 4th August, 1914.

(Station)............... *Pretoria*

(Date) .... *9. 1. 18.*

assistant Officer in Charge of Records,
Union Imperial Service Contingents.

Capt.

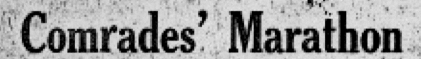

Comrades' Marathon

(Under the N.A.A.A. and N.C.U. Rules)

MARITZBURG TO DURBAN

(Approximately 54 Miles).

May 24th, 1921. (Empire Day).

Start at 7 a.m.

Starter :
His Worship the Mayor
of Maritzburg.

Judge :
His Worship the Mayor
of Durban.

"Times of Natal" Sporting Printery, Maritzburg.—681.

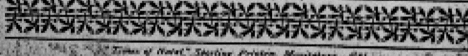

Announcement of a dream come true, which would later become an international institution

The Clapham home at 31 Greyling St, Pietermaritzburg,
where the first Comrades Marathons were organised

A triumphant Arthur Newton with exultant supporters

Robert Mtshali, courageous but unofficial, in 1935

Albert Marie's place in Comrades history

Big Bill Payn, Springbok legend,
who ran the 1922 Comrades Marathon
in rugby boots

Bust of Vic Clapham at
Comrades headquarters

Comrades Marathon House in Pietermaritzburg

Comrades marathon 1921 — DOWN

Position	Name	From	Time	
1	W. Rowan.	Koster. RHODES 10H	8 has 59 mins.	
2	H.W. Phillips.	P.M.B.	9. 40	
3	J. H. Annan.	Durban.	10. 10	
4	R.S. Skinner.	Durban.	10. 17	
5	H.C. Purcell	Greytown.	10. 37	
6	R.R. Main	Durban.	10. 44	1.
7	L. Metcalf.	Tongaat	11. 6	3
8	A. Marie	Durban.	11 - 4	2.
9	H. H. Imray.	P.M.B.	11. 13	
10	L. M. Moran.	P.M.B.	11. 13	3
11	J. A. Goodricke	Durban.	11. 20	
12	H. Herschfield.	Durban	11. 20	36
13	G. E. W. Palmer.	Durban.	11. 20	30
14	C. E. Atkinson.	Durban	11. 26	24
15	B. B. Freeman	P.M.B.	11. 27	16
16	F. K. Wade	Durban	11. 31	1.
17	P. E. W. Pearson.	Durban.	12. 20 X	12
Retd	L. C. Dobery.	P.M.B.		2
"	M.G. Griffiths.	P.M.B.		0
-	C. E. Murden	P.M.B.		6
-	C. Borain	P.M.B.		7
-	S. Wallace	P.M.B.		8

Results of the first ever Comrades Marathon as recorded by Vic Clapham

— 1921 Continued. —

Sition.	Name	From.	Time	No
	L. Botha.	Mooi River.		8
	M. Leish.	P. M. B.		9
	L. W. Delvin.	P. M. B.		10
	R. G. Backewell	P. M. B.		11
	P. Buckinger	P. M. B.		14
	W. Oliff.	P. M. B.		15
	A. Currie	P. M. B.		18
	D. W. Dixon.	Camperdown		19
	J. Kestel	Bellair.		20
	F. J. Davidson	Durban.		26
	B. E. Van-de-Plank.	Durban.		25
	H. Smith.	Durban.		27
	C. E. Nooman.	P. M. B.		28
	R. A. St George	P. M. B.		29
	T. E. Clausen.	Durban.		31
	W. M. Eley.	P. M. B.		32
	H. A. Howard.	P. M. B.		33
	F. Pearse	P. M. B.		37
	H. L. Farrant	P. M. B.		38
	G. Wheelwright	P. M. B.		39
	P. R. Pitcher	P. M. B.		40
	W. Mason	P. M. B.		41

Position	Name	From	Time
Retired.	C. Halstead.	P. h. B	
"	H. W. Soames	P. h. B.	
"	F. W. Taylor	P. h. B.	
.			

Summery and Remarks. - 1921 -

No	of	entries.	47
No	of	finishers.	17
No	to	retire	30

Time limit to win an enscribed silver
medal   12 hours

X P. E. W. Pearson   arrived   20 minutes late
  awarded a bronye medal.

Weather conditions   Fine & Warm.

comfortable lead, breasting the tape in 6.41.05. Although his time was 19 minutes slower than the 'down' record, he had achieved a far more notable landmark. In recording a fifth victory, he became, with Arthur Newton, one of the Comrades Marathon's two most successful athletes to date.

Twenty-year-old Reg Allison came in second, more than 42 minutes after the winner. Allison's experience would prove useful two years later, when he mounted an even more determined challenge. Eddie Hofmeyr, later to become an international rugby referee, was third. Among the other finishers were a few who would leave a lasting impression on the race. Morris Alexander came tenth. Novice Ian Jardine thought better of a mid-race decision to retire, carried on and completed the event in 10.11.30. Aged 45, he would stay away for some years only to come back in 1956 and initiate the great tradition of blind Comrades runners. Hofmeyr and other rugby referees were not officially recognised as belonging to this category! Elderly veteran Edgar Marie, who needed to be medically certified fit before being allowed to compete, started out in slippers and finished successfully in army boots, hastily borrowed en route.

As ever, the 1947 Comrades Marathon had many tales to tell. Most important, a 'down' run had succeeded the 'up' run of the previous year, confirming that the race had survived the Second World War. Comrades was back in business.

1947 COMRADES MARATHON RESULTS

1. H. R. Ballington	6.41.05
2. R. E. Allison	7.23.30
3. E. W. N. Hofmeyr	7.42.17
4. L. A. Nel	7.57.52
5. G. W. Moloney	7.59.07
6. C. R. A. Pace	8.02.41
7. W. D. Parr	8.06.04
8. F. J. Morrison	8.17.52
9. C. C. J. Joubert	8.46.40
10. M. B. Alexander	8.56.02

1948 COMRADES MARATHON
COMRADES SURVIVES AS THE COUNTRY TAKES THE LOW ROAD

This was the year that signalled the start of South Africa's descent into pariah status. In the general election of 28 May 1948, the 'Herenigde' (Reunited) National Party, led by D. F. Malan, defeated the United Party of Jan Smuts by a slender majority and cruelly inflicted their narrow-minded policy of apartheid on the nation. Malan triumphantly proclaimed, 'Today South Africa belongs to us once more.' Sadly, his 'us' excluded the vast majority of South Africans. For the next four decades, the Nationalist government would ruthlessly impose a racist ideology that was in total conflict with the inclusivity of the Comrades Marathon. Comrades organisers and participants, like most white South Africans, were slow to recognise what was being done to the country. In 1948, hardly anyone realised the long-term significance of the election result.

How did the Comrades Marathon runners regard the change in government? They voiced no opinion on the subject, either individually or jointly. This was hardly surprising. The race took place on Monday, 24 May, just four days before the most ill-fated election in the nation's history. The result of the election came as a total surprise to most Comrades runners, who were largely unaware of what was happening in the political arena. The athletic challenge dominated their thinking.

With Hardy Ballington and Bill Cochrane in retirement, the 1948 race had no outright favourite. Reg Allison, runner-up the previous year, was fancied by some, but his 1947 time of 7.23.30 was hardly menacing. Hofmeyr, who had finished third behind Allison, had his supporters until he withdrew just before race day.

Max Trimborn's famous cockcrow signalled the start of the race. Forty-five hardy souls (most wearing soft soles) responded. Maritzburg runner Len Wootton made the early running. At Cowies, the first of the major hills, he was two minutes ahead of the unfancied Bill Savage, whose 1932 victory had largely been forgotten by so-called pundits. Allison was in fourth place.

Wootton predictably met the fate of most front-runners. Savage, displaying all the determination that had earned him his first Comrades victory, took the lead just after Gillits and surged ahead. Allison moved into second place on the ascent of Botha's Hill and seemed to be timing his challenge sensibly. At halfway, Savage was just over ten minutes ahead of Allison.

Fairly early in the day, it became clear that this was not going to be an easy Comrades. It was hot, very hot. As Professor Tim Noakes would later point out, when the wet-bulb globe temperature – a composite measure reflecting the effect on humans of temperature, humidity, wind chill and solar radiation – reaches a particular level, certain runners are adversely affected. This was definitely the case in 1948. Allison surrendered second place to the Germiston pair, Burdett and Moloney, and lay down in the shade of Inchanga for a while, until urged to get up and resume combat by 1940 champion Allen Boyce. This he did, quite remarkably under the circumstances.

A strange feature of torrid conditions is that some people appear unaffected while those around them wither and fade. Bill Savage, apparently unconcerned by the heat and lack of a cooling breeze, ignored the human debris in his wake and powered through Camperdown 18 minutes ahead of Burdett and Moloney. Allison, now fully recovered, was 14 minutes further back in fourth place.

Savage continued to dominate in the closing stages, although he did slow down just a little. Allison's recovery was almost complete. He swept past Moloney and Burdett to claim second place once again. In doing so, he showed that he had the mental strength to win the race. He would be better prepared next year.

The day, however, belonged to Bill Savage. In the most testing of conditions, he led the race for virtually the last two-thirds. It was a superb performance from a great competitor whose credentials had been largely ignored in pre-race speculation.

Very notable was the fact that all three races since the Second World War had been won by pre-war champions: Bill Cochrane (1935), Hardy Ballington (1933, 1934, 1936 and 1938) and now Bill Savage (1932). The 16-year gap between Bill Savage's two victories leaves no doubt that he was one of the great Comrades champions.

1948 COMRADES MARATHON RESULTS

1. W. E. R. Savage	7.13.52
2. R. E. Allison	7.35.55
3. G. Burdett	7.42.06
4. G. W. Moloney	7.42.45
5. W. D. Parr	8.18.05
6. A. H. Ferguson	8.20.37
7. L. Wootton	8.27.47
8. L. A. Nel	8.42.12
9. W. A. C. Rufus	8.52.40
10. P. L. Christie	8.59.30

1949 COMRADES MARATHON
A WELL-DESERVED VICTORY

It is fair to say that 1949 was one of the most significant years in South African sporting history. May was the month of the Comrades Marathon, but this May the great race was all but ignored as Fred Allen's All Blacks became the first international rugby team to tour South Africa since the Second World War. For a few months, rugby dominated the sports headlines. The Springboks registered a whitewash in the series and several players were well on their way to legendary status.

In the political arena, the Prohibition of Mixed Marriages Act signalled the determination of the new government to divide the nation totally on racial grounds, but there was still no realisation of just how far they intended to go.

Despite the counter-attraction of rugby, 54 runners answered the call of the starter, Councillor G. C. Jolliffe, mayor of Pietermaritzburg, and set off on the long journey to the coast. The entry represented an increase of nine over the previous year and seven over the last 'down' run. The numbers might not seem impressive in comparison with the huge fields of present times, but they spelt out a welcome message: the Comrades Marathon had survived its six-year wartime break. There was a solid core of enthusiasts (runners, administrators, helpers, spectators) whose devotion to Comrades was such that the future of the race was far more secure than statistics might suggest.

At last, a Comrades Marathon once again featured a defending champion: Bill Savage was back. He would certainly not be having an easy ride. Frail-looking Reg Allison, twice a runner-up, had shown conclusively the previous year that his appearance belied an inner steel. He now recognised that he was capable of victory, and his training regimen indicated that he was single-minded in his approach this year. A further threat came from 29-year-old John Ballington, younger brother of the great Hardy. Transvaal runners Alan Ferguson and the consistent Gerry Moloney could not be discounted either.

After the Durban runner A. S. Bodill enjoyed a brief stint at the front, the race quickly took on its natural formation. As the leaders commenced the descent of Polly Shortts, Reg Allison and John Ballington were in front. They ran in tandem for the first part of the race, right up until Harrison Flats.

On the ascent of Inchanga, Allison made his move. At Drummond, Allison was over four minutes ahead of Ballington, whose halfway time was just 44 seconds slower than his brother Hardy's best time to Drummond. The pace was hot, competition was strong and the race record was under threat.

Unsurprisingly, the leader's speed and determination put paid to the aspirations of some of those who were trying to match him. Defending champion Savage could not keep up with the flying leader and retired. John Ballington felt the pressure and, utterly demoralised, decided to pull out. Elder brother Hardy, in attendance, had harsh words for his sibling: 'No Ballington has retired yet. If you do, you change your name to something else. Finish and you're still a Ballington.' The younger brother obeyed: he had no option.

Allison, meanwhile, had built up an unassailable lead, so that he was running against the clock in the final third of the race. His main problem now came, not from those following, but from agonising blisters on his feet. The pain visibly diminished his speed, and he lost further time stopping to receive medical attention.

Nothing, however, would prevent Reg Allison from a most well-deserved Comrades victory. Had it not been for the blisters that troubled him towards the end, he would surely have broken the 'down' record: he only missed it by 76 seconds. All doubts about his ability to prevail in a competitive race at express speed were erased. Reg Allison had posted one of the great Comrades victories. John Ballington made one of the great recoveries to finish second.

John Bennee, a medical doctor and a fit rugby player, had been asked to certify 62-year-old Edgar Marie as healthy enough to attempt the marathon. He did this and proceeded to run the race himself. When the 29-year-old doctor collapsed at the finish line, his venerable patient (having finished the race some time earlier) was on hand to render assistance. Marie was presented with the Eddie Hagan Trophy, which became his permanent property as a result of his being the oldest finisher on three occasions.

A major milestone was achieved by 40-year-old Liege Boulle, later to be known as 'Mr Comrades', who became the first Comrades Marathon runner to register ten finishes. Recognition of such feats would in time become one of the great Comrades traditions.

1949 COMRADES MARATHON RESULTS

1. R. E. Allison — 6.23.21
2. J. R. Ballington — 6.52.54
3. A. H. Ferguson — 7.02.52
4. M. B. Alexander — 7.18.06
5. G. Moloney — 7.22.19
6. F. von Hell — 7.31.12
7. W. D. Parr — 7.56.34
8. W. Cunliffe — 7.57.01
9. L. L. Boulle — 8.03.54
10. E. W. N. Hofmeyr — 8.14.26

7

THE WALLY HAYWARD ERA
(1950 to 1954)

This was a time when one could be a proud South African, when people didn't speak of 'The Second World War' but simply of 'The War', as if no other had ever taken place.

It was an era of heroes and villains with no room for in-betweens. War heroes still held pride of place, immortalised in dozens of books and films: Douglas Bader (*Reach for the Sky*), Guy Gibson (*The Dambusters*) and Richard Pape (*Boldness be my Friend*) were the British heroes, and America had Audie Murphy. South Africa's shining star was airman 'Sailor' Malan.

But now the need to respond to the challenges of post-war life was felt throughout the Western world. A new brand of heroes rose up, men whose exploits would inspire the re-establishment of societies built on solid values and noble character amidst a shattered world.

In the field of physical endeavour, there are three heroes in particular whose achievements in this period stand out. On 29 May 1953, a New Zealand bee-keeper, Edmund Hillary, and Sherpa Tensing Norgay became the first mountaineers to reach the top of Mount Everest and return home safely. A year later, British medical student Roger Bannister became the first man to run the mile in under four minutes.

In the latter half of 1953, South Africa's Wally Hayward produced a series of record-breaking performances, at home and in the United Kingdom, that hardly seems possible today. Even before this, in 1951 Hayward had been awarded the coveted Helms Trophy as the outstanding amateur athlete on the African continent.

At stages in its history, the Comrades Marathon has needed an injection of extra interest. Each time, a super-athlete of significant character has emerged. The first was Arthur Newton, who used the event to draw attention to his farming problems, and thereby promoted the race itself. Hardy Ballington continued the process. Now, in the post-war reconstruction period, Wally Hayward brought lustre to the Comrades and to South Africa. His active running career would cover approximately 60 years.

1950 COMRADES MARATHON
HAYWARD RETURNS

The year 1950 featured two of South Africa's all-time sporting heroes, Vic Toweel and Wally Hayward.

On 31 May, Union Day as it was then, a South African fought for a world boxing title for the very first time. In those days, before the proliferation of rival boxing organisations, a world champion truly was a world champion in his weight division. Manuel Ortiz was the reigning champion, an experienced 33-year-old fighter with 111 bouts to his credit. Challenger Toweel was only 22 years of age, with a mere 13 professional fights behind him. Understandably Ortiz was outright favourite to retain his crown.

This was no ordinary pugilistic encounter. On the eve of the fight, champion and challenger, both devout Catholics, attended Mass together.

But this spiritual sharing did not make the following day's world title bout any less fearsome a battle. Toweel's superior fitness and speed were decisive. After 15 rounds, South Africa had its first world champion. An evening debate in Parliament was interrupted by an announcement, to prolonged applause, that Vic Toweel was champion of the world.

Toweel may have won the fight, but his physical state belied the fact. His face was an awful mess. In fact, it was the new champion who was hospitalised. Ortiz visited his conqueror in hospital and presented him with a suit of clothes in a grand gesture of sportsmanship not normally associated with their rather brutal game. The sportsmanship exhibited by these two gladiators suggests that they would have made wonderful Comrades champions if they had directed their competitiveness into a more masochistic arena.

This year's Comrades Marathon saw the return of one of its greatest ever participants, Wallace Henry (just call me 'Wally') Hayward, a sportsman of the highest calibre in every sense. Winner of the tenth Comrades in 1930 at the tender age of 21, Hayward had since then limited his efforts to the standard marathon and less, performing with distinction at provincial and national levels.

While Hayward's return to Comrades elicited a fair amount of interest, it wasn't enough to cause a huge increase in competitor numbers. In fact, the opposite happened. Sadly, only 29 runners faced starter Ken Clarke, mayor of Durban. Interestingly, in view of his subsequent achievements, Hayward was not regarded as race favourite. Defending champion Reg Allison held that honour. Many regarded Hayward as a welcome diversion but, athletically, something of a middle-aged relic from the past. Nobody could have imagined that he would record his greatest triumphs in the next few years, or that he would produce his finest performance 38 years later, just short of his 80th birthday.

Political and medical requirements have limited entries over the years. The Comrades way around the problem was to turn a blind eye and allow the victims of such restrictions to run unofficially. Thankfully, due recognition was given to many such individuals decades later, when laws were changed and medicine advanced. This year, a twosome took part without any hope of official acknowledgement: Miss Jackie Newmarch attempted the ride on her horse 'Night'. In Parliament, exclusivity that was totally contrary to the

Comrades ethos was being legislated. This was the year in which the Group Areas Act, the Suppression of Communism Act, the Population Registration Act and the racial provisions of the Immorality Act became law.

As he had done two years before, Pietermaritzburg runner Len Wootton set the early pace. This time, he was not on his own. Defending champion Reg Allison was at his shoulder, with Hayward following in third place. This formation continued over 45th Cutting and Huntley's Hill and down into Pinetown. John Ballington, Liege Boulle, Bill Rufus, Trevor Allen, Morris Alexander and Max Trimborn, plus a few others, were maintaining contact with the leaders.

Hayward's superior strength on the upward sections started to tell. On the ascent of Field's Hill, he passed Wootton, who had not been able to keep pace with Allison on the longest climb in Comrades. At the crest, second-placed Hayward was only 50 yards behind, and well in sight of, leader Allison. On the relatively flat stretch after Kloof, the lead changed hands and Hayward went through Hillcrest 300 yards ahead of Allison.

Hayward's halfway time suggests that he might have been en route to a new record had conditions not dictated otherwise. It was hot, and becoming increasingly hotter, while a strong wind added to the difficulties of the second half. Nevertheless, he was more than six minutes ahead of Allison and well in control of proceedings. Wootton was third, followed by Allen, Ballington and Alexander. Miss Newmarch and her horse Night dropped out on the ascent of Inchanga while still in sight of race leader Hayward.

Once Inchanga had been successfully negotiated, Hayward set about establishing an insurmountable advantage. At Camperdown, his lead over Allison was 21 minutes. The race was effectively over. All that remained was the record. The clock hinted optimistically, but conditions and the lack of a serious challenger were visibly slowing the leader. Polly Shortts was the killer: Hayward was reduced to a walk.

It soon became apparent that a record was not possible. Hayward was exhausted but still had a huge buffer between himself and Allison. Victory was assured and victory was achieved in a time of 6.46.25. Hayward's return was gloriously successful. Twenty years after his first Comrades run, Hayward was unbeaten in the great race.

He later explained his strategy: 'Reg Allison was the favourite to win. As usual he went off fairly fast, which I had proved to myself I couldn't do, so

I decided to run steadily from the beginning, which paid rich dividends. I was catching him up on the hills, then when we got to the top he would up the gap again.

'I eventually passed Allison at about 20 miles. At Drummond, I had a lead of about 21 minutes and felt very good. A little further on, we ran into a very strong, hot headwind which took its toll on me. Polly Shortts proved a formidable hurdle where I slowed to a walk. However, once over Pollys, I perked up and finished comfortably with a lead over Reg of 13 minutes. My winning time was 6.46.25.

'As I had run against Reg in a number of races, I felt that had he stuck with me from the beginning, he would have beaten me. Perhaps I was lucky that he didn't stay. He is a great lad and a fine sportsman.'

Allison held on for second place, in fact finished the stronger of the first two, cutting eight minutes off the lead in the final stretch from Camperdown. Trevor Allen took third place after a tussle with Wootton.

First-time runner Laurie Barnes was provided with tea on Inchanga by a spectator who encouraged him to persevere as there was a prize for the youngest finisher, 'If you carry on, you will win the cup because all your 18-year-old rivals have dropped out.' That same spectator, Lyle Lightbody, presented Barnes with the trophy for first novice.

1950 COMRADES MARATHON RESULTS

1. W. H. Hayward	6.46.25
2. R. E. Allison	6.59.35
3. T. N. Allen	7.32.37
4. L. Wootton	7.38.47
5. M. B. Alexander	7.44.36
6. J. Ballington	7.47.48
7. L. L. Boulle	7.59.14
8. B. A. Danckwerts	8.20.40
9. W. K. Vorster	8.21.00
10. D. Spencer	8.27.53

1951 COMRADES MARATHON
THE HAYWARD ERA ON TRACK

The successful return of Wally Hayward in 1950 certainly did a great deal to elevate the status of the race and the reputations of its participants. Perhaps, though, this enhancement of importance was overdone. The Comrades Marathon has always been an event for the unathletic plodders as much as for the super-athletes who adorn the race statistics. This has not always been generally recognised, despite the humility shown by virtually all great Comrades champions, starting with Arthur Newton.

Wartime hierarchy was still very much part of life. Officials and 'other ranks' were so far apart that the word 'sir' was used on the sports field. Managing directors were too important to exchange civil greetings with secretaries. Children 'should be seen but not heard'.

However, long-distance road-running was and is the most egalitarian of sports, as Tim Noakes remarked in March 2005. In fact, it could be claimed that the Comrades Marathon is the most egalitarian of all sporting events. The camaraderie, shared by gold medallists and 'tail-end charlies' as equals, remains one of the most distinguishing features of the race.

Outsiders struggle to come to terms with this aspect of Comrades. Perhaps that partly explains why there are so many outsiders, South Africans who haven't experienced the wonder of Comrades. Wally Hayward went to the start of the 1951 Comrades Marathon as a humble, friendly man, keen to share his love of the event with others. He also started as Wally Hayward MBE, war hero and supreme athlete. South Africans were in awe of the man and his achievements even then.

This year's 'down' run was the last to be held on Empire Day as the holiday was being discontinued. First to show was Bill Savage, one of an elite group to have recorded victories both before and after the war. As the leaders reached Polly Shortts, he held a 300-yard advantage.

Savage's lead was short-lived. Reg Allison, ever the front-runner, went past and set about running away from his pursuers. Hayward followed and everything pointed towards a repeat of the previous year. At Umlaas Road, Allison was three minutes ahead of Hayward. By Camperdown, the lead had stretched closer to four minutes. At Cato Ridge, it was nearly five minutes.

With Hayward looking in trouble, this was clearly Allison's opportunity to put himself out of reach.

Halfway was reached in 2.49.23, 2 minutes 22 seconds faster than the previous stage record, set by Harry Phillips in 1925. The race record was clearly under threat. This was emphasised when Hayward, now fully recovered from his bad patch, went through Drummond running strongly and having closed the gap slightly.

Hayward later described his tussle with Allison: 'At Camperdown, he was about three minutes ahead of me, but I was still unconcerned. However, at Cato Ridge, I hit a bad patch with cramp in my calves and fell back a few more minutes behind the leader. For a fleeting moment, I considered dropping out, but determination took control. At the Inchanga climb, I had recovered and got back to my usual rhythm. I shortened the gap by a couple of minutes by the time we reached Drummond. I continued to close in on the hills out of Drummond, and when we reached the station at Botha's Hill, I drew alongside Allison. I called out "Bon jour!" to which a tiring Reg responded, "Wally, the French for goodbye is 'Au revoir'!" I chuckled, shook hands and pressed on.'

Allison had conceded defeat. Hayward drew rapidly ahead. At Hillcrest, he was four minutes ahead. By Emberton, the lead had grown to nine minutes and, by Field's Hill, to 22, with Allison a full seven minutes ahead of third-placed Trevor Allen. It was now a race between Hayward and the clock.

Before long, the clock was in trouble. Hayward arrived at Pinetown five minutes faster than Coleman had done in his record-breaking run of 1939. Instead of weakening in the closing stages, Hayward appeared to be gaining in strength. When he crested Tollgate, the final climb, with plenty of time in hand, it was clear that the record would change hands.

Hayward was already approaching legendary status. Thousands of admiring spectators lined the road as he approached the Track Ground with hundreds of vehicles in his wake. A crowd of 3 000 warmly applauded him as he crossed the line in 6.14.08, 7 minutes 57 seconds inside the previous record. His time for the second half was also a new record, 38 seconds faster than that of Allen Boyce in 1939.

While having his legs massaged afterwards, Hayward reflected on the bad patch that had very nearly put him out of the race: 'The cramp got me only

17 miles from Maritzburg. I'll tell you I was really worried. I have never had cramp as badly as this before. I was thinking I might have to call it a day. It was very close.'

The 1951 race was the sixth and final one for Reg Allison. He took second place for the fourth time to go with one fifth and his great victory in 1949. If disappointed at being the runner-up again, he did have the consolation of leading the Collegians Harriers to the Gunga Din team trophy. His teammates were the consistent Morris Alexander (eighth), B. de la Rey (14th) and K. E. Cohen (20th).

The novice prize went to former national champion Arthur Hampton, who claimed fifth position in a time of 7.20.13. Prior to the race, he expressed his feelings about the event: 'No one in South Africa can call himself a marathon runner until he has completed the Comrades Marathon.'

Wally Hayward's stature was not only recognised in South Africa. The rest of the world was also taking note of this remarkable sportsman. In 1951, the prestigious Helms World Trophy, awarded to one outstanding amateur athlete from each continent, was presented to Frank Sedgman (Australia), Adolpho Consolini (Italy), Robert Richards (USA), Adhemar Ferreira da Silva (Brazil), Shigeki Tanaka (Japan) and Wally Hayward (South Africa).

1951 COMRADES MARATHON RESULTS

1. W. H. Hayward	6.14.08
2. R. E. Allison	6.38.40
3. T. N. Allen	7.00.15
4. J. R. Ballington	7.16.53
5. A. C. Hampton	7.20.13
6. L. L. Boulle	7.33.39
7. F. J. Morrison	7.38.44
8. M. B. Alexander	7.52.06
9. A. H. Ferguson	8.01.24
10. J. H. P. Ayres	8.20.57

1952 COMRADES MARATHON
SLOW, BUT SURE

This was an Olympic year. The Helsinki Olympic Games, the second post-war Olympics, dominated all athletic endeavour.

The Comrades Marathon would take place. It had to. But at what price? The cost was Wally Hayward. The great man, winner in 1930 at the age of 21, had returned as a 'middle-aged man' and won the 1950 'up' and the 1951 'down' runs. He had become the face of Comrades. His humility and sportsmanship emulated the virtues that had become associated with Vic Clapham's great race. His world-class athletic ability epitomised the quality of performance that had come to be expected on Comrades day.

Nevertheless, Comrades had to give way to the Olympics. The great South African went to the start of the Olympic marathon acknowledged as the greatest long-distance runner in the world. Sadly, he also started with a calf injury, which put paid to his chances of a top finish. Despite this handicap, he courageously claimed tenth place in one of the most remarkable of races won by one of the most remarkable of super-athletes, the great Czech Emil Zatopek.

Comrades of 1952 had to make do without its reigning champion. Who would take his place? And would his successor be worthy of the position of Comrades champion? Much was in doubt and the date of the race added to the confusion. As Empire Day was no longer a holiday, it was decided that this year's race would take place on Monday 14 July, the day on which the Queen's birthday was celebrated. Such a day was reasonably acceptable for those living in Natal. For those on the Highveld and in the Cape, however, midwinter training at the level required for Comrades was not a happy prospect. A July date was not sustainable.

Without Hayward, the 1952 Comrades Marathon had no real favourite. It was anyone's race, though there were a few notable entries. Trevor Allen, third in 1950 and 1951, was back, hoping to improve his podium position. At the age of 34, he had the maturity and the experience. Allen Boyce, 1940 champion, was also in the field. Would he become another (after Ballington, Cochrane, Savage and Hayward) to record victories both before and after the Second World War?

At 6 a.m., 32 athletes responded to the official send-off from Durban's deputy mayor R. A. Carte and set off for Pietermaritzburg. Understandably, with no real favourite in the field, the leaders played a watching and waiting game. Nobody made a serious effort to get ahead in the early stages. At 45th Cutting, Rufus, Spencer, Luckin, Martin, White and Hampton were virtually within touching distance of each other.

The pace was slow, which was unusual for Comrades. Front-runners have been a tradition of the race. They haven't won very often – in fact, they've hardly ever won – but their efforts have added to the tactical demands of those who would vie for line honours.

Eventually, 38-year-old Don Spencer made a move at Huntley's Hill and gradually eased ahead through Westville and over Cowies Hill. At Pinetown, he was three minutes ahead of Martin, Luckin and Hampton, with Ferguson fifth and Gerald Walsh sixth. Despite the lack of speed, experienced campaigners Trevor Allen, Allen Boyce and Morris Alexander were content to bide their time and leave the front-running to the lesser knowns.

On the ascent of Field's Hill, the novice Martin put in a surge and temporarily reduced Spencer's lead. It wasn't the right time or place to make such an effort, and Martin soon paid for his folly, dropping back and right out of contention on Botha's, the next big climb. Spencer was still running smoothly and led the field through Drummond in 3.30.42, approximately 16 minutes slower than the record for the first half. Well before halfway, it had become apparent that there was no chance of the race record being threatened.

Gerald Walsh was second at Drummond, just over three minutes behind the leader. He was closely followed by Hampton and Allen, with Ferguson a further five minutes behind. As the athletes commenced the second half, they encountered uncomfortably cold and windy conditions with intermittent rain.

Inchanga, regular graveyard of the overenthusiastic, posed no severe problems for Spencer, but it was here that the race started to take shape. In the absence of Hayward, Trevor Allen knew that this year's 'up' run was his big opportunity. He was well prepared and had approached the first half cautiously and sensibly, conserving his energy for a second-half assault.

After cresting Inchanga together with Walsh and Hampton, Allen broke away on Harrison Flats in pursuit of Spencer. At Cato Ridge, he was only a minute behind the leader. At Camperdown, the gap was 30 seconds. Allen was stalking his man relentlessly but carefully, making sure that he didn't overextend himself in the chase.

On an uphill shortly after Camperdown, Allen at last caught his quarry and moved ahead. Spencer, however, was not ready to concede and reclaimed the lead on the downhill approach to Umlaas Road. The prize was the Comrades crown. Both men desperately wanted to win and were determined to hang on, the finish line almost within scent.

There were, however, two significant obstacles to be overcome. Ashburton (or Little Pollys) and Polly Shortts itself lay ahead. Allen, having gone in front for the second time, was 300 yards ahead at the start of the long descent to Tumble Inn. Spencer fought back and reduced the gap to 100 yards on the downhill section. Walsh, having recovered from a bad patch, was moving up, ready to pounce should the two leaders falter.

Allen was the uphill specialist and took full advantage of this ability on the final two climbs. He moved significantly ahead on Ashburton and increased his lead on Pollys itself. At the top, he was three minutes ahead and relatively safe. He crossed the line in 7.00.02. It was the last time that a Comrades Marathon would be won in a time of more than seven hours.

Spencer, exhausted after his tussle with Allen, now had to hold off a fast-finishing Gerald Walsh to claim the runner-up position. This he managed to do by just over a minute. He explained his motivation afterwards: 'I just had to beat Walsh. The third prize was a cuckoo clock featuring the Harry Lime theme. Imagine hearing the combination of that theme and cuckoos, twice every hour for the rest of your life!'

Spencer, a survivor of the Battle of Dunkirk and past chairman of both the Natal Society Drama Group and the Pietermaritzburg Philharmonic Society, paid tribute to his conqueror: 'There was a lot of uphill and nobody can hold Allen on that.' Allen, relieved to have finally achieved his ambition, said simply, 'I had no trouble at all and did not have to stop once.'

Although it wasn't realised at the time, there was a particular significance in the awarding of the novice prize. Red-haired Jackie Mekler, seventh in 7.45.03, would become one of the greatest of all Comrades champions.

1952 COMRADES MARATHON RESULTS

1. T. N. Allen	7.00.02
2. D. Spencer	7.06.17
3. G. Walsh	7.07.23
4. A. H. Ferguson	7.13.15
5. J. Woods	7.35.38
6. A. K. Boyce	7.37.18
7. J. Mekler	7.45.03
8. F. J. Morrison	8.07.32
9. A. J. C. Gillespie	8.13.13
10. M. Farrant	8.38.41

1953 COMRADES MARATHON
HAYWARD ACHIEVES THE IMPOSSIBLE

This was one of the most memorable years for the Comrades Marathon and for the British Commonwealth, of which South Africa was still a member. It was the year of Queen Elizabeth II. It was the year of Edmund Hillary and Tenzing Norgay. It was also the year of one of the world's greatest ever athletes, Wally Hayward, who produced performances during 1953 that defy understanding over half a century later.

Within hours of the coronation of Queen Elizabeth II on 2 June 1953, news was received of a major British triumph. A mountaineering expedition, led by Briton John Hunt, had succeeded in one of the planet's greatest challenges, the first ascent of Mount Everest. New Zealander Edmund Hillary and his Sherpa colleague Tenzing Norgay became the first people to set foot on the highest point on Earth and return home safely.

Although the new queen had been born on 21 April 1926, her birthday was celebrated officially in South Africa on 13 July, and it was on this day that the Comrades Marathon took place. This year's was a much anticipated event: Hayward was back. Although he turned 45 just three days before the race, he had already dispelled the myth that middle age was a time of slowing down. (It would be another 35 years before he produced an even more profound lesson about age.) Wally Hayward was already a living legend. Comrades followers wondered what he might dish up this year.

To begin with, Hayward was expected to give some sort of credence to his startling statement, after winning the 1951 'down' run in 6.14.08, that a sub-six-hour Comrades was possible. Notwithstanding the huge respect that he had earned, most thought that such a claim verged on the ridiculous. He would have to justify his controversial prediction, which, incidentally, echoed a suggestion by Arthur Newton a few decades earlier.

Whether or not the derision with which some had greeted his sub-six-hour claim was motivating him, Hayward showed from the start that he was a man on a mission. After the crowing Max Trimborn, the city hall bells and the starting gun had announced the start of the race, Hayward swiftly shot to the front and commenced the descent of Pollys with a 30-yard lead over Allen Boyce and Trevor Allen.

Weather-wise, it was a typical 'down' run, cold at the start but warming gradually as the sun made its presence felt. After an hour or two, extra garments were discarded and tossed to the side of the road, where they were swiftly claimed by ululating well-wishers. At Tumble Inn, Hayward was over a minute ahead of second-placed Allen Boyce. Mercer Davies, Syd Luyt, Liege Boulle, Jackie Mekler and a host of others were in reasonable range of the leader.

Hayward's early pace was significantly faster than that of his rivals, yet, at the same time, relatively cautious. At Umlaas Road, he was three minutes ahead of second-placed Boyce. At Camperdown, the gap was three and a half minutes. Although well in front, he was nearly a minute behind his own time during his record-breaking run of 6.14.08 two years previously. By Cato Ridge, Springbok marathon athlete Syd Luyt had overhauled Boyce to go into second place.

As Hayward powered his way through Harrison Flats, his 17-year-old daughter Gwendolyn was heard to call out, 'Keep going, Dad, you're terrific!' She was right. He was terrific. He was also sensible. Still running well within himself (as Bruce Fordyce would do some 30 years later), Hayward reached Drummond in 2.53.02, nearly four minutes slower than Reg Allison's halfway time two years earlier.

Hayward's relatively cautious first-half effort was visibly rewarded as he confidently and powerfully negotiated Botha's Hill and arrived at Hillcrest more than five minutes ahead of second-placed Luyt. He was also a minute and a half inside his 1951 time. By the time the flying Hayward reached Pinetown, the race was effectively over. His lead was seven and a half minutes and he had improved his 1951 time by a full seven minutes. Unless something went drastically wrong, he was going to improve his own record. Furthermore, his forecast of a sub-six-hour Comrades was beginning to appear reachable.

When Hayward reached Westville in 5 hours 2 minutes with Luyt trailing by over a mile, it was clear that Comrades history was being made. There was ample time available and Hayward showed no sign of slowing. He was fully aware that destiny was beckoning him as he reached the new finishing point of Hoy Park – a mile further than the old Track Ground! – and crossed the line in the remarkable time of 5.52.30. His record, which would survive for ten years, was achieved in tennis shoes bought for 75 cents on a tougher course than the one that challenges present-day runners and without the benefit of scientific preparation and fancy diets. He did, however, acknowledge one dietary preference: 'Honey – I firmly believe in it and put it in my porridge, bread and whatever I can.'

In his moment of triumph, Hayward found time to pay tribute to Syd Luyt, second in 6.05.08: 'I am only sorry that I had to clash with, and perhaps take a little edge off, the performance of Syd Luyt. It has taken 32 years for someone to beat six hours in the race, and here Luyt comes along and misses the mark by five minutes at his first attempt. His performance suggests that my record will not stand for long.'

Trevor Allen, reigning 'up' run champion, claimed third place for the third time but did have the distinction of beating the seven-hour barrier for the first time. The first five all managed to do so, and all of them (Hayward, Luyt, Trevor Allen, Allen Boyce and Jackie Mekler) have attained special status in Comrades history. With 'Mr Comrades' Liege Boulle and Mercer Davies taking seventh and eighth places, and Nick Raubenheimer 17th, it seems strange that only 26 completed the course.

South African Comrades champions had twice previously visited the United Kingdom to challenge world records and demonstrate the long-distance prowess of their nation. Arthur Newton did so in 1924, winning the London-to-Brighton race in a record time of 5.53.43 and setting a new world best time of 5.48.42 for 50 miles. In 1937, Hardy Ballington won the London-to-Brighton and Great West Road races. In so doing, he established new world records for 50 miles and 100 miles. In each of the events, he was seconded by Arthur Newton, the man whose world records were being beaten. In no other sport does camaraderie extend so far.

In 1953, it was the turn of Wally Hayward. This was his golden year. In September, while staying at the home of Arthur Newton, he won the London-to-Brighton race in the record time of 5.29.40 and was part of the winning team, his colleagues being South Africans Fred Morrison and Jackie Mekler. In October, he annihilated all challengers in the Bath-to-London 100-miler, taking 1 hour 53 minutes off the previous record, held by fellow Comrades legend Hardy Ballington. In second place was 21-year-old Jackie Mekler, a future Comrades luminary who also finished within the old record.

Without the benefits of modern sports science, Hayward was not aware that recovery and rest periods were advisable in order to attain peak performance at the right time. In July, he had shattered the Comrades Marathon record, most definitely beating the world 50-mile record along the way although his time was officially unrecorded. In September, he had broken the London-to-Brighton record and in October the Bath-to-London 100-mile record. He wasn't quite finished. On 20 November at Motspur Park, Hayward set new world records for 100 miles (12.46.43) and for 24 hours (159 miles 562 yards). On this occasion, one of the timekeepers, later to emigrate to South Africa and become a legend in his own right as a broadcaster, was a gentleman named Charles Fortune.

1953 COMRADES MARATHON RESULTS

1. W. H. Hayward	5.52.30
2. T. S. Luyt	6.05.08
3. T. N. Allen	6.28.15
4. A. K. Boyce	6.45.11
5. J. Mekler	6.52.59
6. F. Mare	7.04.57
7. L. L. Boulle	7.25.37

8. M. J. Davies	7.36.25
9. M. L. Farrant	7.53.55
10. L. R. Barnes	7.55.24

1954 COMRADES MARATHON
FIFTH WIN FOR HAYWARD

On 29 May 1953, Edmund Hillary and Tenzing Norgay had reached the summit of the world. Almost a year later, on 6 May 1954, another 'Everest' was achieved. On the Iffley Road track in Oxford, helped by his co-athletes and close friends Chris Brasher and Chris Chataway, medical student Roger Bannister ran the first sub-four-minute mile.

South Africa's ultra-distance pioneer, Wally Hayward, having demonstrated his outright supremacy the previous year, once again set his sights on the event most closely associated with him, the Comrades Marathon. At this stage of his life, Hayward enjoyed hero status such as few other South Africans had known. In the minds of the public, all he had to do was turn up and victory would be assured. The only speculation concerned his finishing time and the prospect of yet another record.

Such one-sided thinking was encouraged by the absence of two formidable rivals. Syd Luyt, so promising in his debut run the previous year, of whom Hayward had predicted great things, did not return. He would never fulfil the potential he had demonstrated in 1953. Young Jackie Mekler, whose previous year's performances in the United Kingdom had suggested that he would make a worthy successor to Hayward, had been chosen to represent South Africa in the British Empire and Commonwealth Games marathon in Vancouver. The race was due to be run on 7 August and Mekler had no option but to postpone his Comrades ambitions.

Hayward wasn't quite bereft of challengers. In fact, the field was rather a strong one. Reigning 'up' champion Trevor Allen was back to defend his title. Gerald Walsh, third in 1952, was determined to win a Comrades Marathon. Frans Mare, Mercer Davies and Liege Boulle, among others, ensured a high level of competitiveness. Victory wasn't Hayward's only target, although a win would put him alongside Ballington and Newton as five-time champions. He also had the opportunity to become only the second man, after Newton, to hold both 'up' and 'down' records.

Around this time, there was no fixed date for the race. Empire Day was no more and the Queen's official birthday of 13 July was unsuitable. Saturday 12 June was chosen for the 1954 race. This was a centenary year for both Durban and Pietermaritzburg, and celebratory lights proclaimed the occasion as the early leaders crested Tollgate in the breaking dawn.

First to take the lead was Mercer Davies, who went through 45th Cutting 150 yards ahead of Wootton with the formidable trio of Allen, Hayward and Walsh a further 30 yards back. Davies and Wootton were unable to maintain their early advantage, and Allen, Hayward and Walsh, still running together, began the first major climb, Cowies Hill. On the descent, Walsh moved ahead and reached Pinetown, shortly ahead of Hayward and Allen, in the fast time of 1.28.38. Although early in the race, the time was inside record target.

Field's Hill is the steepest and longest climb in the 'up' run. Generally regarded as too early in the race to make a challenge, it can nevertheless cause problems for those who may have started a little too fast. It was here that Walsh lost his early lead, being passed by Hayward and then by Allen.

Front-running was not a problem for Hayward. Most of his running career had been spent in the number one spot. On this occasion, he did have a little problem, the resolution of which bore testimony to the special sportsmanship of Comrades. In 1954, race marshals were not as plentiful as today and runners, particularly leaders, could go off course. On this occasion, Hayward took the correct road but second-placed Allen, incorrectly believing him to have gone astray, called the leader back. Hayward complied. When they realised the error, Allen waited until Hayward had built up the equivalent of his previous lead before resuming his challenge.

Despite the time lost in his little excursion, Hayward was keeping within reach of a record time. Furthermore, his pursuers were staying in touch. A fast time seemed assured. At Hillcrest, Hayward was just 22 seconds ahead of Allen, with Walsh a minute and a half further back. Hayward's halfway time of 3.11.41 was a new record for the Durban-Drummond leg, but Allen was less than two minutes behind. Walsh had dropped back and was almost five minutes behind Allen. Frans Mare (fourth) was a further 15 minutes adrift.

Inchanga is invariably significant in the gradual unravelling of the contest of the 'up' run. On this occasion, front-runner Hayward showed not a scintilla of vulnerability as he steadily overcame the problems posed by the frightening hill. Once over the top, he opened up. No one else had a chance. The great man simply outclassed all comers. He wasn't sprinting. He was merely running at his own natural pace, which was far too fast for the rest.

Hayward comfortably negotiated the relatively boring undulations of Harrison Flats and the subtly testing section between Cato Ridge and Camperdown, reaching Camperdown in 4.32.04. Allen, looking just as comfortable, arrived more than 15 minutes later, such was the superiority of the leader. Third-placed Walsh was another 11 minutes back. It was, clearly, no contest. Hayward's fifth win was safely in the bag and a new record was all but guaranteed.

Prior to the race, five-time winner Hardy Ballington (as qualified a judge as any) had predicted a winning time of between 6.10 and 6.15 for Hayward. When he reached the top of Polly Shortts in 5 hours 40 minutes, Hayward looked likely to justify Ballington's confidence. He did this in emphatic style, breasting the tape in 6.12.55 and lowering the record by 19 minutes 31 seconds. Hardy Ballington had held the previous record for 16 years, the longest such time to date and only to be eclipsed when Bruce Fordyce set a time in the 1980s that would survive for a full two decades.

A new floating trophy, the Founder's Trophy, donated by race founder Vic Clapham, was presented for the first time to the oldest finisher. The oldest finisher happened to be the oldest competitor, who also happened to be the first finisher. His name, of course, was Wally Hayward.

Trevor Allen took second place, with Gerald Walsh third. For the first time in an 'up' run, the first three all finished in under seven hours. Frans Mare, fourth, crossed the line in 7.05.21. The Pietermaritzburg runner R. H. Strachan established his name as one of the characters of Comrades. When his seconds arrived at his home in the early hours of the morning, they found him drinking gin and vermouth with his wife. Fortified by his somewhat eccentric breakfast, Strachan took sixth place in 7.48.44, 14 minutes ahead of next man Liege Boulle.

The 1954 Comrades Marathon should have been the happy ending to the Wally Hayward fairy tale. It wasn't. The war hero, holder of records for both the 'up' and 'down' runs, became persona non grata in possibly the most outrageous blunder by officialdom in the history of South African sport.

In his book, *Just Call me Wally*, published in 1999 (the year he turned 91), Hayward gave his account of the wrong that had been done:

'Unfortunately (and I have never forgiven them for this) the South African Amateur Athletic and Cycling Association, in its misguided wisdom, decided on 12 August 1954 to declare me a professional.

'The SAAA gave permission to Germiston Callies to raise funds for a trip to England for my record attempts, provided the money was channelled through them. They alleged I broke the rules by accepting funds directly from donors.

'The amounts I received were £110 pounds from the Olympic and Empire Games Association, an equal sum from a liquor company, a donation from the SA Boxing Association and some private contributions. The total was about £286. The cost of the trip was just short of £400.

'The chairman of my running club in Germiston (Callies Harriers Athletic Club) Mr J. M. Botha took up the fight – "The greatest runner South Africa has produced has been dismissed from his sport, without even a hearing."

'I had the shock of learning on the radio that I had been declared a professional. I hadn't asked for the money, it was donated to me so that I could represent my country in the record attempts in Britain.'

It might well be accurate to suggest that, at this point in his life, Wally Hayward was more enthusiastically admired abroad than he was in his own country (although it must be acknowledged that public opinion did not approve of his banning). Harold Abrahams, winner of the 100 metres in the Paris Olympic Games of 1924 (as immortalised in the film *Chariots of Fire*), became one of the athletics world's most respected administrators and was, in fact, the chief organiser of the 1948 London Olympics. When asked whom he considered to be the world's finest all-round athlete, he replied, 'Wally Hayward'. Other notables expressed similar sentiments.

1954 COMRADES MARATHON RESULTS

1. W. H. Hayward	6.12.55
2. T. N. Allen	6.45.14
3. G. Walsh	6.58.38
4. F. Mare	7.05.21
5. J. J. Smit	7.46.12
6. R. H. Strachan	7.48.44
7. L. L. Boulle	8.02.32
8. J. Goldie	8.06.14
9. D. B. Chase	8.07.00
10. G. J. Davis	8.15.50

8

AN INTERIM PERIOD
(1955 to 1957)

With Wally Hayward having retired – or, rather, having been retired by uninspired officialdom – concerns about the future of Comrades were being voiced. After all, it was largely the legend of this extraordinary man that had put long-distance running, including the Comrades Marathon, on the sporting map, both nationally and abroad.

Fortunately, the aftereffects of the Hayward era were all positive. The 1955 race drew a record entry of 92. Hayward had brought a sense of national pride, an enhancement of the traditional camaraderie and a personal glamour to Comrades. Although he would no longer compete, the spirit of Hayward was deeply etched into the soul of his favourite event.

Of course, Hayward's absence provided an opportunity of Comrades success for those who had played supporting roles during the reign of the great man. Two of these were Gerald Walsh and Mercer Davies.

Walsh had commenced his Comrades career with a 15th-place finish in a time of 9.18.43 in 1951. He soon showed that he was capable of greater things. In his second and third runs, in 1952 and 1954, both 'up' runs, he had claimed third place. In 1952, his time was 7.07.23. Two years later, he broke the seven-hour barrier in a time of 6.58.38. He was ready to improve his position and managed to do so.

Mercer Davies's Comrades career was remarkably similar to that of Walsh. Both completed 13 races. Their permanent numbers were 112 (Walsh) and 121 (Davies). Walsh's tally of medals is made up of seven golds, four silvers and two bronzes, whereas Davies won five golds, six silvers and two bronzes.

Each produced a positive progression of results before he was able to challenge for first place, which both achieved in fine style. They were both popular champions even though their efforts were understandably overshadowed by the genius of their predecessor Wally Hayward.

1955 COMRADES MARATHON
WALSH AT LAST

Racial polarisation was the most significant aspect of life in South Africa in 1955, but few on the privileged side of the fence seemed to notice. Two years previously, the Bantu Education Act had been passed. Introducing the bill to the Senate, the Minister of Native Affairs, one H. F. Verwoerd, had made the notorious statement, 'What is the use of teaching the Bantu child mathematics, when it cannot use it in practice?' The long-term effects of that disgraceful excuse for legislation still haunt South Africa today.

In 1955, black South Africans spelt out their vision of the future in the Freedom Charter, formally adopted at a national convention called the Congress of the People. The country's first Nobel Peace Prize laureate, Chief Albert Luthuli, called the charter an attempt 'to give a flesh and blood meaning, in the South African setting, to such words as democracy, freedom, liberty'. It contained the famous declaration, 'South Africa belongs to all who live in it, black and white.'

Most white South Africans were unaware of such developments. Their minds were on their favourite pastime, rugby. Robin Thompson's British Lions became one of the most popular sporting teams to visit the country. The series captivated rugby supporters. Lions players Tony O'Reilly, Jeff Butterfield, Phil Davies, Bryn Meredith and Cliff Morgan, among others, became household names. The first test at Ellis Park was won 23–22 by the visitors before a record crowd of 95 000 when Jack van der Schyff narrowly failed to convert a try by Theunis Briers with the last kick of the match. In the second test at Newlands, Tom van Vollenhoven scored a hat-trick of tries as South Africa fought back. The Lions won the third test and the Springboks took the fourth and final one. The series was shared and most agreed that it had been as exciting a tour as any in living memory. Some also noticed that black South Africans tended to support the opposition.

There was, of course, another diversion in 1955, specifically designed for those prepared to endure pain and discomfort in order to achieve a worthy goal. The Comrades Marathon took place without Wally Hayward, who had been disqualified by athletics officials. There was no doubt that the extraordinary achievements of Hayward, both at home and abroad, had focused public attention on Comrades. Nevertheless, the record entry of 92, approximately twice the average field of recent years, did come as a pleasant surprise to the organisers. A further bonus was the entry of a foreigner, Allen Nelson of the United States.

Without Hayward, there was no outright favourite. Trevor Allen, 1952 'up' winner, was certainly in with a chance. In the build-up to this year's race, he came third in the National Marathon Championship and won the Pieter Korkie Ultramarathon from Pretoria to Germiston. His preparation had gone well and it would take a tough man to beat him. Then there was Gerald Walsh, second bridesmaid on a couple of occasions. Would he spend the night of the race in the honeymoon suite? Time would tell.

A new date was set for the race, 31 May, a public holiday. This date would continue to be Comrades day until the early days of the new millennium. A pistol shot commenced proceedings and sent the record field on their way. Early leader Bill Savage of Albion Harriers brought back memories of earlier days – he had won the 1932 Comrades Marathon.

Savage's early effort wasn't just a show for the spectators. He remained a significantly talented athlete, although he certainly wasn't the runner he'd been in his heyday. He was first to the top of Polly Shortts (not quite as significant as this might have been in an 'up' run), and gradually pulled ahead, going through Camperdown 1 minute 31 seconds ahead of second-placed Gerald Walsh.

For the leader, all went well for one-third of the race. Then came Cato Ridge and the demanding Harrison Flats. Savage's advantage didn't survive this testing section. Walsh claimed the lead around Cato Ridge, and ever-competitive Trevor Allen moved into third place. At the crest of Inchanga, just before the long descent to Drummond, Walsh held a three-and-a-half minute lead over Allen, now running in tandem with Mercer Davies. Savage had slipped back to fourth and would hardly be noticed henceforth.

Walsh went through halfway in 2.59.25, almost three and a half minutes ahead of Allen, who had Davies snapping at his heels. Over Botha's Hill and on to Hillcrest, there was no stopping Walsh, although pursuers Allen and Davies continued to try to convince themselves (if no one else) that they were potential winners. Although Allen and Davies were adopting menacing positions, Walsh managed to extend his lead by half a minute over the hilly section from Drummond to Hillcrest.

From Hillcrest to Kloof, the road is gently undulating, with more 'down' than 'up'. It is probably the easiest and least damaging part of the 'down' run into which to put extra effort. Walsh seemed to agree. Towards and over Kloof and down Field's Hill, he pulled ahead of his rivals and reached Pinetown seven minutes ahead of second-placed Trevor Allen.

Walsh appeared to be struggling over Cowies Hill. It wasn't a serious problem and his lead remained formidable. On the descent and through Westville, he seemed to experience a second wind. Behind him, Allen and Davies were slowing perceptibly, and Davies started to drop right down the order, while Allen yielded second place to David Dodds of Salisbury, who was in turn overtaken by Frans Mare.

Walsh was totally unaffected by all the positional adjustments taking place behind him. With his mind set on the finish line and his chance of glory, he sensibly kept to his natural, easy stride. He had come close before, and in 1955, Gerald Walsh was not going to miss out. He didn't. He crossed the line at the Track Ground in 6 hours 6 minutes 32 seconds, the third fastest 'down' time on record. Although everything had gone according to plan, he did admit to a moment of doubt towards the end: 'Coming into

Pinetown, I was not feeling too bright, particularly with Trevor Allen behind me.' Walsh modestly paid a warm tribute to his second, 1940 winner Allen Boyce, who had helped him throughout the race, 'He coached me all the way and told me just when to make a burst.'

Frans Mare took second place, 12 minutes behind the winner. Ever-reliable Trevor Allen came in third – astonishingly, for the fourth time in six years. On the other two occasions, he had finished first (1952) and second (1954), yet his finest year, 1959, was still some way off.

Rhodesian David Dodds, 25 years old, won the novice trophy. Afterwards, he gave his impression of the unique challenge posed by Comrades: 'The downhills bothered me more than the uphills. At one stage, my legs were jarred so badly, I wondered whether I would finish.' American visitor Allen Nelson, who completed his journey successfully in 9.57.57, also discovered the toughness of the Comrades challenge: 'I have run many long-distance races, but the Comrades is definitely the most gruelling of them all.'

Later in the year, on 3 December, Bruce Noel Stephenson Fordyce was born in Hong Kong, a year after Wally Hayward had completed his final victory and claimed the prize for being the oldest finisher. Thirty-three years later, on 31 May 1988, Bruce Fordyce would produce arguably his finest ever Comrades performance. Amazingly, on the same day, so would Wally Hayward, just days short of his 80th birthday.

1955 COMRADES MARATHON RESULTS

1. G. Walsh	6.06.32
2. F. Mare	6.18.34
3. T. N. Allen	6.24.13
4. D. Dodds	6.25.15
5. D. Sansom	6.55.30
6. M. Davies	7.04.28
7. J. J. Smit	7.06.05
8. K. McMaster	7.08.52
9. A. J. C. Gillespie	7.20.14
10. L. L. Boulle	7.26.47

1956 COMRADES MARATHON
GREATHEART'S RACE

The first multiple Comrades winner, Arthur Newton, by then resident in Britain, was invited by the Marathon Runners Club of South Africa to visit the country in which he had first made his name as a super-athlete in the 1920s. Rather unsurprisingly, it was arranged that he would attend the Comrades Marathon. It was the 36th running of the race that had made him famous – and which, it was also generally accepted, he had helped make famous. In recognition of his influence and stature, the 1956 event was officially named 'The Arthur Newton Comrades Marathon, 1956'.

To Newton's great joy, race founder Vic Clapham was also to be present. Clapham had personally organised the early Comrades Marathons that had been dominated by Newton. Now retired, he had settled in Pietermaritzburg. The news that the two main stalwarts of early Comrades history would witness this year's event added lustre to the occasion.

Understandably, nostalgia was the dominant theme this year. A total of 88 runners reported for duty at the start: four less than 1955's record field and one less than the 'up' run record set in 1922, the year in which 'Greatheart' Newton recorded the first of his five victories. According to tradition, this was an 'up' run as it took place in a year with an even number.

Right from the start, the fancied runners went to the front. Mercer Davies was first through Pinetown in 1.22.37. This was six minutes faster than two years previously, when the winner, Hayward, had posted a new record. Walsh, Pace, Allen, McMaster and Wootton also reached Pinetown faster than the 1954 time. With six runners so well placed, race watchers felt confident that a new record was in the offing.

Thoughts of a best ever time were inevitable after the excitement of Wally Hayward's superb record run two years earlier. Overambitious athletes, as well as followers, had still to learn one of the big Comrades lessons: If you set a goal well within your capabilities and approach it cautiously on race day, you may just achieve it. If, on the other hand, you think that a dream of greatness can be easily fulfilled, you might just fall flat on your face, as so many others have done. If the race is run in adverse conditions, fortune tends to discard the brave.

In 1956, the temperature was hot, very hot. Davies maintained his first-half lead and went through halfway, looking strong, in 3.02.20, more than nine minutes faster than Hayward in his record-breaking run two years before. Gerald Walsh, in second place, was also inside Hayward's time. Trevor Allen was in third place, eight minutes behind Walsh. Timewise, it looked like a two-horse race.

Davies continued to build his lead over Inchanga and through Harrison Flats to Cato Ridge, where he was eight minutes ahead of Walsh, with Allen, still third, 20 minutes behind the second-placed man. On the disconcertingly undulating stretch from Cato Ridge to Camperdown, the intense heat began to tell and the pace of the leaders slowed perceptibly. At Camperdown, Davies was marginally behind Hayward's record pace, and Walsh, looking stronger than the fading leader, was just over six minutes behind.

It soon became evident that Mercer Davies's race was run. He was exhausted. Walsh, realising that his quarry was tiring, found renewed strength as he continued his relentless pursuit. On the downhill stretch from Umlaas Road, Walsh made his move and was two minutes ahead of Davies when he commenced the ascent of Little Pollys. The race was over as a contest, as Walsh afterwards confirmed: 'When Davies was eight minutes ahead of me, I thought I had no chance of winning unless he cracked. He did crack, but far more dramatically than I expected.'

As Walsh purposefully extended his advantage and made certain of his victory, Davies gamely attempted to maintain his second position. He almost succeeded, only succumbing to the challenge of fast-finishing Allen Boyce in central Maritzburg. Nevertheless, his third place, 24 minutes ahead of Trevor Allen, was a notable achievement. Arthur Newton, first ever Comrades strategist, summed up Davies's day: 'Conditions were too hot for a record. Davies went too fast in the first half of the race. If he had started slower, he would have done much better.'

Gerald Walsh was a worthy Comrades winner. In torrid conditions, he had set the third fastest 'up' time to date. Acknowledging afterwards that he had focused on speed training in his pre-race build-up, he admitted that the pace on race day had troubled him: 'The early pace upset my rhythm. Through trying to adjust my pace, I went through a bad patch in the vicinity of Drummond, occasionally walking.'

Second-placed Allen Boyce set a whole host of records. He became the second runner, after Liege Boulle, to win ten Comrades medals. His top finish produced an eighth gold, putting him ahead of Hardy Ballington and Fred Wallace. In taking the runner-up spot for the fourth time, he emulated the hard-luck story of another perennial Comrades bridesmaid, Reg Allison.

One man whose 1956 medal was especially significant was 54-year-old Ian Jardine. In 1947, Jardine had considered dropping out of his debut race. Caught up in the Comrades spirit, he had dragged his weary body along to complete the course, 19th out of 23 finishers, in 10.11.30. Now, nine years later, he was back. There was, however, a big difference: blindness had overtaken him. This year, he followed his guide, John Woods, and finished successfully in 9.57.31, about 14 minutes faster than his inaugural attempt. Ian Jardine would become one of the great legends of the race.

Comrades runners tend to be admired by most, although they are sometimes mocked by those who know them well. In 1956, Don Allison, while battling up a hill, was urged on by a supporter who called him a 'barrel of lard'. An incensed onlooker suggested pointedly to the critical spectator that he should 'try running the race'. She would not have known that he was Don Spencer, a close friend of Allison's, who had finished second in the 1952 Comrades Marathon.

1956 COMRADES MARATHON RESULTS

1. G. Walsh	6.33.05
2. A. K. Boyce	7.12.08
3. M. J. Davies	7.14.10
4. T. N. Allen	7.38.00
5. G. N. Raubenheimer	7.44.06
6. W. E. R. Savage	7.51.50
7. A. J. Gillespie	7.57.53
8. G. J. Davis	8.11.00
9. S. Bezuidenhout	8.13.56
10. L. L. Boulle	8.18.25

1957 COMRADES MARATHON
MERCER DAVIES HAS HIS DAY

Not all Comrades Marathons have produced phenomenal performances or significant developments, but no race has been devoid of special interest. The Comrades is too much part of South Africa's national psyche to ever produce 'just another event'. Important in the evolution of the great race has been the recognition that the middle of the pack and, indeed, the back-runners are just as important as the champions and multiple champions. Arthur Newton, the great champion of the 1920s, was the first to establish this vital aspect of Comrades properly. It is notable that succeeding super-athletes have continued to follow Newton's generous example and emphasise the symbiotic relationship between head and tail.

The 1957 race did not lack top performers. In fact, it featured an attempt by defending champion Gerald Walsh, who had also won the 1955 'down' run, to become the first since Newton to achieve a hat-trick of successive wins. His chief rival appeared to be Mercer Davies, South African representative and first Commonwealth finisher in the 1956 Olympic Games marathon in Melbourne. Davies had become a regular top-ten finisher and had come third in 1956. Walsh and Davies were expected to fight out the result.

In sport, expectation and reality often bear little resemblance. Not so on this occasion. Over time, the Comrades Marathon has produced memorable duels, starting with Phil Masterton-Smith's victory over Noel Burree by just two seconds in 1931. Malone and Kuhn, Fordyce and a host of challengers, Tshabalala and Mtolo, and many others would illuminate various epic Comrades battles. The year 1957, Mercer Davies and Gerald Walsh, rivals for some time, staged their personal showdown.

The field of 81 was 11 fewer than the 92 who had set off on the previous 'down' run in 1955. From the start, it was evident that the main contenders were intent on a battle royal. There was no hanging back, no gentle 'come from behind' strategy, just an all-out effort from gun to finish. Gerald Walsh led the pack out of Pietermaritzburg, reaching the top of Polly Shortts after 32 minutes, with Mercer Davies following 150 yards adrift. The two leaders were already a quarter of a mile ahead of the others, the race still in its infancy.

Comrades tradition suggests that any racing should take place in the final third of the race. Walsh and Davies eschewed conventional wisdom and simply ignored all considerations other than their private contest, which at times resembled a long-distance sprint. Walsh continued to lead, but by the barest of margins. He reached Camperdown in 1.35. Davies was just 15 seconds slower.

Inchanga would so often play a decisive role in any close-run duel, whether it be an 'up' or 'down' run. Not so this time. The duo of Walsh and Davies cruised over the giant hill without flinching. Neither was giving an inch. Walsh continued to lead, with Davies shadowing him. At Drummond, Walsh was just over a minute and a half slower than Hayward had been in his stupendous record-breaking run in 1953. Yet Davies was only ten seconds behind him.

The psychological pressure was now on Walsh. He had done everything possible to break the challenge of Davies, but to no avail. Davies had maintained his threatening presence. Now doubts must have entered the mind of Walsh. What more could he do to shake off his determined rival? Perhaps it was time for Davies to make a move. He did, twice. At the crest of Botha's Hill and on the approach to Hillcrest Village, he edged ahead for a short while, just long enough for Walsh to sense that his opponent was strong and resolute.

The ding-dong battle continued through Kloof and down Field's Hill. Going through Pinetown, Mercer Davies made his decisive move. He had waited a long time. Walsh was unable to respond. Realising that his dream was beckoning, Davies confidently climbed Cowies, the last of the major hills. Going through Westville, he was comfortably ahead.

From now on, it was all Davies. Walsh's hope of a hat-trick was in tatters. Davies drew away and increased his lead virtually with every stride. Once over Tollgate, it was just a question of the winning time. New arrangements didn't help him. The finish had been moved to the Track Ground at King's Park, this adding a little extra distance to the final stage. As it turned out, Davies's 6.13.55 was the third fastest 'down' run to date, beaten only by record holder Wally Hayward and vanquished opponent Gerald Walsh in his victory two years previously.

Although the battle between the top two finishers had been fast and furious throughout, Davies had adopted a sensible approach, allowing his rival to do much of the hard work before pouncing at the most opportune moment. He acknowledged this in his post-race comments: 'I allowed Walsh to set the pace, but I was determined not to let him get out of my sight. I knew I had his measure at Pinetown when I felt him easing up.'

Gerald Walsh did have some consolation. A member of Durban Athletic Club, he was the lead runner in the club's successful bid for the Gunga Din trophy. His victorious teammates were K. McMaster (fourth), Nick Raubenheimer (fifth) and D. A. Wellbeloved (eighth).

At this stage of the race's history, gold medals were awarded to the first six finishers. For the first time, all six beat the seven-hour barrier. Standards were improving.

A notable new personality in this year's race was 26-year-old Clive Crawley. Morris Alexander, author of *The Comrades Marathon Story* and stalwart of the race almost from day one, had generously presented his Comrades number 1 to Crawley, and the fortunate recipient did not let him down. Finishing 15th in a time of 8.02.30, Crawley won the prize for first novice. Today, with over 40 medals to his credit, Clive Crawley still asserts his allegiance to the Comrades Marathon and his gratitude to Morris Alexander.

1957 COMRADES MARATHON RESULTS

1. M. Davies	6.13.55
2. G. Walsh	6.26.33
3. F. Mare	6.46.15
4. K. McMaster	6.51.00
5. G. N. Raubenheimer	6.55.07
6. D. N. McInerney	6.57.45
7. B. L. Walsh	7.09.27
8. D. A. Wellbeloved	7.21.38
9. T. Wang	7.24.20
10. E. G. Gore	7.29.30

9

MEKLER TAKES OVER
(1958 to 1965)

Throughout its existence, Comrades has produced memorable figures just when its continuation as a major annual event has appeared to be threatened. In 1958, a full 37 years since the inaugural run in 1921, just 60 athletes faced the starter. Yes, the field was larger than the 34 who braved the early cold in 1921, but significantly smaller than the 89 who commenced the first 'up' run in 1922.

Fortunately, one of the 60 who reported for duty outside the Durban City Hall in 1958 was the modest, self-effacing Jackie Mekler, a 26-year-old athlete whose versatility over various distances matched his phenomenal strength over the most testing of all challenges, the Comrades Marathon. Furthermore, he turned out to be a man of the highest character, worthy to take over the mantle that had passed down from Newton, through

Ballington, to Hayward. A new and exciting period in Comrades history had been born.

Mekler's love of running stemmed from a desire to be himself and determine his own environment. Although a friendly and willing conversationalist, he, like many other long-distance athletes, found solace in his own thoughts and learnt to enjoy the thrill of running while gradually realising that his own ability was significantly superior to that of your average jogger.

In 1952, Mekler's athletic career moved dramatically forward in an academic sense. He responded to an advertisement for Arthur Newton's books in a magazine and was astonished to receive a reply from the great man himself. The following year, Mekler travelled to England as part of the record-shattering Wally Hayward's support group. Newton, who assisted Hayward in his marvellous achievements, took a liking to Mekler and invited him to stay in his home.

What Mekler learnt from Newton became highly significant in the evolution of Comrades. Such lessons went far beyond the strategy required to win a race. Newton emphasised the importance of personally facing the demands of life in order to succeed, a dictum that has served countless runners well over the years.

Mekler's record, compared with those of other Comrades greats, reveals a strange paradox. While Mekler was unquestionably the finest athlete of his era, he was often beaten, even at the peak of his career. Yet Hayward's five victories without failure from 1930 to 1954 and Fordyce's nine wins out of nine starts suggest that your Comrades superstar should be unbeatable during his best years.

What made Mekler different in this respect? After all, his record of success is impressive. In 1960, he ran the first sub-six-hour 'up' run. In 1963, he shattered Wally Hayward's 'invincible' 'down' record just ten days after running a standard marathon in Greece in 2.36.00, only returning to South Africa the night before Comrades. Perhaps the answer might be found in his running strategy. Mekler, not unlike Alan Robb, simply went out and ran as hard and fast as he could without frills and with total commitment. He will always be revered as one of the true 'greats' of the great race.

As indicated above, Mekler didn't have things all his own way. In 1959, popular Trevor Allen added a 'down' victory to his 'up' triumph of 1952. In 1961, school headmaster George Claassen took the title in a creditable

6.07.07, and Englishman John Smith upset South African hopes in his only attempt in 1962. Nevertheless, Jackie Mekler was the best of his day, and most other days, and his contribution to the camaraderie of Comrades continues.

1958 COMRADES MARATHON
MEKLER ARRIVES

When 60 athletes left the Durban City Hall at the start of the 1958 Comrades Marathon, no one would have realised that a significant new era of the race had just begun. It is true that 26-year-old Jackie Mekler was regarded by most pundits as race favourite. It is equally true that he had established his credentials over a variety of distances, including his early Comrades forays. Yet he had not produced any real inkling of the enormous impact he would have on the race.

Mekler's first Comrades efforts were promising, but not remarkable. In the 'up' run of 1952, he finished seventh in 7.45.03. In the following year's 'down' run, he broke seven hours to take fifth place in 6.52.59. Clearly, such a start suggested significant things to come. For Mekler, however, other challenges would take precedence.

In 1953, at the age of 21, he accompanied Wally Hayward to England and played a supporting role in Hayward's record-breaking conquest of the United Kingdom. In the Bath-to-London 100-miler, Mekler actually beat the race record, held by fellow South African Hardy Ballington. Unfortunately for him, Hayward was first to the finish line and claimed the record for himself. During the UK trip, Mekler became friendly with Arthur Newton, a man he greatly admired and who offered him accommodation should he return to the UK. Mekler took him up on this and spent approximately a year with Newton in 1955. It was a valuable experience for the young South African, who learnt at first hand Newton's views on training, his life philosophies and, very importantly, his understanding of the unique spirit that belongs only to the Comrades Marathon.

Mekler established his international credentials in one of the most notorious and controversial distance races ever, the marathon event at the British Empire and Commonwealth Games run in Vancouver on 7 August 1954. This was the event in which British athlete Jim Peters, undoubtedly the finest distance runner of his era, collapsed on the track with victory virtually in his grasp and was carried unconscious to an ambulance, a non-finisher, only to regain consciousness the following day. In the torrid conditions, Joseph McGhee of Scotland took first place in 2.39.36, with South Africa's Jackie Mekler second just over a minute behind. Third place went to another South African, Jan Barnard.

Mekler was a front-runner who tended to take control of proceedings as early as possible. On this occasion, the 'up' Comrades of 1958, he didn't have things all his own way. Mercer Davies, defending champion, was also a front-runner. In his triumphant run in 1957, Davies had curbed his natural inclination to race from the start, timing his endgame to perfection. We do not know if Mekler's participation might have intimidated him. What we do know is that Davies was the early leader of the 1958 Comrades Marathon.

As the defending champion led the way through Mayville, the rising sun witnessed the close attendance of Mekler, Burnley, Raubenheimer and McMaster. The leaders exchanged places on the undulating stretch between 45th Cutting and Westville. Davies, Mekler and Raubenheimer each enjoyed a little helping of the Comrades lead.

Then came Cowies Hill. The tall Davies powered his way upward and reached the top with Mekler close behind and McMaster and Rauben-heimer next in line, but somewhat 'off the pace' in what was still an early stage. Davies went through Pinetown 15 seconds ahead of Mekler. Although he was out in front, his time was seven minutes slower than two years previously. He could hardly have been criticised for reckless running.

Field's Hill was the decider this year. As the front-runners began the murderous incline, Mekler caught the leader. Very sensibly, he stayed with Davies before pulling away on the flattish section to Hillcrest. Davies, looking distinctly uncomfortable, was just half a minute behind Mekler at Hillcrest. At Hillcrest, Mekler was just six seconds behind Hayward's time four years earlier.

Over Botha's Hill, Mekler extended his lead significantly, reaching Drummond in 3.12.22, still in touch with Hayward's 1954 record run.

Davies was more than eight minutes behind and well ahead of third-placed McMaster. It seemed as though Mekler had only to maintain a degree of momentum to win. The record was, however, a different matter altogether. The weather wasn't favourable. It was hot, although a most unpleasant wind made conditions quite chilly at times, a paradox that many Comrades runners have experienced.

On Inchanga, defending champion Davies's challenge fizzled out. He was reduced to a walk on a few occasions and eventually withdrew. Mekler, meanwhile, was in total command. At Camperdown, he was almost five miles ahead of McMaster, now in second place. Despite the fact that he hadn't trained for Comrades (he only put in his entry two weeks before race day after missing selection for his preferred event, the Empire Games marathon due to be run in Cardiff), Mekler's strength didn't fail him in the closing stages, and he crossed the line at the Collegians Club ground in Pietermaritzburg in 6.26.26, the second fastest 'up' run after Hayward's in 1954.

More than 45 minutes later, the superiority of Mekler was underlined when the relatively unknown Andy Greening of Umbogintwini finally arrived to claim second position. To the delight of the crowd, the strongly built Natalian Nick Raubenheimer, one of the great characters of the race, managed to clinch third place.

Among the lesser mortals, Liege Boulle earned his 18th medal, while semi-blind Ian Jardine successfully negotiated the brutal course by sticking to the heels of his guide, 30-year-old Willie Pretorius of Durban. Once again, the Gunga Din team trophy was won by the Durban Athletic Club.

But the day belonged to Jackie Mekler. In his third Comrades, he had pulverised all opposition. Afterwards, he acknowledged the importance that he attached to his victory: 'Today's win realised an ambition for me. The Comrades Marathon is the one race in this country I have always wanted to win. The race today was as tough as I expected. After five years, you lose touch with long runs. I did not do the training I should have liked to have done, consequently the last 15 miles from Camperdown were an absolute killer to me.'

1958 COMRADES MARATHON RESULTS

1. J. Mekler	6.26.26
2. E. A. Greening	7.11.49
3. G. N. Raubenheimer	7.23.40
4. D. N. McInerney	7.25.04
5. K. McMaster	7.31.43
6. D. Stephenson	7.36.08
7. F. W. E Madel	7.44.19
8. T. N. Allen	7.49.08
9. E. G. Gore	8.07.07
10. J. Strydom	8.11.03

1959 COMRADES MARATHON
BATTLE OF THE CHAMPIONS

In South Africa, 1959 was a year in which various political directions were either confirmed or established. The passing of the perversely named Extension of University Education Act led to the emergence of 'non-white' universities, exemplifying the government's policy of denying proper education to people of colour. During the year, there was a major split in the United Party, the official parliamentary opposition. Several members of Parliament, frustrated at the party's impotence, left and set up the Progressive Party. Black resistance grew with the formation of the Pan-Africanist Congress under Robert Sobukwe.

In a far more harmonious arena, the Comrades Marathon was held on Monday, 1 June. Great news for the organisers was the line-up of 103 starters, the first time that the century mark had been passed. This was the 34th running of the race and, more than ever, its future seemed assured.

The quality of the entry suggested that this could be a race for the long-distance connoisseur to relish. There were three former winners in the field, including defending champion Jackie Mekler. Gerald Walsh, with a 'down' victory in 1955 and an 'up' win the following year, was well prepared, and

1952 winner Trevor Allen had fully recovered from an Achilles tendon operation. They would not disappoint race followers.

It was Walsh who led the way out of Maritzburg, with an unknown Rhodesian, Trevor Haynes, running his first Comrades, in second place. Then came a quartet comprising Trevor Allen, Jackie Mekler, J. Allen and Nick Raubenheimer. The main contenders had all started well and were handily placed.

The unknown factor, Haynes, decided to complicate matters for the favourites and moved past Walsh to take the lead shortly after Tumble Inn. In so doing, he highlighted one fear that lurks in the minds of top runners: no matter how well you study your opposition, there's always a chance that some stranger may come along and upset the apple cart. At Camperdown, Haynes was a minute and a half ahead of Walsh. Mekler and Trevor Allen, along with Nick Raubenheimer, Tommy Gore and Fritz Madel, were a full eight minutes off the pace.

Would Haynes be able to maintain his breakneck speed? It was a question his pursuers had to ponder. If he didn't slacken and they continued their waiting game, they would be hopelessly out of the picture. Mekler and Trevor Allen decided that they could not afford to bank on the leader faltering. Leaving Raubenheimer, Gore and Madel behind them, they strove to close the gap.

Haynes, meanwhile, was showing no sign of slowing. Having increased his lead on the undulating section past Cato Ridge and over Harrison Flats, he tackled the formidable Inchanga with aplomb. When he passed through Drummond in 2.50.16, just 53 seconds outside Reg Allison's halfway record, he had everyone worried. Walsh, still second, was 4 minutes 18 seconds adrift. The gaps from the leader to the next four were Trevor Allen (10.40), Jackie Mekler (11.7), Fritz Madel (11.21) and Nick Raubenheimer (12.41). For the latter four, it would seem as if Haynes would have to hit some kind of problem to allow them to have any sort of victory chance.

In both the 'up' and the 'down' Comrades, the first hill of the second half is a huge test of mind and body. Although Haynes negotiated Botha's Hill quite comfortably, Walsh had closed the gap slightly. By two-thirds distance, it was clear that the young Rhodesian's earlier efforts had exacted a toll. He was still in front at Kloof, but struggled down the punishing descent of Field's Hill.

As they entered Pinetown, Walsh reclaimed the lead. It wasn't long before Trevor Allen relegated Haynes to third place. Then Mekler went past. The Rhodesian, having looked virtually invincible for much of the race, now found himself slipping back. Walsh went through Pinetown in 4 hours 42 minutes, a minute ahead of Allen and four minutes in front of Mekler. The race was on. The three favourites would fight out the endgame. Thousands of spectators lined the route while a few hundred motor vehicles followed the leaders.

At Westville, Walsh was 500 yards ahead of Allen. At Suzor's Bend, with just five miles to go, the gap was down to 300 yards. Mekler was three minutes behind Allen. Although all three were very much in contention, the advantage was clearly with Allen. The knowledge that he was catching the leader gave him renewed energy, while Walsh felt all the anguish of the exhausted prey, fully aware that his pursuer was closing in, ready for the kill. Although Mekler had managed to gain a little ground, he still had quite a lot, perhaps too much, to make up.

On the climb up to Tollgate, Allen pounced. Walsh was unable to put up any real defence. The strongly built Allen quickly pulled out a decisive lead and crossed the line at King's Park in 6.28.11, over five minutes ahead of Walsh, who clung on to second place despite the disappointment of having lost the lead so late in the race. The triumphant policeman Allen proclaimed his joy: 'I had no trouble at all and feel wonderful. The heel never worried me in training and I was able to give of my best.'

Second-placed Gerald Walsh, despite his two victories, was regarded by some as somewhat vulnerable in the closing stages. Perhaps he agreed with this view, as his post-race comment seemed to suggest: 'I had no kick left once we entered Durban, but today I exceeded all my expectations.'

Although the first three had all contributed significantly to a memorable race, there remained a feeling afterwards that Jackie Mekler hadn't quite lived up to his pedigree. Although a winner by nature, he had run the entire race just outside the battle for first prize without challenging the leader at any time. His third place, a huge achievement for most people, didn't quite reflect his latent ability. Never one to decry the accomplishments of those whose superiority on the day proved too much for him, Mekler admitted, 'It was a battle all the way. I could not fight off the determined run of Allen and Walsh.'

Although the race record was at no time under threat, certain other milestones were reached. In addition to the first field in excess of 100, the race produced seven finishers who managed to come in in under seven hours. Among the also-rans (the backbone of Comrades), 70 finished the race, beating the previous record of 64 in 1955. With the number 7 featuring so strongly, perhaps it was appropriate that seventh place was claimed by one of the true characters of the race, Nick Raubenheimer.

There were a few notable achievements on the day. Winner Trevor Allen became the third runner to claim ten medals. 'Mr Comrades', the 50-year-old Liege Boulle, obtained his 19th medal, the most by anyone at this stage. Vernon Jones, the same age as Boulle, won his eighth medal, 22 years after his previous run. The old-timers were doing as much as the race winners to establish the Comrades Marathon, or so it seemed.

One special old-timer was 72-year-old Edgar Marie, now reduced to unofficial status. Marie had run his first Comrades in 1933, finishing 34th in a time of 9.19.30. In 1940, he won his solitary gold medal, claiming fifth place, and in 1949 completed his ninth Comrades at the age of 62 in the creditable time of 10.04.57. Marie reached halfway this year in seven hours and withdrew, acknowledging the hopelessness of his task, 'I knew I could never reach Durban in time.' Sadly, he would never complete a tenth race and earn a permanent number.

One youngster deserves mention. Rhodesian Trevor Haynes, the early leader, tenaciously kept going to finish sixth overall and claim the novice prize. Afterwards, he ruefully commented on his day's big challenge: 'The hills were too much for me and, in the end, cramp set in.'

1959 COMRADES MARATHON RESULTS

1. T. N. Allen — 6.28.11
2. G. Walsh — 6.33.33
3. J. Mekler — 6.35.52
4. F. W. E. Madel — 6.44.13
5. D. N. McInerney — 6.48.14
6. T. S. A. Haynes — 6.49.22
7. G. N. Raubenheimer — 6.52.37

8. E. A. Greening	7.05.43
9. J. R. Strydom	7.19.34
10. J. L. Bernon	7.25.33

1960 COMRADES MARATHON
MEKLER BEATS SIX HOURS

A few months after the 1959 race, Comrades followers were saddened to learn of the death of the event's first superstar, 'Greatheart' Arthur Newton. Newton's five victories in the 1920s were only a part of his overall contribution. Although professionally unqualified, he could be described, albeit loosely, as long-distance running's first 'sports scientist'. Newton's books on ultramarathon running, written about 70 years ago, show an understanding of the demands of long-distance running that makes a lot of sense to our modern, ultra-qualified 'gurus'. Perhaps of more significance in the evolution of Comrades was Newton's modest view of his own achievements coupled with generous acknowledgement of the efforts of others. As Jackie Mekler would suggest in 2005, Arthur Newton, more than anyone else, introduced and fostered the unique spirit that belongs only to Comrades.

In the build-up to the 1960 race, South Africa suffered one of its worst self-made catastrophes, the Sharpeville massacre, when police opened fire on 4 000 protestors marching against the system of passbooks, killing 69 and injuring hundreds more. Dr Carel de Wet, the National Party member of Parliament for the constituency of Vanderbijlpark, where the protest took place, made this appalling statement before he heard full details of the incident: 'It is a matter of concern to me that only one person was killed.'

These were not proud days for South Africa. The nation's political leaders showed a total lack of concern for the majority of the country's inhabitants. The security forces were acting with increasing brutality. This was the year in which the South West Africa People's Organisation was formed, the year in which anti-pass protester Robert Sobukwe was arrested and imprisoned, the year in which British prime minister Harold McMillan made his famous 'winds of change' speech.

For many white South Africans, insensitive to what was happening on the other side of the apartheid fence, this was simply, and for many all-encompassingly, the year of another New Zealand All Black rugby tour of South Africa. A thrilling test series was settled only in the final match, a narrow victory for the Springboks. Their triumph dominated the media, with only the barest mention of the fact that South Africans of colour were supporting the opposition.

In this year of conflicting emotions, the Comrades Marathon appeared unaffected by all the drama surrounding it – perhaps rightly so. It has enough drama of its own, and produces what is arguably the nation's most gripping annual theatrical occasion.

A new record number of 104 athletes went to the start, just one more than the previous year's field. While 1959 champion Trevor Allen was there to defend his crown, 28-year-old Jackie Mekler was the popular favourite. He had won the previous 'up' run by a huge margin and arrived in Durban in prime condition, having trained assiduously for the event.

Gerald Walsh, the 1955 'down' winner, was the early leader, closely followed by Mekler, who wasted no time in announcing his competitive intent. Going through Westville, Mekler passed Walsh and went to the front, perhaps sooner than he might have wished. He was, nonetheless, running his own race and seemed untroubled by the demands of his early ascendancy. At Hillcrest, Mekler's lead over second-placed Walsh was nearly five minutes, with 43-year-old newcomer George Claassen third. Nick Raubenheimer and Trevor Allen were handily placed, not too far behind Claassen.

When the red-headed Mekler sped through Drummond with an advantage of nearly ten minutes over Walsh, it was clear that he would break either the record or himself. The Comrades Marathon had never before witnessed such aggressive running in the feared 'up' run. Over Inchanga, through Harrison Flats, past Cato Ridge and thereafter, Mekler continued to pulverise all opposition. His speed was significantly faster than that of his pursuers, his strength undiminished and his determination relentless.

At Camperdown, which he reached in 4.25.30, he was 17 and a half minutes ahead of Walsh, still in second place, with Claassen maintaining his third position. Behind them, little had changed. Allen and Raubenheimer jointly held fourth spot. At this stage, Mekler was 6 minutes 34 seconds ahead of Wally Hayward's time in his record-breaking run in 1954. Nothing in Comrades can be regarded as certain until the finish line has been reached. Nevertheless, it was now clear that Mekler, having left his opponents far behind, was looking beyond mere victory. An 'up' record was in his sights. It was also seeming more and more likely that the first sub-six-hour 'up' run was within reach.

When Mekler cruised up Polly Shortts in total control of proceedings, all doubts receded. This was one of the greatest of all Comrades runs. It seemed that nothing could go wrong. But something did go wrong, right at the end. Entering the finishing arena at the Collegian Club grounds, Mekler clipped a makeshift board and badly gashed his leg. Blood and pain were ignored as he crossed the line in 5 hours 56 minutes 32 seconds, in the first sub-six-hour 'up' run. His time was 16 minutes 23 seconds faster than Wally Hayward's record of 1954. It had been thought that Hayward's time would never be beaten. There was now no doubting Mekler's credentials. He is one of the all-time greats. Referring to his sensational time, he commented, 'I did not set out to beat Hayward's record, although I had my eye on it after Drummond.'

Gerald Walsh tenaciously held on to second place, finishing in 6.31.07, over two minutes faster than his own winning time in 1956. Walsh's time was the fourth-fastest yet recorded for an 'up' run. Amazingly, despite such a fine effort, he finished nearly 35 minutes behind the winner, such was the utter dominance of Jackie Mekler.

Schoolmaster George Claassen claimed third place in 6.34.07. It was the best performance to date by a novice. Although unheralded, he would demonstrate his true ability the following year. Comrades stalwarts Trevor Allen and Nick Raubenheimer shared fourth place, the first gold medal dead heat in Comrades history.

1960 COMRADES MARATHON RESULTS

1. J. Mekler	5.56.32
2. G. Walsh	6.31.07
3. G. N. Claassen	6.34.07

4. G. N. Raubenheimer	6.42.30
4. T. N. Allen	6.42.30
6. E. J. A. Wallis	6.50.12
7. D. Chase	7.01.42
8. E. A. Greening	7.07.44
9. I. Praamsma	7.09.55
10. M. V. Otto	7.13.05

1961 COMRADES MARATHON
THE HEADMASTER TEACHES HIS PUPILS A LESSON

The day before Comrades is, for many, the most agonising in the year. It's a day of waiting, a day of growing tension. As evening takes over, butterflies invade stomachs. Frightened athletes feel involuntary shudders as the enormity of their impending challenge draws closer.

This year's race was held in unusual circumstances. As each of the record field of 148 put his head on the pillow on 30 May, he knew it would be his final sleep – or attempt to sleep – in the Union of South Africa and in the Commonwealth. Early next morning, alarm clocks welcomed runners to the new, independent Republic of South Africa. The country, though it didn't know it yet, was heading towards the sporting isolation that would dominate the 1970s and 1980s and, as a consequence, raise the domestic status of the Comrades Marathon.

H. F. Verwoerd, by then the prime minister, said, 'It is to us a happy day, but above all, a day of dedication and gratitude.' The Malayan prime minister might have been reflecting the Commonwealth view when he said, 'I think it is good riddance to South Africa.'

Such matters were not in mind as the Pietermaritzburg City Hall clock sent the Comrades field on the long journey to Durban. While Jackie Mekler was rightly regarded as firm favourite, nothing could be taken for granted in such an event. All of the previous year's top five had entered, and the race for line honours was anticipated with a good deal of relish. Unfortunately,

Gerald Walsh had to withdraw at the last moment due to ill health, but the trio of Trevor Allen, Nick Raubenheimer and George Claassen were capable of causing an upset should Mekler not be at his very best.

Regular entrant Fritz Madel, winner of the 1959 London-to-Brighton race, took the early lead. He was another with the right credentials. His lead was, however, somewhat short-lived. At Umlaas Road, Mekler was in front, followed by a 22-year-old novice, Keith Pearce. It looked like the previous year all over again: the unstoppable Mekler would simply pull away and demonstrate his clear superiority over all challengers.

When Cato Ridge was reached, it wasn't happening. Mekler still held the lead, but was not getting away. Pearce had, in fact, closed the gap slightly. Through Harrison Flats and over Inchanga, Pearce gradually moved up to Mekler's shoulder and eventually passed him, reaching halfway with Mekler at his heels. Was Mekler fading or was the novice Pearce simply too strong? It was difficult to tell. Pearce's time at Drummond was 2 hours 47 minutes – 2 minutes 23 seconds faster than Reg Allison's record. In his record-breaking victory 23 years later, Bruce Fordyce would pass halfway in 2.50.02, three minutes slower than Pearce and Mekler. Clearly, they were both flying.

At this stage, a trio of Claassen, Madel and Frikkie Steyn were sharing third place, five minutes behind the leaders. Drawing strength from each other, they were certainly top gold-medal contenders. Such was the advantage of the two front-runners, however, that a double disaster (not unheard of in Comrades) would be required for any of the three to have a real chance of victory.

Things can change, and often do, in the second half of a Comrades Marathon. Ever-reliable Jackie Mekler was the first to succumb. Still nursing an Achilles tendon problem sustained in the 1960 London-to-Brighton race, he was forced to pull out after cresting Botha's Hill.

Now, Pearce was alone in one of the loneliest positions in world sport, leader of the Comrades Marathon. He was a long way from the finish and had yet to experience the physical pain and mental anguish that beset leaders and backmarkers alike in the final third of the race. All he had to do to win the race was just keep going, even at a reduced pace. Those who have been in this position before know how desperately difficult it can be.

Pinetown is the finish before the real finish in the 'down' run. Well placed here, one should be able to capitalise. Pearce appeared in control: his time was a minute faster than that of Hayward in the 1953 race, a race in which Hayward had set an athletic standard that many thought would never be challenged. Pearce was nine minutes ahead of his nearest challengers, Claassen and Steyn. He was all but home. Surely, nothing could stop him now.

Suddenly, Pearce's incredible efforts came to an end. One moment, he was comfortably leading the race; then, without warning, he simply disintegrated. Even though well in the lead as he entered the city of Durban, he had nothing left. Pearce's race was over. The novice runner would not be able to defy Comrades tradition. Instead, he quietly dropped out of the event.

The perseverance of the pursuers was now rewarded. All of a sudden, George Claassen and Frikkie Steyn were the only contenders left. They went through 45th Cutting together in 5 hours 32 minutes. Trevor Allen, third, was 12 minutes behind them. Madel and Raubenheimer, fourth and fifth, were, like Allen, too far behind to challenge for the lead. It was between Claassen and Steyn to decide who would be the 1961 Comrades champion.

After running together for most of the race, it was time for one of the two to make a move and establish seniority. And it was the senior (in years, that is) who took the initiative. Going through Westridge, Claassen put in a surge to which Steyn was unable to reply. On the descent of Berea Road, Middelburg headmaster Claassen pulled away and was first to cross the finish line at the Beach Pavilion in 6.07.07, the fourth-fastest time to date for the 'down' run. Steyn was just two minutes behind him. Allen, Madel and Raubenheimer kept up their efforts and finished third, fourth and fifth respectively.

In this, the first Comrades Marathon of the new republic, it was fitting that a black runner should put in a strong performance. John Mkwanyana did just that. His time of 8 hours 15 minutes should have earned him 31st position, but that wasn't to be. He was an unofficial runner and his effort was not officially recognised. The huge applause he received at the end reflected the gulf that existed between the Comrades ethos and government policy.

Politically, this was certainly a year that emphasised growing differences in a nation purportedly celebrating its rebirth. The African National Congress (ANC), South Africa's most prominent liberation movement, acquired Lilliesleaf Farm in Rivonia, Nelson Mandela proposed the armed struggle, sabotage began and a black South African, Chief Albert Luthuli, was awarded the Nobel Peace Prize.

1961 COMRADES MARATHON RESULTS

1. G. N. Claassen	6.07.07
2. F. C. Steyn	6.09.05
3. T. N. Allen	6.22.49
4. F. W. E. Madel	6.36.10
5. G. N. Raubenheimer	6.36.12
6. D. Chase	6.40.14
7. C. Crawley	6.48.40
8. B. R. Harrison	6.50.02
9. J. D. Kuhn	6.55.20
10. D. N. McInerney	7.08.42

1962 COMRADES MARATHON
FIRST FOREIGN INVASION

The establishment of the Republic of South Africa in 1961 may have been a precursor to a gradual slide into isolation, but this was certainly not reflected in the 1962 Comrades Marathon. Instead, Comrades went international. For the first time, a team of foreign athletes arrived in the country to take part in the nation's premier annual sporting event.

For many years, South African ultramarathon runners had visited Britain and performed with distinction. World records for 100 miles and 24-hour non-stop running had been set by a succession of Comrades champions. The London-to-Brighton race had demonstrated the ability of South Africans to dominate on foreign soil.

This year, the Brits were keen to mount a counter-offensive. The Road Runners Club of England selected their finest four – John Smith, Tom Buckingham, Don Turner and Ron Linstead – to compete against South Africa's best in South Africa's most famous race. Smith, Buckingham and

Turner had taken the first three places in the most recent London-to-Brighton race, and Linstead had comfortably won an ultramarathon on the Isle of Wight.

The visitors were assured of a tough team event. Representing the Marathon Runners Club of South Africa were Jackie Mekler, George Claassen and Peter Clough from the Transvaal, and Frikkie Steyn and Fritz Madel of Durban. Mekler and Claassen had won the previous two Comrades Marathons, while Steyn and Madel were regular top finishers. The South Africans were firm favourites to win the team event and their individual team members appeared likely to contest the ultimate prize, that of Comrades Marathon champion.

Religious considerations led to a change of race day. This year, Republic Day (formerly Union Day) fell on Ascension Thursday, one of the most solemn days in the traditional Christian calendar. Comrades had to make allowances and the annual event took place on Wednesday 30 May.

The starting time was also unusual, but not through any considered decision. The Durban Post Office clock, designated the task of starting the event, forgot to chime – so official starter Jack Gafncy sent the runners on their way two and a half minutes after the scheduled start. Not even the gallinaceous vocal chords of Max Trimborn could help, although his traditional cockcrow did confirm that it was finally time to get moving.

Jackie Mekler was the class act in the field. He was also an established front-runner. Rather unsurprisingly, he took the early lead. Frikkie Steyn, Fritz Madel and the English runner Tom Buckingham stayed with him until Westville. That was enough for Mekler. He preferred his own company and swiftly left the others in his wake. At Pinetown, his lead was two minutes. By Hillcrest, he was six minutes ahead of second-placed Buckingham.

Mekler went through halfway in a new record time (for the first half) of 2.56.57, 5 minutes 23 seconds faster than Mercer Davies's 1956 time. Buckingham was still six minutes adrift of him and had been joined by fellow Englishman John Smith. The gap wasn't widening. Had Mekler gone out too fast? The question would soon be answered.

On the long, undulating stretch from the top of Inchanga to Camperdown (the graveyard of many an 'up' runner), Mekler slowed perceptibly. At the same time, Smith, having left his teammate Buckingham behind, appeared to be gaining in strength and in confidence. It was no longer Mekler's race, although he was first through Camperdown in 4 hours 12 minutes. Despite the fact that this was easily the fastest time for this stage of an 'up' run, Smith was now only two minutes behind and looking the more comfortable of the two.

Smith continued to close the gap and soon had Mekler in his sights. On a downhill section, he made his move. Mekler was unable to respond. Having taken the lead at an opportune time, Smith pushed ahead, trying to stretch his advantage as much as possible before reaching the last and most daunting obstacle, Polly Shortts. His lead was five minutes at the foot of the hill, which he negotiated without undue concern.

Once Smith reached the top, the race was effectively over. Mekler was too far behind to have any chance of catching him and was, in any case, only halfway up Polly Shortts. 'The Englishman with the strange name', as one wag called him, had the race totally sewn up. Two targets remained. First, would he break six hours? The answer was yes. He finished in the superb time of 5.57.05. Second, would he break the 'up' record? Sadly for Smith, the answer was no. His finishing time was 33 seconds slower than Mekler's two-year-old record. It was nevertheless a wonderful performance from a novice running in a totally new environment.

What of Smith's compatriots? How did they fare? They put their hosts to shame. Comrades aficionados were dumbfounded. South African ultra-distance athletes had long considered themselves the best in the world, and performances until now had supported this view. Jackie Mekler (second) was the lone South African in the top five. British runners Turner, Buckingham and Linstead claimed third, fourth and fifth positions respectively. The locals had been annihilated. Afterwards, Mekler sportingly conceded the visitors' unexpected superiority:

'By filling four of the first five places, the British runners shattered South Africa's complacent attitude of invincibility over this Comrades course. I think the visitors were underrated because of South Africa's long string of successes in the London-to-Brighton race, where our top men have always beaten the locals.'

The triumphant visitors were gracious in victory and paid warm tributes to the event that they had enriched with their competitiveness. Fifth-placed Linstead reflected on the demands of Polly Shortts:

'The hill was sheer agony. Here I had to let Turner, who had caught up with me, go, for I was now plagued by stitch and kidney pains. Thankfully, the last four miles were downhill and I was able to recover my composure. The crowds over the last stretch were amazing and full of encouragement. They seemed highly delighted at our success.'

The English team captain Tom Buckingham was equally impressed by the unique Comrades spirit. 'The London-to-Brighton has nothing like it. Now I understand why they call it the Comrades. The crowd cheered us all along the way.'

Apart from crowd encouragement, the visitors were also helped by a very special group of personal attendants. Smith's second was Bill Cochrane, Comrades champion in 1935 and 1946; Buckingham was aided by Comrades doyen Vernon Jones; Linstead by five-time winner Hardy Ballington; and Turner by 1940 champion Allen Boyce. National differences weren't even noticed as the Comrades spirit united visitors and hosts.

The popularity of the race was reflected in the many traffic jams en route. Comrades was growing. Two of its regulars reached significant milestones: Nick Raubenheimer and Liege Boulle both achieved the distinction of ten Comrades finishes in consecutive years. Their records were somewhat different, though. Boulle had run the race several times, but not consecutively, before his ten-race sequence, and his collection of medals now numbered 22. Raubenheimer, on the other hand, had begun his Comrades career in 1953. In his ten-year relationship with the race, he had picked up five gold medals for top-six finishes.

One of the more memorable aspects was a little post-race conversation between winner John Smith and personal attendant Bill Cochrane. Observing crowd enthusiasm as the backmarkers came in, Smith commented, 'I thought I won the race. Those chaps finishing now are getting just as big a cheer.' Knowingly, Cochrane responded, 'You are now witnessing the spirit of Comrades.'

1962 COMRADES MARATHON RESULTS

1. J. Smith   5.57.05
2. J. Mekler   6.04.04
3. W. D. Turner   6.07.08

4. T. Buckingham	6.08.26
5. R. Linstead	6.10.39
6. D. Chase	6.30.42
7. F. W. E. Madel	6.33.13
8. F. C. Steyn	6.43.44
9. M. Davies	6.47.19
10. G. Watt	6.49.02

1963 COMRADES MARATHON
HAYWARD'S RECORD BEATEN

This year's race took place in the shadow of its founder. On 5 October 1962, Vic Clapham died. Clapham was the man who had envisaged the event, who fought against significant odds to have it established, who chose the course, who acted as honorary secretary for many years and whose selfless devotion played a major role in the development of that extraordinary, intangible reality that we know today as the unique 'Comrades spirit'.

No greater tribute could have been paid to the humble founder of Comrades than the record number of 224 who faced the starter alongside the Pietermaritzburg City Hall. It was only in 1959 that the field had reached the magic 100 mark for the first time. The sudden explosion in numbers was almost as daunting for the organisers as it was welcome.

Double winner Jackie Mekler was the crowd's favourite. Accepted running logic nevertheless suggested that this was unlikely to be his year. Ten days before Comrades, he had run a standard marathon in 2.36.00 in Greece. Furthermore, he had only returned to South Africa the night before Comrades. The subsequent mad dash to get him to the start suggested that his chances of a top finish were minimal. 'Resting' and 'peaking' were unknown concepts in 1963. Thankfully, nobody attempted to convince Mekler of the folly of his ambition before he had achieved it and, in so doing, made a mockery of the scientific analysis of the sport that would come in later years.

Whatever Mekler's preparation might have been, he would have expected a tough encounter. Mercer Davies, winner of the 'down' run six years previously in the fast time of 6.13.55, was back and eager to post a second victory. Future winner Manie Kuhn, as strongly built as any Comrades contender, was approaching his prime. Others such as Fritz Madel, Nick Raubenheimer, Frikkie Steyn and newcomer Tim Blankley were all capable of providing an upset.

It was Steyn of Durban who made the early running. First to reach Polly Shortts, he arrived at Tumble Inn nearly a minute ahead of Mekler. A 22-year-old policeman from Pretoria, Pieter de Villiers, running his first Comrades, was in third place. He was about to produce a phenomenal performance that would create enormous problems for all top contenders, particularly the winner. Among those just off the pace were Manie Kuhn, Mercer Davies, Ted Craig, Fritz Madel, Charlie Chase, Nick Raubenheimer, Ken Craig and Tim Blankley.

On the climb up to Umlaas Road, Mekler took the lead, rather early for someone who was hoping to win the race, especially taking into account his recent Greek marathon. However, Mekler, now 31 years old, was a seasoned campaigner who by now should have developed a keen sense of his capabilities and weaknesses. He obviously realised that a slow build-up leading up to a 'come from behind' final effort was not for him.

At Camperdown, Mekler was more than two minutes ahead of De Villiers and over seven minutes faster than Hayward had been in his 1953 run, in which he had set a record that some thought would never be broken. Mekler was challenging such beliefs. If he could maintain his early pace, he would trample all previous records into the Comrades dust. Yet it was still too early to entertain such ideas. Comrades is won and lost in the second half, and the same goes for race records.

Mekler reached Cato Ridge two minutes ahead of De Villiers and three minutes before Mercer Davies. Kuhn, Madel and company were starting to look like also-rans. Mekler made light of Harrison Flats and Inchanga and reached Drummond in a new halfway record of 2.45.25. Mercer Davies, now second, was over four minutes adrift of the flying leader, with newcomer De Villiers at his shoulder.

Drummond observers, in awe of Mekler's previous achievements, took the view that Hayward's record was about to be consigned to history. Mekler, at this stage, wasn't quite as confident. Over Botha's Hill and on the long section from Hillcrest to Kloof, Mekler appeared to be wilting. His Greek odyssey, the international effort to rush him to the start and his first-half exertions seemed to be taking an inevitable toll.

He had another problem. Pretorian Pieter de Villiers, the surprise package of the race, was threatening to destroy all pre-race perceptions. On Botha's Hill, he passed Mercer Davies and began his pursuit of leader Mekler. At Kloof, he was less than a minute behind the leader. At Pinetown, the difference was only 20 seconds. A huge surprise was in the offing.

Then Mekler appeared to have a second wind. He had set out with the intention of beating Hayward's record, and he knew that it was still within his grasp. He was also painfully aware of the presence of challenger De Villiers. This is when the heart of the champion kicked in. All of the great Comrades champions have possessed one particular attribute: the ability to go up a gear in the last quarter of the race, when most others are falling to pieces. This is when mental strength takes over from the physical ability which has, quite simply, been used up.

Going over Cowies Hill, the last of the major climbs, Mekler, first of all, shook off the attentions of De Villiers: to all intents and purposes, that won him the race. Then, with time his only real opponent, he put himself in position to challenge the record that for many had been unchallengeable, Hayward's 5.52.30 set in 1953, ten years before.

From 45th Cutting, Mekler had a significant partner: the crowd. Spectators were willing him on. Much as they had loved Hayward, so too did they accept the red-haired Mekler as one of their own. With victory assured and the record there for the taking, Mekler forgot the pain that was threatening to engulf him and focused his entire being on the only thing that mattered. He could not be denied. An ecstatic crowd at the Royal Durban Light Infantry Drill Hall on Greyville Racecourse acclaimed his finish in 5.51.20. Hayward's record had been beaten by 1 minute 10 seconds.

It was only after the race that the full circumstances of Mekler's participation became known. On the eve of Comrades, having finished fourth in the Greek Memorial Marathon about seven days before, he left Athens at 2.30 a.m. for Johannesburg, where he caught a connecting flight to Durban, and was then driven to Maritzburg, arriving there with just enough time to enjoy a few hours of sleep before the race began. He spelt out the reason for his madness: 'I promised the Comrades organisers I would run it if I could possibly return to South Africa in time.' He made good on his promise in emphatic style.

One of the day's most remarkable performances came from Pretoria's Pieter de Villiers. Despite the devastation of giving his all and finding out that it was not enough, the 22-year-old clung on tenaciously to claim second position in 5.58.45, the third athlete and the first novice to break the six-hour barrier. This was in a race in which a record number of 12 runners finished in under seven hours.

The relatively new Savages Athletic Club won the Gunga Din trophy, their victorious team comprising Craig, Crawley, Kuhn and Madel. Fritz Madel, first of the quartet to finish, took third place in 6.08.05, the sixth-fastest 'down' time on record.

A couple of well-known Comrades stalwarts were among the successful finishers. Legendary blind runner Ian Jardine, accompanied by his pilot Ron Clokie, won the Founder's Trophy for being, at 61, the oldest finisher. Race historian Vernon Jones, making something of a comeback after four years' absence (his first Comrades having been in Hayward's year, 1930), claimed a ninth medal in 10.45.28.

There were many outstanding performances, but none could match the achievement of Jackie Mekler. Acknowledging afterwards that victory and the race record had nearly eluded him, he admitted, 'I gambled for the record and nearly lost the race. At Pinetown, I could hear De Villiers right behind me and catching me up. I was determined not to let him pass.'

1963 COMRADES MARATHON RESULTS

1. J. Mekler		5.51.20
2. P. R. de Villiers		5.58.45
3. F. W. E. Madel		6.08.05
4. J. D. Kuhn		6.18.26
5. T. E. Blankley		6.23.17
6. M. J. Davies		6.23.59
7. D. Chase		6.26.32

8. H. J. Greyling   6.39.15
9. E. V. Craig   6.43.29
10. M. J. Heunis   6.55.04

1964 COMRADES MARATHON
MEKLER DISAPPOINTED IN VICTORY

The 1964 Comrades Marathon took place as the nation's most sensational and politically important court case, the Rivonia Trial, was drawing to a close. Eight defendants, who included Nelson Mandela, were sentenced to life imprisonment, narrowly escaping the death penalty.

Nobody at the time could possibly have imagined that 31 years later, South African President Nelson Mandela would officially present trophies to Comrades Marathon runners – black and white, female and male, South African and foreign (including, horror of horrors in the minds of the previous political establishment, successful Russian invaders).

No such thoughts would have entered the minds of the record starting line-up that congregated outside the Durban City Hall on Monday, 1 June. The name on everyone's lips was Mekler, not Mandela. A three-time winner, twice in 'up' runs, the 32-year-old Mekler, now at the peak of his career, was outright favourite. Yet there were still legitimate doubts about his credentials. An out-and-out front-runner who eschewed a tactical approach, Mekler could be vulnerable. He had been beaten and could be beaten again. At the same time, he would have to be off form to lose. He simply was the class athlete in the field.

If Mekler were to prevail, however, the form books suggested that he would have to be at his best. His opponents included 1957 winner Mercer Davies, 1958 runner-up Andy Greening, 1961 runner-up Frikkie Steyn, the up-and-coming Manie Kuhn and the tried, trusted and feared Nick Raubenheimer, Fritz Madel and Charlie Chase. Although the non-appearance of an exciting recent immigrant, world 25-mile track record holder Barry Sawyer, was a minor disappointment, there was enough ability in the field to make this a Comrades to remember.

On a cool winter morning, the virtually unknown Marty Heunis was first of the record 272 starters to tackle the seldom-mentioned but rather taxing climb up to Tollgate. His time at the front was rather short-lived, though race favourite Jackie Mekler used the second 'minor' hill to advantage and took the lead at 45th Cutting.

As usual, Mekler sought to build an early lead. At Pinetown, he was a minute ahead of second-placed Manie Kuhn, who was followed by a group comprising Charlie Chase, Fritz Madel, Andy Greening, Frank Pearce, Australian Bob Horman and early leader Marty Heunis, who was maintaining contact with the top contenders.

Although the record holder Mekler was setting the pace, it was not a particularly fast one. He must have realised, along with his rivals, that if he ran to the best of his ability, there would be no reason for him to fear anyone. The approach he adopted suggested, however, that he was unsure of the tactics that would suit him. At Pinetown, his time was five minutes slower than in 1960, when he had famously broken Hayward's 'up' record. It was also nine and a half minutes slower than two years previously, when visiting Englishman John Smith had punished him for going out too fast. Instead of looking for a happy medium, Mekler seemed to choose an ultra-conservative strategy that might bring victory – with his talent, any approach had a chance – but would be unlikely to lead to a new record.

Going up Field's Hill, Mekler did stretch the gap a little and was three minutes ahead of Kuhn at Kloof. On the gently undulating section from Kloof to Hillcrest (just about the flattest part of Comrades), Mekler kept his advantage while Kuhn was certainly not dropping back. On the ascent of Botha's Hill, Kuhn closed the gap slowly and Mercer Davies made his presence felt.

Mekler went through Drummond in 3.08.40. This was certainly not the fast and furious Mekler of past years. He was, in fact, 12 minutes slower than he'd been at halfway two years earlier. Unless a miracle occurred, the race record was safe. Kuhn, having closed the gap slightly, was less than two minutes adrift. Mercer Davies, six minutes behind Kuhn, seemed well out of contention. Those behind Davies still had gold medals to aim for, but victory was another matter altogether.

Over Inchanga, Mekler inched further ahead of Kuhn, who was maintaining a competitive pace not too much slower than that of the leader.

The two, now well ahead of the rest of the field, remained between two and three minutes apart as they negotiated Harrison Flats and passed through Cato Ridge at two-thirds distance.

Mekler arrived at Camperdown in 4 hours 24 minutes, three minutes ahead of Kuhn. Now they entered the endgame. Mekler had run well within himself thus far, and he continued to do so. At the same time, he continued to demonstrate his ascendancy over all challengers, including the game Kuhn.

When Mekler reached the foot of Polly Shortts, he was so far ahead that he could have walked up the hill and possibly still retained his lead. Instead, he climbed relentlessly and strongly up the final obstacle and reached the top with victory in his pocket. Like most 'up' winners, he finished with a flourish, crossing the line at the Collegians Club in 6.09.54. It was his fourth Comrades triumph, and he became the third man, after Hardy Ballington and Wally Hayward, to post three 'up' wins.

One would have expected a celebratory mood from the victorious Mekler, but that wasn't the case: he appeared almost downcast. Yes, he had achieved a fourth victory, one less than the magic number of five which belonged to Newton, Ballington and Hayward. Yet he hadn't really done himself justice. He knew that he could have done better and was honest enough to acknowledge the fact: 'Frankly, I am a little disappointed. Every runner has his objective in the race. Obviously, as the record holder, that was what I was after.'

Others, the majority of whom finished hours after the winner, were a good deal happier than Mekler. One was Sam Draai, a man whose skin colour dictated that his participation was unofficial. But that didn't worry him: he would continue to run unheralded until the day sanity took over and he achieved the recognition he deserved. Thankfully, that day did dawn, at last.

Three runners managed to complete their tenth journey and claim their 'in perpetuity' green numbers. They were A. J. C. Gillespie (21st), M. D. C Gierke (22nd) and that great Comrades man Vernon Jones. Once again, Ian Jardine, with the help of his guide Ron Clokie, won the Founder's Trophy and early leader Marty Heunis finished 33rd in a time of 8.07.16.

1964 COMRADES MARATHON RESULTS

1. J. Mekler   6 09.54
2. J. D. Kuhn   6.19.37
3. D. Chase   6.36.19
4. F. W. F. Madel   6.46.22
5. F. Pearce   6.49.31
6. G. N. Raubenheimer   6.50.57
7. E. A. Greening   6.55.17
8. P. T. Shrimpton   7.06.25
9. H. J. Greyling   7.07.40
10. J. A. Dean   7.11.30

1965 COMRADES MARATHON
WET AND MISERABLE

A short paragraph from Morris Alexander's superb *The Comrades Marathon Story* eloquently illustrates the difference between the Comrades of the 1960s and the race we know today:

'The start in Maritzburg looked more like several companies of infantry drawn up on parade, so huge was the field. No fewer than 387 runners toed the starting-line out of 433 who entered (and paid their R2 increased entry fee).'

The year 1965 was a special one for sport-loving South Africans. In golf, Gary Player sensationally beat 'Champagne' Tony Lema at the World Matchplay at Wentworth, in a semi-final play-off after being 5 down with nine holes to play, and went on to defeat Peter Thompson 3 and 2 in the final the following day. In another play-off, he edged out Ken Nagle to win the US Open and famously donated his prize money to cancer research in the USA.

In the swimming pool, a minor miracle occurred. A South African team touring Europe entered the British Championships in Blackpool. The expected highlight was a showdown in the women's backstroke event between British world record holder Linda Ludgrove and South African star

16-year-old Ann Fairlie. It didn't materialise. Instead, 12-year-old South African Karen Muir, chosen for the tour to gain experience, upstaged her elders. Considered too young to participate among the seniors, she entered the girls' event and broke Linda Ludgrove's world record.

Cricket was also in the headlines. Peter van der Merwe's Springboks beat England 1–0 in a three-match series in England. The solitary victory came at Trent Bridge, where Graeme Pollock played one of his finest innings. His brother Peter and wonder fielder Colin Bland also played memorable roles in their country's triumph.

What could the Comrades Marathon offer in this vintage year for South African sport? The answer was not too comfortable for the 387 hardy souls who went to the start. This was the year of rain, rain and yet more rain – and of freezing cold: in short, the most miserable day in the history of the race. Thankfully, for runners as well as feeding-station attendants and spectators, such conditions have not been repeated. Indeed, it is a happy and hardly credible fact of Comrades that unpleasant weather is sometimes encountered the day before or the day after the race, but seldom on the day itself.

For regular Comrades followers this year offered the prospect of a great runner's quest for Comrades immortality. Jackie Mekler, admired and liked by his peers, was aiming at a fifth victory, which would put him in the same league as Arthur Newton, Hardy Ballington and Wally Hayward. Mercer Davies, winner of the 1957 'down' run, was making a comeback and could hardly be discounted. A novice whose challenge had to be taken seriously was 23-year-old Bernard Gomersall, winner of the 1963 London-to-Brighton race, a superb athlete who had been chosen by the Road Runners Club of England to try to repeat John Smith's surprise victory in 1962. Top British runners were acknowledging the supremacy of Comrades in the sphere of ultramarathon racing.

When the race got under way at 6 a.m., Durban runner Manie Kuhn, abandoning his normal conservative strategy, took the early lead and was fully two minutes ahead of second-placed Tim Blankley as he started the descent of Polly Shortts. By Camperdown, it was obvious that Kuhn's intention was to lead from start to finish. While such a strategy is generally regarded as unwise, particularly in the 'down' run, there could be no gainsaying the ability of the muscular Natalian.

At Cato Ridge, Kuhn was three minutes ahead of the formidable trio of Mekler, Gomersall and Davies. At Drummond, his lead was more or less the same. Mercer Davies was now second on his own. Jackie Mekler, not enjoying the most comfortable of journeys, was four minutes behind Kuhn and six and a half minutes slower than his own record-breaking effort two years earlier. Mekler seemed to be out of contention.

British invader Bernard Gomersall had been tailing Mekler, the champion, who was falling off the pace to such an extent that his pursuer had to consider a change of plan. This is precisely what Gomersall did, and events worked out perfectly for him. Mercer Davies temporarily took the lead, passing Kuhn on the relatively flat stretch between Hillcrest and Kloof, but his glory was short-lived.

Going into Kloof and on the long descent down Field's Hill, the Englishman Gomersall, revelling in the wet and cold conditions, blasted past Davies and quickly made the race his own. At Pinetown, his lead over second-placed Davies was more than three and a half minutes. By now, it wasn't just about a victory: the race record was well within Gomersall's grasp. At the Pinetown checkpoint, his time was more than five and a half minutes faster than that of Mekler in 1963. Mekler, meanwhile, was in fourth place, nine minutes behind the leader. Not even the great Jackie Mekler could make up such a deficit.

Nobody would be able to seriously challenge the determined Bernard Gomersall. Weather that South Africans regarded as atrocious was just what the doctor ordered for the Englishman. He simply powered his way over Cowies Hill and on towards Durban. It was now simply the record – yes or no? Gomersall answered in emphatic fashion: not letting up for a moment, he crossed the finish line in the Drill Hall grounds in a new record time of 5.51.09 , just 11 seconds inside Mekler's 1963 time.

After the race, Gomersall reflected on his victory over four-time winner Mekler: 'When the race started, I glanced at Jackie Mekler and he looked most unhappy in the bleak conditions. I soon realised that he would not be able to give his best, and at the halfway stage he was having a bad spell. This was the last I saw of him during the race.'

Mekler was beaten, but certainly not vanquished. His challenge more or less ended on Inchanga, where he was clearly in trouble and losing time. Nevertheless, he grimly kept going and was assured of a top-five finish. In the endgame, he showed his true mettle. Although a win (which would have been his fifth) was now out of the question, he valiantly pitted his strength against that of the other potential gold medallists. Despite the fact that he was underprepared, having only taken part in one race since the previous year's Comrades, he finished strongly enough to claim second place in 5.56.19. It was the fourth-fastest 'down' run to date, achieved on a bad day. Such was the calibre of the man.

There were other notable achievements on the day. Mavis Hutchison became the third woman, after Frances Hayward and Geraldine Watson, to complete the distance, albeit unofficially. Sixty-three-year old Ian Jardine finished his tenth Comrades to claim his green number in perpetuity. He was also awarded the Founder's Trophy (for the eighth time) for being the oldest finisher – not bad for a man without the faculty of sight. Bernard Gomersall, apart from his overall victory, also won the novice prize, and the coveted Gunga Din trophy went to Savages Athletic Club.

1965 COMRADES MARATHON RESULTS

1. B. Gomersall		5.51.09
2. J. Mekler		5.56.19
3. J. D. Kuhn		6.04.24
4. M. J. Davies		6.08.44
5. C. H. Crawley		6.16.16
6. E. V. Craig		6.18.31
7. D. Chase		6.19.24
8. F. W. E. Madel		6.33.35
9. R. C. Molver		6.40.43
10. H. J. Greyling		6.40.43

10

RIVALRY, CAMARADERIE AND LIFELONG FRIENDSHIP
(1966 to 1967)

Although the spirit of the Comrades Marathon is well known and highly esteemed in athletic circles within South Africa and abroad, there is a belief among many that it is this spirit alone that motivates the worthies propping up the rear of the pack, while the athletes in front fight exclusively for glory and money. This isn't at all the case. Keen athletic endeavour prevails throughout the field: personal bests mean as much to those who finish at dusk as to those who enjoy their post-race shower before lunch.

Far more importantly, however, the great champions have been passionately committed to the growth of the unique Comrades culture. As Jackie Mekler recently claimed, it all started with the unselfishness of Arthur Newton. Hardy Ballington, Wally Hayward and Mekler himself built on Newton's initiative, as have more recent winners such as Bruce Fordyce,

Sam Tshabalala, Alan Robb, Frith van der Merwe and Andrew Kelehe.

It is probably true to say that the relationship between athletic contest and camaraderie reached its zenith in the extraordinary conclusion of the 1967 'down' Comrades, and the lifelong friendship that ensued between the two main combatants. Manie Kuhn, the Afrikaner from Durban Savages, and Tommy Malone, the Scot who lived for Glasgow Celtic, were about as unlikely a pair of friends as anyone could imagine. Yet their emotional photo finish was the start of an association almost unparalleled in South African sport.

Those who didn't know them well could have been forgiven for imagining that the relationship after their Comrades runs was not particularly amicable. They spent decades niggling each other, but always in good spirit. Malone would remind Kuhn that he (Kuhn) was the only winner (until Jetman Msuthu) who hadn't carried the winner's baton across the finish line. Kuhn would explain to Malone that if the times of their winning efforts in 1966 and 1967 were aggregated, then he (Kuhn) would be the overall winner by a considerable margin.

Both maintained close links with Comrades after their competitive days. Malone completed ten runs. His debut race in 1966 brought his solitary victory and the first of his two gold medals. His fastest time of 5.54.11 came the following year, when he was pipped by arch-rival Kuhn. Those two golds were followed by eight silvers. His final Comrades was run in 1980.

Kuhn's career was somewhat longer. Between 1960 and 1982, he won 21 medals: eight golds, eight silvers and five bronzes. Along with Malone, he ran his fastest Comrades in 1967. It was the only time that either finished in under six hours. Official records show Kuhn's 1967 margin of victory as one second. Both runners, along with all others who were present at the finish, knew that the difference between the two was rather less than a second.

Even when their running days were over, the pair would return annually to Comrades, not to bask in former glory but to actively support those who followed in their footsteps. They maintained strong friendships with other past winners, including Jackie Mekler, Wally Hayward, Alan Robb and Bruce Fordyce.

Manie Kuhn died in his early seventies, just days before the 2005 Comrades Marathon. A heartbroken Tommy Malone was one of the pall-bearers. A week later, Malone was at the finish of the great race that had brought fame to both of them. When someone suggested to Malone that Wally Hayward, now in his late nineties, would probably not attend another Comrades, the Scot said wistfully, 'Neither will Manie.'

1966 COMRADES MARATHON
A CELTIC TRIUMPH

In 1962, Tommy Malone, a lifelong supporter of the famous Glasgow Celtic Football Club, emigrated to South Africa. A cross-country runner in Scotland since the age of 15, he was soon attracted to South Africa's extraordinary Comrades Marathon, an event made up of two standard marathons plus another mile or two over a mountainous course. It was an irresistible challenge for the tough Scot.

Ever the canny Scot, Malone didn't rush into things. A former winner of the Lanarkshire County Marathon, he won the Southern Transvaal Marathon and came second in the South African Marathon in 1965. The same year he seconded 1957 winner Mercer Davies in the Comrades Marathon to 'learn something about the race first'.

The following year, 27-year-old Tommy Malone was ready. Having just won the Korkie Ultramarathon in record time, he was regarded as leader of the Transvaal contingent. His Natal counterpart, Manie Kuhn, second in the previous 'up' run and third in 1965, would start as favourite. Others in contention were previous winners Mercer Davies and Gerald Walsh, as well as Fritz Madel, Charlie Chase, Dave Box and Robin Stamper. The race featured 365 starters, a record number for an 'up' run.

The experienced Madel took the early lead, reaching Westville after precisely an hour on the road. Together with Hargreaves, Craig and the favourite, Kuhn, he crested Cowies Hill some 25 minutes later. Madel and Craig dropped back on Field's Hill, and Kuhn made a move, reaching Hillcrest 50 seconds ahead of Malone, who had gradually come through the field.

From Hillcrest to the halfway mark at Drummond, Kuhn built up a lead of over a minute, while Malone, going through a bad patch, dropped back to fifth place, nearly two minutes behind the leader. Inchanga, as ever, proved a turning point. Kuhn and second-placed Frikkie Steyn were feeling the burden of front-running, while a recovering Malone started to make up ground.

Having disposed of Steyn on the descent from Inchanga through Harrison Flats to Cato Ridge, Malone set about overtaking the tiring Kuhn. At Camperdown, in his first Comrades Marathon, Tommy Malone took the lead. Kuhn, who shortly afterward collapsed momentarily, was taken aback, as he later explained:

'My seconds told me for some time that Malone was coming closer, but I never realised that he was that close. When he came past me, I was still feeling all right. I thought I would hang on to him for a while. Then I had the blackout. I felt I was dizzy and I stopped.'

The Scot had full control of the race. At Umlaas Road, he was three and a half minutes ahead of Kuhn. When he reached the top of Polly Shortts, his lead was 19 minutes. He had the race firmly sewn up: there would be no stopping him now. Tommy Malone crossed the line in 6.14.07, a winner in his first Comrades Marathon. Acknowledging the challenge posed by the formidable Polly Shortts and admitting the nausea that had held him back just before halfway, he later spoke of the determination that had sustained him on his epic journey: 'I did not walk a yard during the race. I only stopped momentarily several times for a drink of blackberry juice with glucose, or lemonade.'

Unofficially, two women, Maureen Holland and Mavis Hutchison, completed the race and gave credence to the growing suspicion that women were capable of challenging men in the most arduous of physical contests. As ultramarathon running had yet to attain respectability in the minds of the public, the two ladies were generally written off as marginally more insane than their male counterparts.

The 1966 Comrades Marathon had been undeniably successful, with several notable contributors. Clive Crawley (28th) won the Gary Player Trophy, awarded for the fastest combined time in the Comrades Marathon and the Pietermaritzburg-to-Durban Duzi Canoe Marathon. The Savages Athletic Club, comprising Manie Kuhn, Fritz Madel, Dave Box and Roland Davey, won the coveted Gunga Din team trophy.

Most important, Tommy Malone had beaten second-placed runner

Manie Kuhn by over 17 minutes. Their rivalry would continue, and the following year would witness one of the most stirring finishes in South African sporting history.

1966 COMRADES MARATHON RESULTS

1. T. Malone	6.14.07
2. J. D. Kuhn	6.31.46
3. F. W. E. Madel	6.33.45
4. D. Chase	6.36.05
5. P. Hargreaves	6.40.55
6. F. Steyn	6.44.28
7. D. Box	6.45.12
8. D. Gent	6.48.08
9. E. Pritchard	6.57.09
10. R. Davey	6.57.25

1967 COMRADES MARATHON
MANIE KUHN AND HIS CLOSEST FRIEND

Arthur Newton, Hardy Ballington, Bernard Gomersall, Jackie Mekler, Alan Robb, Wally Hayward, Bruce Fordyce and Frith van der Merwe would all surely qualify for a shortlist to identify the greatest of all Comrades winners. But if a duo of champions were to be chosen, recognising their joint achievements and their respect for each other and for the great race, Tommy Malone and Manie Kuhn would have no challengers. In 1967, the ultimate human race produced the ultimate human drama.

The 1966 interprovincial rivalry between Transvaler Malone and Natalian Kuhn, first and second, had captured the imagination of Comrades followers. In the build-up to the 1967 race, both provided their followers with sufficient reason to believe that they were at a peak, in prime condition to establish their individual claims to Comrades greatness. The 1966 London-to-Brighton race was won by 1965 Comrades champion Bernard

Gomersall. Kuhn finished second, with Malone third. Kuhn triumphed in the King William's Town 36-miler, as he had done the previous year. Malone set a record in winning the Korkie Ultramarathon. The stage was set for a battle royal, and that's precisely what materialised.

A record 542 athletes out of 600 entrants faced the starter. The Pietermaritzburg runner Eric Rencken took the early lead. Most of the top runners, including Tommy Malone, Gordon Baker and Tim Blankley, were in a tight bunch, while Kuhn was content to maintain a watching brief, holding back but making sure that his main rivals remained in sight.

Durban runner Blankley led the way down Inchanga to Drummond, Rencken having fallen back on Harrison Flats. By now, Kuhn had joined the leaders and a group of seven (Blankley, Malone, Morrison, Hargreaves, Baker, Craig and Kuhn) were timed at 2.51 at halfway. While this was 5 minutes 35 seconds slower than the record set by Jackie Mekler in 1963, and three minutes behind Kuhn's 1965 time, it was only a minute short of the 2.50 that Bruce Fordyce would set in his record-breaking run of 5.27.18 in 1984. Such comparisons emphasise the reality that the Comrades Marathon is not won before Drummond. The second half is the time to make one's effort: generally the later, the better.

The 1967 race started to take shape on the long climb past Alverstone up to Botha's Hill. Malone and Morrison had broken clear and were establishing a significant lead. On the relatively flat section between Hillcrest and Kloof, Malone made his own move, leaving Morrison in his wake. Running strongly, he reached Kloof more than three minutes ahead of his rivals. By now, Kuhn, also looking strong, had moved into second place. The battle was on.

At Tollgate, the leader, Malone, was handed the baton containing the traditional message from the mayor of Pietermaritzburg to the mayor of Durban. When one considers the closeness of the finish, it would appear with hindsight that this extra burden may well have been crucial to the outcome. By now, Kuhn had cut Malone's lead to two minutes and was looking decidedly the fresher of the two. The gritty Scot, although clearly tiring, was determined to hang on to first place. It was a classic example of a hunter chasing his prey for whom safety was beckoning but tantalisingly out of reach. Or was it?

In the stadium, anticipation among the crowd of approximately 3 000 was at fever pitch. There was no television in those days, no big screen to apprise ground spectators of the drama unfolding in the streets outside. Just the wait. Unbeknown to the expectant crowd, both runners were baulked by motor vehicles just before entering the stadium. Did these unwanted intrusions influence the result? We shall never know.

What we do know is that Malone suddenly appeared on the track, some 75 yards from the finish. The crowd immediately acclaimed the apparent winner. Then a second roar went up. Kuhn appeared, only 20 yards behind. It was a frantic dash for the line, with Malone in front and seemingly in charge of proceedings. Did Malone make a mistake in attempting to sprint home when a gentle canter was all that was required? Unsettled, he fell. Kuhn, sensing his opportunity, crammed on the pace. Malone rose, fell again, rose again and reached for the tape. As he did so, Kuhn flashed past. Second in 1964 and 1966 and third in 1965, Manie Kuhn was the 1967 Comrades Marathon champion.

Kuhn and Malone were the only two finishers who came in under six hours, confirming their status as supreme ultra-athletes. The Pietermaritzburg runner Gordon Baker was third, with Tim Blankley fourth. Frikkie Steyn of Cape Town came fifth and Johannesburg's Dennis Morrison sixth, rounding out the gold medals, limited to the top six at this stage.

The team trophy was won by Durban Savages (Kuhn, Craig, Davey and Molver), while 1957 winner Mercer Davies and his predecessor in 1956, Gerald Walsh, were among those to finish their tenth Comrades and claim their permanent green numbers. Liege Boulle, at the age of 58, finished his 27th Comrades (a record), and Nick Raubenheimer brought his tally of medals up to 15.

A little while after the race, a newspaper rather mischievously sought to cast doubt on the veracity of the result. Under the heading, 'Who was the real winner?' the newspaper suggested that Malone might just have crossed the line first. Carefully chosen photographs suggested that they may have had a case. Without the benefit of television replays from various angles, it can safely be said that the two athletes were in the best position to pass authoritative judgement. Some years later, Malone was asked if he though a dead heat might have been the correct result. His reply was succinct and decisive: 'No. Manie won!'

The race was barely over when Kuhn and Malone started ribbing each other, in good fun. Their teasing continued unabated until Kuhn's death shortly before the 2005 Comrades Marathon. Malone would point out that Kuhn was the only Comrades winner who crossed the line without the traditional mayor's baton – true until Jetman Msuthu was awarded first place in 1992 following the disqualification of Charl Mattheus. Kuhn would counter by claiming that his margin of victory of 17.39 over Malone in 1966, less Malone's one-second triumph in the following year, gave him a clear advantage of 17.38.

Tommy Malone must surely be the only sportsman to have lost a major event in a close finish and yet be thankful that he didn't win. He could never begrudge his great friend's victory in the 1967 Comrades Marathon.

1967 COMRADES MARATHON RESULTS

1. J. D. Kuhn   5.54.10
2. T. Malone   5.54.11
3. G. R. Baker   6.02.32
4. T. E. Blankley   6.10.59
5. F. C. Steyn   6.21.47
6. D. G. Morrison   6.25.15
7. J. M. Potgieter   6.25.17
8. E. V. Craig   6.29.13
9. P. M. Hargreaves   6.32.23
10. R. H. Davey   6.34.58

11

COMRADES GOES INTERNATIONAL
(1968 to 1973)

The Comrades Marathon had begun its existence, proudly and unashamedly, as a purely South African event. This is not to suggest that foreigners were in any way unwelcome. On the contrary, the very nature of the race guaranteed acceptance to all, even those who had to compete unofficially because of prevailing legislation.

As far back as 1962, a visitor, Englishman John Smith, had won the race in his first and only attempt. In 1968, another Englishman, John Tarrant, ran the race as the 'Ghost Runner'. A decision, which presumably made sense to those who were party to it, barred him from running officially outside Britain, but his several unofficial Comrades ventures bore testimony to the growing international appeal of the race. Perhaps it is fortunate that Tarrant never crossed the finishing line first, although his running record clearly marked him as a potential winner.

The most welcome of all British invasions came in 1972, when Mick Orton and the Tipton Harriers team of Staffordshire, England, introduced a new strategy to long-distance running in South Africa: the consumption of vast quantities of cake and beer in the final lead-up to the race was considered crucial to their success. What greater incentive could South Africans be given in their quest for Comrades glory? No longer did they have to run 90 kilometres in order to build up their favourite thirst. Now they could dutifully pour pint after pint of lager down their gullets and earnestly proclaim to their wives and others that they were enduring such hardships purely in order to improve their athletic prowess.

On a more serious note, the success of the Tipton Harriers, in particular race winner Mick Orton, brought a new scientific approach to diet in the final week of preparation. The first half of the week involved 'carbo-depletion', with an accent on protein intake. The final three days were the 'carbo-loading' phase, designed to store maximum quantities of glycogen in the muscles in preparation for the huge ordeal that loomed. The Saltin diet had arrived.

The 1968 winner was one of the great champions. Jackie Mekler, four years after his previous victory, became the fourth man (after Newton, Ballington and Hayward) to post five wins. The sheer coincidence of this group sharing the number five made it the benchmark of Comrades greatness in the eyes of many – which was a little unfortunate for Alan Robb, for instance, who would later achieve just four victories, but certainly ranks with the very best of Comrades champions.

Alan Robb enjoys a unique position as four-time winner, holder of the most gold medals, former record holder for both 'up' and 'down' runs, successful finisher of over 30 consecutive Comrades Marathons, and sportsman and gentleman *par excellence*. Not far behind him was immigrant Dave Bagshaw, unbeatable in a three-year period from 1969 to 1971, in which he too set records for both 'up' and 'down' runs. Perhaps rain and cold suited former Englishman Bagshaw, who took full advantage of the most miserable conditions yet in his hat-trick year of 1971.

The 1973 race provided a winner from an unlikely part of the world, Cape Town. Until now, aside from occasional intrusions by British runners such as John Smith and Mick Orton, the Comrades crown had been more or less the preserve of Natal and Transvaal runners. With Cape Town's first Two Oceans Marathon having been run in 1970, the Mother City entered the Comrades fray with a pair of significant contenders. Former Johannesburger Dave Levick, now with the University of Cape Town, had won the 1971 London-to-Brighton race in record time. Earlier in 1973, he had finished second in the Two Oceans Marathon behind strong-running fellow Capetonian Don Hartley. Levick became one of the superb 'come from behind' Comrades champions. His conservative start led to an irresistible finish.

1968 COMRADES MARATHON
MAGIC FIVE FOR MEKLER

In its early stages, the Comrades Marathon, notwithstanding its all-embracing ethos of inclusivity, really belonged to its home province of Natal: Durban and Pietermaritzburg runners made up the majority of the field. As time went on, and the popularity of the race grew, runners from further afield started to become involved. Johannesburg and Pretoria were, after all, only a few hours' drive away.

During the 1960s, the Comrades web spread further, drawing athletes from all over the nation and, in some cases, abroad. John Smith, an Englishman, had won the race in 1962. Air travel was fast becoming a normal method of getting to the start line, although fear of flying was still a significant deterrent for would-be travellers, particularly this year. On Saturday 20 April, southern Africa experienced its worst air disaster when a South African Airways Boeing with 128 on board crashed shortly after take-off from Windhoek in South-West Africa. Only five survived.

There were a few late withdrawals from the Comrades field – some, no doubt, due to unwillingness to fly, but others for more mundane reasons: influenza, which always crops up just before Comrades, work demands or a dawning realisation that training had been insufficient.

An early disappointment was the news that 'up' run champion Tommy Malone was unavailable due to injury. His 'down' run conqueror of 1967,

Manie Kuhn, had entered and was fit for action. The tongue-in-cheek competitiveness between the two would endure and continue to illuminate the spirit that unites all Comrades personalities, but they would no longer cross athletic swords on the long road that connects Durban with Pietermaritzburg.

The 'up' run is generally regarded as the more difficult, and the number of entrants tends to reflect this: almost inevitably, the 'down' run attracts more entrants. This year, though, the 'up' run attracted 659 entries, in comparison with 600 – itself a record – for 1967's 'down' run. Why was there such a reversal of trend? Certainly Comrades was gaining in popularity. Perhaps the 1967 shoot-out between Kuhn and Malone had whetted appetites – and the great Jackie Mekler was in the field. All these, and other considerations such as a new appreciation for the benefits of an active lifestyle, played their part. But who cared? Comrades was growing, and that was what mattered.

While the spirit of Comrades is probably the aspect of the race most spoken about, it doesn't explain a spectral entrant in this year's event, the so-called 'Ghost Runner', John Tarrant. Tarrant had staked a significant claim to be known as Britain's top ultra-distance runner by winning most long-distance races in the UK in 1967.

In 1968, he accompanied his compatriot Bernard Gommersall, 1965 winner and holder of the 'down' record, to Durban to take part in the greatest challenge of them all, the Comrades Marathon. British runners were among the first from abroad to recognise the unique ethos and challenge of Comrades. For somebody with the credentials of Tarrant, this would be an opportunity to stake a claim for true athletic greatness.

Unfortunately for Tarrant, and for Comrades and road-running in general, such a prospect was extinguished before race day. Comrades followers had already experienced the shocking end of Wally Hayward's competitive career, just over a decade earlier, for allegedly infringing amateur rules. This time the International Amateur Athletics Federation took bureaucratic misguidedness to a global level by suddenly barring John Tarrant from running outside the UK as he had apparently been paid approximately R35 for performances in a boxing ring as a teenager two decades previously. He thus joined female and black participants who had to run unofficially without a race number. He has been known ever since as the 'Ghost Runner'. Would such a decision have been imposed on him if he had been planning to run elsewhere in the world? We shall probably never know.

Nowadays, Comrades competitors are well aware that, if they do not reach two or three checkpoints within a certain time, they will not be allowed to continue. It's a sensible ruling, designed to ensure the safety of those who are so far behind the clock that their chances of finishing successfully are virtually nonexistent. It took a few years for the new regulation, introduced in 1968, to be widely accepted.

South African Airways pilot Robin Stamper wasn't particularly worried about such matters when he led the field out of Durban. His mind was focused on building as big a lead as possible in the opening stages. He did so rather well. Brother of Noel Stamper (who has completed more Two Oceans Marathons than anyone else), he went through Pinetown about a minute and a half behind Jackie Mekler's record for the stage. Davies, Mekler, Gomersall and Baker, among others, were running together well behind the flying leader.

As the front-runners began their ascent of Field's Hill, the day started warming. The heat didn't seem to worry Stamper. At Emberton, with roughly one-third of the distance behind him, he was five minutes ahead of a group that included Mekler, Baker and Gomersall, with Manie Kuhn close behind. Bernard Gomersall, winner of the 1965 race in the wet and cold, seemed badly affected by the African sun and looked the most vulnerable of the potential gold medallists.

Stamper was a strong runner, but he had set his sights a little too high this time. On the ascent of Botha's Hill, he slowed down significantly. His five-minute advantage became two, and then a one-minute lead. Before the top was reached, he had been overtaken and was soon out of the top ten. Comrades does not easily forgive those who underestimate the demands of the event.

Jackie Mekler and Gordon Baker were first through halfway, with Morrison snapping at their heels. Manie Kuhn was only a minute behind the leaders with a game Bernard Gomersall still hanging on. Just over a minute behind Kuhn, Robin Stamper, despite having been pushed aside, continued grimly.

On the ascent of Inchanga, Baker made his move and went into the lead. It was a brave time to do so, but he was looking and feeling strong, and Mekler and Morrison certainly weren't. Stamper appeared to be a candidate for early retirement. When Baker reached Camperdown in 4 hours 26 minutes, two minutes ahead of Mekler and three in front of Kuhn, things were looking good for him.

Suddenly, it all changed. Baker slowed and Mekler took the lead, with Kuhn no more than 100 yards behind him. All of this happened in Camperdown. In a flash, Baker went from first to a struggling third, or was it fourth? The Ghost Runner, John Tarrant, determined to stake a claim to unofficial Comrades greatness, was engaged in a private, unrecognised tussle with Mekler.

Very soon, Mekler had good reason to turn his mind away from his unofficial battle and focus on a very real challenge. Manie Kuhn, the formidable late finisher who had pipped Tommy Malone right at the post the previous year, seemed to be gaining strength, and was quite definitely closing the gap on the leader. Suddenly, it looked like last year all over again: the slightly built Mekler versus the muscular Kuhn became the battle for supremacy. Menacingly, Kuhn closed the gap to just 50 seconds. He was aiming for the double, and an 'up' victory to add to his 'down' win in 1967. Mekler was chasing a fifth victory and a special place in history.

As so often happens in Comrades, particularly in the 'up' run, the little man prevailed. At no time was there much in it. Mekler, however, was the master over the two final hills, Ashburton and Polly Shortts. When he crested the latter with a comfortable lead, the race was effectively over.

Mekler's time of 6.01.11 was the third-fastest to date. In accomplishing a fifth victory, he joined other Comrades immortals: Arthur Newton, Hardy Ballington and Wally Hayward. In one respect, he surpassed them all by achieving a fourth 'up' win. As modest as ever, he made light of his triumph and spoke only of the efforts of his closest challengers: 'Manie and Gordon ran splendid races and each had me worried at times. What a pity there couldn't be three winners!'

The defeated Kuhn expressed similar sporting sentiments: 'As usual, Jackie was too good for me. He was the better runner and I congratulate him on his great effort.' Ghost Runner John Tarrant was the fourth to cross the line, although unrecognised, in 6.18.47. Afterwards, he provided a glimpse of the anguish that he had felt: 'I was so worried about running. I kept wondering whether somebody would try to stop me finishing the course.'

The 1968 Comrades Marathon firmly established Jackie Mekler as one of the all-time Comrades greats. It also featured courageous efforts by those of lesser ability. One example was that of early leader Robin Stamper, who gritted his teeth and kept going as he was being overtaken, eventually finishing 31st in 7.26.45. Bernard Gomersall's seventh place in 6.38.17 might have disappointed him, but not so others. It was regarded by many as even more impressive, given the conditions and his background, than his victory in 1965.

1968 COMRADES MARATHON RESULTS

1. J. Mekler	6.01.11
2. J. D. Kuhn	6.03.54
3. G. R. Baker	6.11.33
4. J. M. Potgieter	6.24.30
5. D. G. Box	6.27.17
6. T. E. Blankley	6.31.26
7. B. Gomersall	6.38.17
8. W. H. Brown	6.38.57
9. P. Anderson	6.40.18
10. D. G. Morrison	6.41.02

1969 COMRADES MARATHON
AN IMMIGRANT RAISES THE BAR

By 1969, the growth of the Comrades Marathon had reached an interesting and important level. It was becoming obvious that a clear vision of the future of the event and its place in the sporting calendar would have to be articulated. Vic Clapham's dream had stuttered along bravely for many years. Great achievements had been recorded, noble principles accepted as integral to the ethos of the race, and the Comrades spirit, ethereal and intangible as it is, was recognised, if not fully understood.

Now participants were being attracted in increasing numbers, and the growing popularity of the event brought new questions into play. Comrades had been regarded as the preserve of a minority of supermen – or nutcases, depending on one's point of view. Ordinary people were now being drawn into the Comrades net, causing ordinary problems such as traffic congestion.

The previous year's race, featuring 581 starters and 435 finishers, had brought things to a head. Comrades traditions were under threat. If no workable solution could be found, the race itself could be vulnerable. One of the strongest and most enduring of early Comrades traditions was the relationship between runner and personal attendant. When small fields were the norm, these seconds were able to travel by car along the race route and satisfy their charges' every need. Larger entries posed safety problems, caused bottlenecks on the roads and necessitated increasing numbers of traffic officers.

Fortunately, practicality prevailed as authorities and organisers sought to accommodate the rapidly escalating event within the parameters of law and order and, most importantly, safety. This year brought new regulations. Personal seconds had to use motorcycles rather than cars, and such vehicles were prohibited from stopping on certain sections of the road. The changes reflected a sensitivity on the part of organisers that would do for the moment. In later years, further developments would almost, but not quite, eliminate the role of personal attendants.

Who would win this year's race? Speculation focused mainly on Jackie Mekler, Manie Kuhn and Dave Box. Mekler, having achieved his fifth victory and a special brand of Comrades immortality in 1968, was hoping to better the five victories of Newton, Ballington and Hayward. Kuhn, winner of the closest ever Comrades in the most recent 'down' run two years previously, and runner-up to Mekler last year, was a physically strong man whose mental strength seemed to be peaking. Box, seventh in 1966 and now holder of the world 100-mile record, had his supporters. Mekler, however, was the outright popular favourite. Amazingly, Ghost Runner John Tarrant would again compete unofficially.

When 703 starters set off down Pietermaritzburg's Commercial Road, they could look forward to a welcome innovation. Three feeding stations awaited them en route, shades of things to come. First to show was John Tarrant. As if to emphasise his 'supernatural' status, he ran at a pace that no ordinary mortal could hope to maintain. By the foot of Polly Shortts, he was nearly three minutes ahead of the field. At Camperdown, his lead was four minutes. Bagshaw, Mekler, Box, Kuhn, Blankley and Dave Venter were all relatively well placed.

Conditions were ideal – cool and windless – as the official leaders reached Inchanga. Thus far, Box, Mekler and Baker had been running together with Kuhn, Bagshaw and others not too far behind. On the ascent, Box decided to make a break. Bagshaw, having moved up to the front, followed him, while an uncomfortable Mekler dropped back.

Unofficial runner John Tarrant was first to reach halfway at Drummond, his time unrecorded, history stifled by officialdom. Box and Bagshaw went through, running together, in the fast time of 2 hours 51 minutes. This compares rather favourably with the 2.50.02 set by Bruce Fordyce in 1984 en route to a record-breaking 5.27.18. Vorster, Baker and Mekler were right behind the leading duo. Kuhn was four minutes adrift of the leaders.

Tarrant had set a suicidal pace from the start. As he left Drummond, he began to suffer the effects of his earlier madness and slowed dramatically on the long, steep climb of Alverstone Hill. Before long, he was overtaken by Box and Bagshaw. With the Ghost Runner well and truly exorcised, the race looked like a shoot-out between the Savages clubmates. Then, without any warning, there was only one in the picture. Near the crest of Botha's Hill, Box found the going too hot and fell off the pace.

The surprise package, Dave Bagshaw, a recent immigrant from Britain, held the lead on his own and seemed well in control. Prior to the race, several past champions were asked to predict the winner of this year's event. Only Allen Boyce, 1940 victor, had plumped for Bagshaw. His prophecy was looking good. So was Bagshaw.

Running at a tempo hitherto unknown in the final third of Comrades, Bagshaw reached the top of Field's Hill five minutes ahead of Box, who was still second and, having recovered from his earlier bad patch, was running strongly, if not quite as quickly as the flying leader. Box was trying to ignore a leg that was causing him pain. His second, who also happened to be his wife, offered advice but no sympathy, 'Tomorrow you can spend all day in bed, but today it's the Comrades.'

As Bagshaw entered Pinetown well ahead of his opponents, he realised for the first time that, in addition to a famous victory that was beckoning, he was also in a position to challenge the race record. At the Pinetown checkpoint, he was over three minutes faster than Wally Hayward had been during the first sub-six-hour Comrades in 1953. Dave Box, continuing gamely, was six minutes behind the leader, with Davis, Baker, Davey and Mekler within two minutes of the second-placed man. If Bagshaw faltered, there were a few talented individuals who would be only too happy to pounce.

Bagshaw, however, had no intention of giving anyone else the slightest opportunity. Having successfully negotiated Cowies Hill, he reached Westville with a seven-minute lead, and this was increasing with every mile. Having planned to run 'an attacking' race, he had put his plan into practice quite perfectly, timed his assault with precision and thereafter stamped his authority on proceedings. His winning time of 5.45.35 was an eye-opener. He had taken over five minutes off Gomersall's 1965 record and posed a question that was on everyone's lips: what is the fastest time possible for the 'down' Comrades?

Hanging on to second place after having contested the lead takes a great deal of character. Dave Box wasn't short of courage. He needed it, plus a bit more. Jackie Mekler, having had a wretched day, made something of a recovery. Box, aware of Mekler's attentions, gritted his teeth and tried to ignore the agony of blistered feet. He succeeded and expressed his relief afterwards: 'Having Jackie only four minutes behind you for miles, and going well, is a nasty experience. Only when I crossed the line was I sure of second place.'

Coming third was frustrating for multiple champion Mekler. This was to be his final competitive Comrades, an opportunity to post a sixth victory and establish a unique place in history. It didn't work out that way. At Gillits, two-thirds into the race, he was in tenth place, having had a miserable day. With all prospect of a win out of the question, he nevertheless managed to fight his way to a third-place finish. Despite his disappointment, he remained a true Comrades sportsman: 'Dave's was a magnificent run, and what a race! I've no excuses. He was just too good.'

Cape Town runners have not made too much of an impact on the Comrades Marathon. This year, two representatives of the Mother City provided a little eloquence. Celtic Harriers runner Dave Venter was singled out by a spectator and asked, 'Cape Town, what do you think of the Natal scenery?' Quick as a flash, Venter replied, 'The scenery's all right, but why the devil don't you change the name to the Valley of Two Thousand Hills?'

Fellow Capetonian Marius Diemont was a debutant. After the event, he expressed his impressions in a way that would be familiar to many other novices as well as old hands. 'It all became something of a nightmare. It was endless. Somehow, I kept going – up and down, up and down. I couldn't give up. At the back of my mind there was always the thought of wasting 600 miles of training and the trip all the way from Cape Town. That, quite apart from the personal let-down. The last 13 miles from Pinetown were undiluted hell. Eventually, after an interminable time, I made it – with the greatest feeling of relief imaginable. I felt really bucked. The fact that I had finished in 9 hours 13 minutes 42 seconds, in 286th position, didn't make me feel insignificant at all. The fact was I had finished. I felt like screaming it all aloud.'

A more local novice, Leo Benning of Natal University, answered the call of Comrades somewhat reluctantly. Benning had 'emigrated' to Durban from Pretoria the previous year. A track-and-field man from his earliest days, he took one look at the Comrades obsession in Natal and thought, 'These people are really mad.' He went as far as to write an anti-Comrades article, citing domestic upheavals and using the expression 'really cuckoo'.

Benning did, however, watch the 1968 race. Something obviously got through to him. During the build-up to the 1969 Comrades, he took part, at the behest of Comrades legends Gerry Treloar and Ian Jardine, in a Pietermaritzburg-to-Pinetown training run.

Inevitably, Leo Benning was hooked. He ran the 1969 Comrades Marathon. After a comfortable first half in 'coolish, drizzly conditions', the race punished him for his earlier derogatory remarks. First one knee said 'no', then the other. Bystanders and attendants of other runners provided various liniments. After a long struggle, things suddenly changed. As he later admitted, 'At 45th Cutting, the pain miraculously disappeared.' Benning finished the first of his eight Comrades Marathons in 8.56.46. In 1977, he would set a personal best of 7.26.00. Listening to him talk, it would appear as if his family didn't really want him to earn a green number, 'The longer the race, the more anti my wife Marie gets.'

The warmest welcome of the day was reserved for 67-year-old Ian Jardine. In his final Comrades, the virtually blind Jardine, linked to his pilot Gerry Treloar by a piece of cloth, won the Founder's Trophy, awarded to the oldest finisher, for a remarkable 13th time. Such was his effect on road-running in South Africa that a club chaired initially by another Comrades legend,

Denis Tabakin, was formed to provide blind runners with sighted 'pilots'. This club became known as the 'Jardine Joggers'.

1969 COMRADES MARATHON RESULTS

1. D. Bagshaw	5.45.35
2. D. G. Box	5.57.57
3. J. Mekler	6.01.30
4. H. E. Rencken	6.03.41
5. B. N. Davis	6.03.45
6. G. R. Baker	6.05.49
7. J. D. Kuhn	6.12.26
8. R. H. Davey	6.14.06
9. P. Anderson	6.22.49
10. R. B. Gardner	6.27.11

1970 COMRADES MARATHON
BAGSHAW BAGS A DOUBLE

The sports pages of the nation's newspapers told a story of triumph and supremacy in 1970. The two sports that really mattered, judging by the press coverage, were rugby and cricket. Many South African sports lovers, enthralled by their favourite international rivalries, appeared quite unaware that rugby and cricket, in a global perspective, are minor, and largely British colonial sports. Nevertheless, they are important in the communities and nations that support them, and South Africa is one such country.

Sporting isolation was just around the corner in 1970. This wasn't recognised in the euphoria that accompanied the nation's achievements against traditional foes. It started with cricket. Bill Lawry's Australians, having disposed of virtually all opponents, most recently India, came to South Africa in the summer of 1969/70 to demonstrate their prowess as unofficial world champions. It didn't work out quite as planned. They were whitewashed 4–0 by Ali Bacher's Springboks. In the first hour after lunch on 5 February 1970, Barry Richards and Graeme Pollock put on 103 runs during a partnership of 173.

Literally and figuratively, this was South African cricket's finest hour. The Australians had been supplanted as the world's number one cricketing nation. South Africans felt assured that they were about to celebrate their unprecedented supremacy and parade their superstars on the world stage. But it didn't happen: isolation took over.

In rugby, 1970 brought the New Zealand All Blacks. It was the final tour of the country by famous All Black Colin Meads, who had shown early promise in 1960, also in South Africa. Meads made no secret of his great ambition: 'To beat South Africa in South Africa! What a dream!' For Meads, it wasn't to be. This was the series of crash-tackling Joggie Jansen, inspirational captain Dawie de Villiers, veteran magician Mannetjies Roux and sensational kicker Ian McCallum. The Springboks triumphed by three tests to one.

On the surface, South African sport was at its pinnacle; in reality, it stood on the edge of near oblivion. Cricket was the central issue, and the pivotal figure was a South African political exile: cricketer Basil D'Oliviera, who had been born in Cape Town, but classified 'coloured' and therefore unable to play for his country. He emigrated to England in 1960 to pursue his cricketing career, and ultimately played the decisive innings for his adopted country in the 1968 Ashes decider.

When D'Oliviera was named as a member of England's team to tour South Africa in 1968/69, Prime Minister B. J. Vorster announced: 'We are not prepared to receive a team thrust upon us by people whose interests are not the game, but to gain political objectives which they do not even attempt to hide.'

Vorster's idiotic comments drew rapturous applause from an audience who had little understanding of the issues involved. The repercussions were swift. England cancelled the tour. Australia did visit South Africa in 1969/70, but that would be the last official tour for over two decades. In 1970, South Africa was expelled from the international Olympic movement. Even in rugby, South Africans were ostracised. Isolation took over, and South African sports followers entered an era in which the importance of the interprovincial Currie Cup rugby competition was elevated out of all proportion. There was a positive side to this sporting starvation, though: the Comrades Marathon, until then a 'gimmick' event in the minds of many, if not most, was able, for the first time, to attract the attention that it deserved.

Politics was, of course, far from the minds of the record field of 759, out of a record entry of 865, who faced the starter outside the Durban City Hall at 6 a.m. on Saturday, 30 May. An indication of the growing appeal of the race, and a potentially bright future for it, was the fact that 26 18-year-olds (more than the entire field in six previous runnings of Comrades) had entered.

Pre-race talk suggested that 1969 champion Dave Bagshaw had only to turn up in order to achieve back-to-back victories. Manie Kuhn, 1967 winner and perennial tough man, was regarded as a dark horse. Another who was accorded outsider status was student Dave Levick, who had come second in the recent Korkie Ultramarathon from Pretoria to Germiston.

There was an awkward moment at the start when the post office clock failed to do its duty, and it was left to non-runner Max Trimborn to start proceedings with his famous cockcrow. Early race historian Vernon Jones was one of the starters. Afterwards he compared this year's field with that of the previous year. His comments might seem a little strange to those who have run in recent times:

'The human congestion at the start had to be experienced to be believed. As one of the old and slow brigade, I lined up at the back. For a full minute after the gun had been fired, I didn't move an inch, and when I eventually did move it was so slowly that I had lost two minutes by Field Street. Only then, after nearly half a mile, was I able to run normally. In 1936, Vic Clapham was so ashamed of the tiny field of 19 that he asked me to run a few miles unofficially and I persuaded another chap to do the same. In that way, we increased the size of the field leaving the start by about ten per cent. So I've run out of Durban in both the smallest and the largest fields. I prefer the latter because it's easy for a poor runner like me to conceal himself in the vast throng.'

Jones had no idea that, some 20 years later, tail-enders would take up to 15 minutes to cross the start line – and he would no doubt be astounded to find that slick organisation in the early years of the third millennium could have a field of over 15 000 properly under way within six minutes.

'Go out quickly and pulverise the opposition from the gun,' was a well-accepted philosophy among contenders at this stage of the race's evolution. Bagshaw had almost done that in 1969, taking the lead for the first time just over halfway. Now, in his assault on the 'up' run, he did what many defending champions have done: trained a little harder, was a little more disciplined, set his sights somewhat higher and took the lead a little earlier. We now know that such a mentality can be a recipe for disaster, but not always.

Bagshaw made no secret of his intentions right from the start. Before leaving Durban, he was already in the lead. The outstanding Pietermaritzburg runner Gordon Baker took up a position alongside him. At 45th Cutting, they were still together. At Westville, ditto. Eric Rencken was third, half a minute behind. In fourth place was a man whose mere participation emphasised the lure and spirit of the Comrades Marathon: John Tarrant, unofficial Ghost Runner the previous year, was back. His banning and hence his unofficial status remained. No matter what he might accomplish, his achievement would not be recorded. Yet he was back, drawn by the appeal of the great race to make another attempt that would not be recognised. He didn't walk to the start from a nearby Durban residence. Instead, he once again flew out to South Africa from his home in Britain, united in comradeship with other runners, but officially nonexistent.

Conditions were ideal as the top runners moved through Pinetown and began the ascent of Field's Hill. At this stage, much to the relief of the race organisers (who were not inviting controversy), Ghost Runner Tarrant was clearly in trouble and would not feature again. Dave Venter and Robin Stamper were nicely positioned, just off the leaders' pace. They had already claimed their places in the nation's road-running history earlier in the year. Venter had organised Cape Town's first ultramarathon, the Celtic Harriers 35-mile road race, which had taken place on Saturday, 2 May. Robin Stamper, one of the early leaders, had claimed fourth place in this inaugural event. Robin's brother, Noel, provided the name for the race: the Two Oceans Marathon, today second only to Comrades in stature.

At the top of Field's Hill, Bagshaw and Baker were still together. They remained glued to each other through Hillcrest, over Botha's Hill and down into Drummond, which they reached in the fast time of 2 hours 57 minutes, seven minutes ahead of Rencken, still in third place. With ideal conditions and two contenders matching each other stride for stride, the prospect of a record seemed realistic.

Inchanga, in traditional fashion, played a crucial role. Bagshaw, still full of running, powered his way up the steep ascent. Baker couldn't maintain the pace and dropped off the lead. Another to drop back was Rencken, who yielded third place to Dave Box.

Alone in front, Bagshaw strove to gain a decisive lead on the descent of Inchanga. He didn't falter. Although he was running unchallenged, he was aware that Jackie Mekler's record would be his if he could only maintain his speed. At Camperdown, which he reached seven minutes ahead of Box (now in second place), the clock suggested that he was on target.

It is seldom that a Comrades runner enjoys an entirely trouble-free run. Bagshaw had his bad patch between Camperdown and Umlaas Road, but it didn't last long. He took the two final hills, Little Pollys (or Ashburton) and Polly Shortts, in his stride. Afterwards, he recalled his feelings: 'I was going well up Polly Shortts, and then I knew the record was on.'

Bagshaw wasn't being over-optimistic. He was fully in control and crossed the line at the Collegians Club in 5.51.27, beating Mekler's record by five minutes. Box was nearly seven minutes behind in second place, with Rencken third. Shortly after he had finished, Bagshaw admitted that it had not been plain sailing all the way: 'For the first ten miles, I could not slip into my normal rhythm. Then things went well until I hit Camperdown. My seconds did a splendid job of work and must take a lot of the credit for my success.'

As the tired victor limped barefoot across the Pietermaritzburg turf, a couple of wags offered humorous comments. One glanced at his feet and said, 'No matter how fast or slow the Comrades runners go, it's always a blistering pace.' A first-aid worker offered him a stretcher and, in so doing, elicited the champion's indignant response, 'You must be joking!'

The Hardy Ballington trophy for the first novice finisher went to student Dave Levick, who finished eighth in a time of 6.34.12, just five seconds slower than the time of George Claassen when winning the same award ten years earlier. A significant aspect of Levick's run was his fast finish. He would display this particular talent somewhat more tellingly in 1973.

Last finisher and recipient of the Geraldine Watson trophy was B. Worsley of East London. Herman Delvin, Secretary of the Comrades Marathon organising committee for many years and committee member of the organising club, Collegians Harriers, eloquently spelt out the import of the award:

'This man is the last man officially to make the grade; the man who has been on the road almost 11 hours; the man who has suffered the most, who has tried the hardest; and it is this man who, more than any other, deserves a reward for not giving in.'

1970 COMRADES MARATHON RESULTS

1. D. Bagshaw	5.51.27
2. D. Box	5.58.07
3. H. E. Rencken	6.10.11
4. G. R. Baker	6.12.01
5. T. E. Blankley	6.15.30
6. R. Davey	6.21.44
7. R. B. Gardner	6.27.29
8. D. Levick	6.34.12
9. P. K. van der Leeuw	6.34.59
10. D. J. Steyn	6.37.07

1971 COMRADES MARATHON
BAGSHAW AGAIN – BUT ONLY JUST

South Africa's history, along with that of its greatest road race, the Comrades Marathon, has been so volatile and so unpredictable that each year has thrown up something different, some new angle to tantalise those who are drawn to identify themselves in some way with the one annual event that is closest to the heart of the nation. Some years have produced political intrigue, others controversy of varying nature. This year provided a spectacle of a kind that tends to crop up quite often: simply a great, great race.

It wasn't supposed to be too much of a contest. Pre-race speculation virtually guaranteed defending champion Dave Bagshaw another victory, his third in a row. When 1970 runner-up Dave Box withdrew because of injury and Bagshaw's preparation was seen to be near perfect, the prospect of an upset seemed too remote to consider.

An event as demanding as the Comrades Marathon does, however, present various intriguing possibilities. On one hand, a bad day, or even just a bad patch, might put paid to even the overwhelming favourite's chances. On the other hand, there is always a possibility, even if remote, that some newcomer, fit and strong and well prepared, may surprise everyone.

Dave Levick, first novice in taking eighth place in his first Comrades in 1970, was not entirely unheard of, but had not yet quite reached the level at which he would be regarded as a significant threat. Nevertheless, it had become apparent that he possessed two significant attributes. In the first place, he was a student and, like most university students, possessed that feeling of absolute self-confidence and disdain for others that has caused nightmares for many parents of students around examination time. Self-doubt would be unlikely to inhibit him on race day. Secondly, Dave Levick's performances in various races were broadcasting a message to his opponents: this young student was a fast finisher.

A record entry of 1 239 proclaimed the irresistible appeal of Comrades. Remarkably, this number included no fewer than seven previous winners: Bagshaw, Manie Kuhn, Tommy Malone, George Claassen, Mercer Davies, Gerald Walsh and Allen Boyce. When the runners went to the start, the field had been reduced to 1061. It was the first time in Comrades history that more than a thousand athletes would begin the race.

Such enthusiasm, welcome as it was, led to particularly onerous terms and conditions for the race. Traffic authorities in the area from Umlaas Road to Cato Ridge demanded certain changes in order to prevent congestion of runners and cars. This resulted in a race distance of 92 kilometres (or 57 miles). Another intrusion came from the weather gods. This year's was one of the most miserably cold and wet Comrades Marathons. To run the 1971 Comrades, you had to be a rather tough individual.

On Monday, 31 May 1971, the 50th anniversary of the first Marathon, a crowd of just over 4 000 bade farewell to a field of just over 1 000 as they left the start outside Pietermaritzburg City Hall. The weather was overcast but, at this early stage, relatively comfortable. That would change significantly during the day.

Favourite Dave Bagshaw was one of those who took the early lead. Other notables – Gordon Baker, Robin Stamper and unofficial entrant John Tarrant – were running together, with Tommy Malone and Tim Blankley not too far behind. The early morning threat of nasty weather was fast becoming reality. Light breeze became cold wind, slight drizzle became real rain, visibility was significantly reduced. Thanks to the elements, survival or submission became a mental debate in the first rather than the third and fourth quarters of the race.

At Camperdown, Bagshaw was joint leader, along with a host of strong contenders, including Malone, Baker, Tarrant and airline pilot Robin Stamper. Stamper, third in the recent second running of the Two Oceans Marathon, was looking strong.

One-third into the race, Cato Ridge loomed and recognised strong performances and disappointing let-downs alike. Bagshaw and Baker led the former, as well as the race, while Malone and Tarrant were among those who were dropping back.

On Harrison Flats, the worst-case scenario set in. Those who had hoped that a little early mist and drizzle would give way to traditional Comrades dream weather discovered that their optimism had been misplaced. It was no longer cold, it was freezing. Rain became torrential and life was sheer misery for the hardy (or foolhardy) souls who continued their quest for Comrades glory.

Amazingly, a large and enthusiastic crowd was at Drummond, eager to welcome the leaders and those following them. An indication of the weather problem was the panic felt by front-runners Bagshaw and Baker as they leapt out of the way of a skidding car whose driver had lost control in the treacherous conditions.

Robin Stamper was the leader at halfway, just two seconds ahead of the duo of Bagshaw and Baker. Levick and Malone were not too far behind, but seemed to be faring somewhat differently. Malone, 1966 champion, had gone out fast and was beginning to slip back. Levick, on the other hand, had started conservatively and was now making his move, gaining ground all the while on the leaders.

Levick wasn't the only one to make a move. On the ascent of Botha's Hill, Bagshaw went past Stamper to take control of the race. At Hillcrest, he was two minutes ahead of Gordon Baker, now in second place. Baker, sadly, had shot his bolt and was, in turn, overtaken by the strong-running Levick.

Unfortunately, Levick appeared to have made his effort too late. At Kloof, Bagshaw was four minutes ahead, apparently out of reach.

In Comrades, nothing is certain until the finishing line has been crossed. This is especially true of the 'down' race. Suddenly, Bagshaw was in trouble – so much so that he would later say, 'I never thought I would finish.'

Levick, meanwhile, seemed to be gaining in strength. His conservative strategy working perfectly, he was running smoothly and somewhat faster than his quarry. Afterwards, he recalled the encouragement the crowd had given him in the closing stages, 'It was like a running march with the throbbing cheering of the big crowd keeping you going faster and faster.'

The race for line honours was on: Bagshaw trying to hang on to a rapidly diminishing lead, Levick attempting to catch him before the end. Bagshaw had slowed significantly, but Levick too was feeling the inevitable fatigue. In the end, Bagshaw's perseverance told, but his winning margin was less than two minutes. Shattered but triumphant, the three-time winner admitted, 'The cold and feel of wet clothes clinging to my body practically all the way was the worst.'

Levick's final effort hadn't quite been successful, but he had learnt how to win Comrades. He would be back to demonstrate how well he had absorbed the lesson of 1971. Elated at his second position, he expressed his joy in true student fashion: 'The crowd was roaring and my head felt as though it was being pounded by huge waves, so loud did it seem. Then it was over – and to the beer, the fun and the happiness.'

Another with a tale to tell was the man who finished at the other end of the field. This is how Bernie Conway described his first Comrades:

'While on a holiday farm in the Orange Free State in December 1970, I was brainwashed by a runner from Natal, namely Andy Crichton, who was training for something called the "Comrades".

'On my return to Johannesburg, my friend, Mike McInerney [the brother of Dennis McInerney of Savages Athletic Club – race number 129, 23 medals], continued the brainwashing. Five months later, at the tender age of 42, I found myself "running" from Pietermaritzburg to Durban on a cold, rainy, misty day, eventually finishing in 10.59.59 [position 925] and the very proud and bewildered recipient of the Geraldine Watson Trophy for "last man home".

'During this ordeal, my seconds (Mike, his wife Pam and my wife Shirley) thought that Dennis was seconding me. He, on the other hand, surmised that they were assisting me, resulting in Dennis helping his Savages club-mate and the other three sitting in the Drummond Hotel sipping sherry to get warm.

'At the finish track at Greyville Race Course, Shirley ran down the home stretch after me, resplendent in her voluminous red coat, white boots and plastered, wet, permed hair – to the cheers of the onlookers. She was a mind-boggling sight.

'Needless to say, I had been bitten by the running bug and thereafter completed another 14 Comrades.'

1971 COMRADES MARATHON RESULTS

1. D. Bagshaw		5.47.06
2. D. Levick		5.48.53
3. G. R. Baker		5.57.26
4. B. Gerber		5.59.10
5. W. H. Brown		6.02.12
6. T. Parry		6.03.03
7. R. B. Gardner		6.08.47
8. R. Stamper		6.09.28
9. W. de Swardt		6.10.15
10. C. Crawley		6.11.19

1972 COMRADES MARATHON
A GREAT WIN FOR ENGLAND – AND BEER

Comrades Marathon runners, particularly those up among the gold medallists, used to be regarded as super-tough, ultra-heroic lunatics. Not for them the ordinary pleasures of life – wine, women and song. Dedication demanded abstinence. Lesser mortals opted for the nation's most popular sport, beer drinking. The 1972 Comrades Marathon changed perspectives. It brought a new respectability to the consumption of lagers. In fact, it provided a wonderful new theory: the secret of a successful Comrades might just be the drinking of as many beers as humanly possible. The following year would see the number of finishers top a thousand for the first time. In succeeding years, there would be a dramatic increase in participants. None of this elicited any complaints from local breweries.

This was the year of the Great British Invasion. The Tipton Harriers of Staffordshire, England, travelled to South Africa to take part in the 1972 Comrades Marathon. Their physical appearance served to distinguish them as highly unlikely contenders. In contrast with the evidence of hours in the sun displayed by well-tanned South Africans, the pale limbs of the English visitors looked starkly incongruous. When it was learnt that striptease shows had played a role in fund-raising for their trip, the locals became positively self-righteous.

Yet it was the culinary preferences of the Englishmen that provoked the most derision. With some of their members already looking almost portly on arrival, they proceeded to spend much of their time consuming appreciable quantities of cake and, of course, beer. Their conduct was regarded by many as disappointingly irresponsible, and some were more forthright in their criticism. Yet these English visitors probably had more reason to criticise their hosts, when they took note of the political climate in which the race was held.

In 1972, South Africa appeared to be heading towards serious internal conflict. The Nationalist government continued to implement its policies of racial segregation amid signs of increasing black resistance. In 1969, Steve Biko had established the South African Students Organisation. In 1972, the Black People's Convention was founded. Strikes were held in protest against low wages at a time of escalating inflation. Biko's Black Consciousness Movement was growing in strength.

White recognition of the inequity and unsustainability of apartheid was limited. While many found the policy abhorrent, government control of the media and of education had been effective in brainwashing the public.

The country's racist laws were in direct conflict with the ethos of the Comrades Marathon. Yet the race was, like other entities, subject to the laws of the land. Legislation barred the majority of the population from taking part. Comrades organisers, facing a dilemma not of their own making, opted for compromise. They decided to turn a deaf ear to the problem and quietly encouraged athletes of colour to participate unofficially. It was not a satisfactory arrangement, but there seemed no viable alternative. In 1972, 22 unofficial entries were accepted. Some of these came from women, still excluded through medical ignorance.

The official entry numbered a record 1 448, of whom 1 180 faced the starter. Among them were 63-year-old veterans Liege Boulle and Vernon Jones, rugby heroes Don Walton and Keith Oxlee, and favourite Dave Bagshaw. Also present, contrary to some pre-race speculation, were the cake-eating, beer-quaffing visitors from England.

The weather was perfect as the starters gathered outside the Durban City Hall. Only a few would have allowed their enthusiasm to be dimmed by the realisation that inevitable route changes had increased the 'up' course to 90.4 kilometres. In fact, start-line fever was so intense that final instructions were inaudible, Max Trimborn's cockcrow was barely heard and the event started two minutes late.

This was supposed to be Bagshaw's race. He seemed to think so too. Together with regular colleague Gordon Baker, he led the way over Tollgate. At Huntley's Hill, he moved marginally ahead of Baker and began to draw away. At the foot of Field's Hill, he was a minute ahead of Baker. Third, a further minute back, was Mick Orton, not the most fancied member of the Tipton Harriers. At the top of the long hill, Bagshaw's lead was still one minute but Orton was now level with Baker. At this early stage, seven of the overseas runners were in the top 40. Whether theirs was a serious effort or not remained to be seen.

What was clear was that Orton was looking ominously strong. At about one-third distance, he moved ahead of Baker and set off in pursuit of the leader. On the long descent to Drummond, Orton drew level with Bagshaw and the pair went through Drummond in 2 hours 50 minutes, over six minutes faster than Jackie Mekler's ten-year-old record.

Inchanga is normally where the men get sorted out from the supermen. The steep climb would surely see 24-year-old Orton, lacking experience of the hilly course and unused to the hot South African sun, pay for his early enthusiasm and fall back as the seasoned Bagshaw took control. The opposite happened. The sturdily built Orton cruised effortlessly up Inchanga while Bagshaw went through a 'bad patch' and was forced to walk a few times.

Orton looked well in control. Maintaining a steady stride, he gradually increased his lead on the descent of Inchanga, through Harrison Flats and on to Cato Ridge. At Camperdown, showing no sign of strain whatsoever, he was three minutes ahead of Bagshaw, who was making a gallant effort to remain in contention.

The unlikely leader simply kept going without faltering for a moment. Even Polly Shortts held no terrors as he steadily kept the same rhythm throughout the fearsome climb. It was only when he reached the top that Comrades followers finally realised that he wasn't just leading the race, he was actually winning it.

Triumphantly holding a Union Jack above his head, Mick Orton completed his final lap of the Collegians College ground and crossed the line in a new record time of 5.48.57. It was an extraordinary achievement by a relatively unknown athlete in unfamiliar territory and adverse conditions. He later expressed his own astonishment: 'I'm flabbergasted. My attitude at the start was that I would be content just to finish the course. My longest race previously was 36 miles and I came 13th.'

Three-time champion Dave Bagshaw lost his unbeaten Comrades record but hung on gamely to take second slot well ahead of third-placed Dave Box. Despite being in discomfort throughout the second half, Bagshaw's time of 5.53.54 was the third fastest 'up' time to date. Although disappointed, he sportingly conceded that the better man had won: 'Orton was too good for me. My legs gave me a lot of trouble. It was a novel experience coming second.'

Different runners expressed varying comments about their feelings during the race. Robert Gerhardt (899th) remembered the struggle: 'What I recall was the grinding punishment of pushing along under the sun for hours, with nothing left in the muscles of my body to help my mind in its task. More than anything else, I wanted to lie down and give up. But I knew that if I did, I would despise myself for the next six months. One thing in this race is that in the beginning you hate the hills but later you get to love them because you have to walk up.'

Clive Crawley, on the other hand, waxed lyrical about an altogether different experience in which he had felt the 'exhilaration of running strongly and effortlessly, the tiredness seeping through towards the end, the agony of Polly Shortts, and afterwards the pleasure of knowing you had not stopped once or walked from the starting gun to the finish line'.

Two Springbok rugby players compared the demands of international rugby with those of the race. Flyhalf Keith Oxlee (762nd) said, 'Never again. I've had some tough rugby matches in my time but the Comrades is sheer murder.' Hooker Don Walton (later to become an accomplished bowler) agreed: 'I'd rather play two internationals in succession than run the Comrades again.'

In 1972, pressure was mounting on authorities to allow the official inclusion of women and people of colour. Although it hadn't yet happened, the crowd gave special welcomes to the brave but officially unrecognised finishers, who included Sam Draai, Melchizedek Khumalo, Maureen Holland and Elizabeth Cavanagh. Mrs Cavanagh spoke of her day's ordeal: 'It was tough going. Every time I topped a hill, there seemed to be another one waiting. The race just didn't level out and the hills are so terribly steep.'

The day, however, belonged to England. The first three home (Mick Orton, Dave Bagshaw and Dave Box) were all English-born. The much-maligned Tipton Harriers justified their unorthodox dietary habits by becoming the first non-South African club to win the Gunga Din team trophy. Worst of all for the locals, John Pullin's team shocked the Springboks 18–9 in a rugby test at Ellis Park.

The triumphant English visitors went home with the spoils, but they did leave something behind: the Saltin Diet, which involves a few days of carbohydrate depletion followed by a period of carbo-loading in the final days leading up to the race. In particular, the idea that beer might be regarded as having a beneficial effect appealed to South African consumers. Although medical science could show that the drinking of beer prior to a marathon was more likely to be detrimental to an athlete's prospects, local enthusiasts were not convinced. Beer had worked for the Tipton Harriers. Beer was the answer. Road-running in South Africa would never be the same again.

1972 COMRADES MARATHON RESULTS

1. M. J. Orton	5.48.57
2. D. Bagshaw	5.53.54
3. D. G. Box	5.59.59
4. F. J. van Eeden	6.02.42

5. G. R. Baker	6.03.06
6. J. G. Malpass	6.06.02
7. W. H. Carr	6.07.46
8. L. W. Jenkins	6.13.43
9. W. H. Brown	6.14.49
10. D. C. Hartley	6.15.05

1973 COMRADES MARATHON
FIRST CAPE TOWN VICTORY

In the build-up to this year's event, it was clear that a resurgence of interest had been generated by the 1972 race, which had emphasised a growing international dimension. It was now five years since the race had last produced a South African-born winner, Jackie Mekler. Was Comrades being taken over by foreigners? Twenty-five years later, a similar concern would be raised as Russians and others threatened to dominate the professional era.

In 1973, there was no question of professionalism. True-blue amateurism was regarded as essential to the integrity of sport. Furthermore, no sporting occasion was more highly regarded for its noble idealism than the Comrades Marathon. There was, however, a patriotic fervour that virtually demanded that a South African once again take pride of place in capturing the nation's most admired and coveted crown, that of Comrades champion.

It was soon clear that another foreign assault, though perhaps not as well orchestrated as that of 1972, was on the cards. Defending champion Mick Orton of Tipton Harriers was a surprise late entry. After his maiden success the previous year, he had indicated that his Comrades career was over. Thousands of others have expressed similar sentiments only, like Orton, to return – over and over again, in many cases. Such is the call of Comrades!

Orton was back. Furthermore, he brought with him a bevy of top-class British athletes, including his Tipton Harriers teammate Ken Rock and the great Scottish athlete Alistair Wood. Wood had beaten Orton into second place in the 1972 London-to-Brighton race, finishing in a new record time. He certainly looked the part of a top British runner who had triumphed over another top British runner, who just happened to be the defending Comrades champion. The British contingent were certainly in the picture with a realistic chance of success.

There was, however, another previous London-to-Brighton winner in the field. He was a South African. University of Cape Town athlete Dave Levick had himself set a course record in the 1971 London-to-Brighton race. Levick had also demonstrated his fitness and strength in this year's Two Oceans Marathon, coming second behind record-breaking Don Hartley. Both had entered Comrades. Each was considered a potential winner.

South Africa's traditional bugbear, the question of skin colour, featured strongly in discussion before, during and after this year's race. The dilemma was easy to identify: government policy was all about segregation, and Comrades fostered integration. The solution, obvious in the long term, was not easy to apply in the short term, so black athletes, as well as women, continued to take part unofficially. It was by no means satisfactory. Those who have travelled the Comrades journey and have suffered its unique pain can only marvel at the extraordinary fortitude and resolution of those whose similar achievements were officially unrewarded.

The issue was real, even if it was seldom expressed. When it was mentioned, it was usually in muted tones, as evidenced by the following excerpt from a Natal newspaper editorial:

'There has always been something special about the Comrades, qualities summed up in the very name, which says it all. Let it also be said that as long as these qualities endure, the event and those who organise it or participate in it, have nothing to fear from the currents of social change in which the race has, like so many other South African institutions, been caught up. If viewed with a sense of tolerance and historical perspective, and handled wisely, the impending changes can only enrich the spirit of the Comrades. And happily there is plenty of evidence that out on the road at least, where this motley band of comrades annually share their agonies and their triumphs, there is both the capacity and the desire for sensible change.'

Somewhat more forthright was the Comrades multi-winner Hardy Ballington, whose comments were more enlightened in the context of 1973 than they seem from today's perspective:

'Before the war, non-whites used to have their own annual race between Durban and Maritzburg. I believe that the non-whites should again organise their own event, but that the top ten runners to finish should be allowed to compete in the white Comrades on an official basis. By the same token, the leading whites from the Comrades should compete in the non-white race, also as official entrants.'

The pattern of this year's race was set almost from the start. On the descent of Polly Shortts, defending champion Mick Orton suddenly shot to the front, clearly determined to pulverise his opponents and take control in the early stages. Sprinting down Polly Shortts certainly conflicts with accepted Comrades wisdom. Knowledgeable commentators raised their eyebrows, but had to admit that Orton and his Tipton Harriers teammates had prevailed the previous year despite their unorthodox approach. Orton would either teach Comrades hopefuls a new lesson or learn a painful one himself.

After 15 kilometres, Orton's lead was already half a kilometre. At Camperdown, he was four minutes (a full kilometre) ahead of Gordon Baker and Alistair Wood, who were keeping each other company. Levick was running in a group close behind them. At Cato Ridge, the flying Orton had stretched his advantage to five and a half minutes. At Drummond, the lead was eight minutes. A record was clearly on the cards.

Sporting legs that looked suitable for the front row of a scrum, Orton powered his way up the formidable Botha's Hill. Most of the hard climbing now behind him, he reached the top almost three kilometres ahead of his nearest rival, Gordon Baker. Through Hillcrest and all along the fairly benign stretch to Kloof, he looked strong, confident and totally in control.

Perhaps it was Field's Hill that changed things. On the other hand, it might have been the rather reckless dash down Polly Shortts in the early stages. Whatever the cause, Orton's lead at the bottom of Field's Hill had been reduced to seven minutes. It was still a substantial advantage, almost two kilometres with just over 20 kilometres to go. Nevertheless the challenge of Comrades is largely about making maximum use of fading strength. How much fuel was left in the Orton tank?

Orton dragged his weary body over Cowies Hill. The fluency in his stride, the jauntiness of his body language were no longer there. He was in survival mode and his speed was slower than that of his pursuers, although they were beset with their own travails. At Westville, Durban's Chris Hoogsteden was just over five minutes adrift of the leader. The gap was closing, but

Hoogsteden was running on an empty tank himself.

On the ascent of 45th Cutting, with about ten kilometres left, Gordon Baker moved past the shuffling Hoogsteden and took over second place. He was informed that Orton was in trouble and realised that a lifetime's opportunity was beckoning. Well placed and biding his time sensibly, Baker now moved strongly and steadily up to the shoulder of the early leader. When he passed him with seemingly effortless ease, the crestfallen Orton was reduced to a beaten walk-shuffle routine.

With just over five kilometres to go, Baker could hardly believe his good fortune. He was about to win the Comrades Marathon, or so he thought. Unbeknown to him, another challenger was about to make his effort.

Prior to the race, Cape Town student Dave Levick had encouraged his fellow Capetonians with inspiring words born of his own experience: 'It's a long and hilly race, but on race day there are many, many people camouflaging it. So relax the first 30 miles, make jokes, talk – but, whatever the outcome, enjoy the race.'

For much of the event, Levick appeared to be ignoring his own advice. There was little to suggest that his Comrades was a particularly enjoyable occasion. Although never too far behind the leaders, he experienced bad patches and was overtaken by others. Here and there throughout the day, he seemed well placed for a top-five finish but nothing more.

Almost without warning, Levick passed a walking Orton and was told that he was moving faster than the leader. He later recalled the moment when his miracle suddenly seemed possible: 'I smelt the possibility of a win and my strength came flooding back.'

Baker was closing in on the stadium and mentally composing his acceptance speech when he was suddenly rendered speechless. Too late, his attendants warned him of Levick's threat. He later described his anguish: 'I nearly fell on my back. I didn't know he was anywhere near me. I turned around and there he was coming. He went past me with a tap on my back and that was that.'

With just over two kilometres to the end, the result was settled. Levick had timed his challenge to perfection and crossed the line at the new finish venue, the sports stadium at the University of Natal. Exultantly, he described his feelings: 'I still can't believe it. I only wish my mother could have been here. What an indescribable feeling! I'm thrilled to have won the Comrades. It was a great finish and I enjoyed the race immensely. I felt surprisingly fresh in the late stages, which could have been due to the drop to sea level.' At long last, Cape Town had produced a Comrades champion. Furthermore, Levick was the new record holder. His time of 5.39.09 was 6 minutes 26 seconds faster than Bagshaw's 1969 effort.

Gordon Baker managed to hang on to second place with McBrearty third. The vanquished Orton limped home fifth, exactly nine minutes behind Levick. Now firmly committed to the great race, he promised, 'I'll be back in 1975 for the 50th Comrades Marathon.'

Comrades traditions were growing in importance. The Durban Savages team of McBrearty, Preiss, Kay and Gerber won the Gunga Din trophy. Among those who achieved immortality by earning their 'in perpetuity' green numbers were such Comrades legends as Gerry Treloar, Tim Blankley and Mick Winn.

One Comrades stalwart who endured a rather difficult day was 64-year-old Vernon Jones, running his last Comrades. In the vicinity of Camperdown, he took a tumble, injuring an ankle and badly cutting a hand on barbed-wire fencing as he struggled to stay upright. At the top of Botha's Hill, he again fell heavily and suffered ugly lacerations as well as bumping his head. Undeterred, but in great discomfort, he persevered and was rewarded with his 17th and final medal in 10.35.00.

The unofficial runners also showed their mettle. Female athletes Maureen Holland, Mavis Hutchison, Elizabeth Cavanagh and Lettie van Zyl finished well within the time limit. Zwelitsha Gono, a 21-year-old student, was the first black runner, followed closely by Simon Mkhize. Sadly, Sam Draai (already a Comrades legend) gave up halfway. An interesting comment on the denial of official status to black runners came from winner Dave Levick: 'The more exclusive a race, the less meaning it has.'

1973 COMRADES MARATHON RESULTS

1. D. Levick	5.39.09
2. G. R. Baker	5.42.53
3. J. P. McBrearty	5.46.18
4. J. J. Sutherland	5.47.49

5. M. Orton	5.48.09
6. C. C. Hoogsteden	5.48.49
7. T. Parry	5.52.17
8. D. C. Preiss	5.54.35
9. R. B. Gardner	5.56.09
10. D. H. Carter-Brown	5.59.42

12

DEREK PREISS –
THE ONE-MAN BAND
(1974 to 1975)

When Comrades aficianados contemplate those special runners who have contributed more than just victory, more than special athletic performance, some names stand out. One is that of Derek Preiss, a man whose performances in 1974 and 1975 have not been approached, let alone surpassed.

Comrades wisdom, built up over 80 years, states emphatically that it is just about impossible to compete successfully in two ultramarathons as close together as Two Oceans and Comrades. In the 1980s, Bruce Fordyce would firmly establish his view of peaking, running only two major events per year with sufficient time between the two to rest and recover before attempting the second challenge. Even he found that prudence eventually ruled out the second event if he wished to give full attention to his one major event, generally Comrades.

There are, of course, those who arrive on the scene with an ability and a maturity that set them apart from others of their or any other generation. Derek Preiss was such a runner. In a short period at the very top, spanning just two years, Preiss established standards of excellence that place him in a category all his own. On 13 April 1974, Preiss set a new Two Oceans Marathon record of 3.21.40. On Friday, 1 June, just less than seven weeks later, he became the first runner in history to achieve a Two Oceans and Comrades double win. His time of 6.02.49 was not remarkable, but his achievement was.

The following year, Preiss did even better. Once again, he won the Two Oceans Marathon, successfully meeting the challenge of Scotsman Allister Wood, world record holder for 40 miles on track, as well as record holder for the London-to-Brighton race, having beaten Dave Levick's record by more than ten minutes in 1972.

Preiss chose the Golden Jubilee Comrades Marathon, held on 31 May 1975, as the day on which he would stake his claim for everlasting glory. Despite the exhaustion that inevitably accompanied his second successive 'double' (which no other man has achieved before or since), he set the third-fastest 'up' run to date.

Two other runners staked their claims for historical recognition. The popular Lesotho athlete Vincent Rakabaele became the first official black finisher, taking 20th place in a time of 6.21. The women's race was won, officially for the first time, by Elizabeth Cavanagh in 10.08.

1974 COMRADES MARATHON
NOT A HAPPY YEAR

South African newspaper readers will testify that the country has, over the years, been dominated by two forces, rugby and politics. This year, both were at the forefront of the nation's consciousness. Both would play significant roles in the escalating racial polarisation within which the Comrades Marathon community gradually came to the uncomfortable realisation that all was not well in the world of Comrades.

For rugby followers, the visit of the 1974 British Lions shattered long-held beliefs that Springbok rugby had a right (for some, a divine right) to achieve victory over all challengers. Willie-John McBride's visitors became the first team in the 20th century to defeat South Africa in a four-match home series. Opponents such as Gareth Edwards, J. P. R. Williams, Fergus Slattery, J. J. Williams, Phil Bennett and the skipper himself became better known to South Africans than our own Springboks. Never before had such humiliation been inflicted on a country that measured its state of health in terms of the gold price and rugby results.

The Comrades Marathon had its own problem, the familiar South African one of race. There were various forces at play. From day one, under Vic Clapham's leadership, the ethos of Comrades had encompassed all that its name suggested. It was, by nature, all-inclusive. Yet this inclusivity existed only in an unofficial, peripheral manner in a country whose laws were based on a philosophy of racial exclusivity.

For much of the 20th century, South African – and, indeed, Western – culture had been built around unquestioning discipline. The two World Wars had been won, in the minds of participants, by heroic soldiers, sailors and airmen who obeyed the great military dictum, 'Wait, obey and don't think.'

In the aftermath of the Second World War, South Africa took the opposite road to that of its wartime allies. Most, horrified by the racism of Hitler and the Holocaust, took steps to protect the rights of all, minorities and majorities alike. Despite that fact that South Africa's wartime leader, General J. C. Smuts, had played a major role in establishing the United Nations, the ruling National Party, after ousting Smuts's United Party, had adopted a policy of apartheid uncomfortably reminiscent of Nazism.

As the world moved into the mid-1970s, the times, as Bob Dylan told us, were a-changing. Instead of having to fight desperately for survival through war and depression, nations enjoyed unprecedented prosperity. 'Make love, not war!' became an international slogan. Flower power and Woodstock were terms that signified a new attitude to authority. Suddenly it was right to ask the question 'Why?' and expect an answer. Why were Americans dying in Vietnam? Why were women and black athletes excluded from the Comrades Marathon?

Younger generations tend to ask searching questions of their elders with devastating timing, as parents know. The Comrades organising club, the Collegians Harriers of Pietermaritzburg, were as ill-prepared as any bewildered parents when challenging questions became confrontational demands. In fairness, they couldn't win: while they sympathised with those whose expectation of non-racialism reflected true Comrades culture, they were subject to a government and a legal system strongly opposed to radical change.

This was without doubt the most controversial year in the history of the great race. Many Comrades regulars remember 1974 with a good deal of displeasure. The media, quite naturally, were happy to report and encourage controversy. Differing viewpoints were published. Some stressed, quite correctly, that the unique spirit of Comrades did not lend itself to racial discrimination. Others, sympathetic to this argument but with a slightly different agenda, emphasised the importance of non-racialism as a prerequisite to readmission to the Olympic Games.

Those who favoured retention of the status quo spoke of the need to operate within the laws of the country. Even though these were changing, government directives still required separate change-rooms, social facilities and toilets. Fear of numbers loomed large in the minds of those who resisted change. 'The numbers game' was a phrase used frequently by frightened whites who were concerned that their favourite annual event might eventually be swamped by those they failed to recognise as fellow South Africans.

Prior to race day, various approaches were mooted: two equal but different races on the same day; black armbands to be worn by those advocating change (seven years later, a black armband would win the race and the hearts of the nation); the use of motor vehicles to disrupt the race; and so on. The organising club held a referendum among members. By a large majority, it was decided to continue the race as a whites-only event. While the decision, in retrospect, invites condemnation, it can be said in its defence that many of the club's members were in favour of total inclusivity, but felt that such change would be premature, and that a defiant disregard of government policy would jeopardise the entire future of Comrades.

Perhaps the heated debate stimulated interest in Comrades, for a record entry of 1 557 was received. Among the well-known entrants were boxer Bernie Taylor, canoeist Graeme Pope-Ellis (already a multiple champion) and South Africa's 'galloping granny', Mavis Hutchison. Hardy Ballington, five-time winner and one of the true Comrades greats, died shortly before race day.

Of the 1 557 entries, 1 350 (another record) reported for duty outside the Durban City Hall on Friday, 31 May. The feared political protests did not materialise. Unofficial black runner Vincent Rakabaele, later to represent Lesotho in the Olympic Games and become the first black winner of the Two Oceans Marathon, briefly demonstrated his considerable prowess by taking the early lead.

Rakabaele's tenure at the front was, despite his considerable ability, somewhat brief. Merv Myhill, a local runner, took over, but not for long. R. K. Brimelow, a Johannesburg visitor, claimed the lead in Westville and maintained his advantage over the first major obstacle, Cowies Hill. Going through Pinetown, Brimelow remained in control, with Rakabaele and poet Derek van Eeden in close attendance.

A local radio station, Radio Port Natal, arranged for progress reports to be supplied by helicopter, another indication of growing public interest in the race. The spy in the sky was able to observe the relentless advance of the determined leader, Brimelow, who passed through Hillcrest four minutes ahead of Two Oceans legend Don Hartley. Also visible was Rakabaele, who was right up with the leaders, but not for long. His challenge faded halfway.

Brimelow, still going strongly, went through Drummond in 2.55.05. Don Hartley, whose Two Oceans record had been broken by Westville's 21-year-old Derek Preiss earlier in the year, was second, three minutes behind the leader, with Koos Sutherland, third, a further minute adrift. Seven minutes behind Brimelow, a quartet comprising Baker, Hoogsteden, Preiss and the novice Alan Robb remained just in contention.

For once, Inchanga did not bring a radical change in fortunes. Still looking comfortable, Brimelow actually increased his lead slightly. Behind him, there was little change, although Preiss put in a brief surge and then dropped back, clearly experiencing a bad patch. At Cato Ridge, two-thirds into the race, Brimelow still held a three-minute lead over Hartley, with Sutherland a further two minutes back. Preiss, now fully recovered, had moved up to fourth and was running strongly.

The section from Cato Ridge to Camperdown is one of the most difficult parts of the course, even though it may not look all that demanding. It was here that the battle for supremacy began to develop. At Camperdown,

Hartley and Sutherland, now running together, were just a minute behind the leader. Preiss was a further three minutes back, with Baker and Robb a minute behind him.

Hartley was the first casualty. When he sat down and rested at the roadside, his dream of victory was over. Sutherland, freed of his erstwhile companion, soon claimed the lead and forged ahead. Demoralised, Brimelow was reduced to walking at times, and shortly yielded second place to Preiss. Understandably, Brimelow, struggling with physical and mental pain, started to slip back. Robb moved up into third place.

Victory would almost certainly be contested by Sutherland and Preiss. At Lion Park, Sutherland was two minutes ahead. At the foot of Little Pollys (Ashburton), the lead was two and a half minutes. He appeared to be drawing away, but there was another formidable obstacle to be overcome.

At the foot of the dreaded Polly Shortts, Sutherland's advantage was one and a half minutes. Preiss was making inroads. On the ascent, Sutherland maintained a consistent, businesslike stride. Preiss, however, had moved into overdrive. Already feared as a fast finisher, he now had the bit between his teeth. No leader of a Comrades 'up' run at the top of Polly Shortts had yet been overtaken on the run-in to the finish. It was shortly before the crest that Preiss, demonstrably the stronger of the two, shot past the tiring Sutherland and sprinted for glory.

There was no stopping Preiss now, as he surged to victory in 6.02.49, with the Vanderbijlpark runner Sutherland gamely hanging on to second place. Interviewed after the race, Preiss made the same error that so many others have made when he said, 'Definitely not again. The Comrades is not for me. I favour the shorter races up to the standard marathon distance. I'm delighted to have won. I decided to lie handy until Drummond and push things a little bit in the later stages. I didn't feel at all well for much of the race. My problem was really my hands, feet and face around my mouth, which became pretty numb. It was rather bad over the last 20 kilometres. I couldn't feel the road properly. I didn't fancy my chances of winning, but, once I saw Koos Sutherland was in trouble on the top of Polly Shortts, I felt I could do it.' Preiss became the first athlete to win both Two Oceans and Comrades in the same year.

Alan Robb, the 20-year-old Germiston Callies newcomer, claimed third spot less than four minutes behind the winner. In so doing, he claimed the Hardy Ballington trophy for first novice. Despite his youth, Robb ran a remarkably mature race, following the experienced Gordon Baker until he felt the confidence to make his own move. While he was noted as one to watch in the future, few would have realised that they had just witnessed the debut of an athlete who would become one of the great Comrades legends.

While defending champion Dave Levick's half-hearted approach included a beer on Polly Shortts, his Cape Town rival Don Hartley had pushed himself to the limit, eventually taking 13th place. In typically eloquent style, he described the mental trauma of the last few kilometres: 'My leaden stride, laden with pain. The mind weakly calculated the time. Seconds slip by. My attendant, unknowing, urges me on, tells me I'm slowing down too much. I am blank. I drink. I run. My legs are jellyfish floating along this never-ending canal. I'm strongly aware of everything. The people stare. Do they know? My small world of pain jerks along. There, at last, is the end.'

1974 COMRADES MARATHON RESULTS

1. D. C. Preiss		6.02.49
2. J. J. Sutherland		6.04.25
3. A. G. Robb		6.06.45
4. G. R. Baker		6.12.32
5. B. Gerber		6.13.37
6. T. Parry		6.14.25
7. D. A. Rogers		6.18.19
8. F. J. van Eeden		6.21.47
9. R. K. Brimelow		6.23.22
10. H. B. Saayman		6.27.21

1975 COMRADES MARATHON
FIFTY YEARS – AND A 'DOUBLE' DOUBLE

The Golden Jubilee running of the Comrades Marathon featured many changes, some permanent and welcome, others thankfully discarded since. Perhaps the least controversial issue was the decision to reverse the direction of the race. Traditionally, 'down' runs took place in odd-numbered years and 'up' runs in even-numbered years. In recognition of the part that Pietermaritzburg had played in the establishment of the race, it was decided that the 50th marathon should finish there, meaning two 'up' runs in successive years. A minor tradition was broken.

The second alteration was the opening up of the race to black and female runners. This was also relatively uncontroversial, although there were obviously some South Africans who opposed such a reversal of the country's political policy. These individuals did not represent the true spirit of Comrades, as established right from the start in 1921.

The real controversy lay in the decision to limit the number of competitors to 1 500 runners who had completed a standard marathon within 4 hours 30 minutes. This was anathema to Comrades traditionalists, many of whom, legends of the great race, made their feelings known. Blind runner Ian Jardine, oldest finisher on no fewer than 13 occasions, lamented, 'This is the end of the Comrades Marathon. It will never be the same again.' Mr Comrades himself, Liege Boulle, with 36 medals to his credit, commented that the whole spirit of the race was being ruined by the restrictions: 'There will be no more atmosphere and the race will die slowly.'

Gentle giant Nick Raubenheimer, veteran of 21 successful runs which included six gold medals, pronounced his judgement in eloquent fashion: 'Gone are the days when a man walked into his local pub and bet his mate a case of beer that he could not make it as far as Drummond. That is how many of us came to be running and it is the way things should be still. But these are the sort of men, the bar-room betters, the new regulations will keep out. Those left out must be in the throes of utter dejection, and only a runner knows how it feels. Arthur Newton's ghost must be undergoing a pretty bad patch in the celestial joggers' stadium.'

One of the most poignant criticisms came in the form of a letter from a parent to a local newspaper:

'My son's continuing effort over the past year to train in rain and shine takes a deep dedication. He has lost all excess weight, looks trim and healthwise he is a different person. To what purpose? To compete with the other joggers in that goal of all joggers – the Comrades Marathon. But now he has been told that his time is not quite good enough and that he cannot run. He is quite lost. After being geared for a year towards this goal, the let-down is terrible. Surely, for this one day in the year, and a public holiday at that, motorists can allow the runners (all of them) on the road and not complain about it.'

Mick Winn, chairman of Collegians Harriers, the organisers, attempted to justify the limitation while, as a Comrades runner himself, voicing his heartfelt sympathy for those who were excluded from taking part:

'We all agree it would be fantastic to see the Comrades Marathon with a field of 5 000 as the world's greatest road race. We were, however, faced with the choice of cutting the field down ourselves or facing a far more drastic restriction by the provincial and municipal road authorities. Restricting the numbers is a sad necessity. I feel sorry for the chaps who plead to be accepted after they have missed the qualifying standard by a minute or two, and it's especially rough if they have run 2 000 kilometres in preparation.'

Local government and the organising committee had inadvertently conspired to produce an event largely bereft of the unique Comrades spirit that unites those who respond to the Comrades call. While women and athletes of colour were rightly welcomed into the bosom of the race, others were excluded by the arbitrary cut-off. Comradeship had been denied to potential Comrades in the past on race and gender grounds. In the very year that these unjustified impediments were set aside, the 'numbers game' came into play.

Records disclose that 1 686 entries were received, of which 186 were rejected in order to bring the field down to the required number. Of those 1 500, only 1 352 started the race. If we add the 186 who were discarded to those who took part, we reach a figure of 1 538, just 38 over the prescribed ceiling. Who could blame those who felt somewhat miffed by their non-acceptance?

There was a further mishap, perhaps symbolic of the bizarre effects of unnatural classification, which was what apartheid was all about. Present-day runners would find it extraordinary that race labels were given to black runners in order to identify them by ethnic group, for instance as Xhosa or Zulu. As if this indignity was not repulsive enough, there were insufficient Zulu labels, and some Zulu runners were given Xhosa labels, to their extreme dissatisfaction. Black South Africans had been required to carry passbooks, reflecting their inferior status in their own country. The insensitive tagging of black runners in 1975 was one of the low points of Comrades history. It should be fully recognised that this abominable action came, not from the organisers, but from politically motivated officials who could hardly call themselves 'Comrades'.

With television lights and cameras on hand, the 1 352 starters responded to the official pistol shot and the traditional cockcrow from Max Trimborn and began their demanding journey. First to take the lead in this, the inaugural open Comrades, was, quite appropriately, a black South African, Pius Khumalo, a Durban policeman, who had the identifying word 'Zulu' tagged to his running vest. He clung to the lead throughout Pinetown and Westville.

On the ascent of Cowies Hill, a gentle and pleasant incline for those who are properly prepared, regular Comrades runner Dave Rogers relieved Khumalo of the front spot. Rogers went through Pinetown with a lead of 200 metres, but his advantage was short-lived. On the ascent of Field's Hill, longest and steepest of all the event's fearsome obstacles, last year's first novice, Alan Robb, took over and reached the top with a lead of half a minute over the semi-defeated Rogers.

Comrades spectators had their first glimpse of Alan Robb in the lead, a spectacle they would become accustomed to in forthcoming years. Robb went through Drummond in 2.56, with McBrearty and Van Eeden less than a minute behind. Defending champion Derek Preiss was handily placed, looking cheerful and full of running.

Inchanga has proved the undoing of many an overenthusiastic halfway leader. This year, the man in the firing line was the promising Johannesburg youngster Alan Robb. Robb, tough as teak right from the start of his Comrades career, moved steadily up the daunting hill, but had clearly lost the spring in his very individualistic stride. Had he gone out too fast? He certainly wasn't the type to give up and retained a lead of one minute as he crested Inchanga.

Defending champion Derek Preiss was now in second place. On the descent of Inchanga and through the undulating Harrison Flats, Preiss moved closer to the leader and, at the most appropriate moment, shot past him and drew away at some speed. The crestfallen Robb was vulnerable to further attack from the rear. At Cato Ridge, with one-third to go, Preiss led from Sutherland, Shaw and McBrearty, with Robb down in fifth place.

The leading quintet, although spaced fairly well apart, maintained their positions until Camperdown. Here Preiss, in 4.07, was three minutes ahead of Sutherland and Shaw, who were running together. McBrearty, Robb, Levick, Van Eeden, Deeney, Brimelow, Blankley, Rogers, Atkins and De Swart were all within 12 minutes of leader Preiss. Lesotho runner Vincent Rakabaele was 30th, 24 minutes behind Preiss. The stage seemed set for a photo-finish, although Rakabaele was now too far back to be regarded as a potential winner.

Preiss decided to make the finish line judges' job as easy as possible. Over Ashburton and on the descent thereafter, he extended his lead significantly. At the foot of Polly Shortts, he was six minutes ahead of second-placed Shaw, with Sutherland another two minutes further back.

When Preiss crested Polly Shortts with a substantial advantage over his nearest rival, the race was effectively over. In 1974, he had become the first athlete to win the double: both Two Oceans and Comrades. Twelve months later, he repeated the feat, and he remains the only male runner to have done so once, never mind twice.

After the race, Preiss explained his strategy: 'I had no set plan other than to hold back earlier on to see what the other runners would do, how they intended to run their race, who would set the pace and who would blow up. In the Camperdown area, I was worried about Levick's fast finish, so I pushed ahead hard. Pollys I did not find too bad. Although this year I thought I would have to push myself hard to win, I ended up feeling fresher than in previous years. Running in a different make of shoe, I had less pins-and-needles sensation in my feet. All in all it was an enjoyable run.'

Second-placed Gordon Shaw also expressed satisfied sentiments: 'I've never felt so good. Tired, but not that excruciating, painful tiredness that is normally the Comrades story. The biggest thrill in my life was in passing Dave Levick near Drummond. Nobody passed me in the race. Running through Westville with Derek Preiss, I wondered how a man like him ever won the Comrades. Little did I know. He's a better man than I am!'

Vincent Rakabaele, 30th at Camperdown, powered his way through the field in the closing stages to finish 20th in 6.27. He would never win Comrades, but his top-class effort reflected a rare talent that would flower in other events. He would, for instance, take first place in the Two Oceans Marathon in 1976 and 1979.

The women's event produced a rather interesting question about the value of qualifying times. Three women started the race. Mavis Hutchison pulled out shortly after halfway. Lettie van Zyl became the first woman to cross the finish line in a year in which women could run officially. Unfortunately her achievement, in the excellent time of 8 hours 50 minutes, was not recognised, as she had been unable to meet qualifying standards. Elizabeth Cavanagh, in 10 hours 8 minutes, became the first official female finisher.

Past winners Allen Boyce, Mercer Davies, George Claassen, Tommy Malone, Bernard Gomersall, Dave Bagshaw, Dave Levick and Derek Preiss all took part in this Golden Jubilee run. Other former champions – Darrell Dale, Wally Hayward, Bill Cochrane, Trevor Allen, Gerald Walsh, Jackie Mekler and Manie Kuhn – graced the occasion with their presence.

1975 COMRADES MARATHON RESULTS

1. D. C. Preiss	5.53.50
2. G. W. Shaw	6.03.15
3. J. J. Sutherland	6.06.40
4. J. P. McBrearty	6.07.25
5. A. G. Robb	6.09.24
6. D. A. Rogers	6.10.14
7. D. Levick	6.11.00
8. F. J. van Eeden	6.12.26
9. T. E. Blankley	6.12.48
10. R. G. Deeny	6.13.35

1975 COMRADES MARATHON WOMEN'S RESULTS

1. E. C. Cavanagh	10.08

13

THE ALAN ROBB ERA
(1976 to 1980)

The Comrades Marathon is so integral a part of South Africa's annual sporting calendar that one almost forgets the threats to the survival of the race as recently as 1976.

The problem wasn't a lack of interest, a shortage of athletes willing to take part. In fact, it was the precise opposite. The number of runners and supporters, and consequently motor vehicles on the route, was becoming a safety hazard. It was so serious that a newspaper launched a 'Save the Comrades Marathon' campaign.

Happily, the move to protect the great race was well received. Equally positive were two separate initiatives by medical researchers from Cape Town and Natal universities that would, in time, promote the benefits of a healthy, exercise-related lifestyle. In particular, Cape Town's running doctor Tim Noakes was emerging as a future world leader in the field of sports science.

On 16 June 1976, black children in Soweto protested against the imposition of the Afrikaans language in their schools. The ensuing violence reflected the rejection by black South Africans of the entire apartheid system and the unsustainability of racial domination of the majority of South Africans by a minority whose ideological hold on the population was undermined by wholesome activities such as the Comrades Marathon.

With the ill-judged ban on black and female runners now consigned to history, those previously barred from Comrades demonstrated, through their performances, the ridiculous nature of previous regulations. Black South Africans would henceforth strengthen the event with their talent, dignity and patriotism. Women would shatter misconceptions when sports scientists were forced to admit that, the longer an endurance event, the more competitive women became in relation to their male counterparts.

One runner totally dominated this era. Alan Robb was significantly more competitive than any of his rivals. When he was at his peak, all others raced for second place. Very few athletes display such mastery in their peak years. Robb's victory in the 1978 'down' run remains one of the top Comrades performances.

Yet Robb's domination of his era was not limited to athletic excellence, nor was his tenure at the top his sole, or even his major, contribution to Comrades. For many Comrades followers, Alan Robb personified the idealism of Vic Clapham, Arthur Newton and the race itself in his impeccable sportsmanship, respect for his fellow competitors and total commitment to the spirit that belongs uniquely to Comrades. He remains an excellent runner, still capable of a silver medal. In fact, a finish by Alan Robb, wearing his customary red socks and Liverpool Football Club hat, continues to be one of the highlights for those fortunate enough to be at the stadium.

Any regular sporting event needs not only the successes of those whose brilliance illuminates the occasion, but also the occasional triumph of the surprise winner. In 1979, Piet Vorster's win was unexpected yet highly meritorious, and enduringly highlighted by the record that he set.

Television, to a minor extent, recorded the achievements of the second half of the 1970s, but the real involvement of television in Comrades commenced in the 1980s. Alan Robb provided a foretaste of the forthcoming media feast.

1976 COMRADES MARATHON
THE ROBB ERA BEGINS

If the limit of 1 500 entrants caused consternation in 1975, the build-up to the 1976 race was even more controversial. The burgeoning numbers of motor vehicles on and around the Comrades course created a nightmare for traffic officials. Despite the regard in which the race was held nationally, its future was in jeopardy, so much so that the *Sunday Tribune* newspaper convened a 'Save the Comrades Marathon' symposium. Good sense prevailed, and it was decided that the race would continue indefinitely, with prudent management of motorised transport.

This was also a significant rugby year. Andy Leslie's All Blacks invaded the country in an attempt to become the first New Zealanders to win a test series in South Africa. They brought a capable and exciting side, but their efforts were in vain.

In the world of long-distance running, women were becoming more active in marathons and ultramarathons. The general view was that women would always lag far behind men, but nobody was really sure. In 1976, the men's world record for the standard marathon was 2.08.33, set by Australian Derek Clayton in May 1969. The women's record, belonging to American Jacqueline Hansen, stood at 2.38.19. In South Africa, the gap was even greater: medical student Ferdie le Grange had produced a best time of 2.12.47 in 1974, almost an hour faster than the 3.05.02 set by Suzanne Gaylard. There was, however, a significant difference between the two: Gaylard was only 15 years old. It was still early days, but South African women runners were on the move.

In the mid-1970s, as the worldwide running explosion reached significant numbers, medical experts were starting to research the benefits of sustained physical exercise. Two medical faculties decided to study the 1976 Comrades Marathon: the University of Cape Town's Ischaemic Heart Disease Laboratory was looking into coronary disease while the University of Natal Medical School focused on renal problems and fluid consumption. Runners had long believed in the positive effects of their lifestyles, and many members of the medical profession were enthusiastic disciples of the sport. In this year of medical investigation, there was an added safeguard, as Comrades legend Nick Raubenheimer commented: 'There would be so many doctors running that it was a comforting thought that at any moment in time, there would almost certainly be a doctor either with, just behind or just ahead of you.'

Firm favourite for this year's race was defending champion Derek Preiss, aiming to become the third person to achieve a hat-trick after Arthur Newton and Dave Bagshaw. Preiss wouldn't be able to repeat his 1974 and 1975 feat of winning both Two Oceans and Comrades, because a hamstring problem had confined him to third place in the recent Two Oceans. Now well recovered, he would surely take some beating in the Comrades.

New Two Oceans champion Gabashane Vincent Rakabaele was clearly a big threat. Twentieth in his debut last year, he had the confidence of knowing that he had vanquished both Preiss and second-placed Alan Robb in the Cape race. Would he become Comrades' first black winner? If so, he would be warmly acclaimed. Following his Two Oceans victory, Charlie Savage wrote in the *Sunday Times*, 'Gabashane Rakabaele, the 26-year-old from Marievale in the Transvaal, won three trophies and a million hearts yesterday.'

Alan Robb, beaten by Rakabaele by just six seconds in the Two Oceans, was another who had the credentials to challenge for line honours. Already a Korkie champion, he had displayed consistency, mental strength and significant speed in his two Comrades runs to date. Another to be watched was 28-year-old Cavin Woodward from Leamington in England. World record holder for 50 and 100 miles and current London-to-Brighton champion, he had taken fourth spot in Two Oceans. His record suggested that the extra distance of Comrades would suit him, although his pre-race comments did raise a few eyebrows. Claiming that his motto was to run as fast as he could for as long as he could, he said that he would 'start fast, carve a lead and hold it'. Most Comrades pundits did not regard such tactics as advisable.

Ian Jardine, one of the greatest of all Comrades characters, died a few months before race day. Not only was Jardine the oldest person on record to have completed the race, he had also won the Founder's Trophy as the oldest finisher 13 times. Even more remarkably, he had achieved this despite requiring a sighted 'pilot' to guide him through the course. Such incredible commitment inspired another Comrades stalwart, Denis Tabakin, to institute the Jardine Joggers (later to become affiliated to the Achilles Track Club), an organisation providing sighted runners to assist those unable to see. Vernon Jones eloquently captured Jardine's nature and contribution to road-running when he said, 'He will be remembered as a quietly spoken gentleman, a man of incomparable courage who made light of the great handicap of blindness.'

Rather unusually for Pietermaritzburg, runners reported to the start outside the City Hall in pleasant, almost warm, conditions. Extra clothing was discarded before the gun. When the race got under way, Englishman Cavin Woodward made good his stated pre-race intention by grabbing the early lead and extending it as rapidly as he could. At Umlaas Road, he was five minutes clear. By Camperdown, the lead was up to six minutes. Preiss, Atkins, Hensman, Robb, Rakabaele, Hoogsteden, Rogers, Ashworth, Qokweni and Gerber shared second place, a group of ten who were unsure whether to watch each other or to chase the flying Englishman.

On the relatively easy stretch from Camperdown to Cato Ridge, Woodward maintained his advantage. Wearing sunglasses, he continued his domination through Harrison Flats. Then he faced two formidable obstacles. Inchanga loomed, a climb as daunting as any to be found on just about any course. At the same time, as the morning continued to unfold, the hot South African sun began to exact its toll. For the first time, Woodward showed signs of discomfort. He kept going quite strongly, but his pursuers, for the first time, began to make inroads into his lead.

Although he was clearly under severe pressure, Woodward overcame the problem of Inchanga and went through halfway in 2.46.00. Hoogsteden, in second place, was still five minutes adrift, with Atkins, Preiss, Robb, Hensman, Ashworth and Rakabaele a further minute behind him. Now came the second half.

Botha's Hill proved to be the turning point. Although Woodward held on to first place, Hoogsteden was only 90 metres behind him at Hillcrest, with the formidable trio of Preiss, Robb and Rakabaele close behind. Then things changed rapidly. Hoogsteden went into the lead and enjoyed a fleeting moment of glory. Preiss, Robb and Rakabaele passed both earlier leaders. The threesome, all great runners, now controlled the destiny of the race. One of them would surely be the winner.

At Kloof, with the leading trio running shoulder to shoulder, a phenomenal battle seemed on the cards, but it didn't work out that way. Something better happened. On the descent of Field's Hill, Alan Robb made the move that would establish his career as one of the all-time greats of Comrades. A strong downhill runner, Robb surged ahead and entered Pinetown with a lead of one minute over Rakabaele and Hoogsteden, with Preiss a further minute behind them.

Robb had made his move. It was up to his pursuers to try to catch him, but only one seemed strong enough. Vincent Rakabaele, Robb's conqueror in the Two Oceans, went into overdrive as he raced through Pinetown, reducing Robb's lead quite significantly. As the leaders reached Cowies Hill, Robb was just 200 metres ahead. It was all that he needed. In customary style, he powered his way up the last of the major climbs as Rakabaele began to slow. Robb was now in full control, but not for too long.

Going through Westville, with officials and signboards conspicuously absent, Robb took a wrong turn. A spectator pointed out the error but Robb was advised by his seconds to keep going. Despite the fact that he was not responsible for the confusion, disqualification was considered. Thankfully, organising chairman Mick Winn ruled that his unfortunate detour had added to the distance he had covered. Robb's post-race comments were in agreement: 'I was running along the road when I came to a junction which seemed to fork about four different ways, and, as I didn't know the area, I took what seemed to be the most likely road. I think I may have added a couple of hundred metres to the distance.'

Extra distance or not, Germiston's Alan Robb became the new Comrades champion. He overcame the extension of an already extended course, the challenge of an exceptionally talented field and cramp, which caused him severe problems in the final few kilometres, as he later explained: 'I tore and bruised the tendons in my left foot. This, I think, must have happened over the last eight to ten kilometres. I was getting a lot of cramp in my leg, and so to try and get rid of it, I was stretching my foot and toes and moving my ankle around while running. I think this caused the injury. I felt very tired over the last few kilometres. I struggled up some of the hills, but I went down all of them very well. I can still hardly believe that I've won.' He certainly had won, and a new era in Comrades history had just begun.

The visiting Englishman, Cavin Woodward, displayed extreme courage in taking second place after his front-running strategy had failed him. Dave

Rogers of Westville claimed a superb third place. Vincent Rakabaele received warm applause when he finished in eighth place, as did Derek Preiss, the vanquished champion, who came in 14th.

The womens' race was not particularly exciting. Lettie van Zyl took first place in 9.05, 30 minutes ahead of Lettie Kleynhans. Their efforts did, however, inspire younger women, some of whom would play leading roles as future generations of local female athletes put South African women on the international map.

Capetonians enjoyed a successful trip to Natal this year. A contingent of 20 from Celtic Harriers managed 20 finishers. One of them, Mike Francis, completed his tenth Comrades. Another Capetonian, UCT's Tim Noakes, participating as athlete and medical researcher, finished in a creditable 117th place.

1976 COMRADES MARATHON RESULTS

1. A. G. Robb	5.40.43
2. C. Woodward	5.49.19
3. D. A. Rogers	5.52.41
4. J. J. Sutherland	5.53.26
5. S. Atkins	5.54.39
6. C. C. Hoogsteden	5.56.02
7. R. Ashworth	5.59.01
8. G. V. Rakabaele	5.59.02
9. D. L. Hensman	6.01.08
10. D. van Eeden	6.02.54

1976 COMRADES MARATHON WOMEN'S RESULTS

1. A. S. H. van Zyl	9.05
2. A. C. Kleynhans	9.35
3. L. C. Oberholzer	9.53

1977 COMRADES MARATHON
AN 'UP' RECORD FOR ROBB

Barely two weeks after the running of the 1976 Comrades Marathon, an event had taken place that would forever change both the country and the great race that pulsated to the heartbeat of the nation.

The deliberate denial of proper education to black South Africans had planted a resentment that was bound to grow and, at some point, explode. This happened on 16 June 1976, the catalyst being the imposition of the Afrikaans language as a medium of instruction in black schools.

What began as a protest march by schoolchildren in Soweto led to confrontation and violence that spread through much of the country. In the next six months, more than 500 died in the violence, according to official figures. One of the first schoolchildren to die was Hector Pieterson, whose lifeless body, carried by Mbuyisa Makhubu, was captured in an iconic photograph.

The pupils who lost their lives are today remembered as fallen heroes, and 16 June is commemorated as Youth Day. It is on this day that the Comrades Marathon was run from the mid-1990s until 2007, when a new breed of politicians interfered. The Comrades community sought to honour the memory of these victims of the Soweto uprising, just as they had remembered those who perished in the two world wars, the Korean War and the Angolan conflict.

By now, the world was unifying in opposition to South African racial discrimination. In the run-up to this year's Comrades, the International Amateur Athletics Federation issued a proclamation that effectively barred athletes from other nations from participating in the Comrades Marathon.

It would be incorrect to claim that the Comrades community was united and steadfast in opposing racism. Certainly, the ethos of Comrades, inherited from founder Vic Clapham, would have supported such a stance. However, there was also a strong feeling, in the country as a whole and within Comrades itself, that sport and politics should be kept separate. No matter how unjust prevailing laws may have been, such thinking went, they were still laws and had to be respected and obeyed. In 1981, a new Comrades champion would display a much less acquiescent attitude.

Meanwhile, the 1977 Comrades Marathon went ahead amid speculation that a new era of dominance by a super-athlete might be emerging. Such thoughts were not just figments of the imaginations of Comrades romantics. Alan Robb's superb win in the 1976 Comrades and his subsequent performances in other road races signified that a special talent had emerged.

The overall limit on the number of runners had been discarded, but the age restriction of 65 remained. Liege Boulle, who almost certainly would have become the first to achieve 40 medals, was disqualified by age. Organisers of ultramarathons were becoming more and more concerned that the growing popularity of such events, evidenced by ever-increasing fields, would result in unfit hopefuls risking their lives in pursuit of personal glory, which might reflect adversely on a race should their unwise efforts lead to serious health problems, or even death.

The 1977 result emphasised something that has not generally been recognised by Comrades followers. Alan Robb has been typecast over the years as a 'shuffler' whose style was tailor-made for downhill running. While there is some truth in this, Robb's very economical stride belied the fact that he was a very fast athlete, capable of victory in record time in both the 'up' and the 'down' races. His performances in 1977 and 1978 mark him as one of the true greats.

The morning of Tuesday, 31 May, was pleasantly cool as the record field of 1 963 went to the start. Max Trimborn started the race with his cockcrow, and then, his competitive days behind him, jogged along with the runners as they proceeded up Smith Street.

Even before the advent of television, there had been a tendency for some unfancied and rather unlikely runners to sprint into the lead and stake a claim for fleeting recognition. This time, the early front-runners had a distinctly serious look about them. Francis Koos, a talented novice, and Dolf Dampies from Paarl shared the lead with the redoubtable Gabashane Rakabaele, who had finished eighth the previous year. He had also won the 1976 Two Oceans Marathon, finishing just six seconds ahead of Alan Robb.

Rakabaele certainly had the credentials to challenge for line honours. Together with Koos, he led the field through Westville, ahead of a group that included defending champion Alan Robb. At the top of Field's Hill, Koos was marginally ahead of Dave Wright. Not far behind were Henry Nyembe, Rakabaele, Robb, Malcolm Ball, Anton de Koning, Tim Blankley and a host of highly capable performers.

Dave Wright was comfortably ahead when he crested Botha's Hill. Some two and a half minutes behind him came the formidable trio of Robb, Rakabaele and Steve Atkins, with Gordon Shaw not too far behind. It seemed likely that the winner would be one of this talented quintet. At Drummond, the order was unchanged, although Wright, the bit firmly between his teeth, had stretched his advantage to four minutes.

As ever, Inchanga would sort out the men from the supermen. Wright and Atkins both slowed perceptibly, while Rakabaele and Robb looked strong and eager. The order was about to change. Going through Harrison Flats, Robb and Rakabaele had Wright in their sights. At Cato Ridge, the lead was down to 300 metres. Shortly before Camperdown, Wright was finally passed. It was now a two-horse race.

For a while, Rakabaele adopted his favourite position, so close to Robb's heels that a collision seemed imminent. It looked as though the race might end in a sprint finish, but Robb was the stronger. On the downhill stretch to Tumble Inn, he made his move. Rakabaele had no answer. When Robb crested Polly Shortts, it was merely a question of whether or not a record was possible. The determination of Alan Robb soon erased doubts. His time of 5.47.09 was 1 minute 48 seconds inside Mick Orton's 1972 effort. The record once again belonged to South Africa. Afterwards, Robb discussed the closing stages: 'Rakabaele's shadowing me probably gave me added drive because he always runs behind me like that. I was just determined to really push him this time. I'm used to Rakabaele running hot on my heels.'

Once he'd conceded the lead to Robb, Rakabaele faced one of the most difficult challenges of Comrades: hanging on to second place in physical and psychological pain over the toughest imaginable stretch of road. It was too much. His competitive spirit sapped, he offered minimal resistance as Steve Atkins and Dave Wright both passed him. Atkins claimed second place, finishing in a state of exhaustion. 'Dancing' Dave Wright risked calves and hamstrings as he waltzed across the line third. Fourth-placed Rakabaele succinctly put Robb's achievement in context: 'He was just wonderful!'

The third official women's race was won by popular Lettie van Zyl, who repeated her victory of the previous year. In so doing, she became the first woman to officially break nine hours, although she had unofficially set a sub-nine-hour time in a previous race, and also became the first winner

Hardy Ballington, followed by bikers of his era

Hardy Ballington in 1947

First multiple champion, Arthur Newton and founder, Vic Clapham reminisce

Mercer Davies at halfway in 1957

The Natal Witness

Wednesday June. 1st. 1960

COMRADES MARATHON RECORD SHATTERED

Trevor Allen and Nick Raubenheimer in 1962

Charlie Warren (100) and Gerry Treloar (151) with blind legend, Ian Jardine

Unbelievably, Savages Manie Kuhn is about to
overtake Tommy Malone on the line in 1967

Dave Bagshaw bags a hat-trick of wins in 1971

Max Trimborn's cockcrow signals another start

John Ballington assisted by Bill Cochrane

One of five victories for Jackie Mekler

Jackie Mekler as drawn by Jock Leyden

Vincent Rakabaele: first official black finisher in 1975

Dave Levick records a rare Cape Town victory

'Dancing' Dave Wright waltzes across the line

of the new Rose Bowl women's trophy. Novice Thea Claassen took second place ahead of Marie-Jean Duyvejonck, the Two Oceans champion. Well-known international athlete Mavis Hutchison was among the finishers.

Duyvejonck was not the only Two Oceans winner to have a successful day. Don Hartley, former record holder of the Cape's classic race, finished 25th in 6 hours 32 minutes. Other Capetonians to feature among the silver medallists included veteran all-rounder Leo Benning and Paarl's Dolf Dampies.

The 1977 Comrades Marathon included its fair share of characters, among them well-known comedian Len Davis, former Springbok soccer star Eric Logan, airline pilot Robin Stamper and former champions George Claassen and Tommy Malone. All achieved their main objective of finishing, as did Clive Crawley and Kenny Craig, both of whom were building up impressive records as Comrades regulars.

There was a notable newcomer in this year's field, a second-year Witwatersrand University student who had been so upset by the brutality meted out to protesting black pupils on 16 June 1976 that the next day he had simply run and run to get the anguish out of his system. He soon discovered that he had a significant talent for long-distance running, confirmed when he ran his first Comrades in 1977 and finished 43rd in a time of 6.45.00. Bruce Fordyce had arrived.

1977 COMRADES MARATHON RESULTS

1. A. G. Robb	5.47.09
2. S. Atkins	5.57.48
3. D. R. H. Wright	5.58.43
4. G. V. Rakabaele	6.03.50
5. H. G. Jean Richard	6.09.54
6. B. Gerber	6.12.48
7. M. C. Ball	6.14.00
8. N. Wessels	6.14.41
9. S. A. de Koning	6.15.38
10. J. J. Sutherland	6.16.14

1977 COMRADES MARATHON WOMEN'S RESULTS

1. A. S. M. van Zyl   8.58.00
2. S. D. Claassen   9.18.00
3. M. J. Duyvejonck   9.51.00

1978 COMRADES MARATHON
ROBB AT HIS BEST

This year's race will always be remembered for one of the greatest performances by one of the greatest athletes in Comrades history. Alan Robb had earned a reputation as a tough competitor, a very strong downhill runner, a strong uphill runner, a man of immense mental powers, and a gentleman and sportsman in the finest tradition of the great race. Yet something was missing. Largely because of his distinctive running style, he had come to be known as a shuffler. Some shuffler! Robb's 1978 Comrades achievement proclaimed his undeniable status as one of the world's finest ever ultra-distance athletes. He was fast!

A great 1978 Comrades Marathon was a positive reminder of what was good about South Africa at a time when there was a great deal happening that could certainly not be regarded as admirable. A few months after the 1977 event, political activist Steve Biko died in police custody 26 days after being detained at a roadblock. At a congress of the ruling National Party, Minister of Justice Jimmy Kruger, stated that Biko's death 'leaves me cold'. Another delegate declared that Biko had exercised his 'democratic right to starve himself to death'. The autopsy revealed that violent blows to the head had caused the death of Biko, whose existence had been unknown to the vast majority of whites.

While there was no place for racism in the culture of Comrades and of road-running in general, people of colour understandably rejected everything that smacked of white management. One amateur athletic association forbade 28 of its members, who had qualified for Comrades, from taking part in the event. Comrades organisers were unable to monitor the protest as they did not record details of skin colour.

While Comrades remained a largely white, male event, an increasing number of participants came from sections of the population that had previously been barred. On the female side, a few wives of male runners were following cautiously in their husbands' footsteps. Joan Clark, wife of Errol, succinctly voiced her self-doubts: 'I am not so sure that I can do it now that the day is looming near. It gives me butterflies to think about it.'

While female newcomers were hoping to show the world that they were capable of finishing the race within the time allowed, black athletes were somewhat more ambitious. From the moment participation became open to all, speculation centred around who would be the first black winner. Right from the start, there existed a possibility in the person of Gabashane Vincent Rakabaele. He certainly had the ability to win the race, as he had shown on several occasions, including his victory in the 1976 Two Oceans. In this year's Two Oceans, he had finished second behind Brian Chamberlain. Unfortunately, Rakabaele was just about as unpredictable as any sportsman could be.

Another strongly tipped participant was local favourite Derek Preiss, seeking a third win after his victories in 1974 and 1975. He knew how to compete in Comrades. He knew how to win Comrades. There were, however, serious doubts about his motivation. It appeared as if he had been dragging himself through recent races rather than committing himself fully. A case in point was the 1978 Bergville-to-Ladismith, where he had dropped out after 25 kilometres.

While Preiss and Rakabaele were rightly regarded as potential winners, Alan Robb was the outright favourite. Should he prevail, he would become only the third runner to secure a hat-trick, three victories in a row, after Arthur Newton and Dave Bagshaw. His toughness as a competitor was well respected by his rivals. His preparation had been thorough. He had run 3 500 kilometres in training since the start of January. When he let it be known that his target time was 5 hours 35 minutes (which would constitute a new record) some felt that he was overreaching himself.

Towards the end of April, a tragedy occurred that highlighted the physical vulnerability of road-runners. Three athletes taking part in a Sunday morning training run in the vicinity of Johannesburg were struck by an out-of-control vehicle. Rocky Road Runners club member Dave Isaacs was assisting Ronnie Steenberg and Alan Niehaus, who was recently married with a pregnant wife. All three were killed. Johannesburg runners were incensed. Witwatersrand University athlete Steve Novis recalled an incident shortly after when a clubmate picked up a stone and hurled it at a vehicle that was being driven in threatening fashion. The angry runner would finish 14th in this year's Comrades.

The weather forecast for 31 May announced a heatwave – but it was wrong. As usual in a 'down' run, cold conditions greeted the record number of 2 721 starters as they assembled outside the Pietermaritzburg City Hall. During the day, the temperature increased, but remained cool with occasional light rain. Conditions were ideal for a fast race.

The city hall clock, the starter's pistol and Max Trimborn's famous cockcrow sent the field on their way. When the early 'show ponies' had enjoyed their brief flirtation with an unsustainable lead, the field began to settle down. By now, Rakabaele had become known as Robb's 'shadow'. In many races, he would position himself at Robb's shoulder, almost clipping his heels as he followed him. On this occasion, he went as far as to follow Robb in obeying a call of nature. Derek Preiss was right there with them. At Camperdown, the trio trailed leader George Williams by about two minutes. They were handily placed. Atkins, Wright and Gerber were also ahead of them.

On the approach to Cato Ridge, Preiss dropped back slightly. Although he didn't appear to be in trouble, he went through Cato Ridge 30 metres behind his erstwhile companions. Meanwhile, Steve Atkins was making a move as Williams began to tire. Going through Harrison Flats, Atkins took over the lead.

There were further developments on the ascent of Inchanga. Rakabaele was unable to keep pace with Robb and dropped back. He and Preiss were both overtaken by Piet Vorster, Anton de Koning and physiotherapy student Graeme Lindenberg, who were running together.

Up front, Atkins had been joined by Dave Wright. Robb, having shaken off his main rivals, now set his sights on the leading duo. Powering his way down the steep descent, he soon caught them. Running together, the threesome went through halfway at Drummond in 2 hours 48 minutes. Gerber, Strydom, Ball, Lindenberg, De Koning, Vorster, Briscoe and Williams were all within three minutes of the lead. Wits (University of the

Witwatersrand) student Bruce Fordyce, running in his second Comrades, was ten minutes off the pace.

In ideal conditions, the leaders began the climb past Alverstone up to Botha's Hill. Robb's superior strength was evident as he drew ahead of Wright, firstly, and then Atkins. At Kearsney College, the top of the hill, Robb's advantage was 200 metres. He was determined to put as much distance as possible between himself and his opponents. He succeeded in doing so. At Kloof, the lead was up to 300 metres.

Racing down Field's Hill is not generally recommended. The pounding that the legs endure is likely to cause a significant slowdown in the closing stages. Robb paid no attention to such conventional wisdom and simply flew down the hill. When he reached Pinetown Flats seemingly none the worse for wear, he, and race followers, were aware that a new record was a distinct possibility.

Cowies Hill, the last major obstacle, now loomed ahead. Robb made light of the challenge and reached Westville eight minutes ahead of Wright, who had claimed second place from Atkins. Wright had survived a nasty scare on Cowies when he had to jump out of the way of a speeding car. Afterwards, he made light of the incident, saying, 'It's something we get used to in training – you have to be agile.' Agility after more than 70 kilometres of hard running is somewhat rare, but 'Dancing' Dave Wright would prove his point by waltzing across the finishing line.

Meanwhile, Robb had a new target. The first sub-five-hour-30-minutes Comrades was within his grasp. Experienced campaigners know how difficult it is to keep agonised legs moving quickly in the closing stages of the 'down' run. Robb seemed oblivious of pain as he ignored all distractions and maintained his steady pace. The large crowd at Kingsmead cheered him to the tape, which he broke after 5 hours 29 minutes 14 seconds.

Alan Robb became the third man to achieve the hat-trick of three consecutive victories. He was the first to finish in under five and a half hours. He was the holder of both the 'up' and 'down' records. His place in Comrades history as one of the true greats was secure. Looking remarkably fresh, he explained his tactics: 'I was going to crack on the pace from Field's Hill, but I just felt good at Drummond, so I took a chance and pushed it from there.' Acknowledging that perfect conditions had played a part, he paid tribute to his attendants: 'I've got two great seconds, Charles and

Richard Perrie, who always help me. They know me inside out and therefore play a big part.'

An indication of Robb's supremacy is the fact that, when he crossed the line, second-placed Wright was in Mayville, over four kilometres from the end. Wright eventually finished, performing his customary jig, in 5 hours 48 minutes 40 seconds, which was 19 minutes 26 seconds behind Robb. Anton de Koning came third, with Piet Vorster fourth. Trompie Strydom, in fifth place, was the first novice home. Bruce Fordyce finished 14th and realised for the first time that he was capable of achieving gold.

In the ladies' race, 23-year-old novice Sue Wagner of Harlequin Harriers took the early lead and was first through Drummond in 4 hours 1 minute. Defending champion Lettie van Zyl was ten minutes behind her, with Elizabeth Cavanagh a further three minutes back. Wagner maintained her advantage and was still ten minutes ahead with 30 kilometres remaining. From then on, Van Zyl gradually closed the gap and finally went ahead at the top of Cowies, eventually taking first place in 8 hours 25 minutes. Although the women's race had not yet reached the competitive level that it enjoys today, Germiston Callies Harriers could claim all four individual records, male and female, 'up' and 'down', courtesy of Robb and Van Zyl.

While rugby Springbok Wilf Rosenberg and cricket star Peter Pollock received warm ovations as they successfully completed their journeys, the runners who captured the hearts were those who had overcome severe adversity. Jack Piek won his fifth medal six years after suffering a serious stroke. Timothy Treffry-Goatley, who had barely survived a hang-gliding accident in 1975, obtained his first medal. Blind Ron Clokie, a Comrades character and regular, finished in 10 hours 47 minutes.

1978 COMRADES MARATHON RESULTS

1. A. G. Robb	5.29.14
2. D. R. H. Wright	5.48.40
3. S. A. de Koning	5.49.39
4. P. F. Vorster	5.52.04
5. W. P. Strydom	5.54.14
6. S. Atkins	5.55.58

7. M. C. Ball	5.57.19
8. B. Gerber	5.57.38
9. W. J. J. Vermeulen	5.59.15
10. H. W. Schubert	6.02.07

1978 COMRADES MARATHON WOMENS' RESULTS

1. A. S. H. van Zyl	8.25
2. S. D. Wagner	8.43
3. J. P. Clark	8.53

1979 COMRADES MARATHON
A YEAR OF SURPRISES

As the race grew in numbers and in stature, so did the demands on organisers. There simply wasn't enough room for all the vehicles and runners that wanted to be there, so, the runners being the focus of the occasion, the vehicles had to give way. This year therefore saw a major departure from past relations between athletes and attendants: no unauthorised vehicles were allowed on the course at all.

Feeding stations, the only possible alternative, did not materialise out of nowhere. They had to be set up, and sponsors were needed. Organising committee member Dave Jack approached Wesbank manager Pat Fletcher, who readily agreed to commit his bank to the event. Comrades runners of that era will recall the rather attractive young female feeding station attendants, whose outfits were perhaps a size too small.

Pat Fletcher was an astute businessman who believed in a quid pro quo. He asked to have the Comrades trophies displayed on the Wesbank stand at the Pietermaritzburg Royal Show. The committee agreed and Dave Jack went along to have a look. While chatting to Pat Fletcher, he became aware of an elderly couple whose attention was focused on the Anderson Trophy (for second place). When the woman indicated that her husband was a previous holder of the trophy, Jack joined in the conversation, as he recently recalled:

'"What year was that?" I asked. The old man chipped in and said, "It was 1931 – a long, long time ago, young man." Having more than a passing interest in Comrades, it didn't take me more than a few seconds to put a name to the person who had finished second in 1931 in what is still the second closest finish in the history of the race.

'"Noel Burree finished second that year – but I thought he was dead," I said, inserting my foot ever so gently into my mouth. "No, I'm not dead," the old man said, very seriously. While I was trying to figure how best to correct the embarrassing situation I had caused, *Sunday Tribune* reporter Ronnie Borain came strolling past. Precision timing!

'I called Ronnie and introduced him to Burree. The lead story in the next *Sunday Tribune* was the story of Noel Burree, his 1931 run and where he was at that time. Burree had been living in the caravan park at Ifafa Beach down the South Coast for years, and every year without fail he hitched his caravan to his car and towed it to Pietermaritzburg to watch Comrades – and nobody knew he was there!

'Noel Burree was an instant VIP at Comrades in 1979 and for several years after that. A charming and humble man.'

In the early build-up to this year's race, one man's name was on everyone's lips. The great Alan Robb was at his peak. Winner of the previous three races, he was once again in tip-top condition. With his no-nonsense approach and mental toughness, he was regarded by many as close to invincible. He realised this and acknowledged the extra pressure that he felt, 'Being considered some sort of superman is preying on my mind. That's my one problem. People expect too much of me. They don't seem to realise I'm human and I, too, can be stopped by cramps, stitches or injury.'

Then the picture changed, and pressure of a different sort was brought to bear on Robb. Johnny Halberstadt entered the fray. Although a Comrades novice, his all-round running record at home and abroad was awesome. A sub-four-minute miler, he had won national championships at various distances from cross-country to the standard marathon. His marathon time was 2.25.18. In America, he had won the National Collegiate Athletic Association's ten-kilometre race and taken third place in the Boston Marathon.

Halberstadt was initially cagey about his plans to enter the race. When his participation was confirmed, he introduced a competitive edge to the pre-race build-up, saying, 'If Robb is only five minutes ahead of me at halfway, he won't have it sewn up.' Somewhat uncharacteristically, the reserved Robb responded, but in gentle terms, 'I won't let him influence my plans at all. He must be really fit to contemplate winning. Only a few novices have won, but Johnny is capable of doing it. If he does, he'll have to run very hard. I'm not going to give over without a fight.'

Interestingly, Robb spoke of another threat, a runner he couldn't name. 'The man I fear is the unknown runner who suddenly comes to light in the race, as has so often happened before.' There were a few who had limited Comrades experience who were worthy of respect. Vincent Rakabaele's second place in the recent Two Oceans suggested that he was one to watch. Piet Vorster had progressed from 21st to fourth in the previous two Comrades Marathons. Wits University's Bruce Fordyce had likewise advanced from 43rd to 14th, not sufficient to cause him to be feared at this stage.

On the eve of the race, it appeared as if Vorster would not even make the starting line-up, as he had been suffering from an ankle injury for some time. Despite a cortisone injection, the discomfort remained and he decided to withdraw. His supporters persuaded him to have a little jog and test the ankle an hour before the gun. Still the pain persisted and he confirmed his earlier decision to pull out. This time, his friends convinced him that he should at least start the race. Piet Vorster was among the 3 001 athletes who responded to 79-year-old Max Trimborn's cockcrow.

Soon after the gun, Halberstadt threw down the gauntlet. Steve Atkins followed him. At 45th Cutting, they were half a minute ahead of a group that included Robb and Dave Wright. Halberstadt was not in the mood for conversation. At Westville, he was nearly a minute ahead of swiftly discarded Atkins, with Robb half a minute further back in third place.

Having proclaimed his tactics so eloquently, Halberstadt had no option but to establish an insurmountable lead and, in effect, win the race in the first half, a tall order indeed. He was certainly running at a faster pace than anyone else. At the crest of Field's Hill, he was over three minutes ahead of Atkins, still second. Rather surprisingly, Piet Vorster was now third and looking good. Properly warmed up in the heat of battle, his ankle was no longer troubling him. A little further back, Alan Robb did not appear comfortable.

Botha's Hill posed no problem for the flying Halberstadt, who sprinted the downhill section from Alverstone to Drummond. His halfway time of 2.45.30 was a new record for an 'up' run. Vorster, now second, was four minutes behind the leader but over three minutes ahead of third-placed Atkins. Robb, more than ten minutes off the pace, was now out of contention.

Halberstadt's strategy had worked to perfection. If he could maintain the speed differential between himself and his pursuers, his advantage would soon be such that he could experience a bad patch without being threatened. Those chasing him had their own problem. Could they bank on him 'hitting the wall'? On the other hand, was it time to change their chosen tactics and try to hunt him down? Halberstadt had sown confusion among his opponents. At this stage, only Vorster seemed strong enough and close enough to mount a challenge.

Halberstadt took Inchanga, traditional graveyard of the overambitious, in his stride, but he still wasn't extending his lead over the more strongly built Vorster. On the deceptively demanding section between Cato Ridge and Camperdown, the gap between the two front-runners came down to under four minutes. Was something happening? Dave Wright was only a minute behind Vorster. The race was hotting up.

As he passed through Camperdown, it was clear that Halberstadt had lost his customary jauntiness. His pace had slowed perceptibly. Vorster, on the other hand, recognised his chance of Comrades glory. Near the Dardanelles turn-off, cramp reduced Halberstadt to a walk and Vorster flashed past to take control. Shortly afterwards, Wright claimed second place from the stricken Halberstadt, who was at this point lying down at the roadside. Halberstadt lost about eight minutes before courageously rejoining the race.

A member of Collegians Harriers, Vorster was racing on his regular training route. He knew every step of the way and received all the support from spectators that any hometown contender could hope for. Determinedly, Vorster overcame the last two hurdles, Ashburton and Polly Shortts itself, while behind him a revitalised Halberstadt had reclaimed second spot from Wright.

There was no stopping Vorster now. With all his pre-race travails consigned to the past, he was aware that no 'up' race leader had yet been passed on the run-in from the top of Polly Shortts. He also knew that the race record was within his grasp. With the crowd urging him on, Vorster crossed the line at

Jan Smuts Stadium, a surprise but popular winner in a new record time of 5.45.02. He expressed his thoughts afterwards:

'The weather was nice. It helped me. I wasn't worried about Halberstadt's early lead because I just didn't think he'd go the whole distance. But I was only sure I'd win it at the finishing line. I really was surprised to win after all the trouble I've had. I was not even in the right frame of mind to run, let alone win.'

Warm applause greeted Johnny Halberstadt, who fought back bravely. In describing his setback along the way, he used words that will be understood by others who have had similar experiences:

'The differing temperatures along the route troubled me. At one stage, I was close to freezing. I feel that I diluted my body salts and drank too much water.'

The man who made everyone sit up and take notice was third-placed Bruce Fordyce. In addition to the progress and consistency he had shown to date, he exhibited a very special ability that singled him out as a potential winner. His second-half time was the fastest of all and was significantly faster than his own first-half effort. He was learning his trade and would soon demonstrate just how much he had learnt.

Fordyce acknowledged this some years later in his book *Run the Comrades*:

'The 1979 "up" Comrades Marathon will always be my favourite race. It was the year I first realised I had a talent for long-distance races over hilly courses. It was the year I first struck gold. And it was the year that I realised that it was actually possible to run up Polly Shortts.'

An innovation this year was the award of a silver medal to the first woman finisher. Although there were only 17 women in the field, they welcomed this recognition. Lettie van Zyl, thrice the victrix, didn't make it this time. Johannesburg's Jan Mallen was a worthy winner in 8.22.41, the fastest time to date.

Certain old-stagers distinguished themselves this year. Seventy-year-old Liege Boulle defied those who had brought in an upper-age restriction by completing his 38th successful run. Among those who attained their green numbers and 'in perpetuity' status were Comrades stalwart Barry Varty and originator of the Two Oceans name Noel Stamper.

1979 COMRADES MARATHON RESULTS

1. P. F. Vorster	5.45.02
2. J. P. Halberstadt	5.50.30
3. B. N. S. Fordyce	5.51.15
4 S. A. de Koning	6.00.18
5. A. G. Robb	6.01.12
6. M. C. Ball	6.01.52
7. E. G. Deeny	6.02.40
8. D. L. Hensman	6.03.38
9. N. Wessels	6.04.16
10. D. R. H. Wright	6.04.58

1979 COMRADES MARATHON WOMEN'S RESULTS

1. J. R. Mallen	8.22.41
2. M. L. Hornby	8.29.10
3. A. S. H. van Zyl	8.32.55
4. J. P. Clark	8.37.18
5. G. H. Ingram	9.02.43
6. M. J. Duyvejonck	9.05.30
7. N. F. de Beer	9.53.40
8. H. D. Hobbs	9.58.34
9. D. C. Ledlie	10.10.28
10. J. M. Pretorius	10.11.07

1980 COMRADES MARATHON
ROBB WINS, BUT THE LADIES CREEP CLOSER

Rugby fever gripped South Africa in 1980. Bill Beaumont's British Lions arrived in the country, determined to emulate the success of their predecessors under Willie-John McBride six years previously. Few favoured the Springboks. It was an unusual contest. The Lions won the tight forward battle, but the South Africans took the series, largely through a strategy of counter-attack that perfectly suited them. Beaumont acknowledged this and named elusive fullback Gysie Pienaar and speedy flanker Rob Louw as the key players. One of the test matches was played on the same day as the Comrades Marathon.

Comrades was going through a period of change. The race was growing significantly. Long gone were the days of a field of under a hundred enjoying the services of personal attendants. In order to look after the 4 208 starters, 52 refreshment stations and extra sponging points were set up along the way. Many old-timers resented the change, but acknowledged that there was no real alternative. One explained his feelings clearly: 'I don't like it. I can't have my family with me. I'm not looking forward to it. The feeding stations do the trick, but they are too impersonal.'

Along with the increase in numbers came a strengthening of the competition up front. This year's was a very open race, although the newspapers disagreed. Johnny Halberstadt, back to try to erase his previous year's disappointment, was the overwhelming press favourite. He certainly fancied his chances, but his pre-race comment was a little less confident than the previous year's: 'I don't say I'll win, but anyone who finishes ahead of me will have run the race of his life.' He certainly couldn't be discounted, and this was underlined by his amazing Korkie victory, about which Bruce Fordyce said, 'His Korkie 3.11 at altitude is better than his Two Oceans 3.05 over the same distance.'

Alan Robb had not been at his best in 1979, but had nevertheless finished among the golds. He was the defending 'down' champion, and his 1978 record run will forever rank as one of the great Comrades achievements. Robb's sequence of victories had been broken the previous year, and he was determined to get back to the top.

Then there was Fordyce. In his three previous Comrades, he had graduated from 43rd through 14th to third. In 1979, he had run fastest of all over the second half. Was he ready to set his sights higher? Last year's winner, Piet Vorster, hadn't really featured since then, but his build-up to the 1979 race hadn't been too impressive either. Geoff Bacon, cross-country and standard marathon star, had recently won the 56-kilometre Arthur Newton Memorial Race. Hoseah Tjale was bidding to become the first black winner. He had plenty of support, as did others too numerous to name.

These and other leading contenders would have to accept that they were competing for medals that lacked the monetary, if not the symbolic, value of previous years. Silver medals coated with gold replaced solid gold medals, and silvers were demoted to 'silver-plated over high-quality gilding metal'. This, along with greater exposure given to sponsors, confirmed the growing cost of staging the great race.

As usual, the start of another 'down' run was another cold experience. Television floodlighting drew sprinters like moths to a temporary position at the front of the pack. At Ashburton, the leaders were Aaron Gumbi, Elliot Dlamini, Chris Mkize and Gordon Kruger. Of the four, only Mkize could be realistically regarded as a minor threat. The real battle was being fought further back. Bacon, Halberstadt, Robb and Vorster kept each other company, two minutes off the pace.

While Lawrence Hlophe took the lead shortly before Camperdown, there was little change among the favourites. Halberstadt's tactics were hard to fathom. He was obviously determined to ensure that he didn't burn himself out as he had done last year. He appeared to be taking his cue from Robb as the early morning chill gave way to pleasantly warm conditions.

Hlophe maintained his lead up Inchanga, but, on the descent, was overhauled by Deon Holtzhausen, 16th in 1979. Now the race was on in earnest. Holtzhausen went through Drummond in 2.45.16. Hlophe, Bacon, Tjale, Robb, Donnelly, Ball, Halberstadt and Vorster were all within two minutes of him and handily placed. Although Fordyce's halfway time was 2.53, his strength in the closing stages had to be respected. His progress was according to plan.

The race moved into the second half with no clearly discernible pattern. This was a chess match in running shoes. Someone would have to make a move at some stage, but this was only the middlegame. The grandmasters of Comrades were still in the process of positioning themselves and encouraging their adversaries to make potentially fatal errors.

On the ascent of Botha's Hill, the first few exchanges took place. Geoff Bacon took the lead, then Holtzhausen reclaimed it, only to lose it to Bacon for a second time. The gates of Kearsney College are generally regarded as the top of Botha's Hill. Here, Geoff Bacon was in front, while Hoseah Tjale had taken second place from Holtzhausen. Robb and Halberstadt, with Vorster closely behind, followed menacingly.

Then came a change that the Comrades family had anticipated with relish. On the short but steep climb from the foot of Botha's Hill to Hillcrest Village, Hoseah Tjale overtook Bacon and became the first black leader in the 'business section' of a Comrades Marathon. Bacon was running in his footsteps. Robb, in third place, was a minute back, half a minute ahead of Halberstadt, with Holtzhausen dropping back and presently occupying fifth place. But what was happening to Halberstadt? The dominating front-runner should surely have made a significant move by now.

History beckoned for the popular 25-year-old Hoseah Tjale, 'Hoss' to his friends. With just one-third of the race to go at Gillits, he was seemingly in control. Bacon was second and Halberstadt, at last making his presence felt, had wrested third place from Robb. A mouth-watering endgame lay in store.

At Kloof, with the downhill of Field's Hill and thereafter just over 20 kilometres to go, Tjale was looking so good that the possibility of a new record entered the minds of hopefuls. Such thoughts were a little premature, as Bacon was just over a minute behind and races have to be won before records can be set. Robb was back in the picture, having once again passed Halberstadt to take third position. Halberstadt remained in contention, as did Malcolm Ball, just ahead of him, and Piet Vorster, a few metres behind.

As the race finally reached its endgame, Comrades, as usual, randomly punished those who had dared to try to meet its challenge. Halfway leader Holtzhausen pulled out. His successor as leader, Geoff Bacon, dropped back. Then came the big one. Johnny Halberstadt had at no time looked like a potential winner. He certainly didn't while lying at the roadside. As had happened the previous year, his attendants did their level best to get him back on the road, but to no avail. Halberstadt was out of the race.

Hoseah Tjale remained very much in contention, if not quite in control. At Pinetown, he was two and a half minutes ahead of Robb, with excited spectators willing him on to his dream. Then came Cowies Hill, the last major obstacle. Tjale slowed perceptibly. Robb did not. At the top, Tjale's lead was less than two minutes.

Robb, like other Comrades greats, took control while still behind. He knew, and so did Tjale, that he was the stronger of the two. Gradually, he whittled away at Tjale's lead. At Westville, he was almost within touching distance of his quarry. Just before Konigkramer Road, Tjale was left nursing his aching thighs and damaged pride as Robb surged into the lead, his customary position.

Although he remained strong until the end, Robb was unable to relax for a moment. He had about two kilometres to go when his watch told him that he had already gone beyond his record time of 1978. His attendants told him that Fordyce was now in second place and going like an express train.

Robb was not going to fail. Maintaining his steady but fast pace, he delighted admiring spectators by recording his fourth win. Acknowledging afterwards that he had been in a tough race, he told of his concerns about his rivals: 'Halberstadt came past me at Hillcrest and then he just seemed to battle. I then passed him again, and that was the last time I saw him. I was sure I had the race after I overtook Tjale, but it was a battle holding on the last 20 kilometres. I was worried about Fordyce because he finished so fast last year when coming third.'

Fordyce finished fast again this year, although, perhaps, not fast enough. On the other hand, maybe he had left himself too much to do in the closing stages. Ever since, Fordyce has felt that this was the one that got away, that he hadn't seized an opportunity that was there for the taking. I have my doubts. We were witnessing the beginning of the end of the career of one great champion, Robb, and the start of the phenomenal reign of another, Bruce Fordyce. For the moment, Robb had his nose in front. Next time they crossed swords, the advantage would lie with Fordyce.

The women's race served notice that the so-called gentler sex would not be playing second fiddle for much longer. Defending champion Jan Mallen was back, as were three pioneers of the official and unofficial past: Lettie van Zyl, Elizabeth Cavanagh and the Galloping Granny, Mavis Hutchison. Moving the women's event into a more competitive mode were two youngsters, 26-year-old Gail Ingram and 20-year-old Irish lass Isavel Roche-Kelly of the University of Cape Town.

It was the ever-smiling Roche-Kelly who set new standards. After running in company with, and under the guidance of, running guru Tim Noakes, she simply took off at Kloof and became the first woman to finish within the silver limit, her time being 7.18.00. Second-placed Cheryl Jorgensen, an immigrant from the USA, also achieved silver. Oh, to beat the record while finishing second!

Organising chairman Mick Winn had the unenviable task of disqualifying someone who had not adhered to the rules. In announcing the decision, he spoke of the true ethos of the sport:

'Long-distance running is based on an honour system. If an athlete wants to cheat, it's not that difficult. But if we catch someone, we'll most certainly take action. If a man does get away with it, he's cheating himself. He just wouldn't experience the sense of achievement Comrades runners feel when they finish.'

1980 COMRADES MARATHON RESULTS

1. A. G. Robb	5.38.25
2. B. N. S. Fordyce	5.40.31
3. M. C. Ball	5.40.45
4. T. A. Briscoe	5.46.20
5. A. M. Abbott	5.47.27
6. H. Tjale	5.50.12
7. D. E. Ryan	5.52.46
8. J. E.W. Claase	5.53.33
9. T. K. Bilibana	5.56.49
10. I. T. Emery	5.57.42

1980 COMRADES BOWL RESULTS

1. I. Roche-Kelly	7.18
2. C. L. Jorgensen	7.22
3. R. Smit	7.50
4. G. Ingram	7.52
5. J. P. Clark	8.04
6. G. I. Faure	8.10
7. M. J. Duyvejonck	8.39
8. J. M. Pretorius	8.47
9. O. A. Anthony	9.10
10. S. Stevens	9.17

14

THE FORDYCE YEARS
(1981 to 1988)

The Comrades Marathon has long been recognised as an event that both influences and reflects relationships among the groups that make up the 'Rainbow Nation'. The 1980s spanned a period in which more and more white South Africans patiently but firmly told their government that apartheid must come to an end.

There were many, black and white, who played significant roles in this seminal period, which paved the way for the release from prison of Nelson Mandela in 1990 and the present hopeful, if imperfect, dispensation. As the Comrades Marathon and the nation demonstrated by recognising the date of 16 June, the heroic rising of black school pupils in 1976 marked a pivotal point in the country's evolution. It was now up to white youth to respond.

Five years later, a door opened that enabled this to happen. At the start of the 1980s, the government were eager to celebrate their magnificent achievement of a republic in which most inhabitants were regarded as non-citizens and providers of cheap labour on account of their skin colour. The Comrades Marathon of 1981 was chosen as an official part of the 'celebrations'.

White university students, many of them of the same age as the black schoolchildren who had rebelled and, in many cases, lost their lives in 1976, regarded the government initiative as, aside from being outrageous, an opportunity to express solidarity with their black counterparts and denounce the abhorrent system of apartheid. As providence would have it, a Witwatersrand University student strongly opposed to any form of racial discrimination was about to enjoy a decade-long domination of the Comrades Marathon, and also of ultramarathon running worldwide.

It's difficult to imagine what was going through the mind of 25-year-old Bruce Fordyce when he went to the start of the 1981 Comrades Marathon. We know that he was abused by spectators and runners alike for his famous black armband. We know, with hindsight, that he won the race and has been revered ever since for his athletic brilliance and steadfast promotion of human dignity. We don't know what self-doubts might have brought him close to aborting his demonstration. We don't know how ineffective his stand might have been if he'd similarly attempted to influence people in earlier years, when he came second and third. Was being the victor crucial?

It doesn't matter. We know that Bruce Fordyce, throughout his running career and after, consistently stood up for those who were disadvantaged. We know that he had the courage to promote his views when still a hopeful and rather timid young athlete, unaware of the extraordinary career that lay before him. We have seen him disregard, and thereby jeopardise, the obvious benefits of popularity in order to use his fame as a platform for the claims of the underprivileged. We have witnessed the significant gains of the Sports Trust, providing facilities for those in need, under his stewardship.

Yet it would be folly to judge the contribution of Bruce Fordyce purely in terms of his benevolence. Fordyce was an athlete of supreme quality who maintained domination over all comers, at home and abroad, for a full decade. In his Comrades career alone, he successfully repelled the efforts of three generations of challengers.

His career statistics are astonishing. In the decade from 1981 to 1990, he entered every Comrades Marathon apart from that of 1989. Of the nine he entered, he won every single one, setting records on no fewer than five occasions. His one omission, in 1989, was a result of his participation in the Standard Bank Ultra 100-kilometre race, which he won in world record time. He competed in three London-to-Brighton races from 1981 to 1983. He won them all, setting a world record for 50 miles en route in 1983. He won the United States 50 Mile Championship in Chicago in his only attempt, duly setting a US record that was second only to his own world record for 50 miles. He twice ran the Nanisivik Midnight Sun Ultra 84-kilometre race, 800 kilometres inside the Arctic Circle, setting a new record on both occasions. He received many awards, far too numerous to mention.

Victories and records don't tell the full story of the athlete Bruce Fordyce. It is the manner in which he achieved his successes that will long be remembered by those privileged to have seen this phenomenal running machine in action. At his peak, he could be criticised for teasing the nationwide Comrades television audience almost cruelly. Virtually every year, he would be so far behind that it seemed impossible for him to overcome the advantage of the mid-race leader. Yet, with panache and a sense of timing that was pure theatre, he would emerge triumphant and disarmingly surprised by yet another victory.

Of course, there were the battles. Like Edberg and Becker, Navratilova and Evert, Fordyce fought many duels. In the early days, Alan Robb and Johnny Halberstadt were mighty adversaries. Then came Hoseah Tjale and Bob de la Motte, both providing epic contests. When they had been dispatched, a new breed came along: Mark Page, Shaun Meiklejohn, Nick Bester and Charl Mattheus. They had a better chance. Old man Fordyce was reaching the end – but he wasn't yet ready to relinquish his crown.

1981 COMRADES MARATHON
THAT ARMBAND

Few Comrades Marathons have been awaited with quite as much anticipation as this year's race. Four legendary champions, Arthur Newton,

Hardy Ballington, Wally Hayward and Jackie Mekler, had each posted five wins, with the result that Comrades followers saw five as some kind of magic number, a criterion of Comrades greatness.

Pre-race speculation therefore focused on Robb's attempt this year to join the ranks of the five-time winners. It would be no easy task. He had two very serious challengers, both 25 years old: Johannesburg Wanderers runner Johnny Halberstadt, a sub-four-minute miler with a distinguished record of successes nationally and in the USA at distances from ten kilometres up to the standard marathon, and Witwatersrand University student Bruce Fordyce, who, from his very first race, had focused his efforts on the world's foremost ultramarathon. His Comrades record had improved dramatically year by year, from 43rd in 1977 to second in 1980. An intellectually gifted athlete, he had made a serious study of the complex demands of the race. Some felt that a tentative approach might have cost him victory in 1980, but this year, he was ready.

Fordyce very nearly didn't make it to the start. The government had announced that the marathon would form part of official Republic Day celebrations. Students at English-speaking universities, traditional opponents of apartheid policies, were outraged, and many decided to boycott the race. Others preferred to make a visible protest. Fordyce was undecided until the night before. At the last moment, he resolved to take part, believing that a stay-away protest would not be noticed. By now, the students had chosen black armbands as a symbol of protest. Not having one to hand at this late stage, Fordyce borrowed a friend's yellow hairband and dyed it black.

Nowadays, stringent regulations forbid the display of political or unauthorised commercial messages by athletes. The official Comrades rules state: 'Under no circumstances may a runner display a political slogan.'

One might ask: What is a political slogan? A catchphrase? An emblem? An inflammatory statement? The 1981 Comrades Marathon saw one of the most eloquent, though restrained, political comments in the history of South African sport. Gentle as it was, it constituted a powerful statement of opposition to the racial policies of the Nationalist government.

Other students also wore armbands, but Fordyce, as one of the race favourites, was singled out by Comrades purists who resented the intrusion of politics into the noble event. These people found it easier to direct their frustration at long-haired student demonstrators than at the government, which was attempting to gain respectability by associating itself with the marathon, while its apartheid policy utterly contradicted everything that Comrades represented. In the few minutes before the starting gun, Fordyce was subjected to angry abuse. He even had tomatoes thrown at him.

The starter's gun, which traditionally releases pre-race tension, also relieved pre-race animosity this year. Once into the race, competitors and plodders were able to focus their minds on the journey ahead and forget distractions. But Fordyce was not so fortunate. Warned by his chief second Godfrey Franz (whose brother was a member of the Bureau of State Security) that an attempt would be made to spike his drinks, he also had to endure the attention of two cameramen on motorcycles filming his every step. By nature a positive thinker, Fordyce decided that their attempts to fault his adherence to race regulations would only strengthen his acceptance of, and commitment to, the rules and spirit of the great race. Instead of being intimidated, he felt even more determined to broadcast his message loud and clear.

The warning Fordyce received about his drinks was serious, as new seconding regulations had come into effect this year. Any athlete who accepted drinks from a moving vehicle would be summarily disqualified. By now, it was well known that Fordyce had assembled a strong team of attendants who catered for his every need, providing him with much-needed sustenance and supplying him with information about his main rivals. They would have to be on their toes today.

The regulation change was unacceptable to many traditionalists. Runner and second had constituted an indivisible entity in the past. Comrades stalwart Vernon Jones was one of the more flexible of the old-timers, saying, 'It was a lonely road between Durban and Pietermaritzburg in those early days and nobody had regular seconds. But you can't bring back the old times.' Possibly the most heartfelt and eloquent response came from a relieved wife who pronounced herself delighted at not having to get up 'at an unhealthy hour to drag sleepy and unwilling children from their warm beds, spend the day accepting abuse from her bad-tempered runner, suffer all sorts of discomfort and exhaustion, and then in the end stand back, a nonentity, while her medal winner brushed off the compliments of adoring fans with false bravado'.

At the front, the battle between three favourites soon became a contest for two. Alan Robb was not well, although, in typical Robb style, he was up among the leaders for much of the first half. Chris Mkize, having gone to the front early, led the way through Drummond. The big guns, Fordyce and Halberstadt, were well placed. It was going to be one of them.

Having negotiated Inchanga quite comfortably, Fordyce felt strong and in command of proceedings. Suddenly, he was passed by a seemingly jet-propelled Halberstadt. His well-considered pre-race strategy now threatened by the class athlete in the field, Fordyce was confused. Should he stick to his own game plan or should he chase his flying adversary?

Ever the deep thinker, even at this early stage of his Comrades career, Fordyce accepted that Halberstadt would win the race if he could maintain his breakneck speed. On the other hand, if he was going too fast, he would pay the penalty. The canny Fordyce decided to stick to his chosen game plan. It was the right decision.

Going through Harrison Flats, Halberstadt slackened his pace slightly, while Fordyce did the opposite. Soon they were running together, shoulder to shoulder, testing each other's strength. Shortly after Cato Ridge, they passed Chris Mkize and took over joint lead of the race. Fordyce sensed that Halberstadt was struggling. On an awkward little ascent before Camperdown, he put in a little surge. Halberstadt failed to respond.

Bruce Fordyce was now in total command of the race, but not of himself. Somewhat overprepared, he was below his optimum weight, and there was still a long way to go. The pressure of leading the race earlier than expected, along with other distractions, weighed heavily on him. Desperate to maintain and increase his lead, he put in surges until he was told by a second, 'Bruce, you're leading and pulling away from the field. You don't have to push.' It was a timely reminder to a man whose approach was all about common sense.

At the top of Polly Shortts, Fordyce was more than five minutes ahead of Halberstadt. At last, he was safe. Now he could focus on the record, which was well within his grasp. Despite his weariness, he sped through the final six kilometres and proclaimed victory, black armband held eloquently high, in a new record time of 5.37.28. Afterwards, he spoke about the Halberstadt challenge: 'He was running away from me downhill, but I would come back very fast uphill. I was trying to run an even race. I think Johnny raced too many races before Comrades.'

Halberstadt was modest in defeat: 'Bruce was definitely the best man out there today.' He also expressed a new understanding of the challenge: 'The Comrades is more akin to a mountaineering event. It requires specialised training because one needs an excess of stamina to handle the hills and distance. I love running and compete in various marathons as often as possible, but Bruce made the right decision to concentrate on the Comrades. The race is such an adventure that I want to experience it again.'

For a change, Alan Robb was not among the gold medallists, finishing in 6.21.53 and joining fellow former champions Manie Kuhn and Dave Levick among the silvers. Kenny Craig successfully completed his 23rd consecutive Comrades, beating the record previously held by Liege Boulle.

The smiling Irishwoman Isavel Roche-Kelly produced one of the great Comrades performances, finishing 76th overall in a time of 6.44.35, two minutes faster than Wally Hayward's winning time in 1950, when women were considered too frail to compete in such arduous events. Roche-Kelly beat the previous women's 'up' record by an astonishing 1 hour 38 minutes and announced that she had run her last Comrades. She turned to cycling. Very sadly, she was knocked off her cycle by a car and fatally injured in 1984, after returning to Ireland.

As had been the case in 1980, Roche-Kelly was followed home by American Cheryl Jorgensen, who repeated her previous year's time of 7.22. It seemed likely that she would go one better in the near future.

Opinion on the success or otherwise of the new feeding station regulations was divided. Malcolm Ball found the race 'a bit lonely at times' without personal attention, while Tony Abbott felt that it had been 'easier without a second'. One thing was certain: there could be no turning back. Rapidly increasing fields dictated this.

1981 COMRADES MARATHON RESULTS

1. B. N. S. Fordyce	5.37.28
2. J. P. Halberstadt	5.46.00
3. A. M. Abbott	5.52.41
4. C. B. Mkize	5.53.29
5. D. R. Biggs	5.54.08

6. G. A. Fraser	5.54.12
7. G. Bacon	5.54.50
8. D. R. H. Wright	5.56.02
9. D. C. B. Anderson	5.57.07
10. J. E. W. Claase	6.03.02

1981 COMRADES BOWL RESULTS

1. I. Roche-Kelly	6.44.35
2. C. L. Jorgensen	7.21.55
3. R. Smit	7.46.34
4. G. H. Ingram	7.46.49
5. L. W. Warren	7.48.51
6. B. J. Gilfillan	8.16.16
7. C. M. Hooke	8.29.44
8. C. I. Faure	8.30.17
9. M. O. Quirk	8.32.29
10. L. M. Fourie	8.41.32

1982 COMRADES MARATHON
FORDYCE vs ROBB

Comrades backmarkers tend at times to be envious of the top runners, who finish before lunchtime while they toil from dawn to dusk. In 1982, there was no reason for the also-rans to feel jealous. The first two athletes to cross the line indulged in a battle that was as painful to them as it was breathtaking to the privileged spectators who witnessed their contest.

From a management point of view, this was a Comrades with a difference. During the latter part of the previous year, the organising club, Collegians Harriers, had sensibly acknowledged that Comrades had simply become too big for a club to organise. A special general meeting of the club in September 1981 paved the way for an independent organising committee. Thus it was that the 1982 marathon was the first to be arranged by the new

Comrades Marathon Association. Fortunately, continuity was assured with Mick Winn as chairman, Dr John Godlonton as his deputy and 'Bullet' Alexander as secretary. Others on the committee were Piet van der Leeuw (treasurer), Cathy Rogers, Derek Palframan, Rob Lambert, Dave Barrow and Allen Callaghan. Comrades remained in good hands.

When all the background issues had been settled, the reality of this year's race became apparent. The mercurial Halberstadt, feared and respected by all his contemporaries, was not in the field. Faced by local sporting isolation, he had turned professional in order to make a living abroad. Vincent Rakabaele and Hoseah Tjale, although vying to become the first black winner of Comrades, were also non-entrants.

When all was said and done, this was, barring mishap, going to be a shoot-out between two of South Africa's finest ever long-distance runners, Bruce Fordyce and Alan Robb. Alan Robb was approaching the end of his illustrious career at the top. While he was undoubtedly one of the greatest of all Comrades greats, he did have one problem: he was the only member of the unofficial association of greats who had to contend with a future great, on the verge of achieving Comrades immortality, while he himself was just starting to feel the effects of nature's natural decline. Fordyce, on the other hand, had all the determination of a great athlete who was beginning to realise his true potential and was ready to claim his position in the pantheon of Comrades superstars.

Each contender had a somewhat erratic build-up to this year's race. Fordyce won the 1981 London-to-Brighton, but suffered a leg muscle tear in February. Professor Tim Noakes helped him, in rather painful fashion, by reintroducing him to a fellow ex-Witsie, physiotherapist Graeme Lindenberg, who was using a new method of treating muscle sprains called 'cross-friction'. It wasn't pleasant, but it worked. Fordyce took third place in the 56-kilometre Korkie behind winner Hoseah Tjale and John Claase. Robb, king of the Korkie, finished five minutes behind. He did, however, return to form and win the Bergville Marathon. Fordyce supporters were well advised to remember that Robb had triumphed in all three previous 'down' runs in which he had participated, and that his 1978 record of 5.29.14 was the only sub-five-hours-30-minutes Comrades yet.

A record field of 4 887, out of 5 501 entrants, assembled outside the Pietermaritzburg City Hall in extremely inhospitable conditions. Overnight rain had not abated. The beginning of a 'down' run is generally colder than a Durban start, and this year, it was positively freezing. It was not at all comforting to the shivering athletes to consider the awesome fact that the 1982 Comrades was 91.4 kilometres, one of the longest ever.

In fact, the only relief was the starting gun, which allowed sodden runners to get some movement into their aching limbs. It wasn't too much fun for the brave spectators either, although one did raise a laugh with the comment, 'Fordyce, you need your black armband to keep you warm.' First to show were Johannes Tsetseng, Israel Kutoana and Henry Nyembe. Of the three, only Nyembe could be regarded a realistic contender.

Experienced Comrades runners are aware that the temperature at the foot of Polly Shortts is generally a degree or two colder than that at the start. This year was no exception. Still-cold athletes were astonished to find, at the bottom of Pollys, a bed occupied by a couple who toasted them with champagne as they passed. It was said afterwards that the pair had just spent their honeymoon night there.

Humour helped many runners overcome the discomfort they were feeling. Any sort of diversion that would distract troubled minds from their present dilemma was welcome. 'Dancing' Dave Wright, well known for his Fred Astaire-like finish, sang 'Waltzing Matilda' for the benefit of the press vehicle. Taciturn Alan Robb passed the sign reading '56 kilometres to go' and, somewhat uncharacteristically, said, 'OK, boys, only Two Oceans to go.' Two or three disconcerted souls were so overawed that they pulled out.

Despite his quip, Robb clearly meant business. He showed his hand as the leaders went through the perversely named Harrison Flats, putting in little surges on the downhill sections and drawing others into his race strategy. A few casualties fell by the wayside, among them Danny Biggs, fifth in 1981, and a Comrades newcomer by the name of Bob de la Motte.

Despite Robb's aggressive tactics, aimed largely at his major rival, Fordyce, it was the relatively unknown Henry Nyembe who was first through halfway in 2.48.32. He was followed by a pack that included virtually all the big guns: Robb, Fordyce, Wright, Abbott, Tivers, Metcalfe, Holtzhausen and Vorster. The race was now well and truly on.

Nyembe stayed in front, accompanied by the Fordyce/Robb 'bus', until the top of Botha's Hill. Then Robb put in another surge on the descent of Botha's. Fordyce and Nyembe were the only ones who responded. Nyembe couldn't maintain the pace and dropped back. When they reached Hillcrest, Robb and Fordyce had shaken off all other opposition and had only each other to worry about.

For the next 20 kilometres or so, Robb and Fordyce fought a private battle of frightening intensity. The stretch of road from Hillcrest to Kloof is regarded as relatively flat, yet it is subtly undulating. Each of the two leaders was fully aware of his strengths and (minor) frailties. Robb was the downhill specialist, Fordyce master of uphill running. On the downs, Robb would surge. On the ups, Fordyce would pull ahead. Each time one made a move, the other would counter. They were traveling at breakneck speed, each trying to break the other. The sheer pressure was clearly unsustainable. One of these two great athletes would have to concede.

As they approached Kloof, Fordyce observed a weakening of Robb's resolve. Instead of coming back alongside his rival after a Fordyce surge, Robb was content to tuck in behind him. The canny Fordyce reasoned that the showdown was beckoning. At Kloof, he put in another surge. Robb again responded. Immediately, Fordyce surged again, now on the descent of Field's Hill. Despite his downhill strength, Robb was unable to answer. Fordyce had shrewdly put in his challenge where it would be least expected. It was a masterstroke.

In Pinetown, Fordyce was half a kilometre ahead of Robb, whose pace was visibly slackening. The after-effects of the titanic battle were starting to tell on both athletes. Fordyce wearily dragged himself up Cowies Hill. His rivals now knew that he was weakening, and he was unaware that they were struggling to keep moving.

At the top of Cowies, Fordyce held a seemingly insurmountable lead of four minutes. By Westville, his advantage had increased to seven minutes. Barring accidents, he was now relatively safe, although extremely uncomfortable. He felt that he was hardly moving, yet his lead was steadily increasing. Near Westridge Stadium, he wanted to walk. The desire to do so was almost irresistible. He said later, 'I thought it would look a bit ridiculous for the winner to be walking, and I realised that, if I walked, my chances of getting going again were slim.' Nevertheless, he did broach the subject of walking to one of his seconds, Alan Edwards, whose response was rather firm: 'You walk one step and I'll kick your backside all the way to Durban!'

Fordyce found the advice quite convincing. He didn't walk as he gently eased his weary body to a finish in 5.34.22. Afterwards, he incorrectly stated that he would never again take part in a 'down' run and gave his view of his tussle with Robb: 'I did about the time I expected. I prefer going up. I couldn't believe that no one caught me. I was almost jogging on the spot. It wasn't easy to get away from Robb. It was a long battle.'

Even in defeat, Alan Robb managed to impress all with his courage and determination. Never before had he been beaten in a 'down' run. After Fordyce had passed him, he fell back into fourth place behind the Hillcrest Villagers duo of Graeme Fraser and Tony Abbott. Summoning up every ounce of his reserves, Robb fought back and tenaciously took second place just 29 seconds ahead of Fraser. His post-race comments were typically brief: 'Coming down Field's Hill, I tried to hang in, but my thighs were playing up. At Tollgate, I felt good so I went after Fraser and Abbott. I'll be back next year.'

Fraser and Abbott finished third and fourth ahead of fifth-placed 'Dancing' Dave Wright. Sixth place went to Piet Vorster, popular record-breaking winner of the 1979 'up' run who ran in the colours of his new club, Celtic Harriers of Cape Town. Another Celtic Harrier, Chet Sainsbury, completed his fifth silver in 7.15.45. Derrick Tivers, ninth, and Errol Ackerman, 15th, joined forces with their more senior Hillcrest Villagers clubmates Graeme Fraser and Tony Abbott in successfully retaining the coveted Gunga Din team trophy.

This year, the women's race started off with a clear favourite. Former American Cheryl Jorgensen had finished second in 1980 and 1981. Surely this would be her year. It certainly seemed to be going that way when Jorgensen, well ahead of her rivals, went through Drummond in the fast time of 3 hours 24 minutes. She continued to dominate the women's 'race within a race', but found the excruciating downhill of Field's Hill a real problem. Nevertheless, she overcame that particular hurdle and set a new women's 'down' record of 7.04.59, finishing over 46 minutes ahead of second-placed Lisa Warren. A highly elated Jorgensen, a worthy winner after her previous efforts, spelt out her tactics rather succinctly: 'I ran my own race. After the start, I didn't see another lady.'

Jorgensen's effort was a significant step forward in the development of women's ultramarathon running. She was the only female recipient of a silver medal, which she had earned with 25 minutes to spare. It was also her third successive silver in a race in which she finished 229th overall, with over 4 000 runners behind her. Women's running was still short of quantity, but the quality was changing mindsets.

Mr Comrades, Liege Boulle, successfully finished his 38th Comrades at the age of 73 with almost an hour to spare. Hopes were expressed that Boulle would hang in and become the first to win 40 medals. As usual, there were tales of those who had overcome adversity on their way to Comrades success. Helderberg Harrier Justin Swart, 25 years old, was one such runner. He had endured two years of suffering after having been diagnosed with cancer of the lymphatic glands. Swart finished comfortably with over 35 minutes to spare.

1982 COMRADES MARATHON RESULTS

1. B. N. S. Fordyce	5.34.22
2. A. G. Robb	5.41.26
3. G. A. Fraser	5.41.55
4. A. M. Abbott	5.42.32
5. D. R. H. Wright	5.46.49
6. P. Vorster	5.50.20
7. H. G. Holtzhausen	5.52.44
8. H. M. N. Nyembe	5,53,29
9. D. R. Tivers	5.55.10
10. D. C. B. Anderson	5.55.25

1982 COMRADES BOWL RESULTS

1. C. L. Jorgensen	7.04.59.
2. L. W. Warren	7.52.26
3. R. Smit	8.01.16
4. P. A. Carlisle	8:03:05
5. J. A. Saunders	8:04:14
6. L. P. Spence	8:11:25
7. S. Stevens	8:12:48
8. S. H. van Wyk	8:14:48

9. J. A. Cadman   8:17:33
10. H. E. Hairs   8:22:13

1983 COMRADES MARATHON
FORDYCE'S HAT-TRICK

On Friday, 20 May 1983, just 11 days before the Comrades Marathon, runners throughout the country were going into traditional pre-race hypochondria, with severe paranoid complications. Colds and influenza were all around. Family members and work colleagues seemed to have only one objective in mind: sneeze, sneeze and sneeze again, sending as many aggressive germs as possible in the direction of poor, innocent, healthy Comrades hopefuls.

On this, the second-last weekend before the big day, runners would be winding down: no more long runs, no more attempting to build up strength and stamina. It was too late now. All the hard work had been done. All that remained was the waiting. Staying out of trouble was the only thing that mattered.

Staying out of trouble suddenly became impossible for those working in central Pretoria. Shortly before 4.30 p.m., as office workers were leaving for the weekend, the city erupted. A huge bomb had exploded outside the headquarters of the South African Air Force. It was clearly aimed at a defined military target, although peripheral casualties were inevitable. There were 19 fatalities and 217 reported injuries. It was a clear reminder that the nation was uncomfortably close to civil war. There were a few late withdrawals from the Comrades line-up as fear led some to cancel flights.

Comrades itself had a problem that for a while seemed to imperil the holding of the 1983 race: the Natal province was experiencing its worst drought in recorded history. Households were subjected to severe restrictions on water usage, as were businesses. Visitors were informed, on arrival, of regulations affecting their conduct during their stay.

In such circumstances, how could more than 6 000 lunatics be allowed to engage in a self-destructive road race in which each would consume approximately six litres of liquid along the way? The anti-Comrades brigade were up in arms. Fortunately, there weren't too many of them – and furthermore, the water crisis in Natal, and particularly the Comrades response to it, underlined the importance of the race. Desalinisation machines were set up in Durban to purify sea water. The Cape Town municipality arranged to transport containers of water to Durban. The show had to go on.

The show did go on. If anything, the water issue brought home to many the realisation that the Comrades Marathon was an integral and essential part of South African life. The runners didn't have to be persuaded. Despite all the problems, a record number of 6 636 submitted their entries. There was also an enthusiastic response to the 'Buy a Brick' campaign introduced by the Comrades Marathon Association in order to entrench the permanent nature of Comrades in the minds of South Africans. An office and a museum were envisaged. Recognising the changing circumstances of the sport, Comrades chairman Mick Winn succinctly spelt out a concern of the association: 'We must avoid the possibility of a major sponsor taking over the race and prefixing the word "Comrades" with its name.'

The campaign was to prove a huge success in various ways. Today, Comrades House, an imposing Victorian building in Pietermaritzburg, serves as a museum, containing and preserving Comrades records and memorabilia of inestimable value. Next door, the Comrades office handles the administration and marketing of the event. On the course, the Comrades Wall of Honour registers the names and race records of runners whose association with the race means more to them than mere medals.

Seventeen days before the 1983 marathon, a very special event took place: a reunion of all available past winners of the race. It is widely believed that a motivating factor was the advancing age of supreme Comrades hero Wally Hayward. As he was approaching 75, it was felt that he should be honoured, along with his fellow champions, while he was still around. Whether or not this is true, he would go on to outlive some of his co-winners by a couple of decades.

The official reunion was held at a Johannesburg hotel on 14 May. Attendance was extraordinary, considering that some of the winners had been visitors from abroad and a couple of South Africans had emigrated. Of those still alive, only Bill Savage was unavailable through ill health. Present were Darrell Dale, the only surviving winner from the 1920s, John Smith,

Dave Levick, Bernard Gomersall, Piet Vorster, Dave Bagshaw, Allen Boyce, Mick Orton, Reg Allison, Bill Cochrane, Trevor Allen, Wally Hayward, Gerald Walsh, Tommy Malone, Manie Kuhn, Derek Preiss, Jackie Mekler, Johannes Coleman, Mercer Davies, George Claassen, Alan Robb and current champion Bruce Fordyce. Those who were no longer alive – Bill Rowan, Arthur Newton, Harry Phillips, Frank Sutton, Phil Masterton-Smith and Hardy Ballington – were suitably remembered.

During the event, the long-standing but entirely friendly rivalry between Tommy Malone and Manie Kuhn surfaced. It was decided that a showdown would take place in order to establish which of the two was the better runner. Late in the evening, or perhaps early the following morning, they were escorted a few blocks away from the hotel in order to stage their decider. Alan Robb was the official starter and Bruce Fordyce the line judge. Perhaps as a result of the night's celebratory nature, both lost their way and entered the hotel premises from separate entrances. They were both disqualified and, rather thankfully, the rivalry continued.

Pre-race speculation was all about Fordyce. Now champion of both the 'up' and 'down' runs, he was threatening to establish a new era of dominance. Despite his triumphs in the preceding two years, however, doubts lingered as to how good he really was. Somewhat shy and retiring by nature, Fordyce was beginning to break out of his shell, thanks largely to the media attention that had followed his recent successes. Not only was he the 'up' and 'down' champion, but he had also won the two previous London-to-Brighton races. Furthermore, he went to this year's start as the record holder for the 'up' race and as South Africa's 1982 Sportsman of the Year. He had made a study of the race and was fully aware of the strengths and weaknesses of his opponents. With well-founded confidence in his ability, Fordyce was ready.

A total of 5 862 gathered outside Durban City Hall and set off on the long journey to the capital city. This year, the race was actually a little shorter than usual: minor route alterations had reduced the distance to 87.7 kilometres. A crowd of 20 000 well-wishers provided a festive atmosphere as the large field moved away from the city centre and began the first climb of the day, the ascent of Berea Road, with further spectators providing encouragement until the top at Tollgate.

The initial 'dash for TV glory' was becoming a feature of Comrades starts. A few brief moments of recognition were all that some seemed to desire.

Wildebeest athletes Bernard Posholi, Johannes Makgotsi and Johannes Tsetseng were the first to show. They were followed by Rakabaele, Selkonyela and John O'Byrne. None would leave a lasting impression on this year's Comrades.

At 45th Cutting, the same bunch continued to lead the race, with top runners Graeme Fraser and Colin Goosen not too far behind. Closely following them was a large group including Piet Vorster, Danny Biggs and Alan Robb. Bruce Fordyce was a further two minutes behind. He had set himself three early aims: 'to have Alan Robb in sight, not to be left too far behind at the gun and, at the same time, not to be caught up in the initial rush'. So far, so good. Fordyce's plan was right on track.

The threat of Robb soon disappeared. He wasn't really at his best, although he would never admit that to himself. He was suffering from blood poisoning, which had adversely affected his preparation. Going through Westville, he fell heavily. Clearly in pain, there seemed no rational reason to continue. Nevertheless, 'submission' did not exist in Alan Robb's vocabulary.

Colin Goosen was first through Drummond in 2.49.15, an exceptionally fast time, yet four minutes slower than the 'mad' time set by Johnny Halberstadt in his unsuccessful 1979 run. Vorster, Fraser, Shaw, Biggs, Fordyce and Tjale were all virtually within shooting distance of the leader. The struggling Robb was more than three minutes behind the lead group.

Inchanga invariably has an effect on the outcome of an 'up' run. Gordon Shaw, feeling strong and aware of the Fordyce threat, pushed ahead. Graeme Fraser and Colin Goosen were unable to answer. Fordyce and Tjale, running together, gradually made up ground and caught Shaw. The effort was too much for Tjale, who dropped off the pace. Shaw and Fordyce were left to fight out the battle for supremacy.

The decisive moment came unexpectedly. A marshal, whose knowledge of the rules was somewhat short of adequate, saw Fordyce take a drink from one of his personal helpers and immediately confronted him: 'Bruce Fordyce, I'm a marshal. You have just been seconded. I'm disqualifying you.' Fortunately, Fordyce's chief second, Godfrey Franz, witnessed the exchange and quickly reassured him, 'Don't worry, Bruce, we'll take care of the problem. Just calm down.'

If the unwelcome intrusion achieved anything, it was to galvanise

Fordyce into possibly the most determined mood of his career. He simply took off and pulverised any opposition that might have challenged him. Gordon Shaw had no answer as the defending champion stamped his authority on the race. Utterly devastated, Shaw lay down on the side of the road. Afterwards, he lamented the untimely intervention of the misguided official: 'It was the worst thing that marshal could have done.'

Fordyce kept his emotions to himself and channelled his anger into a controlled assault on the course. He was on his own and nobody would come close to contesting his dominance of the event. At the foot of Polly Shortts, he was told that a record was out of the question. When he reached the top, he heard that a new record was within his grasp. Tim Noakes described Fordyce's triumph in words that have become part of Comrades folklore:

'The television broadcast bore witness to one of those supreme moments in sport: a vision of athletic perfection that is unlikely to be equalled. I am happy to admit that watching Bruce running up Polly Shortts, with the strains of Vangelis's famous music in the background, moved me to tears of joy. Never before had the Comrades seen such poetic running, nor had such fast running ever been achieved so effortlessly in the last third of the race. Bruce's running expressed an intangible beauty: the now great runner, oblivious of the camera, content with his own most private thoughts, proving that man is beautifully made and indeed the wonder of the universe.'

Tim Noakes's eloquence was matched by Fordyce's finish. At the foot of Pollys, a record wasn't on, but by the time he reached the top, it had become possible. His finishing time of 5.30.12 beat his own record by 7 minutes 16 seconds. Any doubts about Fordyce's credentials had been well and truly erased. Clearly, he was one of the all-time Comrades greats. As for Noakes – well, he finished this year, but somewhat undertrained, not in anything approaching his best time.

Fordyce's victory put him in a special category. He became the fourth man, after Arthur Newton, Dave Bagshaw and Alan Robb, to record three successive victories. Afterwards he spoke of the mental demands of the race: 'I had a very bad first half and I felt the pressure. It's always bad because you never know what the others are doing and going to do. At halfway, I was running with Hoseah Tjale. He was a great help and relaxed me a lot. I think I helped him too.' It had been a wonderful effort of Fordyce, but the result wasn't totally satisfactory. His time of 5.30.12 was a new record and by a considerable margin, but he had failed to break five and a half hours, as Alan Robb had done in the 1978 'down' run. Fordyce would have to return and make amends.

In the women's race, defending champion Cheryl Jorgensen was expected to contend for line honours with the young Natal University student Lindsay Weight. Weight it was who triumphed on the day, her winning time of 7.12.56 being the second-fastest yet for a woman. Jenny Wilson took second place, with Gail Ingram third. Ever-reliable Cheryl Jorgensen was fourth, while Moira Hornby, in the nick of time, brought the women's silver tally to five, a new record.

1983 COMRADES MARATHON RESULTS

1. B. N. S. Fordyce	5.30.12
2. G. W. Shaw	5.45.48
3. G. A. Fraser	5.46.20
4. A. M. Abbott	5.54.26
5. E. Ackerman	5.55.27
6. H. Tjale	5.59.25
7. P. Vorster	5.59.34
8. J. F. Dixon	6.00.17
9. A. M. D. Dearling	6.00.25
10. C. A. Goosen	6.02.14

1983 COMRADES BOWL RESULTS

1. L. M. Weight	7.12.56
2. J. A. Wilson	7.23.45
3. G. H. Ingram	7.27.00
4. C. L. Jorgensen	7.29.41
5. M. L. Hornby	7.29.59
6. L. W. Warren	7.32.42
7. R. Smit	7.35.36
8. H. E. Hairs	7.44.36

9. A. J. Steyn   7.53.37
10. P. A. Carlisle   7.54.14

1984 COMRADES MARATHON
A FAMILY DAY FOR THE VILLETS

In 1984, the Springboks played a two-match series against England. Errol Tobias was selected at fly-half, the usual incumbent Naas Botha having temporarily given up local rugby for gridiron football in the U.S.A. In the first test in Port Elizabeth, Tobias played superbly in a 33-15 South African victory. Danie Gerber, Carel du Plessis and Rob Louw scored tries for the Springboks. Gerber's was a gem. His centre partner, John Villet, making his debut, straightened the line, broke incisively and timed his pass to perfection to put Gerber in behind the posts. Villet's parents, John senior and Anna, were not at the ground to witness their son's triumph. They had their own challenge that day. While the test match was being played, they were running the Comrades Marathon.

More often than not, the Comrades Marathon has been run on a public holiday. The first race was held on Empire Day, 24 May 1921. In recent years, Republic Day, 31 May, had been regarded as a natural successor. But South Africa in 1984 was a nation in conflict. Religious and moral leaders were becoming increasingly vociferous in their rejection of the government's apartheid policies. So there was a sense of unease among the Comrades faithful when it was realised that Ascension Thursday coincided with Republic Day this year. There was consequently a sense of relief when Friday, 1 June, was declared a public holiday and became, effectively, Comrades day.

All eyes were focused on Bruce Fordyce in the build-up to the 1984 Comrades Marathon. As defending champion, with three successive victories, he was hoping to emulate Arthur Newton and become the second runner to record four straight wins. No one doubted his ability to do so. Although he regarded himself as something of an 'up' run specialist, the record books suggest that he was equally adept in both directions.

The manner in which he had achieved his 1983 victory lent him an aura of invincibility. As if that were not enough, he had won the London-to-Brighton race for the third successive time in 1983, setting a new world record for 50 miles along the way.

One of the challenges facing those seeking a place among the greats is the need to achieve athletic and psychological mastery over the top runners of one's era. Fordyce had already done this. When he became a main contender, Alan Robb was the top man, with Piet Vorster another champion and record holder and the awesome Johnny Halberstadt looking like heir apparent to the Comrades throne. While one should acknowledge that Robb was not only one of the all-time greats, but also the only great champion whose declining years coincided with the rise of the next superstar, the simple fact is that Fordyce overcame those early rivals and established himself as number one.

Now longevity beckoned and, with it, the prospect of an extended tenure as Comrades champion. A new batch of contenders would have to be faced and repelled. That was the challenge facing Fordyce as he prepared for this year's race. Yet there were no obvious threats, and this itself posed a problem: whom should he watch? Hoseah Tjale had been around for a while. He would certainly have made a worthy champion, but Fordyce seemed to have the measure of him. Bob de la Motte was a strong runner who had come second in this year's Korkie. He commanded respect, but was a relative newcomer to Comrades.

Then there was the gnawing fear that haunts every favourite: the unknown runner or, perhaps, the experienced athlete who has the pedigree but hasn't tried his hand at ultra-distance racing. Three top runners fell into this category: standard marathon stars Bernard Rose, Willie Farrell and Kevin Shaw. Fordyce allowed the trio to constitute, in his mind, his main opposition on the day. It was a mistake that very nearly cost him dearly.

Final instructions from the organising committee specified that official race numbers had to be visible, front and back, at all times. Novices turned up fully compliant. Seasoned campaigners, though, wore old jerseys, tracksuits and, as was the new custom, black refuse bags. The temperature was zero. The naively obedient nearly shivered to death as they watched the city hall clock move closer to 6 a.m., listened to *Chariots of Fire* and Max Trimborn's cockcrow, and eventually shuffled forward at the gun.

The freezing start must have contracted bladders already swollen in response to the current medical advice: 'Drink, drink, keep on drinking! Don't become dehydrated!' Evidence of this was the hundreds of male runners lining the side of the road, watering flowers and shrubs. At the foot of Polly Shortts, approximately ten kilometres into the race, the temperature was -1°C.

Fortunately, the sun did make an appearance. After about two hours on the road, life became pleasant. Frozen limbs thawed. Extra clothing became an unwanted burden and was discarded. Zulu women ran alongside the road, picking up jettisoned garments and ululating. Runners picked out those who they felt had the greatest need and were rewarded with the most grateful of smiles. Comrades was at its best.

Early leaders Sithembele Ndamase and Velemseni Nyandeni might have looked impressive to onlookers and television viewers, but they would not feature in the outcome of the race. At the commencement of the descent of Polly Shortts, Kevin Shaw was right up with the front-runners. The marathon stars had split up, although Farrell and Rose were together.

At Camperdown, Mike Symonds of Johannesburg Harriers became the first realistic race leader. At Cato Ridge, he was still in front, with Kevin Shaw, Wellington Njozwana, Chris Reyneke and John Hamlett close behind. Following them was another group that included Graeme Fraser, Tony Abbott, Arthur Lemos, Karel Liebetrau, Deon Holtzhausen and Bob de la Motte. Fordyce was in yet another bunch, along with Rose, Hoseah Tjale, Alan Robb, Mike Horn and Danny Biggs.

At this stage Fordyce was asked by a television interviewer to reveal how he was feeling. He responded, 'At the moment, it's still pretty cool, but it's going to be very hot, so I think everybody's drinking quite a lot. So far it's a very tactical race. It's rather slow so I don't think a record will be on.' Evidence of the tactical nature of proceedings was the manner in which the main contenders had become sucked into various 'buses'. They were watching those they had identified as their rivals. Fordyce's eyes were on Rose.

Over Harrison Flats and on the ascent of Inchanga the race began to develop in earnest. Firstly, Shaw and Reyneke took the lead from a tiring Symonds, with Hamlett third and De la Motte, making an early move, in fourth spot. On Inchanga, Reyneke broke away from Shaw. Reyneke was wearing white gloves to help his family identify him on their television screen. He needn't have bothered: being in first place was quite sufficient.

Reyneke went through halfway in 2.44.20, with Shaw second and Hamlett third. Bob de la Motte was about four minutes behind the leader and two minutes ahead of Fordyce. Asked by a television commentator at Drummond if he was concerned about being six minutes adrift of Reynecke, Fordyce replied: 'I'm not worried about the leaders. I'm quite happy with my time.'

His happiness didn't last very long. His seconds managed to convince him that he had been watching the wrong men, Farrell and Rose. His real opponents, Reyneke and De la Motte, were way ahead. Both realised that they had successfully pulled out a significant lead over the defending champion. Both knew that it was vital to extend that lead, and each set about doing so. Each had a healthy respect for the strength and speed of Fordyce in the closing stages of an ultramarathon.

Bob de la Motte knew that this was his big opportunity, and Bruce Fordyce was fully aware that De la Motte was capable of grasping it. At Hillcrest, De la Motte had taken two minutes off Reyneke's lead and maintained his advantage over Fordyce. He saw the relatively flat section from Hillcrest to Kloof and the steep descent of Field's Hill as the ideal section to push hard, and did so. Shortly before Kloof, De la Motte took the lead for the first time. Fordyce, mindful of the damage he had suffered in his epic duel with Robb two years previously, eased his way gently down Field's Hill.

At Pinetown, De la Motte's lead over Fordyce had been stretched to 2 minutes 10 seconds. Although Reyneke was still second and Shaw and Tjale were only a minute behind Fordyce, most realised that the victor would be one of the two Johannesburgers, leader De la Motte and chaser Fordyce. Nursing a painful toenail, Fordyce was concerned that he wasn't getting any closer to De la Motte.

On the ascent of Cowies Hill, Fordyce went past Reyneke into second place. At the top, De la Motte's lead was still two minutes. The news gave him fresh heart and he pressed ahead, determined to keep his pursuer at bay. Fordyce, too, felt renewed resolve as he tried to close the gap. Finally, after about 75 kilometres on the road, De la Motte showed signs of weakening and his pace dropped perceptibly. At Westville, he was only a minute ahead of the greatest of all finishers.

Ever the tactical master, Fordyce timed his takeover bid in order to exploit his main asset, his uphill strength. On the climb up to 45th Cutting, he finally took the lead. As he passed De la Motte, he called out, 'Bob, you're running like a star.' Soon afterwards, reaction set in. The battle for supremacy had been won, but nearly ten kilometres still needed to be negotiated with weary legs. Fordyce slowed, but the vanquished De la Motte was in no condition to challenge him.

Kissing the winner's baton with relief, Fordyce entered Kingsmead to the acclaim of thousands and crossed the finish line in a new record time of 5.27.18. Afterwards, he said, 'It was a tough race and Bob ran very well. I learnt a crucial lesson running against Alan Robb a couple of years ago, and that was to be as relaxed and casual as possible. I realise today what a fantastic time Robb's 1978 record time was.' Fordyce was also swift to point out that Robb's record had been set on a longer course.

Bob de la Motte, although exhausted, managed to cling on to second place and was welcomed, as he described it, as a 'loser being given a victor's ovation'. The same could be said in respect of all ten gold medallists, with special attention given to Hoseah Tjale, fourth, and local university student Danny Biggs, who followed him home. Ninth place went to Varsity Old Boys' Eric Bateman, who earned a rare gold medal for Cape Town. Early leader Kevin Shaw claimed tenth spot.

The women's race was regarded beforehand as fairly open, although defending champion Lindsay Weight, now of UCT, Ralie Smit and Moira Hornby were singled out as potential winners. Weight took an early lead, but was later joined by Smit, who moved ahead shortly before Inchanga. Weight fought back, however, and was first to Drummond in 3.18, a time that she regarded as too fast, although she was feeling strong. Ralie Smit was still second, ahead of Cheryl Jorgensen, Gail Ingram, Anneline Pieterse and Priscilla Carlisle.

In the second half, there was simply no one to challenge the defending champion. Lindsay Weight outclassed the field, coming home in a new record time of 6.46.35. She became the first woman to break the seven-hour barrier in the 'down' run, although, rather amazingly, fellow Ikey Isavel Roche-Kelly's 'up' record was even faster. A thoroughly exhausted Priscilla Carlisle crawled her way to the finish, where she took second place ahead of Gail Ingram. Sandy Stevens came fourth ahead of the 1980 winner, the consistent Cheryl Jorgensen, who won her fifth successive gold medal.

Liege Boulle was the big disappointment of the day. Race chairman Mick Winn admitted recently that one big error made by the Comrades Marathon Association was the announcement that a special medal had been struck in order to record Boulle's 40th successful Comrades. Unfortunately, Boulle pulled out of the race when almost in sight of the finish. He didn't ever get to complete a 40th run.

When John Villet had showered and dressed after playing a significant role in the Springboks' rugby victory over England, he had a moment or two to find out how the senior members of his family had fared. The news was positive. Both had successfully completed their fifth Comrades Marathon, John senior in 10.35.50 and the speedy Anna in 9.14.35.

1984 COMRADES MARATHON RESULTS

1. B. N. S. Fordyce	5.27.18
2. R. A. L. de la Motte	5.30.59
3. J. C. Reyneke	5.34.39
4. H. Tjale	5.37.24
5. D. R. Biggs	5.47.11
6. H. G. Holtzhausen	5.48.14
7. G. A. Fraser	5.48.22
8. A. P. Lemos	5.48.58
9. E. D. Bateman	5.50.37
10. K. R. Shaw	5.51.56

1984 COMRADES BOWL RESULTS

1. L. M. Weight	6.46.35
2. P. A. Carlisle	7.15.32
3. G. Ingram	7.15.51
4. S. Stevens	7.18.04
5. C. L. Jorgensen	7.20.35
6. H. E. Hairs	7.24.20
7. G. Buhrmann	7.29.08

8. L. W. Warren	7.31.43
9. G. M. Rawson	7.34.11
10. C. M. Bauer	7.42.35

1985 COMRADES MARATHON
FORDYCE'S FIFTH

South Africa was in the middle of the most challenging decade in the nation's short history. This was the period in which whites were asked by the more enlightened of their compatriots to consider the possibility that the privileged status that they enjoyed was both unjust and unsustainable.

While attempts to make the white electorate see reason were gaining ground, the divisions caused by the government's apartheid policies were becoming more pronounced in 1985. This was the year of President P. W. Botha's disastrous 'Rubicon' speech. It was the year in which the disinvestment campaign became a reality and British and American companies introduced new employment policies for their South African operations. It was the year in which concerned religious leaders produced their 'Kairos' document. It was the year in which the Congress of South African Trade Unions was established. It was clearly a year of increasing racial polarisation.

It was also the year of the Comrades Diamond Jubilee, the 60th running of the great race that remained true to the nobility of human ideals inclusive of all. The occasion was marked by defending champion Bruce Fordyce's attempt to join Arthur Newton, Hardy Ballington, Wally Hayward and Jackie Mekler as a five-time Comrades winner. In the case of Fordyce, however, there would be a significant difference should he succeed: his victories would have been achieved in consecutive years.

Following his 1984 triumph, Fordyce had abandoned his erstwhile practice of taking part in the London-to-Brighton race. Instead, he went to the USA to compete in the American Medical Joggers Assocation 50-miler in Chicago. As usual, he finished first, his time for the distance being second only to his own world record for the distance set in England the previous year.

During 1985, Fordyce produced a book entitled *Comrades*, in which he gave advice on how to tackle the event, including this: 'Caution should be applied to both training and racing. It means not "flying off" at the sound of the Comrades gun; it means experimenting carefully with new ideas long before the race; and it means not falling into the trap of excessive training mileage.'

Fordyce failed to follow his own advice and, contrary to character, almost recklessly overdid early-year racing. After a tough January, he came third in Cape Town's Peninsula Marathon in 2.18. The following month, he entered the Pieter Korkie Ultramarathon. Despite his oft-repeated belief that racing twice within a few months is 'suicidal', he responded as most athletes would when he unexpectedly found himself in the lead. A time of 47 minutes over the final 14 kilometres secured victory, but could have thwarted his Comrades ambitions.

A severe cold in April curtailed the reigning champion's hectic schedule, perhaps saving him from Comrades self-destruction. The experts seemed to think so. They could see only one possible winner, Bruce Fordyce – or, as some were saying, Bruce 'Fivedyce'. Tommy Malone, 1966 Comrades champion, admiringly referred to Fordyce as 'the Einstein of long-distance running'.

There was no doubt that Fordyce, in addition to the natural athletic ability inherited from his parents, had a mindset that was totally positive and optimistic. As fear of the awesome Polly Shortts spread among novices, Fordyce expressed his view of the famous last obstacle of the 'up' run: 'I actually feel very positive about Pollys. When I see it, I'm on a physical low but a mental high. I know I only have that one hill to get over and then I'm home and dry.'

On a mild and relatively windless morning, 9 058 athletes set out on the epic journey to the provincial capital. First to show up on the nation's television screens was local runner Patrick Maphumulo of Pinetown. He was soon supplanted by Zacharia Makukumare, who was a far more serious runner.

Makukumare led the field over Cowies Hill, the first of the Big Five. Behind him, early sensibility started to come to the fore. About half a kilometre behind the obviously temporary leader, Capetonian Bruce Matthews led the real race, with Aaron Jama and Chris Reyneke close behind. Hoseah Tjale kept in close contact with the leading bunch, while Fordyce was closer to the early action than one had come to expect of him.

In Pinetown, Makukumare's period of glory came to a sudden end as Matthews, Jama and Reyneke went past. In addition to Matthews, a few other Capetonians were close to the lead. Eric Bateman and Mike Horn kept the Mother City's hopes high.

Jama and Matthews continued to lead the field, having jettisoned the hapless Makukumare, over Field's Hill and onto the fairly long and relatively flat section from Kloof to Hillcrest. The following bunch, quietly biding their time, included the big names: Tjale, Gordon (not Kevin) Shaw, Thobejane, Fordyce, Biggs, Van Staden, Tivers, Fraser and Gqele. Mike Horn and Chris Reyneke were both looking uncomfortable and a little off the pace.

On the ascent of Botha's Hill, Matthews put in a surge, to which Jama was unable to respond. The fancied Capetonian led the pack through halfway in 2.54, nine minutes slower than Halberstadt's record for that section. Tjale was second, with Oberholzer third. Then came the real contenders, still together and well placed to mount an attack at the appropriate moment.

True to form, Inchanga proved a pivotal point in the race. Matthews started to wilt and was soon passed by Tjale. Biggs, Fordyce and Tivers moved up into contention while Matthews gradually slipped back, eventually to finish 15th in 6.07.34, a year after claiming 14th position in 5.58.32. With 20 medals to his credit, he didn't ever crack that elusive gold. Now living in New Zealand, he was asked on a recent visit to Comrades if impetuous front-running had cost him his chance of gold. His response was swift and firm: 'Absolutely not. I ran to the best of my ability. If I could do it all again, I wouldn't change anything.'

Going through Harrison Flats, Tjale, Fordyce, Biggs, Tivers and Oberholzer were out in front, exchanging positions almost as if they were slipstreaming cyclists. For a short while, Fordyce felt confused. Tjale, possibly the most experienced and the strongest of his rivals, was in front. Meanwhile, Siphiwe Gqele, three-time Two Oceans winner and arguably the most intellectual of all in his tactical approach, was behind and menacing. Unfortunately for race enthusiasts, the threat from behind did not materialise. When Gqele fell back, the defending champion realised that Tjale was his one real threat.

From Cato Ridge, the two rivals matched each other and tested each other, looking for signs of weariness. Eventually, on the awkward climb up to the bridge over the highway on the approach to Camperdown, Tjale took a drink and lost a few metres. Fordyce surged. Tjale didn't respond. Fordyce surged again. Soon, a significant gap was evident. The strong man had timed his move perfectly and would now stride away to victory.

Actually, the strong man was feeling decidedly weak, even though his advantage over Tjale was growing. At the Dardanelles turn-off, he was over a minute and a half ahead. Conscious that he would be vulnerable to a strong attack, he felt threatened by the overhead television helicopter pinpointing his position, seemingly for the benefit of his pursuers.

There was no letting up for Fordyce, whose dictum, 'Training is a science, racing is an art,' had caused him to take the lead with approximately 25 kilometres to go. The loneliest position in ultramarathon racing was his. He was uncomfortable but determined to keep going. At the foot of Polly Shortts, he was just 1 minute 22 seconds ahead of Hoseah Tjale, who had Derrick Tivers snapping at his heels.

In boxing, when world title fights were fought over 15 rounds, the final three were sometimes referred to as the 'championship' rounds. With physical energy expended, it was the stronger willpower that would prevail. In a sense, this was true of Comrades. No 'up' run leader who has reached the top of Pollys first has been overtaken on the run-in to the finish.

The champion Fordyce would not succumb in the final moments of his race of destiny. His winning time of 5.37.01 was almost seven minutes slower than his record-breaking effort two years previously, and his victory margin over second-placed Tjale was more than five minutes. Bruce Fordyce had edged ahead of his predecessors in the quest for all-time Comrades glory. His five wins, equalling the feats of Newton, Ballington, Mekler and Hayward, had been achieved in consecutive years. Could he go one better? His response was swift and to the point: 'I'll be back!'

The glamorous duo of Bruce Fordyce and Lindsay Weight had triumphed over all opposition over the past two years. Both were highly intelligent academics. Both combined disarming shyness with the rare ability to express themselves eloquently and authoritatively. During their joint reign as Comrades king and queen, their crowns seemed to fit naturally, if not quite timelessly.

When Fordyce took line honours, Weight was still locked in combat, and things weren't going all that well. She knew beforehand that hers would not be an easy task. The strong New Zealander Helen Lucre, twice a Comrades finisher, had broken the women's record in this year's Pieter Korkie. Already the Two Oceans record holder, she would clearly provide serious opposition to the defending champion.

And so it proved. After a period in which the two ran together, Lucre moved ahead in the first half and stamped her authority on the race over the huge challenge of Inchanga. Thereafter, she gradually eased further ahead and broke the tape in 6.53.24, a fast time but nearly nine minutes slower than the 1981 record of Isavel Roche-Kelly. Jubilantly, Lucre expressed her feelings: 'I had a very nice run. I had a few worried moments up to halfway because Lindsay Weight always looked better than I did. The crowd were fantastic. My helpers were great.'

Weight was obviously disappointed to come second and lose her opportunity to claim a permanent number via three consecutive victories. She was, nevertheless, generous in defeat: 'It wasn't a good day. I'm just so glad to finish. Really, that's all that counts. I won't attempt it again. My congratulations to Helen.' Actually, she did run the race several times afterwards – but that's just the way it is with Comrades.

As always, there were those who didn't get to stand on the podium but whose day's outing turned out to be particularly memorable, among them the silver medallists including Richard Venniker, Tammie Bilibana, Brian Chamberlain and Chet Sainsbury. Opposition parliamentarians Ken Andrew and Mike Tarr finished in the fast time of 9.29. Winner of the 1961 Comrades George Claassen had the pleasure of welcoming home his son, 1981 Springbok rugby captain Wynand.

Bruce Fordyce, in addition to his personal victory, managed for the first time to be part of the team winning the coveted Gunga Din shield. His Rand Athletic Club teammates were Tony Dearling, Trevor Metcalfe and Alan Day, and they deserved all the recognition they received. Equally meritorious was 62-year-old Sam Draai's seventh finish in a time of 9 hours 34 minutes. The majority of his successes had fallen outside government parameters for record-keeping – another way of saying that he had been of the 'wrong' skin colour.

1985 COMRADES MARATHON RESULTS

1. B. N. S. Fordyce	5.37.01
2. H. Tjale	5.42.40
3. D. R. Tivers	5.53.53
4. I. T. Emery	5.54.53
5. D. C. B. Anderson	5.55.11
6. D. R. Biggs	5.57.55
7. F. D. van Staden	5.59.14
8. J. D. Oberholzer	5.59.22
9. A. G. Robb	5.59.26
10. G. A. Fraser	6.00.04

1985 COMRADES BOWL RESULTS

1. H. C. Lucre	6.53.24
2. L. M. Weight	7.01.23
3. P. A. Carlisle	7.24.07
4. R. Smit	7.24.56
5. H. E. Hairs	7.26.07
6. M. Sassenberg	7.38.39
7. A. L. Clemson	7.52.26
8. C. A. Torr	7.56.10
9. M. J. Baird	8.00.04
10. A. M. Margolin	8.03.08

1986 COMRADES MARATHON
FORDYCE MAKES HISTORY

On 13 April 1986, Winnie Mandela, whose husband Nelson was still imprisoned, spoke to a large crowd in Kagiso, just outside Krugersdorp, and delivered her message of racial hatred: 'We work in the white man's kitchen. We bring up the white man's children. We could have killed them at any time we wanted to. Together, hand in hand, with our sticks and our matches, with our necklaces, we shall liberate this country.'

This was a time of apparently insurmountable division in the country, a time when positive, constructive people were close to despair.

Yet it was also a time in which optimists sought to bring understanding and reconciliation to those, on both sides, who preferred confrontation. There were individuals and organisations bringing people together in a spirit of comradeship despite diversity. The country was approaching a crossroads. The Comrades Marathon, born of triumph over adversity in the aftermath of the First World War, remained an institution of hope, confidence and unquestioning acceptance of all who were prepared to accept its all-inclusive idealism.

This year's Comrades was the ultimate test for a man who had had the courage to promote transformation years before such ideas became fashionable among whites. His name was Bruce Fordyce. He had already joined the select circle of five-time winners, but could he go one better and reach a stature all of his own? This was the question that was uppermost in the minds of Comrades followers as the big day approached.

How much pressure was Fordyce feeling? If his comments at the time are anything to go by, he was quite relaxed about it all: 'What motivates me in training is that I enjoy my running. Whatever you do, it has to be good fun. And it is good fun. It's challenging. It's interesting, and it remains so even though this is my tenth run, particularly in the "down" run, where I don't think that I've run to my full potential.'

The fact that it was Fordyce's tenth run was noted with a degree of extra admiration when he was observed reporting for duty on race day wearing a yellow number, which signifies that the wearer is attempting to obtain his or her permanent green number. With five victories and seven golds to his credit, he had already earned his permanent number 2403 twice. Asked why he was running in a yellow number, he showed his appreciation of Comrades camaraderie: 'This is my tenth Comrades. I want to earn my green number the proper way.'

Tradition and sadness jointly got the 1986 Comrades show on the road. Max Trimborn's cockcrow had been synonymous with the start of the race since the 1930s. As he grew older, so did his vocal cords, and in later years a recorded rendition of his call annually heralded the beginning of affairs.

During 1985, Trimborn had passed away at the age of 83, thankfully leaving the recording as a link between modern technology and early comradeship. The Comrades Marathon Association can be congratulated for carrying on this particular tradition.

Pre-race speculation focused on two issues. Firstly, there was the prospect of yet another 'come from behind' dramatic victory for the great Bruce Fordyce. Secondly, there was the annual tentative thought that the previously unassailable champion might show sufficient frailty for one of his challengers to be strong enough, on the day, to upset the Fordyce apple cart. While the credentials of Hoseah Tjale and Danny Biggs demanded respect, it was generally believed that Bob de la Motte was the one real obstacle that Fordyce faced in his quest for historic greatness.

Nobody respected the threat posed by De la Motte more than Fordyce himself. In 1984, he had had to pull out all the stops in order to prevail against his tall rival. Since then, De la Motte had grown in stature and in confidence. Not known as someone who tried to motivate his opponents, Fordyce nevertheless said admiringly, 'Some runners hope that they can win. Bobby de la Motte knows he can.'

The first half went according to plan, ensuring that the second half would provide the type of dramatic contest that most spectators hoped for. The tactical battle was played out exactly as expected. Front-runner De la Motte sought to build up a substantial lead. The 'come from behind' specialist Fordyce, having been bitten two years previously, tried to keep within reasonable distance of the leader without extending himself unduly. The jokers in the pack, such as Hoseah Tjale and Danny Biggs, positioned themselves sensibly, hoping to strike once the two favourites had succeeded in destroying each other.

At the crest of Botha's Hill, all the contenders were well positioned without anyone having a distinct advantage. De la Motte was in front, approximately 200 metres ahead of Deon Holtzhausen, who had Tjale, Biggs and Fordyce, together, trailing in his wake. To television viewers, it looked like history repeating itself yet again. Fordyce appeared to be in control. He was running smoothly and confidently, content to spend time behind his colleagues Tjale and Biggs, and making sure that De la Motte did not get more than two minutes ahead of him.

The 32-year-old De la Motte, an accountant by profession, was too intelligent and streetwise to allow anyone, let alone his arch-rival, to dictate strategy to him from behind. At 1.7metres and 70 kilograms, he was considerably taller and nearly 20 kilograms heavier than Fordyce. What he lacked in power-to-weight ratio, he made up for in tactical acumen. He couldn't expect to compete on equal terms with Fordyce on the uphills, so he had to take maximum advantage of the downs.

On the flattish but slightly downhill stretch from Hillcrest to Kloof, a key section for racers and plodders alike, De la Motte upped his pace and attempted, with partial success, to pull away. Fordyce, well served by his seconds, was soon made aware of what was happening. He responded. So did those around him, to the best of their abilities. Holtzhausen was the first casualty: the pace was just too hot for him. Soon after, to the disappointment of local spectators, their man Biggs began to fall back. Now there were only three, but what a trio: De la Motte in front, followed by Fordyce and Tjale.

Going through Pinetown, Fordyce and Tjale ran shoulder to shoulder. Fordyce looked effortless. Tjale's naturally laboured style gave no clue of how he was feeling. Together they moved on to the last of the so-called Big Five, Cowiess Hill, without either showing any sign of weakness. Further up the hill, leader De la Motte suddenly slowed. The battle of wills, which would determine the outcome, was just beginning.

At the top of Cowies, De la Motte's lead had been reduced to 40 metres, but now he was on another downhill. Once again, he quickened his pace, but to no avail: Fordyce and Tjale had him in their sights. In the television studio, Tim Noakes, who knew that Fordyce had repeatedly stated that he would be happy if his winning streak were broken by Tjale, surmised that the defending champion might at this stage be regarding Tjale as his major threat.

Certainly, Tjale was up there with him, and De la Motte was showing telltale signs of wilting. In the vicinity of Westville, Fordyce demonstrated his formidable strength in the final stages. Almost in a flash, he left Tjale and moved up, gradually, to the shoulder of leader De la Motte. Now came one of the most riveting sessions of ultra-distance running ever witnessed on South African television.

For approximately five kilometres, Fordyce and De la Motte ran side by side, De la Motte looking (as he was) fiercely determined, while Fordyce tried to appear as casual and comfortable as possible. They were running at record speed. In fact, they were running faster than record speed. A new record was almost guaranteed unless they both cracked, which seemed a real possibility. Surely, one of them would have to yield. Yet they continued their relentless battle. Amazingly, Tjale, in third place, was keeping in touch with them.

The resolution of this titanic struggle was remarkable for the prophetic accuracy of the television commentary as much as the contribution of the two great athletes. In the commentary box, Tim Noakes, watching proceedings, stated confidently, 'I think on the next hill, going up 45th Cutting, Bruce will pull away. We saw earlier how much stronger Bruce is on the hills, and 45th Cutting is a long hill. I'm sure Bruce will break through there. He knows he has the race under control.'

South Africa's foremost running guru was absolutely spot on. On the ascent of 45th Cutting, Fordyce went to work. He moved ahead. De la Motte dropped back slightly. Fordyce kept going. His opponent was soon five metres off the pace, then ten, soon 50. Effectively, the race was over. In total admiration of both, Noakes commented, 'I just can't emphasise enough that we are now seeing Bruce really at the peak of his powers. He's running a phenomenal race. For Bob to be that close, it just shows what a fantastic run he's had today. There's no other runner in the world who could stay this close to Bruce on a day like this. Bob really made the race.'

When Fordyce serenely crested Tollgate, the final hill, he was in total command, not only of the race, but also of his remarkable athletic frame. Adoring crowds cheered their hero on the last few kilometres to Kingsmead, where he crossed the line in 5.24.07, the fastest time ever for a Comrades Marathon – in fact, a record record, as it remained intact longer than any other Comrades record. In the tally of victories, this sixth triumph moved him ahead of all others. He was now master of the masters. The media called him the 'Comrades King', a title he seems unlikely to relinquish.

Tim Noakes's praise of Bob de la Motte was certainly not misplaced. The tall accountant took second place in 5.26.12. He would have set a new record if Fordyce had not finished ahead of him. Hoseah Tjale's third place time of 5.29.02 was also highly commendable. It would have been good enough to secure victory in all previous 'down' runs apart from the 1984 race, in which Fordyce had set the previous record. The three leading runners made this year's race the greatest athletic contest in Comrades history.

There was a shining example of Comrades courage and camaraderie further back in the field this year. Magnolia runner Tony 'Duckles' Horne had been driven to the start by his brother-in-law, Ronnie Bester, along with running friends Jack van der Westhuizen, Billy Masemola and the legendary Liege Boulle. After the race, there was no sign of Van der Westhuizen. Bester located the missing runner, after a long search, in a medical tent outside Kingsmead and was instructed, 'Take him to Addington Hospital.' At Addington, Van der Westhuizen was given pills and told, 'You runners are mad.'

The next day, Horne, Masemola and Van der Westhuizen drove to Pretoria. Van der Westhuizen, in agony, was put in his wife's care, and she took him to hospital the following day. A newspaper article disclosed the nature of Van der Westhuizen's pain:

'Not even a broken hip bone could keep a courageous 37-year-old man from Kilner Park in Pretoria from earning a bronze medal in this year's Comrades Marathon. Mr Jack van der Westhuizen was operated on in the Eugene Marais Hospital after he completed the murderous race with a broken hip bone. Doctors expressed their disbelief at the courage he had shown.

'While still enduring a lot of pain a few hours after the operation, Mr Van der Westhuizen said that he was about 40 kilometres from the finish when he felt hip pain. About four kilometres from the end the bone gave way completely. Thanks to two other participants he was able to complete the race. He spoke glowingly of their camaraderie: "In spite of the pain, I knew I would finish thanks to the moral support of the other runners."'

In the women's race, the popular former Kiwi Helen Lucre notched up her second straight success. Having disposed of previous double winner Lindsay Weight the previous year, she now claimed a 'down' victory in 6.55.01, a time that was, interestingly, slower than her winning time in the previous year's 'up' race.

Perhaps the reason for her slower 'down' time in the year in which conditions were such that Fordyce was able to post the fastest ever Comrades time is that she did not have to contend with the threat of Lindsay Weight. Nevertheless, a win is a win, and Lucre had posted two successive sub-seven-hour victories. Ralie Smit took second place in 7.07.40 with Lettie Greeff third in 7.14.49.

1986 COMRADES MARATHON RESULTS

1. Bruce Fordyce	5.24.07
2. Bob de la Motte	5.26.12
3. Hoseah Tjale	5.29.02
4. Boysie van Staden	5.37.00
5. Deon Holtzhausen	5.40.13
6. Alan Robb	5.41.09
7. Ian Emery	5.42.35
8. Danny Biggs	5.45.57
9. Steven Hollier	5.46.48
10. Leon Swanepoel	5.51.11

1986 COMRADES BOWL RESULTS

1. Helen Lucre	6.55.01
2. Ralie Smit	7.07.40
3. Lettie Greeff	7.14.49
4. Lorraine van der Poel	7.20.51
5. Hazel Hairs	7.22.46
6. Hester Kotze	7.23.52
7. Angie Longman	7.26.24
8. Lynne Spence	7.27.50
9. Suzanne de Villiers	7.29.29
10. Tilda Tearle	7.29.59

1987 COMRADES MARATHON
HELEN LUCRE'S HAT-TRICK

In the build-up to this year's race, an undercurrent, of which the public were largely unaware, was building up in the background, ensuring that change was just around the corner. Comrades had been caught up in the so-called 'shamateurism' that plagued most sports in the 1980s. Even though many refused to accept the message (some with good reason, as they tried to preserve noble traditions), the writing was on the wall: professionalism, like it or not, was the future.

The country's international sporting relations were dominated at this time by the effects of isolation. Rebel tours had kept South African cricketers and rugby players in touch with the latest developments in their sports and had maintained South Africa's position as a world-class power in these two sports at enormous cost to sponsors and taxpayers. Players, particularly visitors, were paid vast sums of money.

The Comrades Marathon had enjoyed a very different existence through-out the turbulent 1980s. Regarded as a sport that attracted individuals rather than teams, it was nurtured by the authorities, much as Adolf Hitler had used the 1936 Olympic Games in his attempt to portray Germany to the Germans as the world's dominant nation. In the 1980s, Comrades had few real media rivals. The country's historical sporting opponents, mainly British or members of the Commonwealth, were under strong pressure from their governments to cut or at least suspend sporting ties with South Africa. The majority of South Africans, being people of colour and therefore denied basic human rights, supported the boycott. Because they were also the poorest South Africans, however, their protests were largely ignored, while most white sports followers, who were generally not short of money, were only too happy to hear that their sporting personalities were the best in the world.

During this period of double standards, certain cricket and rugby stars, while still officially recognised as amateurs, became multimillionaires simply by playing their sport at the highest (generally unofficial) level available to them. While those who left the country in order to earn a significant living playing professional sport legitimately were often branded as unpatriotic, traitorous prostitutes, there were a few instances of such individuals being surreptitiously welcomed back into South African sport when their overseas contracts were terminated. The hypocrisy of 'shamateurism' was real and significant.

At the same time, rebel tours were unpredictable, had to be arranged at short notice and could not come close to adequately satisfying the requirements of a sport-loving nation. Consequently, certain local sportsmen and sportswomen who could be relied upon to entertain the public as true-blue amateur stars were used and abused. Among them were Currie Cup rugby players and Comrades Marathon specialists.

The 1980s saw one of the most important changes in Comrades history. Television brought the race into the living rooms of people throughout the land. Television proclaimed the extraordinary (for many) news that running the Comrades Marathon was within the capabilities of most people. Television allowed viewers to follow the fortunes of family members, social friends and work colleagues, many of whom lacked competitive athletic ability but were still able to meet the Comrades challenge. In 1977 a record field of 1 963 had started the race. In 1986, thanks to television and to the personal appeal of Bruce Fordyce, the number of starters exceeded 10 000 for the first time. Sponsors were having it all their own way. Sportsmen who had built their entire year around this one day went home with medals and trophies and paid for their own beers, as well as travel expenses.

Six-time winner Bruce Fordyce was well aware of the role he was playing in promoting the Comrades Marathon. He had become arguably the nation's number one sporting celebrity and was in constant demand for television interviews, always making himself available. He also enjoyed a central position in the upper echelon of the country's sporting heroes. He was well aware of the disparity between his relatively meagre earnings from sponsors whose products he endorsed and the vast sums paid to semi-professionals from other sporting codes. Not prone by nature to envy, he largely accepted the status quo, but did make a concerted effort to introduce professional rewards in order to attract foreigners and maintain the highest possible standards after his career at the top had ended. Tim Noakes, commentating on the 1987 race, aptly summed up Fordyce's contribution:

'Bruce has really made this event and put something into running that we didn't have before. I remember when I first started, we were the eccentrics, and now in fact it's gone the other way around. We're not so eccentric now. I think it's because of people like Bruce that credibility has been brought to the sport.'

At this stage, Bruce Fordyce was the face of Comrades. Unlike any of his rivals, past or present, he had become one of the most recognisable sporting personalities in the country, as Tim Noakes had suggested. The 1987 Comrades Marathon might as well have been called 'Fordyce's latest challenge', such was the extent of his domination.

The only person who seemed to disagree with this sentiment was Fordyce himself. As the years of dominance produced ever-growing expectations, he alone could feel the wear and tear of the demands that he had made on himself. He knew he wasn't invincible, but was well aware that anything other than another Fordyce 'come from behind' finish would cause huge disappointment. He was also intensely aware that the Comrades Marathon Association, for whom he had the greatest admiration, and race sponsors, for whom his feelings were rather ambivalent, relied on him to provide the annual drama that was almost a duty for him. The strain of expectation was beginning to weigh heavily on his shoulders, as evidenced by a casual comment he made to his father: 'Dad, it's just a numbers game nowadays.'

Fordyce, by now, had given up his academic studies, which had taken him to the brink of a Master's degree in Archaeology. He was actually a full-time amateur runner, whose earnings were derived from sponsorship, motivational speaking and the sale of an energy supplement named FRN in partnership with Bernard Rose and Tim Noakes. Some expressed the view that he held an unfair advantage over someone like Bob de la Motte, a chartered accountant who had professional responsibilities to fulfil. The truth is that both were able to train to the nth degree while also earning a reasonable living.

Bruce Fordyce did, however, hold one special advantage this year. He had formed a friendship with a young Wits student who was not only a dedicated athlete, but also a faster runner. Mark Plaatjies helped Fordyce increase his speed as they ran back-breaking laps at the university's Charles Skeen Stadium. To his credit, Fordyce persuaded Plaatjies that his talents were better suited to shorter distances, advice the younger runner acknowledged after winning the world standard marathon championship some years later.

One of Fordyce's favourite build-up runs was Cape Town's Peninsula Marathon. In 1981 and 1985, he had completed the Peninsula in 2.18 and had gone on to win Comrades in 5.37.28 and 5.37.01, respectively. When he recorded yet another 2.18 in the 1987 Peninsula Marathon, he was confident that he was well on track.

The start of the 1987 Comrades Marathon was enough to fill virtually everyone with trepidation. The runners lining up just didn't look right. There was almost a total absence of black refuse bags. A kaleidoscope of running club colours greeted spectators. There was no need for extra clothing. The temperature was 18°C and was expected to exceed 30°C during the day. Those who followed the advice of Tim Noakes – which included just about everyone – accepted that ambitious finishing times would have to be adjusted and plenty of liquid consumed.

Pre-race speculation was rather muted. Fordyce would win. That was taken for granted. Tjale and De la Motte would probably contest the other two podium places, while Alan Robb, Johnny Halberstadt, Danny Biggs and Graeme Fraser, among others, would probably end up with gold medals. Fordyce wasn't overconfident. He had great respect for Tjale and De la Motte as well as the others, and he always had, in the back of his mind, the fear that some unknown runner would come along and surprise everyone. Furthermore, the heat introduced a real sense of unpredictability.

Riaan Oberholzer took the lead after the early front-runners had been sorted out. Boysie van Staden, Deon Holtzhausen, Hoseah Tjale and Sam Tshabalala, among others, were well placed. Fordyce, slightly more cautious than usual in the heat, was just inside the top 20, with De la Motte snapping at his heels. Oberholzer was first through Drummond, where Fordyce and De la Motte, still together, were starting to move into contention.

As ever, Inchanga and Harrison Flats brought a change in proceedings. The pundits had been spot on with their predictions. At Cato Ridge, Tjale was in front. Fordyce had moved up to second, but was four and a half minutes behind the leader. The third member of the trio, De la Motte, wasn't far behind Fordyce. On the stretch from Cato Ridge to Camperdown, Tjale's lead was cut to three and a half minutes. History was repeating itself.

Fordyce the hunter was, as usual, utterly implacable. When, with approximately 20 kilometres to go, he caught sight of his quarry, the race was effectively over. There were two hills left, Little Pollys and Pollys itself. Tjale, De la Motte and Fordyce were all well aware that Fordyce was the absolute master over this section. On Little Pollys, he pounced. Putting on the pressure, he pulled out as much of a lead as he could before reaching the foot of Polly Shortts. He was now safe. Tjale tried to stay with him, but couldn't. The effort of doing so, as well as the disappointment of surrendering the lead so close to glory, demoralised him so much that he relinquished second place to De la Motte on the run-in to the finish.

Once again, Fordyce's reliance on the Peninsula Marathon as a yardstick of his progress had proved correct. His third 2.18 Peninsula was once again followed by Comrades victory. Amazingly, his time of 5.37.01 equalled exactly his 1985 winning time. With his seventh straight victory, he had achieved total mastery over two generations of challengers. A third group was waiting in the wings.

The women's race generated a great deal more interest than had previously been the case. Uppermost in the minds of supporters were two double champions, each hoping for a third victory and, with it, the 'in perpetuity' recognition of a permanent green number.

The pair, Lindsay Weight and Helen Lucre, had dominated the event over the past four years. Each had both an 'up' and a 'down' victory to her credit. Only one had set a record, Lindsay Weight's 6.46 'down' victory in 1984 having taken 18 minutes off the time set by Cheryl Jorgensen in 1982.

In the first half, the two were in close proximity, at times alongside each other. Comrades is a test of strength, and Lucre was the stronger. She took control in the second half and completed her hat-trick in 6.48.42, ten minutes ahead of Weight. Lucre's consistency had paid off. Another consistent finisher was Ralie Smit, who took third place (her fifth top-three placing in the 1980s) in 7.01.

The relationship between Comrades and Two Oceans has always been positive. Nobody demonstrated this more impressively than Two Oceans chairman Chet Sainsbury. His first two Comrades attempts, in 1978 and 1979, had yielded bronze medals. Since then, from 1980 to 1986, he had registered seven successful silvers. With his whole family in attendance, he was aiming for an eighth silver out of ten finishes.

It nearly didn't work out. In the first kilometre, Sainsbury was tripped and sent sprawling. After being severely trampled, he regained his footing and attempted to continue. His left arm, with a bump the size of an orange, was useless. He had to stop and turn around to take drinks at feeding stations. The damage to his elbow was so severe that he required an operation on his return to Cape Town to repair the joint. Yet he still managed to finish, quite remarkably earning another silver with six minutes to spare. Such is the mettle of the man.

1987 COMRADES MARATHON RESULTS

1. Bruce Fordyce	5.37.01
2. Bob de la Motte	5.43.38

3. Hoseah Tjale	5.44.42
4. Boysie van Staden	5.48.41
5. Arthur Lemos	5.48.41
6. Graeme Fraser	5.50.29
7. Alan Robb	5.51.17
8. Leon Swanepoel	5.53.02
9. Deon Holtzhausen	5.53.21
10. Siphiwe Gqele	5.53.51

1987 COMRADES BOWL RESULTS

1. Helen Lucre	6.48.42
2. Lindsay Weight	6.58.44
3. Ralie Smit	7.01.13
4. Beverley Malan	7.07.03
5. Sally Edwards	7.21.50
6. Frith van der Merwe	7.22.19
7. Priscilla Carlisle	7.22.55
8. Hazel Hairs	7.25.11
9. Lorraine van der Poel	7.25.14
10. Erika Coetzee	7.35.32

1988 COMRADES MARATHON
THE GREATEST RACE OF ALL TIME

Wow! That is just about the only way to express what it felt like to witness the 1988 Comrades. Never had an athletic event captured the hearts of an entire nation and changed previously held beliefs about athletic limitations, gender equality and geriatric decline so dramatically as did the 1988 Comrades Marathon, in a glorious affirmation of the enormous potential of the human spirit. This was a year that would have brought great pride to founder Vic Clapham.

As far as Bruce Fordyce was concerned, the true-blue nobility of amateurism was wearing a little thin. He was essentially an amateur. Yes, he did receive money from certain sponsors who were delighted to have him endorse their products. He was also paid by various organisations as a motivational speaker, a role for which he is well qualified. As a runner, he was not paid. Yet he witnessed the exploitation of top athletes by corporations that were happy to pay substantial sums to sportsmen and sportswomen of other codes. He wasn't exactly jealous, but he would play a resolute role in bringing professionalism into the sport just after his own competitive era ended.

At this stage of his career, Fordyce was, in a way, a tired athlete. When he began his Comrades odyssey in 1977, the top runners were Alan Robb, Piet Vorster and Johnny Halberstadt. He beat them all. Then, in the middle of his Comrades career, came a new bunch of challengers, among them Hoseah Tjale, Bob de la Motte, Graeme Fraser, Tony Abbott and Danny Biggs. They were taken care of. Now, in what was clearly the twilight of his career at the top, another generation of would-be champions arrived on the scene. Some were rather formidable: Mark Page, Nick Bester, Shaun Meikeljohn and Charl Mattheus were about to become household names. Old man Fordyce, now in his 33rd year and having won his first Comrades at the age of 25, had a real battle on his hands. Would he be up to the task?

In the build-up to this year's race, Fordyce meticulously studied the progress of the pretenders to his throne, in his usual thorough manner. He became convinced that his Rand Athletic Club colleague Mark Page would pose the strongest threat to his chances. In the Peninsula Marathon, he had finished behind an impressive performance by Page. In the Two Oceans, on the occasion of Thompson Magawana's world-class record of 3.03.44, Page had put in a sensible performance, coming fourth in 3.16.39. His preparation for Comrades was close to ideal.

Actually, Fordyce's preparation wasn't quite up to standard – not in the last few days, anyway. In his book *Run the Comrades*, he gave valuable advice to fellow runners on how to be properly ready for the big day. Under the heading 'Race Inventory', he made it clear that shoes were the most vital part of a runner's equipment. This year, unbelievably, he had left his own running shoes at home. Fortunately, a family friend who was also running the race was able to deliver Fordyce's shoes to him. The friend's name? Alan Robb.

In the early stages of the race, it became clear that the majority of top contenders were building their strategy around the progress of Fordyce. He was surrounded by a large group that included Page, Nick Bester, Johnny Burgess, Stewart Peacock, Danny Biggs and Johnny Halberstadt. As the television broadcast clearly showed, the reigning champion was disconcerted by the attention from those clinging to him. At times, he was jostled. His heels were clipped from behind. He looked distractedly from side to side, obviously wanting to break the shackles impeding him.

Suddenly, without warning, Fordyce broke away and entered the bushes, either to obey a call of nature or simply to get away from the over-demanding companionship of his fellow runners. When he rejoined the race, he had only Colin Goosen, well known for his crawling finish to the final gold medal in 1983, as an immediate companion. The two clearly enjoyed running together, exchanging pleasantries and greeting supporters along the roadside. Fordyce was visibly more relaxed. He also looked strong and full of running, an ominous sign for his opponents.

Local star Boysie van Staden and the diminutive Jetman Msutu led the way through Drummond, with Philemon Mogashane close behind. Fordyce, having shaken off Goosen, was once again in the pack from which he had earlier been keen to depart. Fortunately, the group had thinned out significantly, with only the likes of Bester, Halberstadt, Page, Biggs and Holtzhausen still in touch with proceedings. Fordyce's halfway time of 2.52.32 was, deliberately, a couple of minutes faster than that of the previous year. He was on track for a special run.

Although Fordyce had looked strong and well in control during the first half, he later admitted to having felt rather bored and impatient. In the second half, he initially exercised patience and restraint. On the ascent of Inchanga, he allowed Bester, Page and Halberstadt to move ahead. He wasn't struggling, just biding his time. On the somewhat easier descent, he gradually rejoined the group.

At this stage, Page made his move and set off in pursuit of joint leaders Msutu and Van Staden. Just before Cato Ridge, Page swiftly passed the halfway leaders and led the Comrades Marathon for the first time. Aware of the threat posed by the champion finisher Fordyce, Page sought to establish as big a lead as possible. Seven-time winner Fordyce was wise to such tactics and upped his own tempo. All others became beaten men fighting for the lesser spoils as the two RAC clubmates, Page and Fordyce, contested the ultimate prize.

Roadside spectators and television viewers looking forward to the annual Comrades drama were not disappointed. Defending champion Bruce Fordyce, after his usual conservative start, had moved up through the field and was stalking his final victim. Mark Page, aware of the Fordyce game plan, had made his move at the most opportune moment and was grimly hanging on to his lead, fully aware of the determined hunter who was chasing him.

Page was more than just aware of the threat from behind. Whenever he reached a group of spectators, he would receive the warm applause that he thoroughly deserved. Some time later, he would hear the selfsame supporters erupt into excited cheering as they encouraged their special favourite, Bruce Fordyce. Leading the Comrades Marathon is never an easy task. Being out in front, with the crowd egging on their darling in pursuit of you, can be an absolute nightmare.

Camperdown is a spot where the crowd is both vast and vociferous. Here, Page had a lead of approximately 300 metres. From here on, the undulating course favours those with experience. Page, running bravely, had never run further than 56 kilometres before. Fordyce knew every uphill, every downhill, every bend, every nuance along the way. On the short little hill out of Camperdown, he crept a little closer to his prey.

The attendants of both runners kept them fully informed of their respective positions. For Page, pressure was mounting. For Fordyce, the serial winner, another victory was beckoning. The champion drew ever closer. The leader, trying to keep his composure and his forward momentum, couldn't help looking behind. The hunt was nearing its climax, and the kill was imminent.

In textbook fashion, Fordyce gradually moved up to his quarry and passed him, without any communication. Page, however, wasn't ready to submit. He hadn't given up hope of winning the race. He responded to Fordyce's challenge and moved up alongside him. Now they did acknowledge each other, shaking hands and putting arms around each other's shoulders.

For a short while, the two gave the impression that, as clubmates, they would help each other to the end. The impression was fleeting. They were racing, as individuals, against each other. Fordyce surged on a downhill. Page came back at him. Fordyce was feeling out his adversary, looking for weaknesses. Page was hanging in. Fordyce was stronger.

On the second-last ascent, that of Ashburton or Little Pollys, Fordyce made the decisive move. Far more muscular than eight years previously, he exuded power as he relentlessly built up a sizeable advantage. At the top of the penultimate hill, he had the race under control. When he reached the foot of Polly Shortts itself, Fordyce's lead was two minutes. The television coverage of his ascent of the hill provides a masterclass of one of the world's greatest athletes doing what he does best.

At the crest of Pollys, victory number eight was assured for the flying Fordyce. The race record became the next target, and it soon became apparent that this was well within his capability. Pulling faces at television cameras and graciously acknowledging the cheers of the adoring crowds, he sped majestically to yet another extraordinary achievement, a new 'up' record of 5.27.42. In so doing, he became the first athlete to achieve five 'up' victories, to set three 'up' records and, of course, to win an unprecedented eight Comrades Marathons. This may well have been his finest triumph – but, remarkably, he was overshadowed on the day, not once but twice.

The women's section will presumably play second fiddle to the overall race until a female athlete performs the unlikely trick of winning the race or at least coming in the top ten. In 1988, we didn't realise that we were getting rather close to an assault by a female runner on what was regarded as a bastion of masculine invincibility.

In 1987, Helen Lucre had notched up a hat-trick of three successive wins. She appeared to be in a class of her own. Not too much attention was given to the debut performance that year of a 23-year-old Benoni schoolteacher named Frith van der Merwe. An initial run of 7.22.10 was meritorious, earning a comfortable silver and sixth position, but not enough to prepare Comrades supporters for what was to come.

This year, for the first time, gold medals were awarded to the first three women. Frith van der Merwe stole the hearts of South Africans by setting a standard hitherto unimagined. Very much a front-runner, she totally dominated the race, winning in a time of 6.32.56, over half an hour faster than second-placed Lettie Greeff and defending champion Helen Lucre, third. Van der Merwe's time beat Isavel Roche-Kelly's Comrades best for a woman by nearly 12 minutes. Her happy finishing smile heralded a new era in long-distance running and drew many hundreds of women to a sport more suited to them than originally thought.

A couple of hours after Van der Merwe's triumphant finish, the ground commentator informed the large crowd at Jan Smuts Stadium in Pietermaritzburg that there was an old man on the course who was close to finishing – a special old man, by the name of Wally Hayward. Most knew that he had started, but hardly anyone could have imagined the remarkable feat that he would accomplish.

The fact that Wally Hayward had even entered the race is quite extraordinary. Comrades winner in his 1930 debut at the age of 21, he had established the credentials of youth by coming first. In a remarkable comeback in the 1950s, he had pulverised all opposition and previous records, demonstrating the capabilities of the middle-aged. He retired undefeated, in his mid-forties. Having been declared a professional on spurious grounds following his 1954 victory, he was discarded indefinitely until sanity prevailed and he was allowed to resume his athletic career, but only after he had passed his allotted three score years and ten. Then, shortly before his 80th birthday, Wally Hayward eclipsed all his earlier achievements and produced a performance that changed perceptions of the reality of growing old.

Qualifying for the race was Hayward's most difficult obstacle. He had a friend, Les Hackett, who looked after his every need, including protection from misguided well-wishers. Together, Hayward and Hackett negotiated the qualifying requirements. Together they set out on their impossible Comrades adventure. People at home waited to hear news of a miracle. Comrades runners witnessed that miracle as the great man, keeping to a constant and relentless rhythm, cruised past many who were half his age, or even a quarter.

One of South Africa's largest ever television audiences joined the crowd at Jan Smuts Stadium in welcoming home Wally Hayward in the extraordinary time of 9.44.15. Just days before his 80th birthday, he became the oldest Comrades finisher ever, with approximately half the field trailing in his wake. In the words of Bruce Fordyce, 'Wally Hayward is, and probably always will be, the greatest Comrades winner, and runner.'

1988 COMRADES MARATHON RESULTS

1. Bruce Fordyce	5.27.42
2. Mark Page	5.38.28
3. Nick Bester	5.39.00
4. Hoseah Tjale	5.41.16
5. Boysie van Staden	5.46.30
6. Jetman Msutu	5.49.32
7. Charl Mattheus	5.49.47
8. Madumetja Mogashane	5.50.31
9. Johan Ebersohn	5.51.40
10. Ephraim Sekotlong	5.51.56

1988 COMRADES BOWL RESULTS

1. Frith van der Merwe	6.32.56
2. Lettie Greeff	7.04.00
3. Helen Lucre	7.07.50
4. Lindsay Weight	7.08.51
5. Lorraine van der Poel	7.17.47
6. Hazel Hairs	7.23.33
7. Tilda Tearle	7.29.02
8. Priscilla Carlisle	7.30.39
9. Ann Margolin	7.42.26
10. Mariana Minty	7.47.13

15

THE BIG CHANGE
(1989 to 1993)

Friends of Bruce Fordyce, who probably had little understanding of the potential consequences of their action, hatched an amazing plan to keep their buddy running competitively in 1989. Out of the blue, they arranged a world 100-kilometre championship race in the Stellenbosch area in February, persuading virtually all the world's leading ultra-distance athletes to take part. It was a huge success. Fordyce proved his mastery winning in 6.25.07, and South Africa looked good in the minds of visitors as well as locals.

Then came Comrades, significantly affected by the Stellenbosch race. Those South Africans who had taken part in the 100-kilometre event were the best that the nation could offer, but they had burnt themselves out. They either gave Comrades a miss or performed well below their true ability. The same applied to visitors who returned for the big one, with one notable exception, Frenchman Jean-Marc Bellocq.

Yet Comrades came out on top. Why? Firstly, because it is Comrades, too big and too important to come second to anything else. Secondly, because an opportunity arose for the race to play a special role in the vital process of transformation that was key to the future of the nation. For the first time ever, a black South African, Sam Tshabalala, won the nation's premier annual athletic event.

What does that mean? When the best were away, the second-stringers had their day – is that what Tshabalala's victory meant? Absolutely not! In the build-up to the 1991 Comrades, Bruce Fordyce feared only one man. Sam Tshabalala had shown him a clean pair of heels in several races. For the first time in his illustrious career, Fordyce felt threatened by someone who had the ability to beat him.

Then tragedy struck. Tshabalala was involved in a terrible motor accident that left him the sole survivor. He recovered sufficiently to earn a silver medal two years later, but would never again be able to run at his previous best. He did, however, make the big breakthrough. His 1989 victory showed the way to his compatriots, but they weren't quite ready to take over his mantle. That would come later.

The period 1989 to 1993 (plus the first half of 1994) was the most dramatic and the most significant in South Africa's history. It wasn't a tranquil time. Change seldom comes easily, and this was major change. It was both the type of change that the country needed and a progression towards a place more in keeping with the ideals of the Comrades Marathon. Since 1981, Comrades had shown that it had the desire and the ability to play a leading role in such change.

In just a few short years, South Africa made the transition from a land run by a minority for the benefit of that minority to a fully democratic society. During the transition, a great deal of blood was shed, and brutal violence became almost commonplace. Yet the peace process remained on track, and, at the end of 1993, President F. W. de Klerk and Nelson Mandela were jointly awarded the Nobel Peace Prize.

Comrades also had to deal with change. The 1980s belonged to Bruce Fordyce. In 1991, he handed the baton to the first of many successors. In 1989, Frith van der Merwe produced the most remarkable long-distance performance by a woman, not just in Comrades, but arguably anywhere, ever. Her brilliant but all too brief time at the top ended with her victory in 1991. She, too, had to make way for a future generation of champions.

In the early 1990s, a new problem appeared at Comrades, threatening to blemish the event's nobility of purpose, dedication and application: disqualification. In 1992, the first man to cross the line was disqualified, not for cheating, but for naively infringing a regulation in a manner that brought him no benefit whatsoever. In 1993, a gold medallist was disqualified for cheating.

The years 1992 and 1993 marked a turning point for Comrades. Two of its greatest champions, Bruce Fordyce and Frith van der Merwe, were no longer competitive at the highest level. These two years could be regarded as an interim period pending the new direction that was needed. The triumph of German Charly Doll in 1993 gave notice of this new direction. The international invasion was about to begin.

1989 COMRADES MARATHON
TWO FIRSTS FOR SAM TSHABALALA

The Comrades Marathon has, virtually from its inauguration in 1921, been the dominant long-distance running event in South Africa. In the months leading up to Comrades, standard marathons tend to be called 'qualifiers', as many runners enter them mainly in order to meet the requirements for participation in the 'big one', Comrades.

In the various provinces, weekend races are scheduled in such a way that they gradually build up to a half marathon, then 32-kilometre and 36-kilometre races, the qualifier itself and thereafter the long slog building up to Comrades preparedness. The Comrades Marathon is both the pinnacle of the road-running calendar and the pivot around which road races are organised.

This year, there was a difference, one that affected those of gold medal ability. Johnny Burgess and Mike Gahagan were friends, running partners and business colleagues of Bruce Fordyce. They realised that Fordyce's enthusiasm for his annual 31 May parade had waned to such an extent that, if he was to be kept involved in the sport, he needed something else to draw his attention and whole-hearted commitment.

They came up with an extraordinary and extremely ambitious idea: a 100-kilometre world championship race to be held in South Africa – and that at a time when sporting isolation was at its most stringent. South Africans were barred from playing sport virtually everywhere. Visiting individuals and teams took part in events on South African soil at their peril, risking life bans in their own countries. South African cricket and rugby administrators had, however, discovered and exploited a significant weakness among the world's best: money. In most cases, people could be bought. This is how rugby and cricket were kept alive and standards maintained during the isolation period. Money spoke a universal language. This new race, therefore, required generous funding and absolute secrecy.

Burgess and Gahagan put their plan together simply in order to keep their friend Fordyce in the running limelight. They did, however, impose a rather exacting demand on their man: he had to win the race, not a simple requirement when his opponents were the world's finest long-distance athletes, almost without exception. Scotsman Don Ritchie was the only overseas runner to decline his invitation, perhaps influenced by his defeat at Fordyce's hands in the 1983 London-to-Brighton race.

Burgess and Gahagan secured the organisational skills of legendary Two Oceans chairman Chet Sainsbury to administer the event. Funding was, of course, a major concern. Sponsorship had been the lifeblood of rebel rugby and cricket tours during the isolation era, which, though nobody knew it, was about to end. Burgess and Gahagan persuaded the Standard Bank to finance the race. The first prize, the main drawcard, was US$30 000. There were also participatory incentives for all visitors, to induce them to brave the opposition to their involvement from their own governments.

What has all this to do with the Comrades Marathon? Quite simply, at the highest level of ultra-distance running in South Africa, the Standard Bank Ultra 100-kilometre race overshadowed the 1989 Comrades Marathon in terms of athletic performance. Those who would normally dominate Comrades were invited to take part, and 20 were chosen.

The clandestine nature of the rebel event gave these runners a huge problem: how did they explain to family and friends why they were putting the same effort into their training over the festive period as they would normally do in the build-up to Comrades?

The secret was kept. News of South Africa's first 100-kilometre world championship event only broke when the visitors were safely in South Africa. On their first night in the country, they gathered at the home of Bruce Fordyce in Johannesburg. The next day, they flew to Cape Town, where they were booked into a hotel in Somerset West.

Although Fordyce was central to the event, he had strong misgivings about the whole affair. Deeply opposed to apartheid, he was not willing to become involved in a rebel race that would take pressure off the South African government. In fact, he had to be persuaded that the race would not undermine the demands of those who sought political change in the country. As it turned out, the apartheid regime was effectively ended within 12 months.

The race clearly proved South African superiority in ultra-distance running. Bruce Fordyce won the event in what was said to be a world record. There is some doubt as to the accuracy of this claim, as no official records of ultra-distances were recognised at the time. The major fact is that he proved himself superior to global challengers in torrid conditions. He simply was the best at distances between 80 and 100 kilometres.

Afterwards, Fordyce announced that he would not take part in this year's Comrades Marathon. He was convinced that it was quite impossible to race competitively in two such events within three months. He added that those (there were a few) who attempted to do both would not feature prominently in Comrades. He was quite correct. The South Africans who took part in the 100-kilometre race were Johan Ebersohn, Ian Emery, Bruce Fordyce, Johnny Halberstadt, Steve Hollier, Deon Holtzhausen, Arthur Lemos, Thompson Magawana, Charl Mattheus, Philemon Mogashane, Jetman Msutu, Mark Page, Siphiwe Gqele, Meshack Radebe, Alan Robb, Ephraim Sekotlong, Deon Swanepoel, Hoseah Tjale, Boysie van Staden and Louis Harmse. They represented the cream of South African ultra-distance athletes, yet only three made the Comrades top ten: Ephraim Sekotlong (seventh), Charl Mattheus (ninth) and Hoseah Tjale (tenth).

This is not to say that the 1989 Comrades Marathon was a let-down. In fact, it was a wonderful day, which brought about a long awaited break-through for a black runner and an astonishing performance by a woman. In considering their achievements, it is worth bearing in mind that, 15 years earlier, neither would have been eligible to take part.

The absence of Fordyce brought a new dimension to the race: doubt. For the first time in almost a decade, there was no obvious favourite. There was also going to be a new champion. In the past 13 years, there had only been three winners: Piet Vorster (once), Alan Robb (four times) and Bruce Fordyce (eight times). Although the possibility of another 'come from behind' Fordyce victory would be missed, the prospect of an unknown breaking the tape brought a new excitement to the day.

It didn't have to be an unknown, and was unlikely to be one. For some years, there had been speculation about who the first black winner might be. With Fordyce and a few others out of the picture, the opportunity was there. Hoseah Tjale was the name on everyone's lips. He had, however, taken part in the Stellenbosch 100-kilometre race, coming 12th overall (eighth among the South Africans). Had he burnt himself out? Then there was Willie Mtolo, the popular local hero. He lacked Comrades experience, but was certainly a marvellous athlete.

It proved to be a race of surprises. Shaun Meiklejohn, a relative newcomer some saw as a Bruce Fordyce lookalike, led the way into Pinetown. Meiklejohn would earn a reputation for consistency and reliability over the next decade, but that would have to wait a while.

Just before Cowies Hill, Sam Tshabalala took over the lead. Was this the breakthrough that Comrades had anticipated for so long? Would Tshabalala be the first black winner? Before long, however, Tshabalala was joined at the front by Willie Mtolo. Now there had to be a black champion, surely. It was between the two as they exchanged the lead several times.

Mtolo seemed to be the crowd's favourite in the closing stages. He was cheered and, at times, impeded by excited spectators. Whether such distractions affected him adversely, we do not know. What we do know is that he experienced severe cramps, which reduced him to walking on a couple of occasions. It was all that Tshabalala needed. He took his opportunity and became the first black Comrades champion in the relatively slow time, for a 'down' run, of 5.35.51, while Mtolo courageously kept going to take second place ahead of Jean-Marc Bellocq, a Frenchman who had taken part in the Stellenbosch 100-kilometre race. Bellocq was the only foreigner in the top ten. How times would change! Also among the gold medallists were Nick Bester, Shaun Meiklejohn and Charl Mattheus, all future winners.

While the men's race provided a fascinating spectacle, the women's section produced a performance that overshadowed everything else. In the 1988 race, Frith van der Merwe had set a new 'up' record. During the build-up to 1989, she displayed form that astonished road-running followers to such an extent that male superiority began to be questioned.

The 1989 Two Oceans Marathon had witnessed one of the world's greatest ever performances by a female athlete. The maximum temperature officially recorded was 31°C. In accordance with prevailing medical opinion, runners were advised to slow down and readjust their targets in these conditions. It had been suggested that races should be called off in such heat, but everyone realised that this was out of the question. In these torrid circumstances, Frith van der Merwe came 22nd overall in a new women's record time of 3.30.36. En route, she set new world records for 30 miles (3.01.16) and 50 kilometres (3.08.39). A further indication of Van der Merwe's amazing achievement was the fact that second-placed Helen Lucre, former Two Oceans record holder and triple Comrades champion, was eight kilometres short of the finish when Van der Merwe crossed the line.

As everyone knows, it is unwise to run a hard Two Oceans in a year in which one has significant Comrades aspirations. Such opinion would suggest that Van der Merwe had ruled herself out of contention for the 1989 Comrades Marathon. Fortunately, she seemed unaware of any such problem. She also had the public on her side. The smiling, ponytailed Benoni schoolteacher had become the darling of the South African road-running community. In fact, she was probably the nation's most popular female athlete.

When Frith van der Merwe went to the start of the 1989 Comrades Marathon, the country went with her, and she did not let the nation down. Although the battle between Tshabalala and Mtolo was enthralling and the female race emphatically no contest, the sheer brilliance and personal appeal of Van der Merwe captivated not just Comrades followers, but the whole country. Someone asked whether she should not be awarded two gold medals, one for the overall top ten and the other for the women's race, if she managed a top-ten overall placing. She didn't quite make that happen, but her 15th place overall caused observers to ponder how little we humans understand the difference between male and female. Second-placed Valerie Bleazard, over an hour behind Van der Merwe, performed superbly, but in a different dimension.

In his supremely authoritative book *Lore of Running*, Professor Tim Noakes pointed out that Van der Merwe's time of 5.54.43 would have won every Comrades Marathon until 1963, when women were still barred. Noakes went a little further. Citing the performances of triathlete Paula Newby-Fraser, as well as Van der Merwe's, he wrote:

'The performances of Newby-Fraser and Van der Merwe raise the possibility that men and women are indeed not equal and that, relative to their respective performances in shorter-distance races, women perform better than do men in very prolonged exercise. This is in line with the anthropological evidence that, in traditional societies, the women performed the chores requiring endurance.'

As was the case the previous year, Van der Merwe had to compete with the greatest scene-stealer of them all, Wally Hayward. This time, she beat him, but only just.

Shortly before the start, Hayward, a few weeks short of his 81st birthday, fell awkwardly as he stepped off a pavement in Pietermaritzburg. Many of us have witnessed the consequences of a fall for an octogenarian. Often it is what concerned family members tend to call 'the beginning of the end'. Hayward's response was somewhat different. He got up, dusted himself off and proceeded to complete the Comrades Marathon. It wasn't his most impressive run. He only just beat the time limit and was hospitalised for a few days. But he made it!

1989 COMRADES MARATHON RESULTS

1. Samuel Tshabalala	5.35.51
2. Willie Mtolo	5.39.59
3. Jean-Marc Bellocq	5.42.28
4. Nick Bester	5.43.05
5. Shaun Meiklejohn	5.44.50
6. Anton Hector	5.46.15
7. Ephraim Sekotlong	5.46.53
8. Lucas Tswai	5.47.03
9. Charl Mattheus	5.48.58
10. Hoseah Tjale	5.50.16

1989 COMRADES BOWL RESULTS

1. Frith van der Merwe	5.54.53
2. Valerie Bleazard	6.56.08
3. Naidene Stewart	7.00.09
4. Pat Lithgow	7.11.32
5. Hazel Hairs	7.13.44
6. Tilda Tearle	7.14.35
7. Ralie Smit	7.16.50
8. Priscilla Carlisle	7.27.36
9. Gail Buhrmann	7.29.21
10. Rae Bisschoff	7.35.05

1990 COMRADES MARATHON
AN OLD WINNER IN A NEW ERA

Between the 1989 and 1990 Comrades Marathons, the world changed dramatically and positively. South Africa was very much part of the change. Communism, the scourge of much of the world through most of the 20th century, collapsed spectacularly in Europe. The fall of the Berlin Wall symbolised a return to freedom for millions after decades of totalitarianism during which human rights were denied, national economies were virtually destroyed and utter misery became a way of life for millions.

Although South Africa's Nationalist government had strongly opposed communism since taking power in 1948, its own apartheid policies had also denied basic human rights to black South Africans, the majority of the population, who were denied citizenship purely because of skin colour. During 1989, the leaders of the Soviet-dominated Eastern Bloc and those of apartheid South Africa were admitting privately that their policies were wrong, unjustifiable and unsustainable.

Fortunately for the South African government, communism in Europe collapsed before the apartheid regime did. The Nationalist leaders, although deeply divided, had the opportunity to exploit the downfall of communism in facing up to their own wrongdoing. They needed some prompting, and this had been provided throughout the turbulent 1980s.

Serial Comrades winner Bruce Fordyce had been one of the leaders with his famous 'black armband' in 1981, the first of his victory years. In 1985, liberal opposition politician Helen Suzman had arranged for Lord Bethell, a member of the European Parliament, to visit Nelson Mandela in prison. This not only raised the status of Mandela in the minds of European politicians, but also gave him the opportunity to share with Lord Bethell his firm commitment to ending the violence and negotiating a peaceful future for all South Africans.

The following year a former leader of the opposition, Professor Frederik van Zyl Slabbert – a Celtic Harrier who finished the 1982 Comrades Marathon in the commendable time of 9.37.00 – infuriated State President P. W. Botha by leading a delegation of prominent South Africans including politicians, academics, sports administrators and church leaders to Dakar in Senegal, where they met top officials of the ANC and discussed their respective hopes, fears and aspirations.

P. W. Botha's anger was positive, in that it enhanced the status of the initial meeting and those that followed. Botha made further contributions through error rather than inspiration. He offered to release Nelson Mandela from prison provided that he renounced violence. In response, Mandela, by letting it be known that he would not accept any conditional release from Botha, cemented his position as leader-in-waiting of the ANC. Shortly before the general election of September 1989, F. W. de Klerk, a member of the National Party cabinet, ousted Botha from the leadership of the National Party.

On Friday, 2 February 1990, President F. W. de Klerk opened Parliament with a speech in which he unbanned political organisations including the ANC and effectively ended apartheid. Bruce Fordyce, feeling renewed justification of his 1981 armband protest, summed up the feeling of the moment: 'It was full of hope.' When Mandela was released nine days later, Fordyce watched, along with the rest of the world, and voiced his emotions: 'I wanted to know what he looked like. Nobody really knew until the TV cameras caught him. I had no idea he was so big. He looked so gentle.'

With a sense of optimism for the future of his country, as well as the encouragement of sponsorship from Allied Bank, Bruce Fordyce committed himself to an attempt at a ninth Comrades victory. It wasn't an easy decision. He had won an unprecedented eight in a row. Then, in 1989, he had made himself unavailable in order to take part in, and win, the world 100-kilometre championship in Stellenbosch. While he shared the euphoria of a South Africa committed to change, in the back of his mind he realised that a ninth victory would lead to pressure for an attempt at an unlikely tenth.

He soon realised that his doubts were realistic. At 34 he was still relatively young, but the the 1980s had taken their toll. Following his favourite dictum, 'Training is a science but racing is an art,' he once again relied on his tried-and-tested training schedule. Everything went well except for one rather important consideration: his times were slower. There was nothing he could do about it. Grateful for what he'd been able to achieve over the past decade, he recalled the words of South Africa's foremost expert: 'Tim Noakes says you have five or six great runs. I'm fortunate. I've had more than twice as many. Perhaps that Stellenbosch 100-kilometre run was just one race too many.'

Nevertheless, he had committed himself to Comrades and was determined to win, even though he knew that a record was out of the question. He had passed his peak, and victory would depend on his challengers being unable to maintain a sustained assault in the closing stages. As had happened two years previously, front-runners Boysie van Staden and Jetman Msutu took the lead once the TV hopefuls had been discarded. On the descent from Botha's Hill to Drummond, Mark Page caught the leading duo, and the three of them went through Drummond five minutes ahead of the defending 'up' race champion.

Fordyce was feeling nauseous at halfway and had all but given up his challenge. Nevertheless, he kept going, albeit somewhat uncomfortably. At Camperdown, Page and Msutu, having dispensed with the threat of Van Staden, were four minutes ahead of Fordyce, who had Meshack Radebe for company. Remembering how Fordyce had caught him at this stage of the course two years previously, Page put in a surge and increased his lead to four and a half minutes by the foot of Little Pollys. He was now in control and only had to keep going in order to win.

If Page had known how weak Fordyce was feeling at this stage, he might have put in a final decisive effort. Fordyce, in joint third, with nausea still troubling him, was concerned that his companion, Radebe, seemed stronger than he felt. In desperation, Fordyce thought of the women who had assisted him throughout his Comrades career, particularly his mother, Nancy Whittaker, who had taught him to be a winner. His sister, Oonagh, had flown out from London to support him in Comrades for the first time. She had seconded him in the London-to-Brighton race many years before. He thought of the stern comment from his wife, Gill, when he had shown pre-race nervousness: 'Bruce, you've been a Comrades record holder since 1981!'

Their support sustained his faltering self-belief as the leaders reached 'his' part of the course. On Little Pollys, Msutu bailed without any warning. Soon afterwards, Radebe dropped off the pace. Fordyce was second, but a full four and a half minutes behind Page, with 15 kilometres to go. At the top of Little Pollys, five kilometres later, the gap was just over three minutes. Fordyce was making inroads, but was about a kilometre behind with just ten kilometres to go. Page should be almost safe by now.

No leader at the top of Polly Shortts has yet surrendered his lead in the closing stages. Fordyce was conscious of this when he reached the foot of Pollys. His great friend, former Comrades champion Tommy Malone, called out to him, 'Bruce, the lead's 2.25. You're going to catch him. You'll get him in Maritzburg.' These were heartening words, but Page was over half a kilometre ahead and would surely use that gap to his advantage when he crested the hill with mainly downhill running ahead of him.

Then Page made his fatal mistake. On the ascent of Pollys, he looked back and saw the advancing Fordyce. His legs cramping, he walked for a while. Fordyce, the supreme hunter, recognised the vulnerability of his quarry. His own strength, which had been close to deserting him, came surging back. Television captured the hopelessness of the contest. Page was a beaten man. When Fordyce drew alongside him, he tried to encourage Page. They were, after all, teammates, and the Gunga Din trophy was within their grasp.

Page was simply unable to respond. Fordyce moved confidently over the top of Polly Shortts and seemed to have the race wrapped up. His seconds knew otherwise. They didn't want to frighten him by telling him that a fast-finishing Hoseah Tjale had passed Page and was now in second place. It didn't matter anyway. Fordyce finished strongly, although his time of 5.40.25 was the slowest of his nine wins. Tjale duly finished second and

Meshack Radebe grabbed third place from a devastated Mark Page.

Fordyce was convinced that his days of dominance were over. At the finish, he ran into the arms of his sister Oonagh and told her, 'It's over.' He knew. When, some time later, he looked back on the race, he acknowledged candidly, 'I won by default.' He realised that Page should have been the victor.

What was happening much further back in the field? Well-known silver medallist Marius Kuhn provided this account of his questionable advice to a clubmate:

'Standerton Marathon Club members travelled far and wide to run. We camped out at various venues, ran races, drank too much and returned to Standerton the next day. One of our members was an ex-British Airborne soldier by the name of Peter Murphy. When I moved to Nelspruit and joined the Nelspruit Marathon Club, Peter stayed at my house whenever he travelled to the Lowveld. He would dive into a pool after any run, regardless of the water temperature. This sometimes involved near-freezing stuff in midwinter. He merely shouted "Airborne!" and went for it.

'Peter had a camping stove and made his own pasta the night before a race. He did not like crowds, and many a Comrades was run on his own concoction. I also avoided the masses and really enjoyed the bunny chow, a curry speciality, sold by an Indian fellow from a take-away caravan outside the old Newton's Amusement Park. Real hot and greasy, but divine. I actually believed it worked for me on Comrades Day.

'While carbo-loading with copious quantities of Castle Lager two days prior to the 1990 Comrades, I bumped into Peter, who immediately joined me in this very important ritual. During the session I convinced Peter that the bunny chow provided more stamina than pasta and was the reason for my improved times. The next day we walked down to the caravan, but he was not as convinced as the previous evening. Intervention was required, and I reminded him that he should have no fear, being ex-Airborne. So, with the familiar shout, Peter got stuck into the bunny chow.

'I did not see Peter at the start as I was a seeded runner. I later learnt that the bunny chow caused six pitstops. Apparently Peter shouted "Airborne!"during the first three and "F#%$ you, Marius!" thereafter. Peter finished in time.'

Female participation in the Comrades Marathon was undergoing transformation. The superb performances of Lindsay Weight, Helen Lucre and Frith van der Merwe had inspired women from all over the country to take part in long-distance running and to discover for themselves what medical science now knew: the longer the distance, the better women seemed to perform relative to their male counterparts. More and more female entries were received. More and more women finished Comrades and other gruelling events with a smile.

At the front of the field, however, something of a lull was being experienced. It wasn't surprising. Lettie van Zyl had achieved a hat-trick of victories from 1976 to 1978, at times of 9.05.00, 8.58.00 and 8.25.00, respectively. Jan Mallen's 1979 victory was attained in 8.22.41. In 1980 and 1981, Isavel Roche-Kelly posted times of 7.18.00 and 6.44.35. Cheryl Jorgensen's 7.04.59 win in 1982 kept the standard high, and Lindsay Weight followed up with 7.12.56 and 6.46.35 in 1983 and 1984. Helen Lucre produced remarkable consistency with times of 6.53.24, 6.55.01 and 6.48.42 from 1985 to 1987. Then came Frith: 6.32.56 in 1988 and an unbelievable 5.54.43 in 1989. In a decade and a half, the winning time had been reduced by over three hours. There had to be a reaction.

That came in 1990. It wasn't a particularly slow race. In fact, it was a highly entertaining race, with the lead changing hands several times, and Newcastle runner Naidene Stewart's victory was well received by the locals. Nevertheless, her winning time of 7.02.00 was the last to exceed seven hours. Annette Schoeman was second in 7.07.35 and Di Terreblanche third in 7.09.42.

1990 COMRADES MARATHON RESULTS

1. Bruce Fordyce	5.40.25
2. Hoseah Tjale	5.45.19
3. Meshack Radebe	5.45.40
4. Mark Page	5.46.42
5. Jean-Marc Bellocq	5.47.32
6. Ephraim Sekotlong	5.48.01
7. Boysie van Staden	5.48.37
8. Shaun Meiklejohn	5.48.58

| 9. Gary Turner | 5.49.11 |
| 10. Nick Bester | 5.52.43 |

1990 COMRADES BOWL RESULTS

1. Naidene Stewart	7.02.00
2. Annette Schoeman	7.07.35
3. Diana Terreblanche	7.09.42
4. Tilda Tearle	7.11.16
5. Jean Cooper	7.17.37
6. Denise Lorenzen	7.20.57
7. Heather Grobler	7.25.57
8. Carol Crosley	7.27.12
9. Lindsay Weight	7.27.26
10. Hazel Hairs	7.29.02

1991 COMRADES MARATHON
BESTER'S BIG DAY

During 1991, it was at times difficult to believe that reconciliation was on the national agenda. Newspaper headlines such as 'Mob rampage after 35 die' and 'Necklace back in bloody Alex' hardly painted a picture of optimism and goodwill.

In May 1991, Winnie Mandela was sentenced to six years' imprisonment after being convicted of kidnapping and of being an accessory to assault. A newspaper report pulled no punches:

'The uncontested facts of the Winnie Mandela trial are simple – and few. Four youths staying at a Methodist manse in Soweto were picked up on the night of December 29, 1988, by associates of Mandela and brought to her home in Diepkloof Extension. The brutally assaulted body of Stompie (Seipei) was found in the veld a few days later.'

About two weeks after the sentencing, a section of the nation celebrated Republic Day. A press report of the event illustrated the great divide that still needed to be overcome:

'Right-wingers listened reverently as the taped voice of Dr H. F. Verwoerd was played to 1 500 people at a Republic Day festival in Pretoria. Guest of honour was Betsie Verwoerd, who was present at the birth of the Republic on May 31, 1961. She had been at her husband's side when he introduced C. R. Swart as the first State President.

'"Lank sal hy lewe in sy gloria" (long may he live in his glory) erupted from the crowd that day when Dr Verwoerd had finished his stirring speech to the nation.

'Rev Mossie van der Berg, chairman of Friday's meeting, told Mrs Verwoerd: "Till the end of time, the Afrikaner volk will cherish being associated with the name of Verwoerd."'

Rather than dwell on Van der Berg's ludicrously inaccurate prediction, perhaps we should focus our attention on another event that took place on the same day, the 66th running of the Comrades Marathon, an activity that brings together people from all walks of life in an annual pilgrimage honouring those who have sacrificed their lives for their country and forging the relationships needed to build the new nation.

Comrades week, however, began in a sombre mood. Sam Tshabalala, hailed as the first black winner of the race just two years previously, had travelled to Pietermaritzburg with other members of the African Zionist Church in their annual Easter religious pilgrimage. The minibus in which he was travelling was involved in a horrific accident. All occupants were killed, apart from Sam, whose condition, complicated by pneumonia, remained critical for some time.

As the 1991 entrants lined up for registration at the Comrades Expo, they walked past a box placed there to receive donations for the benefit of Tshabalala. One can assume, from the interest shown, that contributions were generous. Thankfully, Tshabalala recovered sufficiently to be able to run Comrades again, but not at the very top level.

Most eyes were on Bruce Fordyce as the runners went to the start. He was aware that the public viewed him as a kind of running Peter Pan and expected yet another dramatic last-gasp success, this time to claim his tenth title. He didn't share their view. As the years continued to take their toll of his physical and mental strength, he became more and more conscious of his human frailty. He wasn't expecting to win, but he didn't want to let anyone down.

The first half went more or less as expected. Although Fordyce was known to be a cautious starter, he did have the rather unusual experience of catching up to a woman, Frith van der Merwe, after about 15 kilometres. This, however, had more to do with her ambitious mindset than his lack of pace. After exchanging a few pleasantries, he moved ahead and joined one of his closest running friends, Hoseah Tjale. They ran together for a while, enjoying each other's company for the umpteenth time along that long, long road.

When spectators at the halfway point of Drummond saw Fordyce pass through three and a half minutes behind the leaders, they felt relieved. Their man was doing it again. In fact, Fordyce at that stage, was well in contention. All he had to do now was maintain his pace to the end – something that had never been a problem for him – and he would win the race.

Spectators and experts seldom know the inside story of the battle taking place in the minds of combatants. Boxing commentators can tell you who is landing the most punches, or the harder punches, but they can't tell you who is gaining the mental ascendancy, or who is wilting. Going over Botha's Hill and on to Hillcrest, Fordyce was wilting. Those ahead – Bester, Morake, Matthews, Meiklejohn and others – were watching each other, racing each other. They weren't concerned about the nine-time champion.

Fordyce suddenly ended all speculation. He had had enough. He walked off the road. It wasn't a call of nature, as many surmised. It was a symbolic capitulation, an admission of defeat. Ten years after his first victory, the reign of Fordyce had come to an end. The media were in attendance to hear the words for which he will always be remembered: 'If this was any race other than the Comrades, I would bail. But because it's Comrades, I'm going on to the end.'

In true Comrades fashion, Fordyce plodded on to a relatively sedate (for him) finish in 6.57.02

Stunned television viewers throughout the country had to accept that, while an era had come to an end, there was still a race to be decided. Up front, it wasn't particularly fast, but it was certainly furious. It was no longer a battle for second place: the main prize was up for grabs. Even though news of Fordyce's capitulation hadn't filtered through to the front, his non-appearance in a challenging position sent a sufficiently eloquent message.

Of all the contenders, Nick Bester had the most impressive credentials. A gold-medal winner for the three previous years, including third place in a time of 5.39.00 in 1988, he had the strength and the determination. His winning time of 5.40.53 was the slowest 'down' victory since Bagshaw's 5.47.06 in 1971, but was nevertheless well merited. Shaun Meiklejohn came second in 5.43.55, with Colin Thomas third in 5.45.13.

A special cheer was reserved for ever-popular Alan Robb, who arrived in eighth place in 5.51.49, just over ten minutes behind winner Bester. Seventeen years after his debut third place in 6.06.45, and with four victories to his name, Robb was still sufficiently strong and committed to Comrades to manage a top-ten finish. In so doing, he earned his 12th gold medal, the most of any athlete.

As ever, the appearance of Frith van der Merwe brought its own brand of excitement. The charismatic 27-year-old had brought a new dimension to the sport of long-distance running. Miracles were still hoped for, but greatness would be an acceptable substitute. Among the ultramarathon community, there was a growing fear that Van der Merwe was overdoing things and, frankly, pursuing a mission of over-ambitious self-destruction.

An indication of Van der Merwe's high hopes this year was the fact that it took Bruce Fordyce, running at more or less his normal early race-winning pace, approximately 15 kilometres to catch up with her. Such early speed was indicative of an attempt to better her extraordinary 15th place overall in the previous 'down' run. The fact that she managed to throttle back and adjust her effort to a mere winning pace does, however, suggest a sensible mid-race assessment of what was prudent.

While Van der Merwe's performance was not quite up to her phenomenal 1989 record-breaking run, she did nevertheless pass one male runner after another during the second half. This was quite a normal occurrence for her, but she had the shock of her life when she suddenly realised that the man she was about to overtake was none other than Bruce Fordyce.

Sadly, this was the final victory for Frith van der Merwe in her remarkable, but disappointingly short, career. She would make several comebacks, with a few non-finishes, and would always brighten Comrades day, no matter how she fared. Evidence of Frith's standing is the fact that her 1991 finishing time of 6.08.19, while falling short of the expectations of many, was still the second-fastest female time yet, after her own 5.54.43 in 1989. Top visiting female runners who dominate long-distance running throughout the world have come to South Africa, run Comrades, and all expressed their awe at Van der Merwe's Comrades record.

1991 COMRADES MARATHON RESULTS

1. Nick Bester	5.40.53
2. Shaun Meiklejohn	5.43.55
3. Colin Thomas	5.45.13
4. Israel Morake	5.45.43
5. Gary Turner	5.46.28
6. Charl Mattheus	5.47.31
7. Lucas Matlala	5.48.33
8. Alan Robb	5.51.49
9. Simon Tshabalala	5.53.17
10. Madumetja Mogashane	5.54.15

1991 COMRADES BOWL RESULTS

1. Frith van der Merwe	6.08.19
2. Heleen Reece	6.54.17
3. Tilda Tearle	6.55.01
4. Diana Terreblanche	7.00.13
5. Frances van Blerk	7.04.49
6. Gail Claase	7.10.09
7. Naidene Harrison	7.11.47
8. Rae Bisschoff	7.12.05
9. Val Bleazard	7.21.06
10. Berna Daly	7:23:57

1992 COMRADES MARATHON
JETMAN, THE FORGOTTEN MAN

What do Mark Page, Johnny Halberstadt, Hoseah Tjale and Bob de la Motte have in common? Most followers of ultramarathon running in South Africa could answer without hesitation: all four were famous for taking second place in the nation's most prestigious annual sporting event, the Comrades Marathon, and none ever won the race.

The 1992 winner does not enjoy the public acclaim due to a Comrades champion, nor even the status reasonably accorded to a runner-up. Jetman Msutu was the major victim of an unfortunate decision thrust upon the Comrades Marathon by 'higher authority'.

Ordinary citizens sometimes wonder about a secret relationship between government and big business. Is this paranoid, or is there really an ongoing relationship between the two which dictates much of the lives of the people and perhaps, to an extent, defeats the theoretical objectives of the democratic process?

Such questions were being asked in 1992, the year of the Barcelona Olympic Games. During the late 1980s, senior executives of some major companies were assured by their top managers that South Africa would be readmitted to the Olympic movement in Barcelona. Was this accurate conjecture, or did captains of industry have advance knowledge of an international sporting breakthrough at a time when P. W. Botha was still head of government and Nelson Mandela was still in jail? To take matters further, could there be any truth in the rumour that the country's impending participation in the Olympics might have influenced the result of the 1992 Comrades Marathon?

With the Fordyce era consigned to the record books, the search was on for his successor. Fordyce himself would have a bird's-eye view of stage one: he was one of the 1992 television commentators, a role for which he was as well equipped as he had been for racing. In fact, his performance on television with Tim Noakes proved to be one of the enduring Comrades highlights.

Who would take over Fordyce's mantle as number one Comrades athlete? There were a few pretenders to his throne: Nick Bester, Charl Mattheus,

Jetman Msutu, Mark Page, Shaun Meiklejohn, Gary Turner, Boysie van Staden and sensational Two Oceans record holder Thompson Magawana. Fordyce had shown his superiority over all of them. Would one of them now break out of the pack, show that Fordyce wasn't that special after all and set new standards? Time would tell – and finishing times would be interesting.

The 1992 race was an 'up' run, slower than the 'down' run for most, but the version favoured by Fordyce. The main contenders went through Drummond in fairly conservative fashion. As expected by most Comrades watchers, Bester, Page, Msutu, Van Staden, Meiklejohn and Mattheus led the assault. Bester, winner of last year's 'down' run, and Page, Fordyce's closest challenger in the last two 'up' runs, had the most impressive track records.

Page, aware that his tactical approach would, in all probability, have secured victory in the last two 'up' runs if Fordyce had been absent, sensibly adopted the same strategy that had almost worked on those occasions. At approximately two-thirds distance, he crammed on the pace and swiftly built up what looked like a winning lead.

His main adversaries seemed unable to raise their tempo at this stage. Bester, looking rather forlorn, dropped back and appeared to be out of contention. Mattheus kept going, but looked ill at ease. Page seemed to be in control and about to claim the victory that had only just eluded him in the previous two 'up' runs.

In the final third of the race, all the leaders went through 'bad patches'. The lead changed hands several times, and nobody looked in command until the very end. With about 24 kilometres to go, Mattheus, until now in a settled, if not particularly confident, second place, hit trouble and dropped back, Bester, who had all but given up five kilometres earlier, passed him somewhat gingerly. So did Thompson Magawana, fastest marathon runner in the field and holder of the Two Oceans Marathon record.

While the others were floundering, Mark Page pressed serenely onward, his dream of Comrades victory coming closer to fulfilment with every kilometre. No leader of an 'up' run at the top of Polly Shortts has as yet failed to win the race. As he had done two years previously, Page reached the foot of Pollys with a substantial, and apparently winning, lead. Two years ago, he had faltered and allowed Fordyce through to complete his ninth and final victory.

Having learnt his very painful lesson on that occasion, Page surely couldn't fail again, not at this late stage. Unbelievably, he did. Once again, he was struck by his old bugbear, cramps. In an almost impregnable position, he once again stopped running and clutched his painful hamstring, before resuming a cautious walk-shuffle motion. All eyes looked back to see if another challenger might be moving into contention.

To the astonishment of most, it was Charl Mattheus, all but dead and buried 15 kilometres earlier, who suddenly emerged in fine fettle, looking for all the world like someone coming to the end of a half-marathon. He shot past an almost motionless Page, moved effortlessly up the most feared hill in road-running and strode strongly onward to finish in 5.42.34. There he revealed the secret of his strength in the closing stages: he produced an engagement ring that he had carried throughout the race and proposed to his girlfriend. She accepted, and the whole country enjoyed the most romantic ending of a Comrades Marathon.

While the main contenders had faltered and recovered during the second half, one little man kept going with a consistency that he was the only one to display on the day. Tiny Jetman Msutu moved almost unnoticed through the pack to finish second in 5.46.11, three and a half minutes behind Mattheus. Mark Page courageously fought back to be the third finisher in 5.48.58, with Shaun Meiklejohn just behind him in 5.49.37. Nick Bester, 1991 'down' winner, finished sixth in 5.52.25.

Frith van der Merwe had not retired, but she was unavailable owing to injury. This was the start of a pattern: recurrent injury wouldn't hasten her retirement – her love of Comrades was too great for that – but her competitive days were now more or less over.

In Van der Merwe's absence, the women's race was open. As expected, Frith's phenomenal performances were not repeated. Pretorian Frances van Blerk took first place in a time of 6.51.05. Local favourite Tilda Tearle, third in 1991, came second, with Susan Robertson third.

Without doubt, the most poignant moment of the race was the arrival, in silver medal time, of 1989 men's winner Sam Tshabalala, who had made a near-miraculous recovery from the accident that had nearly claimed his life the previous year. His 1992 finish in a time of 6.23.39 received a standing ovation from the huge crowd, who were amazed to see him claim 65th place after all that he had been through.

A few weeks after the event, the 1992 Comrades Marathon suffered a setback not deserved by the organisers or the runners involved. The race, which had never before been associated with drug abuse or cheating or scandal of any sort, suddenly found itself under scrutiny when Charl Mattheus was summarily stripped of his victory after having been found guilty of using a substance banned by the International Amateur Athletics Federation.

On the face of it, he did wrong: he disobeyed the rules and had to take the punishment. Are there any circumstances that might exonerate him? In the first place, the background to the offence should be understood. For some time, drug cheating, which largely originated in the German Democratic Republic in the 1960s, had reduced many international athletics events to cynical competitions between opposing pharmacists. International rules were drafted to combat cheating by sprinters, weightlifters and others whose performances could be enhanced by illegal substances, particularly anabolic steroids.

In the early 1990s, there was no substance known to improve the competitiveness of ultra-distance runners. Yet Comrades Marathon runners, through their rather tenuous association with Athletics South Africa, the governing body of South African Athletics, were subject to the same stringent rules that applied to all athletes. Yes, all athletes should have known the rules and made sure that they obeyed them. At the same time, there was no culture of drug cheating in Comrades, and the relationship between Comrades runners and other branches of athletics was so remote as to be virtually nonexistent.

So what really happened? In the last few days before the race, Mattheus felt a throat irritation and went to a pharmacist, where he obtained an over-the-counter remedy. After winning the race, he was asked to disclose any substance that he had taken before the race and was required to provide a urine sample. The two matched up. The medicine he had taken contained phenylephrine, which would not have affected his performance in any way, and a mild sedative, which could have retarded his performance marginally. In other words, he gained no competitive benefit whatsoever from taking an innocuous substance for purely medicinal purposes.

The most logical conclusion is that Mattheus committed a minor infringement of a regulation designed to prevent cheating in the broader realm of athletics. In the interests of fighting the scourge of drug cheating, which certainly does exist in sport, he might reasonably have been severely admonished. But his disqualification, in the words of Tim Noakes, can be regarded as a 'gross miscarriage of justice'.

It is worth noting that the decision to disqualify Mattheus was not made by the Comrades Marathon, but by the national athletics body. Ever since, Comrades followers have asked: was Mattheus disqualified by a politically minded official who thought that his phoney dedication to cleaning up athletics might advance his own career in the Olympic year of 1992?

On the positive side, Charl Mattheus came back and proved his Comrades ability by winning the 1997 race in under five and half hours. He is a genuine Comrades champion, and the record books confirm this.

Jetman Msutu, on the other hand, has never been accepted by the Comrades rank and file or the general public as a true Comrades winner. Sadly, he doesn't even receive the credit which he genuinely deserved for a wonderful second place in 1992. The ill-considered decision to grant victory to the man who was second to cross the line has been far more detrimental to Msutu's reputation than that of the man who legitimately beat him. The forgotten man, Jetman Msutu, deserves better.

1992 COMRADES MARATHON RESULTS

1. Jetman Msutu   5.46.11
2. Mark Page   5.48.58
3. Shaun Meiklejohn   5.49.37
4. Koos Morwane   5.51.21
5. Nick Bester   5.52.25
6. Boysie van Staden   5.52.28
7. Theo Rafiri   5.52.39
8. Lucas Matlala   5.53.51
9. Zephania Ndaba   5.54.08
10. Joseph Mokoena   5.57.27

1992 COMRADES BOWL RESULTS

1. Frances van Blerk	6.51.05
2. Tilda Tearle	7.07.44
3. Susan Robertson	7.11.25
4. Pat Lithgow	7.13.04
5. Denise Lorenzen	7.13.33
6. Sanet Beukes	7.19.15
7. Dalene Vermeulen	7.24.09
8. Astrid Damerell	7.26.41
9. Desiree Botha	7.30.01
10. Annie Vermeulen	7.39.09

1993 COMRADES MARATHON
A GERMAN WINNER

In 1993, South Africa moved significantly closer to a peaceful settlement. Along the way, there was a frightening escalation of violence in which the most outrageous atrocities were committed. Positive and negative headlines alternated in a turbulent year within a turbulent period.

Three political leaders died in April. The passing of ANC chairman Oliver Tambo and Conservative Party leader Andries Treurnicht naturally elicited widely differing responses, but it was the third death that could have blown the peace process apart. Communist leader Chris Hani, previously head of the ANC's military wing, and one of the most influential characters in the transformation process, was shot dead on Easter Saturday, 10 April. Hani had a well-earned reputation as a hard-liner, but had wholeheartedly embraced the process of reconciliation, and was regarded by both political allies and former adversaries as a key figure in that process.

In mid-year, the prospect of a peaceful settlement seemed remote as the two sides drifted apart. At an ANC rally in May, Nelson Mandela threatened to reduce the legal voting age to 14. On 25 June, right-wing militants violently disrupted political negotiations. In July, members of the Azanian

People's Liberation Army attacked a church service in a predominatly white suburb of Cape Town with machine guns and grenades, leaving several worshippers dead and maimed.

But, on the other side of the coin, the peace process continued: in December, F. W. de Klerk and Nelson Mandela jointly received the Nobel Peace Prize, and the 29-year-old grandson of H. F. Verwoerd joined the ANC.

In the middle of all this drama, there was a German invasion, fortunately of an extremely peaceful nature. Charly Doll, a 39-year-old chef from the Black Forest region, entered Comrades – and he wasn't alone. Six foreign athletes – two Germans, two Britons, a Frenchman and a Pole – formed an international team to race against the best that South Africa could offer. Comrades had gone international.

It was Doll who stole the show. A proven 100-kilometre runner with a best time of 6.29, he would not be troubled by the Comrades distance. The hills were more likely to be a factor, but he took them in his stride as well. When Doll went to the front shortly after halfway, locals confidently predicted his collapse. After all, South Africans were the world's best ultra-distance athletes, weren't they? Record books don't lie. No foreigner since Mick Orton in 1972 had won Comrades. Apart from dominating the great race throughout the 1980s, Bruce Fordyce had shown the world that no one could touch him in the London-to-Brighton and other international races. The likes of Wally Hayward and Jackie Mekler had done the same. Who was this Charly Doll?

As the German kept going, another question arose: who was going to catch him? Where were the South Africans? During his lengthy reign, Bruce Fordyce had predicted that the first victory by a black South African would open the floodgates. It hadn't quite happened yet, although six black South Africans had finished among the gold medallists in 1992. One of them was Theo Rafiri, who, in addition to his running ability, was a gifted communicator. In the modern Comrades world, it wasn't enough to be a successful competitor. Sponsors sought real crowd-pleasers with public relations skills to market their wares, and black athletes had been looked upon as lacking in this regard. Not so, Rafiri. He was a character! He had personality, a sense of humour, an instant rapport with spectators. He was also his own man, not afraid to stand up for his beliefs, his values and his friends without concern for the judgement of those who used to (and sometimes thought they still did) control his country.

On Botha's Hill, Rafiri was in second place and looking good. Doll was running steadily, but Rafiri, with those long, powerful legs of his, was running quickly. At Hillcrest, the gap had clearly closed. Doll was aware that he was under attack. He didn't look as comfortable as he had ten kilometres previously. The long, flattish stretch from Hillcrest to Kloof is the most favourable part of the 'down' run for an athlete to make an extra effort without incurring too much damage. It was here that Rafiri made his move and took the lead from the German.

At Kloof, Rafiri had the race in his grasp. All he had to do now was ease his way down Field's Hill and keep his momentum going to the end. Such wisdom, however obvious it may be to the armchair viewer, often eludes the athlete, no matter how sensible he may be. The mindset that has propelled the pursuer to haul in his quarry is difficult to adjust afterwards. Rafiri raced down Field's Hill. He didn't have to, but he couldn't stop himself. Going into Pinetown, he was four minutes ahead of the German, but very close to being a spent force.

On Cowies, the last of the major hills, the tables were turned. Doll was now the chaser and Rafiri, his prey, was beginning to look vulnerable. But Doll wasn't one to become overexcited. He simply maintained his steady pace. It was all he had to do. The gap began to close. Doll waited until Tollgate had been negotiated and then went to business, drifting past Rafiri, who realised he was a beaten man, and crossing the line in 5.39.41 – not a particularly fast time, but a winning one, nevertheless.

Richard Santrucek was a Czech who had emigrated to South Africa and was enjoying a successful business career in his new country as managing director of Conshu, the company that distributed Asics running shoes. Being a true immigrant, he also completed three Comrades Marathons. Santrucek was near the finishing line when Charly Doll won the race. Shortly afterwards, he was within earshot when Doll spoke to his family and friends in German about his impressions of the race. Santrucek had a good understanding of the German language and was able to understand the winner's comments, which went something like this:

'The Comrades Marathon, without any doubt, is the greatest road race in the world. The general atmosphere from start to finish is phenomenal. The support along the way is unlike anything I have ever experienced before.'

We can safely assume that Doll, unaware that he was being overheard, was giving an utterly sincere account.

Theo Rafiri, fast becoming a crowd favourite, was a popular second finisher in 5.42.16, just 25 seconds ahead of Mohala Mohloli. Shaun Meiklejohn, fourth, earned his fifth consecutive gold medal, a superb achievement that earned him a permanent green number. Eloi de Oliveira took ninth place. His wife, Grace, would, in a few years time, become the region's favourite female runner.

The Comrades Marathon has rightfully earned a reputation as the sporting event which, more than any other, encapsulates all that enriches the world of sport: world-class performances, supreme courage, sincere humility, camaraderie and unity of purpose totally devoid of prejudice. Cheating is anathema to the Comrades tradition. Yet human nature has its foibles, and no organisation is immune to personal frailty.

As the battle for the gold-medal positions moved into the closing stages, television commentator Lindsay Weight casually remarked that one athlete looked as if he had only just started the race. Her observation was, regrettably, quite correct. Bellville's Herman Matthee had travelled most of the race in the comfort of a taxi. In the vicinity of Kloof, with just over 20 kilometres left, he had joined the race and gone on to the finish line as an apparent gold medallist. He had no chance of getting away with this deception; in fact, many felt that he had hoped to be caught. Of course he was disqualified and banned from the race for a lengthy period. It was an uncommon Comrades incident, and one that saddened the Comrades community.

If KwaZulu-Natal, as the province was now known, had a favourite woman in 1993, it was probably Tilda Tearle. She had taken third place in Frith van der Merwe's final victory in 1991. The following year, she had come second to Frances van Blerk. She was a regular top-ten finisher. Among other impressive performances, she had recorded two fourth places, in 1990 and 1991, as well as a sixth place in 1989 and seventh in 1988.

Tearle's progression through the ranks suggested that 1993 could be her best year to attempt a win. Her times had been consistent, although far from sensational. In 1986, her tenth place had been earned just within the silver limit, in fact in 7.29.59. From 1988 to 1992, she had returned times of 7.29.02, 7.14.35, 7.11.16, 6.55.01 and 7.07.44. It was an interesting record that probably reflected her own interpretation of her potential: for a couple of years, she just managed a silver, then she reached comfortable silver status before emerging as a potential champion through her 1991 effort.

Tilda Tearle went to the start of the 1993 race aware that she could do it, but probably unaware that it was her last chance. (Foreigners would take care of that from 1994 onwards.) She didn't waste her opportunity. Her time of 6.55.07 was six seconds slower than her own third-place time of two years previously, but it was enough to secure victory ahead of second-placed Rae Bisschoff (7.00.30) and Berna Daly, third in 7.03.32. Tearle wasn't just a popular local winner. Her model looks were featured in the national weekly press as the country celebrated her success.

1993 COMRADES MARATHON RESULTS

1. Charly Doll	5.39.41
2. Theo Rafiri	5.42.16
3. Mohala Mohloli	5.42.41
4. Shaun Meiklejohn	5.46.24
5. Thompson Magawana	5.49.29
6. Rudi du Plessis	5.50.44
7. Zephania Ndaba	5.52.21
8. Deon Holtzhausen	5.52.29
9. Eloi de Oliveira	5.53.27
10. Simon Williamson	5.54.18

1993 COMRADES BOWL RESULTS

1. Tilda Tearle	6.55.07
2. Rae Bisschoff	7.00.30
3. Berna Daly	7.03.32
4. Sanet Beukes	7.06.28

5. Diana Terreblanche　　7.07.24
6. Debbie Menton　　7.11.49
7. Desiree Botha　　7.12.21
8. Marie-France Janse van Vuuren　　7.19.36
9. Denise Dippenaar　　7.22.48
10. Ina Sanders　　7.23.04

A young Bruce Fordyce

Alan Robb's record-breaking 1978 finish

Denis Tabakin: champion of blind athletes

Piet Vorster stunned everyone in 1979

1979 P. Vorster

Former Kiwi, Helen Lucre:
Comrades champion

Octogenarian, Wally Hayward enters the
stadium with half the field in his wake

The nation's favourite twosome: Frith van der Merwe and Bruce Fordyce

Bruce Fordyce defies the
challenge of Mark Page

The agony and ecstacy of
1987 winner Bruce Fordyce

Fabulous Frith breaks the tape in 5.54.43 in 1989

Grishine, Bester, Volgin and Mattheus lock horns in an international battle

Wally Hayward presents green numbers to Ernst Vroom and Barbara Puttick

Sam Tshabalala: first black winner of
the Comrades Marathon in 1989

Charl Mattheus sets the record straight in 1997

Alberto Salazar pulverized the field in 1994

President Nelson Mandela visits Comrades

The late and sadly missed Lindsay Weight

Another success for Sue Brewin

16

THE FOREIGN TAKEOVER
(1994 to 2000)

John Gardener, greatly respected former headmaster of premier Cape Town school Diocesan College (known as Bishops), wrote:

'One of the best metaphors for what schools should be like is that of the Comrades Marathon. What a great name! It's a long, hard slog. Every runner goes at his or her own pace. Their paces vary. Everyone is prepared to help others. Spectators are uniformly encouraging, not critical. Runners respect one another. Even a Wally Hayward or a Bruce Fordyce can run the race much more slowly than he once did but achieve mightily in a new way that contributes to the strength and joy of others. Everyone is a unique winner. Even those who drop out have done a great thing in getting as far as they do, and everyone understands. Finishing is a triumph. Finishing first, or in gold, is just a different kind of triumph.'

John Gardener shows a keen appreciation of the culture of the Comrades Marathon. True Comrades devotees will also recognise the educational significance of his words. Those fortunate enough to have become part of the Comrades family may well have contributed to the legendary spirit of the race, as Wally Hayward and Bruce Fordyce have done. All will have learnt something that holds them in good stead as they travel through life.

Since professionalism and prize money have brought an annual influx of foreign runners to Comrades, there has been much speculation as to how profound their association with the great race may be. Do they just come for the money, or have they too found something so noble that their lives, and those of their families, have benefited? Certainly, some have made it clear that coming to South Africa and sharing our annual adventure has been a mind-altering experience.

One such person was American Alberto Salazar, widely regarded as the world's finest standard marathon runner in the early 1980s, although his 1994 victory was achieved just before the introduction of prize money. In the closing minutes of the race, Salazar, interviewed at the ground, told the huge crowd, 'When I get home, I'm going to tell everyone in the United States that the Comrades Marathon is the greatest road race in the world.'

The years 1994 and 1995 were momentous ones in the history and evolution of South Africa. The nation's first fully democratic election took place in 1994 and Nelson Mandela was installed as president, the first national leader who was totally acceptable to all, at home and abroad. In 1995, President Mandela played a rather significant role in South Africa's winning of the Rugby World Cup. He also paid a surprise visit, the first of three, to the Comrades Marathon and graciously handed out the prizes. The Nelson Mandela Children's Fund was well supported by runners, and there was a growing emphasis on charities.

Three South African athletes distinguished themselves in different ways during these years. Shaun Meiklejohn, as consistent a performer as any, finally showed in 1995 that he could do a little better than be among the golds by claiming the first gold on offer. Charl Mattheus put his 1992 nightmare behind him with a sub-five-hour-30-minutes win in 1997. Among the women, Rae Bisschoff's 1998 win was a triumph for a casual, amateur mindset. Could such an approach ever succeed again? It seems unlikely.

The most significant change was the introduction of prize money. For many years, athletes had received incentive bonuses from sponsors. From 1995, the race was officially professional. Thankfully, the Comrades Marathon Association and race veterans have ensured that the essential spirit of Comrades remains unchanged.

The advent of money brought visitors in increasing numbers. Some left indelible imprints in the Comrades record books. Many Comrades aficionados had considered Bruce Fordyce's 1988 'up' record of 5.27.42 impossible to beat. In 1998, Ukranian Dimitri Grishine shattered such misconceptions with a time of 5.26.25. Two years later, it was the turn of Vladimir Kotov to lower the record even further to 5.25.33. South Africans were still able to feature in the 'down' run, but visitors dominated the supposedly more difficult 'up' race.

Among the women, the overseas takeover was even more pronounced, with only Rae Bisschoff achieving a solitary South African win. Grace de Oliveira and Helene Joubert did perform heroically, but, generally speaking, the locals were outclassed.

In 2000, the special millennium run, 24 505 entered, 23 901 registered and 20 047 finished within the allotted 12 hours. The Bill Rowan medal was introduced for those missing a silver but finishing within nine hours, and was awarded to 3 275 runners, the first being Kabelo Tshabalala. A special once-only extension of the 11-hour cut-off to 12 hours was allowed for the momentous occasion and has subsequently become a permanent feature.

At the end of the millennium, South Africans Bruce Fordyce and Frith van der Merwe held the 'down' records while Belarussian Vladimir Kotov and American Ann Trason were the 'up' record holders.

1994 COMRADES MARATHON
ALBERTO SALAZAR BREAKS ALL THE RULES, BUT WINS

Major excitement came to the Comrades community in the build-up to this year's race. A few athletes in history have guaranteed a packed house wherever they have appeared, among them Sebastian Coe, Roger Bannister,

Carl Lewis, Alberto Salazar, Abebe Bikila, Paula Radcliffe and Robert de Castella. News was received that one of these world greats would be attending the Comrades Marathon, not just as an observer but as a participant.

In the pantheon of athletic superstars, they don't come much bigger than Alberto Salazar, the Cuban-born American who grew up in Massachusetts and became one of the great sporting heroes of the United States. He specialised in the standard marathon and was arguably the finest marathoner in the world at his peak from 1980 to 1983. His major event was the New York City Marathon, in which he achieved a notable hat-trick. His winning times were 2.09.41 in 1980, 2.08.12 in 1981 and 2.09.29 in 1982. His 1981 effort was briefly regarded as a world record, until it was discovered that the course was 150 metres short of marathon distance. In 1982, he won the Boston Marathon in the world-class time of 2.08.51.

From 1983, Salazar's career went into limbo. He failed to qualify for the 1984 Olympic Games, where he had been expected to be one of America's trump cards. Yet, as his performances and his confidence slipped, his reputation increased. Although he was no longer competitive at top level, the legend of Alberto Salazar continued to grow. In American minds, he was simply too big ever to be looked upon as anything other than superlative. The rest of the world agreed.

For almost a decade, Salazar remained virtually uncompetitive. It was a terrible time for someone who was still relatively young and had become accustomed to beating all comers. He went through periods of depression. After failing to make the 1992 United States Olympic marathon team, Salazar announced his retirement from the sport. Soon after, a physician introduced him to the anti-depressant Prozac, which helped him feel better and run faster, the two things that had been missing from his life.

Realising that he was, at best, a slower runner than he had been in his prime, Salazar sensibly looked for a race of longer duration, and therefore slower speed, in which to attempt some sort of a comeback. He chose South Africa's famous Comrades Marathon. Where he lived, weather conditions were anything but conducive to outdoor running in the months leading up to Comrades, so he did most of his training on a treadmill. Despite this disadvantage, as well as the fact that it had been many years since he had achieved anything of note as an athlete, he felt so confident that he wrote to Comrades officials and asked them to donate any prize money he might win to the local Catholic Church. He was politely informed that Comrades was an amateur event without prize money.

Salazar's was not the only entry received from abroad. Defending champion Charly Doll was eager to find out if he could be as competitive in the 'up' run as he had been in the 'down'. He had also made good his declared intention of telling his fellow Europeans all about South Africa's wonderful ultramarathon, and a few decided to join him in 1994. Among the entrants were the world 100-kilometre champion, Russian Konstantin Santalov, Switzerland's Peter Camenzind and Australian Don Wallace.

Never had it been more appropriate for world attention to be focused on South Africa. This was the nation's greatest year, and its greatest day was 27 April, when it held its first fully democratic general election. The mood of the country was unlike anything in its history. As huge queues of South Africans of every imaginable shape, size and persuasion patiently awaited their turn to vote, it appeared as if a blanket of tranquillity had been drawn over the land. Cold, rain and other unpleasant conditions were simply ignored.

Knowing that I would be able to cast my ballot on the 28th, I chose to spend the first day of the public holiday that had been declared for polling on a long Comrades training run. As I ran, I passed scores of black South Africans, dressed in their Sunday best, on their way to exercise the right to vote for the very first time. As I went by, they all greeted me. The words I heard more than any others were, 'God bless you.'

Two weeks later, in his inaugural address as South Africa's first democratically elected president, Nelson Mandela expressed a simple desire for change that embodied ideals that were already in place, at the heart of the Comrades Marathon:

'The time for the healing of the wounds has come. The moment to bridge the chasms that divide us has come. The time to build is upon us.'

Many have acknowledged that sport is the most effective activity in that human beings can 'bridge the chasms that divide us'. The Comrades Marathon has an 80-year record of building bridges in a spirit of camaraderie that no other sport comes close to emulating. The numbers of participants, the diversity of backgrounds, the enormity of the challenge and the reliance on one another make the Comrades Marathon a microcosm of a nation striving together, against enormous odds, to achieve a worthwhile shared objective.

While the arrival of the overseas athletes was a mouth-watering prospect for Comrades followers starved by years of isolation, political unification brought about a brand new sense of patriotism. Jetman Msutu, Nick Bester, Theo Rafiri, Rasta Mohloli and Charl Mattheus were all back to do their individual best and to defend the nation's honour. There was also another who was back, Bruce Fordyce, although nobody really expected him to do what, frankly, was now beyond him. He realised his limitations, but couldn't resist a generous sponsorship from Panasonic. He did, however, tell them very firmly that he was no longer capable of winning.

The 1994 Comrades Marathon was dominated by one extraordinary man, Alberto Salazar. His training had been such that most regarded him as ill-prepared, he was running in a continent that was strange to him, he had never before run further than 42 kilometres, and his race strategy was just about the opposite of what local pundits would have considered prudent.

Tim Noakes described Salazar's day in his book *Lore of Running*:

'During the race, Salazar ran just like the novice ultramarathon runner he was. Ascending Field's Hill after only 20 kilometres, Salazar took the lead. The last runner to win the race after leading from so early was Jackie Mekler 30 years earlier, when there were only 272 entrants (compared to 8 000 in 1994), none of whom could seriously challenge Mekler.

'Salazar passed through the halfway mark in 2.44.00, a new record for the "up" run, and with a lead of some seven minutes. But by 50 kilometres, his early pace was beginning to tell. He wished only to stop running. He began to pray and say his Catholic rosaries. With 16 kilometres to go, his lead had been reduced to five minutes, enough he calculated to allow him to win if he just kept running. He held on to win by two minutes in 5.38.39. It was, he concluded, a miracle; more satisfying than anything he had ever done in his life.'

For the second year in a row, South Africans were left to fight for second place, bewildered and outwitted by Salazar, although many still felt that the American's performance might have been even better had he adopted more orthodox tactics. At various stages, Theo Rafiri, Nick Bester, Rasta Mohloli and Thompson Magawana showed signs of challenging, without quite getting into a threatening position.

Of the locals, Bester fared best. In fact, there were observers who expressed the opinion that Bester might have won the race if he hadn't left his finishing effort until too late. Their argument hinged around a report that he was wearing a heart-rate monitor and ran the entire race in accordance with the information supplied to him by the monitor. Only in the closing kilometres, so they said, did Bester realise that he needed to abandon his technological approach and simply race the man who was ahead of him.

Whether or not that interpretation is correct, there is no doubt that Bester put in a phenomenal surge over the last ten kilometres. Certainly, he finished at a significantly faster speed than Salazar. The patriotic view of South Africans that Bester might have triumphed but for an error of judgement is not quite as compelling as some seem to think. If, for instance, Bester had put in his finishing surge a little earlier, would he not have run out of steam? On the other hand, if Salazar had found himself under attack in the closing stages, would he not have been able to dig deeply and keep his pursuer at bay?

Such ifs and buts are of academic interest. American Alberto Salazar was the new Comrades champion. His margin of victory, 4 minutes 13 seconds, was quite conclusive, representing more than a full kilometre. If we acknowledge that no Comrades leader at the top of Polly Shortts has yet been overtaken in the run-in to the finish, then we have to accept that the chances of a change in tactics bringing success to Bester would have been slight indeed. Just as Bester had been a worthy winner in 1991, so was Salazar three years later.

The Swiss runner Peter Camenzind came in fourth in 5.43.37, while defending champion Charly Doll of Germany was sixth in 5.52.51. Frenchman Denis Gack was ninth in 5.54.30. Bearing in mind the fact that Comrades was still a strictly amateur event – though this was about to change – three gold medallists from different countries signified a growing international interest in South Africa's greatest road race.

In the women's section, the foreign invasion was about to become a virtual takeover. There was no shortage of South African talent, with defending champion Tilda Tearle and perennial local favourite Frith van der Merwe both in the field. In the case of Van der Merwe, her participation was an attempt at a comeback, her last victory having been achieved in 1991. Sanet Beukes, sixth in 1992 and fourth in 1993, strengthened the South African contingent, although both of those top position finishes were accomplished in over seven hours, which was no longer fast enough. Naidene Stewart's

7.02.00 in 1990 was the last female victory above the seven-hour mark.

From now on, the women's race would be dominated by visitors, in particular Eastern Europeans. When Van der Merwe dropped out in the early stages, South African involvement was effectively over. The phrase 'the two Valentinas' would be heard regularly over the next few years as two Russians with the same name made their presence felt. On this occasion, Valentina Liakhova won in 6.41.23 from Valentina Shatyayeva, more than four minutes behind, with Hungarian Martha Vass third. Two South Africans, Sanet Beukes (6.52.21) and Helene Joubert (6.58.53), broke seven hours, taking fourth and fifth places, respectively. Cape Town's Jowaine Parrott was sixth in 7.09.14 and the 1990 winner, Naidene Stewart, took the final gold in 7.14.41.

1994 COMRADES MARATHON RESULTS

1. Alberto Salazar	5.38.39
2. Nick Bester	5.42.52
3. Rasta Mohloli	5.43.15
4. Peter Camenzind	5.43.37
5. Theo Rafiri	5.44.52
6. Charly Doll	5.52.51
7. Jacob Tlhapi	5.53.46
8. Jetman Msutu	5.54.27
9. Denis Gack	5.54.30
10. Livingstone Jabanga	5.54.53

1994 COMRADES BOWL RESULTS

1. Valentina Liakhova	6.41.23
2. Valentina Shatyayeva	6.45.49
3. Martha Vass	6.51.04
4. Sanet Beukes	6.52.21
5. Helene Joubert	6.58.53
6. Jowaine Parrott	7.09.14
7. Debbie Menton	7.10.27

8. Ina Sanders	7.11.34
9. Tilda Tearle	7.14.25
10. Naidene Stewart	7.14.41

1995 COMRADES MARATHON
MADIBA COMES TO COMRADES

Whatever political and ideological differences might have split the country in the past, one thing was absolutely certain in 1995: Nelson Mandela was president. The first democratically elected leader of the nation was its first fully supported, and indeed loved, leader.

President Mandela had one obvious objective on his agenda in 1995: he was going to use sport to help achieve his political ends. South Africans weren't exactly unfamiliar with that strategy, but there was a significant difference this time. Past political leaders had used sport to serve minorities and create division, but Mandela realised that the opposite was possible, in a sports-mad country like South Africa. Sport could be used to build bridges between people who had been separated by apartheid.

He didn't take long to show his hand. Rugby was the major sport for white South Africans, and almost a religion for Afrikaners. This was a Rugby World Cup year and, for the first time, South Africa was the host nation. Imagine if, back in 1985, when apartheid was in full force, someone had predicted: 'In ten years time, South Africa will have a black president who will mobilise all black South Africans to support a Springbok team in winning the Rugby World Cup in order to bring about national unity.' Truth certainly is stranger than fiction.

Before the opening match of the tournament on 25 May, the hosts versus defending champions Australia, the president interrupted a Springbok training session and told his unlikely troops, 'I have the hardest job I've ever had in my life. I'm trying to unite this country. I need your help.' His inspired team answered the call. In one of the great displays of Springbok rugby, Australia were beaten 27–18. In the final on 24 June, Mandela couldn't leave it all to the players, so he donned that famous number 6 jersey. The 15–12

World Cup victory was the nation's greatest sporting moment. In extra time, there was a break in play, during which the crowd sang 'Shosholoza', a traditional song of encouragement. There was a calmness and a confidence bordering on certainty about the manner in which it was sung. South Africa couldn't be denied. Francois Pienaar was absolutely correct when he told a television interviewer that 43 million people had supported the team to World Cup glory.

Between the opening match and the final, another great sporting occasion took place, the Comrades Marathon. The race was, for once, in a state of confusion. Times were changing and a new reality was in place. For many years, when South Africa had been part of the British Empire and Commonwealth, the race had been held on Empire Day. From the early 1960s, Republic Day, 31 May, had been the regular date. Sensitivity – and the fact that the date was no longer a public holiday – demanded a rescheduling of the event, but no regular date had yet been chosen. As a compromise, Saturday, 20 May, just five weeks before the rugby final, was decided upon for the 1995 race. Because it was a Saturday, rather than a public holiday, it was considered inadvisable to run through Pinetown. A detour around the town meant that the total distance was 90.7 kilometres, making it one of the longest races on record.

Another change, one that tore at the heartstrings of Comrades purists, was the introduction of prize money. For many of the old-timers, this was indeed a bitter pill, far more difficult to swallow than the abolition of personal seconds. The Comrades Marathon had been established to commemorate fallen comrades of the First World War. It was an annual event of comradeship, of sportsmanship and of fellowship. It was the most egalitarian sporting event on the calendar. Winners, record-breakers and 'tail-end charlies' were equals. The spirit of Comrades was everything. Who needed money?

There was another side to the argument. During South Africa's sporting isolation, the race had enjoyed a disproportionate level of television exposure. The allure of the annual Bruce Fordyce drama had drawn new followers in their thousands. The numbers of participants had grown phenomenally. Sponsors and advertisers had flocked to the race. Now, in the post-isolation era, other sports had turned fully professional and were back on the international stage. Comrades had to move with the times.

Prize money would only affect the front-runners. For most, there would be no noticeable change. Runners had been consulted, they had spoken, and prize money was now a fact of life.

The starting gun was fired by Pietermaritzburg mayor Rob Haswell, who was then advised that President Mandela was in Durban. He tried to persuade the president's entourage that his presence at the finish would be a positive gesture. When Haswell arrived at Kingsmead, he told Mick Winn, who was looking after the VIPs, that President Mandela might arrive. The phlegmatic Winn thanked him for the information.

Meanwhile, a race was being run. Who would be first to Durban? Would it be a visitor? The late withdrawal of Alberto Salazar and Charly Doll was a disappointment, but Alexei Volgin and Konstantin Santalov (present and past world 100-kilometre champions), as well as the likes of Peter Camenzind of Switzerland and German Kazimierz Bak, constituted a potent invasion force.

It was the South Africans, however, who provided the early pace. Elias Mabane and Aaron Nzimande were in front as the formidable obstacle of Inchanga was reached. This was where the overambitious were prone to fall apart. Not so Mabane and Nzimande, two talented athletes who had paced themselves sensibly. Inchanga was safely negotiated and Nzimande was first through halfway with Mabane breathing down his neck. Charl Mattheus, Livingstone Jabanga and Shaun Meiklejohn were three minutes behind the leaders and about a minute ahead of a huge bunch containing many of the pre-race favourites.

The next major hill, Botha's, posed no serious problems for the leaders. It was on the relatively easy stretch from Hillcrest to Kloof that the real contenders for line honours became apparent. Mabane's challenge ended at Winston Park. Nzimande was out in front on his own, but was showing signs of faltering. Behind him, Mattheus and Meiklejohn, having dropped Jabanga and passed Mabane, now shared second place and looked in command of proceedings. In fact, they soon led the event. Nzimande had run superbly, but simply had no answer when the speedy duo shot past.

At the top of Field's Hill, it was obvious that this had become a two-horse race. Both men had points to prove. Meiklejohn, a perennial gold medallist, needed to show that he had more than just leg speed, that he possessed that indefinable quality that enables a true champion to stand above all others.

Mattheus had already demonstrated his ability to win Comrades by crossing the line first in 1992, only to have the title snatched away from him by officialdom. Nothing short of a fully acknowledged victory for Mattheus would lay the 1992 debacle to rest.

Both highly incentivised, the pair sped down Field's Hill, shoulder to shoulder. It was a repeat of the Fordyce versus Robb duel of 1982. This is the one place on the course where one shouldn't race, but racing is unavoidable when your opponent is right next to you trying to impress you with his strength. Something had to happen. One or the other might make a decisive break or, perhaps, succumb and drop out of contention.

Near the foot of Field's Hill, Meiklejohn took off and established a reasonable lead. On the ascent of Cowies, Mattheus closed the gap, and then he made his move on the descent. He was now in charge and was first through 45th Cutting. Back came Meiklejohn to retake the lead. This time it was permanent. Mattheus was forced to yield. Meiklejohn breasted the tape in 5.34.02, a worthy winner. Mattheus, second, was 59 seconds adrift, with the Russian Alexei Volgin third.

While the locals gleefully celebrated a superb South African victory, the women's race was still in progress and was looking very much like a visitors' whitewash. American Ann Trason, holder of the world 100-kilometre record, was a newcomer to Comrades and was much feared by her opponents – and before long, she demonstrated why. Showing scant regard for the arduous Comrades course, she was soon so far ahead that Frith van der Merwe's 1989 record seemed threatened.

It wasn't destined to be Trason's day, however, as the stomach bug that had disrupted her preparation put paid to her challenge and she was forced to retire. Another novice, German Maria Bak, took over and dominated proceedings, winning in the fairly fast time of 6.22.45. South African Helene Joubert claimed a popular and well-deserved second place, with Russian Valentina Shatyayeva third.

The changing nature of the country was visible in various ways during the race. A group of five backmarkers noticed that someone just ahead of them was wearing a South African Defence Force vest on which he had sewn the old South African flag, which was no longer an official national symbol, but now widely associated with a hankering for the apartheid past. Clearly, this was an individual who had yet to embrace the new reality.

The same group, all white, found themselves in trouble on the detour round Pinetown. They had failed to drink liquids on the descent of Field's Hill and were feeling the heat. Deciding that they had had enough, they looked for a rescue vehicle. But a few black spectators started cajoling them and urging them to get back in the race, even singing 'Shosholoza' with such enthusiasm that a positive response was assured. All five made it safely to the end, two of them claiming their medals in the final minute.

Around noon, official starter Rob Haswell had his second conversation with legendary Comrades administrator Mick Winn. This time, his message was somewhat more definite than the first: 'The president is here.' Imperturbable as ever, Winn simply asked, 'Where?' and was told, 'Downstairs.'

Within minutes, news of Mandela's arrival spread through Kingsmead and the ground was abuzz. The great man generously joined in and enhanced the spirit of the occasion, presenting prizes to the award winners. Women's champion Maria Bak took full advantage, putting her arms around the president and giving him a big kiss.

In an interview published over a decade after the Rugby World Cup victory, 1995 Springbok team manager Morné du Plessis was asked, 'Looking back to the 1995 World Cup, do you think South Africa will ever be able to regain the connection that it so briefly had with the broader population?'

Du Plessis responded: 'That was such a unique and special moment in our history that to replicate it is probably going to be impossible. To have that brief, monumental impact is probably not going to be possible again, but you have to look at a more continuous and stable relationship with the greater population.'

Morné du Plessis is a road-runner who has completed several marathons. Hopefully, he will watch future television broadcasts of the Comrades Marathon and take heart from the efforts being made by Comrades to strengthen and grow the race's association with the broader population for the benefit of all.

1995 COMRADES MARATHON RESULTS

1. Shaun Meiklejohn	5.34.02
2. Charl Mattheus	5.35.01
3. Alexei Volgin	5.40.38
4. Rasta Mohloli	5.41.30
5. Gary Turner	5.42.33
6. Sipho Masango	5.47.09
7. Colin Lindeque	5.48.11
8. Lucas Matlala	5.49.13
9. Nick Bester	5.49.54
10. Theo Rafiri	5.50.33

1995 COMRADES BOWL RESULTS

1. Maria Bak	6.22.45
2. Helene Joubert	6.34.04
3. Valentina Shatyayeva	6.42.21
4. Sanet Beukes	6.57.28
5. Valentina Liakhova	6.57.57
6. Denise Dippenaar	7.00.28
7. Jean Rayner	7.03.22
8. Tilda Tearle	7.04.21
9. Lettie Greeff	7.12.35
10. Rae Bisschoff	7.13.23

1996 COMRADES MARATHON
THE ARTIFICIAL FOOT

As Bruce Fordyce has so often noted, the Comrades Marathon has an almost mystical ability to draw the very best out of human beings on one unforgettable annual journey that equips them the better to fulfil their more mundane responsibilities through the other 364 days of the year. Occasionally, someone answers the call of Comrades with a degree of heroism that can barely be believed. One such was Estienne Arndt.

Arndt ran his first Comrades in 1979, finishing the 'up' run in 8.44.10 in the colours of Bluff Athletics Club. Despite falling in love with the event, he missed 1980, but returned the following year as a member of Germiston Callies Harriers, the club he has represented ever since. He earned a silver medal in 7.26.07. Clearly, he was blessed with some ability.

For most of the 1980s, Arndt was a regular and colourful presence in the race, but his performances dipped somewhat. This didn't worry him. Together with a group of friends, he had discovered a new approach. Dressed in full Scottish gear (including kilts and sandals and carrying bugles and miniature bagpipes), they ran to promote the cause of the Little Eden Home for mentally handicapped children.

They found the answer to the famous question, 'What does a Scotsman wear under his kilt?' Why, running shorts of course! There was, however, an exception who kept the more traditional assumption alive, causing a great deal of mirth. One year, runners were warned that they would be disqualified if they infringed international rules by sporting logos of organisations that were in competition with official Comrades sponsors. Encountering race photographers, our friend turned round, raised his kilt and displayed two offending logos, one on each bare buttock.

In 1988, Arndt successfully completed his ninth journey, now for green. He was determined to make his tenth Comrades a memorable one and started early training. It didn't happen. While he was travelling home from work on his motorcycle, a bakkie pulled out in front of him. He had no chance of avoiding a serious accident and injury. A pin had to be inserted in his shattered femur and, worse still, two-thirds of his right foot was removed, partly in the accident and partly in an ensuing operation.

In hospital, Arndt assured doctors that he would yet complete his tenth Comrades. It was the right spirit of optimism for the recovering patient, but such an outcome seemed hardly likely. The positive approach continued on his return to semi-normal life. Wearing a prosthesis, he took up cycling and canoeing to build up the injured leg. Walking was difficult and running was impossible. Furthermore, he was warned by doctors that back problems would be a likely result if he ever managed to get back into any kind of running. He wasn't convinced.

As he was living and working in Cape Town in 1994, he took an opportunity to visit sports science guru Tim Noakes and asked him, 'Should I run?' Noakes responded with his own question: 'Do you want to run?' Arndt's response: 'Yes, I'd love to run Comrades.' 'Then run,' said Noakes.

Soon Arndt was running, albeit with a rather unusual gait. With the typical drive of a Comrades maniac, he overdid things and tore the ligaments in his good leg. Nevertheless, he was on his way and started looking for a Comrades qualifier, only to find that he was unable to run a sufficiently fast standard marathon. This was a minor setback. He qualified in the Korkie Ultramarathon and actually finished the 1995 Comrades 'down' run, but 15 minutes too late. Such a painful failure would have deterred most, but not Estienne.

Undaunted, he set his sights on the 1996 race. This was an 'up' run, and therefore slower and more difficult to complete. I should know, because I tried – and failed – that year. Sitting in the relative comfort of a rescue vehicle (if a bailer can ever feel comfortable), I watched those ascending Polly Shortts. Most were walking. Suddenly, I spotted the most individualistic running style I'd ever seen. It was Estienne. I looked at my watch. There was still plenty of time. Surely, he'd make it. As our vehicle drew alongside him, I took a close look. On his face, I could see etched every detail of what he was feeling: hope, pain and, above all, an absolute determination that would not be overcome. Now I knew he'd get that green number. In a time of 10.29.18, Estienne Arndt completed his extraordinarily courageous comeback, one that could be rivalled only by Wally Hayward's unbelievable run in 1988.

Arndt wasn't finished. He has subsequently completed three further Comrades Marathons. Nowadays, Estienne and his wife Nadia are well known for their organisation of extreme marathons such as the Kalahari Augrabies and the Addo Elephant 100-miler. He is one of the Comrades legends.

Prize money had been introduced in 1995 in order to lure overseas athletes to the race. The experiment must have been at least a partial success, as the money was increased this year. It seemed to do the trick. Among the foreigners were Alexei Volgin and Konstantin Santalov (again), Mikhail Kokorev, Brazilian world 100-kilometre champion Valmir Nunes, Australian Don Wallace, American Tom Johnson, Ukranian Dimitri Grishine (purported to be an uphill specialist) and an Englishman named

Chris Parkes, who happily predicted that he would run flat out for the full distance. Eyebrows were raised, but the memory of Alberto Salazar's barnstorming run two years previously was still fresh in most minds.

Seventy years of Comrades history had shown that the prudent approach was a gentle first half followed by a tactical battle in which individual skirmishes had to be timed with absolute precision. Prize money, however, seemed to dictate that nobody should be allowed to get too far ahead. Visitors could hardly be expected to know the difference between 'television hares' and real contenders. From the start, this was a fast race.

Englishman Chris Parkes made good the first part of his boast, cresting Cowies in 58.20 together with co-leader Stemmer Lekoto. On Field's Hill, an obstacle greatly respected by the battle-hardened, Parkes sped away from his rivals as if he were running a middle-distance race. He went through halfway in a new record time of 2.38.35, well ahead of Andries Tshekiso (2.44.16), Lekoto (2.44.31), Walter Nkosi (2.45.23) and the 1993 Two Oceans champion Isaac Tshabalala (2.45.27). Defending champion Shaun Meiklejohn was nearly ten minutes adrift of the flying Englishman. If Parkes were to keep up his first-half pace, a finishing time of 5.15 was on the cards. Old stagers simply shook their heads and predicted his imminent demise.

Parkes did maintain his lead over Inchanga, but was clearly slowing. Before long, he had been passed and the race took on a more familiar pattern. The formidable quartet of Mattheus, Volgin, Bester and the novice Grishine took over the lead, with Meiklejohn trying gamely but unsuccessfully to join them. It was apparent that Grishine was enjoying his first Comrades outing, in particular the climbs, where he held a clear advantage. With Ashburton and Polly Shortts looming, he was starting to look ominous.

Volgin was the first to flag, dropping back, but not entirely out of the picture. This gave Mattheus and Bester the opportunity to work as a team. On the downhill before Little Pollys, they took turns to put in surges, trying to shake off the Ukranian. Their joint effort seemed to be working, and they opened a reasonable gap over the visitor.

Then came Little Pollys, second-last of the uphills. Grishine caught up to, and passed, the two South Africans in as decisive a move as Comrades had yet witnessed. Bester and Mattheus were dumbfounded. They had no answer. The race was effectively over. Polly Shortts, the real challenge, was comfortably negotiated by Grishine, who went on not only to win his maiden Comrades, but also to beat the five-and-a-half-hour barrier, finishing in 5.29.33.

Nick Bester, a tough competitor who doesn't know how to give up, took second place in a gritty 5.30.48. Volgin came back to claim third spot from an exhausted Mattheus, with Meiklejohn fifth. Comparisons with the past showed just how competitive Comrades had become in the modern era. No fewer than 30 men finished in under six hours. Money was living up to its reputation and 'talking'. The Comrades Marathon was attracting the foremost long-distance runners in the world.

Much the same could be said of the women's race. American Ann Trason had arrived in South Africa a year ago with the reputation of being the world's number one female long-distance athlete. She had gone home empty-handed. True champions overcome their failures, and Trason was back, eager to make amends. Also in the field was Englishwoman Carolyn Hunter-Rowe, former world 100-kilometre champion and winner of the 1994 Two Oceans Marathon. The South African contingent was led by 'up' and 'down' record holder Frith van der Merwe. Nearly all the regulars were back to contest what was expected to be one of the greatest women's races yet.

Those who were hoping to witness a close race had their hopes dashed. At no stage was it a contest. At the same time, one of the all-time great Comrades performances provided an enthralling spectacle. Ann Trason was in a class of her own. Her tactics were exactly the same as in 1995. The only difference was that this time she was in perfect health. Her halfway time of 3.03 was a new record. Maria Bak, second, was a full five minutes behind her. In third place, Capetonian Jowaine Parrott was a further five minutes back.

The second half was similar to the first. Trason showed no sign of faltering, even taking Polly Shortts in her stride in her first 'up' run. Her winning time of 6.13.23 shattered Frith van der Merwe's 1988 record by 19 minutes 33 seconds. Maria Bak was second in 6.24.08, with Valentina Shatyayeva third. Jowaine Parrott, fourth, was the first of the South Africans. The consistent Berna Daly took fifth position. Sixth-placed Carolyn Hunter-Rowe arrived in 6.57.59. No fewer than seven women beat the seven-hour barrier, with Valentina Liakhova just making it in 6.59.44. Van der Merwe was a non-finisher.

Even though Bruce Fordyce continued to hold both 'up' and 'down' records and Frith van der Merwe's 'down' record remained intact, it was plain that the annual influx of visitors was raising the overall standard markedly. The foreign impact had also introduced a new dimension to the race, one of national pride. Ultramarathon racing had long been looked upon as very much an individual sport, so the sight of Nick Bester and Charl Mattheus working in tandem in an effort to get the better of Grishine was something of an eye-opener.

Would these overseas runners ever become acquainted with the spirit of Comrades, or would they just jet in, make some money and disappear? Chris Parkes's conduct might give an indication of the answer. The halfway leader, having shot his bolt and surrendered his place, lay down on the side of the road, thoroughly exhausted. After a while, he got up, returned to the race and, in true Comrades fashion, continued to the end although well down the field.

Perhaps, one day, visiting runners may learn to covet and appreciate green numbers as much as the locals. In 1996, Barbara Puttick and her husband Ernst Vroom achieved the great milestone. Barbara recalls the day fondly:

'As the most unfit, most unathletic and definitely the most sport-hating girl throughout my entire school career and well into my early thirties, no one was more surprised than I when in 1996 I ran my tenth consecutive Comrades marathon, along with my long-suffering husband and running partner, Ernst Vroom.

'Despite the fact that I would be running my tenth, a highlight of any runner's career, I did not deviate from my usual training schedule of never running more than 50 kilometres per week, indulging in the couch potato life and ingesting large amounts of food and alcoholic beverages. It just goes to show that my unorthodox training methods really do work, as my tenth Comrades was the most wonderful race I have ever run!

'The day was filled with many magical highlights – managing to run up Field's Hill was one; seeing the man who got me through my very first Comrades was another; hearing strangers shout out our names and encourage us to keep going was yet another; as was the amazing support of my two brothers and their families all the way along the route; touching hands with the incredibly supportive disabled schoolchildren alongside the road near Inchanga was another (very emotional) one; but perhaps, rather selfishly, my personal best highlight was being the stronger runner on that particular day and having to keep waiting for Ernst to catch me up!

'Of course in reality I hurt like hell, of course I was tired, of course I felt nauseous at the mere thought of yet another mouthful of sports drink to keep me going, and of course, as usual, I cursed and swore and said some very bad words during the day. But these complaints paled into insignificance in comparison with the wonderful sense of achievement and amazement I felt as the 10 672nd person across the finish line in a time of 10 hours 33 minutes.

'Perhaps THE highlight of the day was having our photograph taken with the great Wally Hayward, who handed us our green numbers.'

1996 COMRADES MARATHON RESULTS

1. Dimitri Grishine	5.29.33
2. Nick Bester	5.30.48
3. Alexei Volgin	5.32.21
4. Charl Mattheus	5.34.56
5. Shaun Meiklejohn	5.39.20
6. Gary Turner	5.40.52
7. Tom Johnson	5.41.57
8. Mikhail Kokorev	5.42.10
9. Moses Lebakeng	5.43.27
10. Donovan Wright	5.45.55

1996 COMRADES BOWL RESULTS

1. Ann Trason	6.13.23
2. Maria Bak	6.24.08
3. Valentina Shatyayeva	6.30.33
4. Jowaine Parrott	6.55.19
5. Berna Daly	6.56.33
6. Carolyn Hunter-Rowe	6.57.59
7. Valentina Liakhova	6.59.44
8. Sanet Beukes	7.05.57
9. Reneé Scott	7.07.26
10. Nurziya Bagmanova	7.09.06

1997 COMRADES MARATHON
VINDICATION FOR MATTHEUS

After every Comrades Marathon, every runner has a tale to tell. The event is so long and so gruelling that it takes ordinary mortals to the limit of their physical, mental and spiritual resources. The story of the last person home is often more enthralling than that of the winner. In 1997, however, it was definitely the winner who attracted everyone's attention.

Over the years, virtually every race has brought untold pleasure to participants, supporters and spectators. Yes, runners endure a great deal of pain, and many feel the disappointment of failure. Yet the pain is generally an exquisite affirmation of the magnitude of the challenge, while disappointment inspires a determination to return.

The 1992 Comrades Marathon was memorably painful for the man who crossed the finish line first – though not physically, and the hurt was only inflicted after the race was over. That was the year in which Charl Mattheus was stripped of his winner's title, not by Comrades Marathon officials but by Athletics South Africa. The facts are set out a few chapters back.

For five long years, Charl Mattheus was forced to live under a cloud. The hurt he endured was numbing, his personal life adversely affected, and he would not be able to rest easy until he came back and proved himself for all to see by winning another Comrades Marathon. When he went to the start in 1997, it was as favourite and not just for sentimental reasons. His two most recent Comrades efforts, in 1995 and 1996, had produced a second and a fourth, respectively. His 1997 training had gone well and he would be hard to beat.

Just under 14 000 runners arrived at the start in near-perfect conditions. The temperature in Pietermaritzburg, often freezing at this time of the year, was a relatively comfortable 6°C. It was windless and expected to remain so for the duration of the race. Weather forecasters expected a pleasantly warm, but not unduly hot, day.

The usual horde of 'television runners' took the early lead. None would be in serious contention to challenge for a win. They knew it, everyone knew it, but nobody begrudged them their few moments of fleeting fame. At least their families would know that they weren't up to mischief and their employers could see that their special leave applications had been valid. They were also able to enjoy the extraordinary thrill felt only by those who lead, even for a short while, the world's number one ultramarathon and who are recognised as top runners by the massive crowds along the route.

Behind them, the real contenders were bunched together in a bus of approximately 40. In a few short years, the nature of the race up front had changed. Virtually all the front-runners were full-time professionals, chasing a great deal of money. The Comrades Marathon Association had increased prize money, but perhaps the greatest incentives came from sponsors who were offering huge bonuses to any of their runners who might earn gold medals, win the race or, above all, break Bruce Fordyce's 11-year-old record of 5.24.07. It was reported that certain athletes stood to gain well over a million rand should they break the record. Many of the top athletes had prepared at high-altitude training camps: Grishine and other Eastern Europeans in Russia, Bester and some South Africans in Dullstroom and Mattheus in Colorado in the United States. Interestingly, Fordyce pooh-poohed such strategy, saying that it was better to stay at home, train as an individual and keep within reason to one's normal lifestyle. He believed that the altitude of his hometown of Johannesburg was quite sufficient.

The first to make a significant move was Mattheus, who attacked the ascent of Inchanga, a tactic one might have expected from Grishine. Grishine followed him, as did Bester, wearing a heart monitor, and others. The new, reduced lead group went through Drummond in 2.43.45, nearly two minutes inside Bruce Fordyce's halfway time in his 1986 record-breaking run. With virtually all the main contenders at or near the front, a new record seemed a distinct possibility. The athletes were determined, while their sponsors trembled.

The race was now well and truly on. Bester was the next to show his hand, making a break on the long climb of Botha's Hill. South African marathon record holder Zithulele Sinqe followed him. They overtook the leading bunch, which included Mattheus, Grishine, Donovan Wright and former winner of the 'Om die Dam' Ultramarathon, Soccer Ncube. The gauntlet had been thrown. The leaders were approaching the fast, flattish section from Hillcrest to Kloof. Anyone with line-honour ambitions couldn't afford to lag behind at this stage.

Mattheus accepted the challenge and set off in pursuit of the leaders. At

Hillcrest, he was alone in third place, having shaken off Ncube. Defending champion Grishine suddenly 'blew'. Soccer Ncube, Andrew Kelehe, Rasta Mohloli and Sarel Ackermann kept each other company, a little off the pace and waiting to pick up the pieces should the leaders hit trouble. Behind them, the Pole Jaroslaw Janicki was steadily moving through the field, looking relaxed and strong. Mattheus, continuing to push strongly, managed to catch Bester and Sinqe at Gillits. It seemed likely that the winner would come from this trio.

Shortly after Kloof, Bester produced the next break and flew down Field's Hill at an astonishing three minutes per kilometre. Sinqe and Mattheus were somewhat more circumspect and allowed Bester to get away, waiting for the flat section through Pinetown before responding. With 20 kilometres to go, the trio were once again running alongside each other. On Cowies, the last of the so-called 'majors', Sinqe, the standard marathon specialist, fell back. He had shot his bolt. It was now a race to the end between South Africa's two favourites, Bester and Mattheus. Once again, it was Bester who made a move, surging on the ascent of 45th Cutting and looking to have the race wrapped up when he reached the top of Tollgate in the lead, with only downhill and a final flat section ahead of him.

For Mattheus, it was now or never. His physical energy having been exhausted, all he had now was mental strength and the conviction that victory today would redress the wrong of 1992. Second place was not an option. Drawing on whatever reserves he still possessed, he surged past Bester with about four kilometres to go and pressed ahead, making sure of his win. His time of 5.28.37 made him only the fifth man to break five and a half hours for the 'down' run. Interviewed afterwards, he said:

'At last, I'm back. I'm pleased with the time. I think I worked very hard in the United States, in Colorado at very high elevation. That pulled me through. At one stage, I thought Nick had it in the bag. On the downhill, I gave everything. I knew I had to get rid of Nick totally and not let Nick sit with me because he is a very tough customer.'

Bester kept going to take the runner-up spot for the third time. With several other gold medals to his credit, he can be considered unfortunate not to have added a second victory to his 1991 triumph and joined the exalted ranks of multiple winners. Janicki, the likeable Pole, came through to take third place ahead of Sinqe, whose fourth position was an excellent effort. Russian Konstantin Santalov, after several attempts, finally claimed the tenth gold. South Africans had reason to feel pleased with seven gold medallists.

The women's race featured an extremely gutsy performance from American Ann Trason, who had undergone serious hamstring surgery the preceding November. Asked about her prospects, she stated emphatically that she wouldn't have come to South Africa if she hadn't fancied her chances. In 1996, she had shattered Frith van der Merwe's 'up' record. When reference was made to Van der Merwe's phenomenal 'down' time of 5.54.43, the American graciously described the record as being 'in another orbit'.

Maria Bak, winner of the 1995 'down' and runner-up to Trason the following year, decided to take the fight to the American and surged ahead after only 15 kilometres. Sensing that Trason would be nursing her injured leg, the German endeavoured to get as far ahead as possible. Trason sensibly ran cautiously, although the pace was anything but slow. At halfway, Bak's lead over Trason was 1 minute 30 seconds, with the Russian Valentina Liakhova in third place.

The pattern continued in the second half, with Bak gradually extending her advantage. At Hillcrest, the gap was up to two minutes, and that's where it stayed all the way to Kloof, down Field's Hill and through Pinetown. Bak was suffering from a bruised heel and began to limp slightly over Cowies Hill and through Westville. As the pair began the final climb to the top of Tollgate, the difference was only ten seconds. Trason swiftly took the lead and kept it. Her winning time of 5.58.25, almost four minutes slower than Van der Merwe's 1989 'down' record, nevertheless made her only the second woman to break the six-hour barrier. In a television interview shortly after finishing, she admitted, 'Maria had a gear I didn't have today,' and added:

'It was very hard for me. I had surgery in November. My surgeon recommended that I didn't come. I promised Carl, my husband, that, whatever I did, I'd do it for him. At the end, I dug deeper than I'd ever dug before because he was here, helping me.'

Over the years, runners have completed the race in various strange forms of attire. We've seen barefoot athletes, those wearing formal dress, Scots in their kilts, the rhino man and more. This was the year of the 'Liquorice Allsorts Man'. Percy Dunn, a 37-year-old South African diplomat, ran the entire race in a costume weighing three kilograms. His aim was to raise funds for, and increase awareness of, the Nelson Mandela Children's Fund.

Dunn's arrival at Kingsmead was greeted with tremendous applause. Despite the extra load, he finished 21st in an astonishing time of 5.56. Asked how he might have fared without the suit, the deeply religious Dunn modestly replied: 'One can only speculate whether I could have got gold without the suit. There are always so many factors and dynamics which come into play at Comrades.'

In three years' time, the Comrades Marathon Association would celebrate the new millennium and the 75th running of the race by extending the cut-off from 11 to 12 hours, as a once-only concession. Although no one knew this at the time, a debate would later ensue as to whether the 12-hour limit, which also applied to the first few races in the 1920s, should be reinstated permanently. One of the arguments in favour of such a move was the view that the event would be able to retain the participation of stalwarts who had been slowed by age. This year's halfway cut-off provided some evidence to support such a proposal: the first person who was not allowed to continue after halfway was Len Taylor, holder of permanent number 125 with 16 medals to his credit.

1997 COMRADES MARATHON RESULTS

1. Charl Mattheus	5.28.37
2. Nick Bester	5.30.41
3. Jaroslaw Janicki	5.32.50
4. Zithulele Sinqe	5.33.18
5. Andrew Kelehe	5.33.24
6. Sarel Ackermann	5.33.27
7. Shaun Meiklejohn	5.34.04
8. Rasta Mohloli	5.34.34
9. Peter Camenzind	5.34.47
10. Konstantin Santalov	5.37.36

1997 COMRADES BOWL RESULTS

1. Ann Trason	5.58.25
2. Maria Bak	6.00.28

3. Valentina Liakhova	6.22.59
4. Valentina Shatyayeva	6.31.38
5. Charlotte Noble	6.45.51
6. René du Plessis	6.45.58
7. Helene Joubert	6.51.15
8. Berna Daly	6.52.37
9. Rae Bisschoff	7.05.04
10. Sanet Beukes	7.07.51

1998 COMRADES MARATHON
NEW RECORD FOR GRISHINE

Those who have accepted the responsibility of organising South Africa's favourite annual event are all people with an abiding love of the race. The Comrades Marathon Association committee has never been slow to give recognition to those who have played significant roles in building the event.

Without any doubt, the most important person in Comrades history is race founder Vic Clapham. It was his vision that led to the establishment of the event. His appreciation of the comradeship he shared with fellow soldiers in long marches through the desert in the First World War remains the basis of the legendary Comrades spirit. For 17 years, he organised the race. Ignoring legislation and medical opinion, he quietly encouraged women and those of colour to take part in his event, albeit unofficially.

The annual Comrades Marathon awards dinner took place in March 1998. Warm tributes were paid to the founder and a bronze sculpture of Clapham was unveiled by his sons Eric and Doug. The sculpture, by Kim Goodwin, stands proudly at the entrance to the Comrades Museum in Pietermaritzburg, where it truly belongs.

One aspect of running that was being closely examined was the question of drinking on the run. In *Lore of Running*, Tim Noakes records that Jackie Mekler had told him that, in one Comrades Marathon, he had taken liquid for the first time after 60 kilometres. In a 160-kilometre race, Mekler's first drink came after 100 kilometres. In the 1980s, when Comrades and road-running in general were growing exponentially, athletes were warned that they would be courting disaster if they failed to drink sufficient liquid before and during runs. Official starters would urge runners to visit refreshment tables as often as possible, particularly on a hot day.

Recent developments, led by Professor Tim Noakes, suggest that Mekler wasn't quite as ignorant as some might have imagined. In fact, his long athletic record of success after success at the highest level in the most strenuous of ultra-distance contests indicates that there wasn't too much wrong with his methods. Noakes identified 24 cases of runners who had drunk too much liquid during the 1987 Comrades Marathon. Some of them were in a critical condition and three barely survived. A new word, hyponatraemia (meaning overhydration), found its way into the runners' dictionary. One thing is now crystal clear: drinking too much is a great deal more dangerous than drinking too little.

There would certainly be no shortage of liquid along the route in 1998. As ever, runners would be pampered in every conceivable way. No fewer than ten physiotherapy stations would be set up for those who would require, or perhaps just enjoy, a stop and a rub. Steve Felsher, the man in charge, spoke of the challenge facing his team: 'It is a tough 11 hours for all of us, and the logistics of manning all ten stations and moving the physios from the first three stations to the finish, where it's like a battlefield, are awesome. We also man the Voltaren Emulgel Comrades Expo stand for three days prior to Comrades. Any injured Comrades runner can come to the stand for a free physiotherapy consultation and treatment.' All told, there would be 30 qualified physiotherapists and 170 final-year physiotherapy students on duty on race day.

Over the years, there have been occasional changes of finish venues. This year was one such occasion. For some time, there had been a feeling that Pietermaritzburg's Jan Smuts Stadium was too confined, and indeed too small, to cope with the huge crowds who congregated each year to welcome the runners home. Not everyone agreed. There was no doubt that the stadium possessed a special atmosphere, as did the approach to the stadium for runners. The short ramp leading into the ground was both loved and hated by athletes. In 1998, the finish was moved to Scottsville Racecourse, a venue that also had its shortcomings.

There was no clear-cut favourite in 1998. The main contenders had all displayed frailty as well as considerable talent in past years. Dimitri Grishine and Charl Mattheus were the names on most lips. Grishine had looked awesome in his debut race two years previously, but had fared badly in the 1997 'down' run. What did that tell us? Was his 1996 win a flash in the pan? Was he unwell last year as he claimed to have been? Was he a one-way man, just an uphill specialist?

For Mattheus, 1997 had taken a huge load off his slim shoulders. He had proven himself to be a worthy Comrades winner, and now he was the defending champion. Could he add an official 'up' to his 'down' victory? He carried the majority of South African hopes, although the stout-hearted Nick Bester's chances could never be ignored.

Right from the start, the majority of the favoured runners formed two groups. The front bus included Grishine, Mattheus, Volgin and Jaroslaw Janicki. It was clear that Grishine and Mattheus were watching each other closely. Nick Bester, Sarel Ackermann and Shaun Meiklejohn were prominent in the second group. Both Bester and Meiklejohn were experienced tacticians who had learnt to leave the punishing early work to others while holding comfortable watching briefs. It seemed likely that the eventual winner would come from one of these two packs.

The status quo remained more or less unchanged throughout the first half, although Grishine, who doesn't mind attacking uphills in the early stages, did test Mattheus's resolve on the long, steep climb of Field's Hill. Mattheus was equal to the challenge, and the battle between the pair caused the gap between their bus and that of Bester to stretch to one and a half minutes at Kloof.

The lead group passed through Drummond in 2.44.38, more or less the time that Mattheus had set as his halfway target. So he hadn't been pushed beyond either his capability or his plan. Grishine was running an extremely aggressive race, trying to shake off all rivals as swiftly as possible. Mattheus, not in the least bit intimidated, stayed with him, but others succumbed to the pressure. Walter Nkosi dropped back, Zithulele Sinqe dropped out and the Bester bus continued to fall further behind. When Ravil Kashapov fell back, there were just three: Grishine, Mattheus and Volgin. In the 1996 'up' run, two South Africans, Mattheus and Bester, had tried to outgun Grishine, but to no avail. Now it was a case of two Eastern Europeans against the lone ranger Mattheus.

Fortunately for Mattheus, Volgin was unable to maintain Grishine's murderous pace and was content to follow in the wake of the leading duo. Unfortunately for Mattheus, however, Grishine didn't need help. He was in awesome form. A couple of years older, stronger and more streetwise since his debut victory, Grishine knew the route and was able to use it to his best advantage.

Suddenly, without any warning, Grishine seemed to be in trouble. It was on the approach to Camperdown, one of the most subtly difficult sections of the 'up' run, when he slowed perceptibly, a worried frown on his face, and allowed Mattheus to pass him. The Ukranian, rubbing his right thigh, took pain killers and drank a great deal of water. While this was happening, Mattheus pulled out a gap of about 50 metres.

Grishine's recovery was swift. Before long, he reclaimed the lead and reached Umlaas Road 20 metres ahead of Mattheus. As they turned right to skirt the chicken farms, his advantage was up to 100 metres. There was just a short downhill before the two final climbs, Ashburton (or Little Pollys) and Polly Shortts itself. Mattheus was already a beaten man.

All eyes turned to Grishine's next opponent, the clock. Although the course had been lengthened slightly by the change of finishing venue, a new record was on the cards. Polly Shortts was unable to slow the flying leader, who was well aware of the prospect of a new record and the riches that would accompany such an achievement. In total control of himself and the race, he sped through Scottsville to set a new 'up' record of 5.26.25, beating Bruce Fordyce's 1988 time by 1 minute 17 seconds. Mattheus gamely held on to take second place ahead of Volgin. Once again, the 'up' run had been won by a foreigner. Among the South Africans, Andrew Kelehe claimed sixth spot and was starting to look like a future champion.

Over the preceding decade and a half, there had been a steady improvement in the women's race, in terms of both winning times and the level of competition among the front-runners. This had been recognised by the Comrades Marathon Association: for the first time, gold medals would be presented to the first ten finishers.

In the absence of Ann Trason and Maria Bak, the 1998 race had no clear favourites, although the two Valentinas, Liakhova and Shatyayeva, would take some beating, particularly in view of their new status as unofficial top seeds. Of the South Africans, Helene Joubert had looked the part before and had posted a second place behind Maria Bak in 1995. Rae Bisschoff also had a second place to her credit, but that was in 1993, when Tilda Tearle took the title, the last time a South African had done so. Joubert and Bisschoff were both consistent campaigners, but there were doubts about either of them having a 'killer instinct'.

It turned out to be a rather unusual race. Rae Bisschoff was the first to show, moving to the front after just ten kilometres. A private person, Bisschoff was known as someone who simply ran her own race, ignoring her opponents. The others couldn't have regarded her as a major threat as they simply let her move ahead unchallenged. The pattern remained unchanged throughout the first half, with Bisschoff gradually extending her lead while the others watched each other.

Early in the second half, Bisschoff's rivals suddenly came to the conclusion that she was a serious contender after all. Alarmed, they set off in pursuit, but Bisschoff held a substantial lead. Liakhova broke clear of the others, but Bisschoff was first to crest Polly Shortts, a huge advantage. In the final stages, Liakhova whittled away at Bisschoff's lead and seemed destined to win. Bisschoff appeared quite content to keep her comfortable pace, seemingly oblivious of the hysterical urging of a crowd trying to will her home. In the end, she got there safely, just 19 seconds ahead of the Russian.

After the race, the quiet Bisschoff explained her unusual tactics: 'I don't wear a watch and have no race plan. I also do not use seconds and never keep a logbook, so I can't tell you about my training. I can't remember when I passed the leaders.' Onlookers could scarcely believe what they were hearing, but the relaxed and popular Rae Bisschoff was the new Comrades Bowl champion.

In 1986, there had been tremendous excitement when Liege Boulle, Mr Comrades, tried to complete his 40th Comrades. Sadly, he was forced to retire just a few kilometres short of his goal. His health deteriorated the following year, and he was unable to make another attempt before he passed away.

This year, two Comrades legends, Kenny Craig and Clive Crawley, were both going for their 40th medals. Both were relatively young and significantly strong, and no one doubted that their 40th runs would be successful – particularly Clive, who had completed several Dusi Canoe Marathons and even climbed part of Mount Everest.

As expected, both made it to the end, each setting a unique personal record. Clive was actually the first ever to complete 40 runs as he arrived in 8.36.22, as against Kenny's 10.15.46. Kenny, quite remarkably, ran his 40 in consecutive years. If one considers that, for most athletes, a successful Comrades requires six months of full commitment, then we can have some idea of the devotion to Comrades that these extraordinary men shared.

When all was said and done, this was Dimitri Grishine's day. He had erased the disappointment of 1997 and had beaten the 'up' record, something that many had considered well-nigh impossible. An indication of his speed relative to others is the fact that he averaged 16.07 kilometres per hour, as against the 13.16 kilometres per hour of leading lady Rae Bisschoff and the 7.94 kilometres per hour of final finisher Henry Jones.

1998 COMRADES MARATHON RESULTS

1. Dimitri Grishine	5.26.25
2. Charl Mattheus	5.31.32
3. Alexei Volgin	5.33.57
4. Igor Tyupin	5.35.23
5. Ravil Kashapov	5.37.26
6. Andrew Kelehe	5.39.40
7. Sarel Ackermann	5.40.49
8. Livingstone Jabanga	5.41.07
9. Shaun Meiklejohn	5.41.59
10. Anatoli Kruglikov	5.42.14

1998 COMRADES BOWL RESULTS

1. Rae Bisschoff	6.38.57
2. Valentina Liakhova	6.39.16
3. Valentina Shatyayeva	6.44.13
4. Sanet Beukes	6.57.15
5. Karen Bradford	7.02.09
6. Amor van Zyl	7.02.51
7. Elizabeth McCaul	7.03.34

8. Berna Daly	7.04.14
9. Ina Sanders	7.06.07
10. Ann Chester	7.10.12

1999 COMRADES MARATHON
THE RACE OF HEROES

The year 1999 was one in which the entire world seemed to be looking forward. A new millennium was looming. The Comrades Marathon Association, in keeping with its nature, decided to look back and honour its past. Chairman Adrian Stowell announced that the 1999 Comrades would be known as the 'Race of Heroes', in honour of the approximately 65 000 who had successfully completed the course, and would be dedicated to one of the most loved of Comrades heroes, Wally Hayward.

Television coverage entered fully into the spirit of the race. Ian Laxton had clearly delved deeply into the South African Broadcasting Corporation archives and found footage going right back to the days of Arthur Newton in the 1920s and Hardy Ballington in the 1930s. There were fascinating glimpses of the slightly stooped, boyish stride of a 21-year-old Wally Hayward, the powerfully muscular stride, with head held proudly erect, of Hayward at his peak in his forties, and the very deliberate and still powerful stride of Hayward the octogenarian in 1988 and 1989. With rugby star Tony Watson anchoring the broadcast, Bruce Fordyce provided personal insights into the careers and personalities of the heroes, while Helen Lucre did the same in respect of the heroines.

Regular Comrades runners expect freezing weather when they prepare for the start of a 'down' run. When they lined up this year, the temperature was 9°C, with 95 per cent humidity. This was indeed welcome, although some athletes feared that a real scorcher lay ahead. The forecast, however, was relatively favourable, with a maximum temperature of 24°C and humidity of 55 per cent expected, as well as a 20-kilometre-per-hour north-easterly wind.

In recent years, South Africans had tended to win the 'down' run (apart from Charly Doll in 1993) and visitors (Alberto Salazar and Dimitri Grishine) the 'up'. Russian ultramarathoners in particular had begun to target Comrades in increasing numbers. Pre-race interviews suggested that some of the top contenders were approaching the race as something of an unofficial international team competition.

The first half of the Race of Heroes was run in extraordinary fashion. Most front-runners seemed by now to have accepted that Bruce Fordyce's method of a gentle build-up, leaving a final effort for the closing stages, was the one most likely to succeed. In 1999, with a few exceptions, such wisdom was largely ignored. Dimitri Grishine seemed to be the reason for this. Despite having won the two previous 'up' runs, his 'down' run in 1997 had been a total disaster. He claimed that he had been ill on that occasion and stated emphatically that he was equally adept at 'up' or 'down' running.

Grishine's race tactics belied such talk. In fact, he seemed intent on turning this year's 'down' into an 'up' run. On each of the uphills, he would put in a surge. Amazingly, most of his main rivals followed. On the downhills, Grishine would slip to the rear of what was a huge leading pack. Two runners who chose not to join in the frenzy at the front were Nick Bester and the Pole Jaroslaw Janicki. Bester was heard to exclaim, 'The leaders are going much too fast.' He was right. At one stage, the projected finishing time was 5.17.02. There was no reason to believe that anyone in the field was capable of running that quickly for 90 kilometres.

Over a six-kilometre stretch approaching Inchanga, the real lead pack (there were still a few 'television runners' ahead) averaged 3 minutes 31 seconds per kilometre. It was a pace that would shatter the record if kept up. Actually, it was more likely to shatter the aspirations of those who tried to keep it up. Grishine was still driving the 'bus', although only going to the front on uphills. Whether he was trying to overcome a downhill weakness or simply chasing a huge cash incentive offered by sponsors for breaking Bruce Fordyce's long-standing record, only he really knows.

As ever, the mighty obstacle of Inchanga brought about a change. Again, Grishine moved to the front of the pack, but this time without the authority that he had shown earlier. Right next to him was Jaroslaw Janicki, who had left Bester behind. Suddenly, there was a breakaway. Letu Rachaka, Anatoliy Korepanov and Capetonian Donovan Wright moved ahead. Grishine was reluctant to respond immediately. Once over the top, the trio sped down to Drummond at 3 minutes per kilometre. Janicki followed, keeping in touch and continuing to run sensibly. Michael Mpotoane – not really a 'television runner', as he would finish 32nd – had led for some time and was first through halfway, followed by the breakaway group, which had been joined by Michael Peace. Janicki was now sixth, and most of the favourites, including Grishine, Alexel Volgin and Willie Mtolo, were still very much in the picture as the race moved into the second half.

Over Botha's Hill and on the fast stretch from Hillcrest to Kloof, the leaders surged and counter-surged, swapping positions and making life as difficult as possible for each other. At Kloof, the contenders for line honours had been reduced to just six: Janicki, Grishine, Volgin and the South Africans Rasta Mohloli, Andrew Kelehe and Lucas Matlala. In Pinetown, Grishine dropped back. He had spent the first half trying to burn off his rivals and had succeeded only in burning himself out.

On Cowies Hill, the last of the Big Five, Janicki made a decisive move. He had looked ominously strong over Inchanga and clearly still felt that way. Virtually the only one of the European visitors known for his downhill prowess, he surprised with the timing of his break. On the descent, he looked confident and comfortable. Increasing his advantage through Westville and over 45th Cutting, he seemed to have the race in the bag.

One man had other ideas. Alexei Volgin had not given up. With three third places to his credit (1995, 1996 and 1998), he was widely regarded as a future winner. Now he saw his chance, an opportunity that might never again present itself. Driven by such reality, he gradually hauled in the leader on Tollgate (the final climb) and went to the front, with but five kilometres to go. But Volgin was in pain. He had been drawn into all of Grishine's first-half surges and now paid the penalty. His legs virtually on fire, he was unable to maintain the pace. When the smooth-striding Janicki reclaimed the lead, Volgin lay down on the pavement, took out a needle and applied acupuncture to his aching muscles.

Now there was no stopping Janicki. He was in peak condition and had run a clever race, biding his time patiently and challenging at the most opportune moments. Although he just failed to break the magic five-and-a-half-hour barrier, a time of 5.30.10 was certainly impressive. He expressed his great joy afterwards, 'It had been my dream to win Comrades, and today my dream has come true.' It was a popular victory with fellow athletes and supporters alike. A quiet man who spoke very little English, he was nonetheless noted for his friendliness and ready smile.

The day before the 1998 Two Oceans Marathon, running shoe executive Richard Santrucek had been approached by a young German woman who asked him for a pair of shoes, as she didn't have any to wear in the race. Not being in the habit of handing out free shoes to all and sundry, he asked her what her target was. When she replied, 'I will win the race,' he had no option but to part with a precious pair. Unfortunately, Birgit Lennartz hadn't told him the truth: she only came second. Today she was running her debut Comrades.

South Africa's big hope, Helene Joubert, took the early lead in the women's race. At no stage did she manage to establish any significant advantage. Lennartz, Berna Daly and the Brazilian Maria Venancio were in close attendance. At one stage, Heidi McIntosh of Hilton, who had only managed an 8.28 before, surprised and delighted the locals by taking a temporary lead.

In a relatively slow race, Lennartz, who looked the strongest contender throughout, went to the front on Botha's Hill and stayed there to the end, breaking the tape in 6.31.03. Afterwards, Lennartz, a seasoned and well-travelled campaigner, explained how much the victory meant to her: 'This has been my absolute delight. I've never experienced a race as great as this. London, New York – I've run all these marathons, but nothing beats the Comrades.'

Along with her male counterpart, Lennartz received a special winner's bonus immediately after the event: they were flown to Pretoria to attend the farewell banquet of President Nelson Mandela, who officially handed over the reins of government to Thabo Mbeki. It was a special occasion for the German: 'Mr Mandela has been my hero for years. It has always amazed me how he could have so much compassion and forgiveness in him after having been incarcerated for 27 years. It has been a dream to meet him. Now, after all the training and the pain of the race, my dream has come true.'

A fellow debutant, KwaZulu-Natal's Grace de Oliveira, ran a sensible race, easing her way through the field to claim second place ahead of Russian Marina Bychkova. A delighted De Oliveira described her first Comrades: 'I listened very carefully to advice, especially from my husband Eloi. I simply raced my own race. I focused on myself and refused to be drawn into racing.

That gave me the strength to come through over the final section of the race after Field's Hill. It was a wonderful experience. I loved every minute of it.'

It was only natural that the Race of Heroes would produce significant new heroes. 'Cancer can be beaten' was the theme of an attempt by Paul Selby and Guido Schromges to raise money for the Cancer Association of South Africa, one of the official four Comrades charities that year, and to promote the idea that the disease could be overcome. After leaving Durban on foot at 7 p.m. on 15 June, they arrived in Pietermaritzburg at 5.26 a.m. Thirty-four minutes later, they responded to the official gun. Amazingly, Paul Selby finished his second back-to-back Comrades in 10.47.11. Schromges didn't make it to the end, but his valiant effort can be regarded as equally commendable.

On the subject of the Comrades Marathon's role in support of charitable organisations, Bruce Fordyce, now a member of the Comrades Charities Committee, drew a comparison with another famous race: 'The London Marathon raises millions of pounds for charity each year in an ethic that elevates the purpose of the event. The spirit of the Comrades also means a great deal more to our country than a mere athletic contest.'

This year's run witnessed a significant female milestone: Paddy Williams, wife of Comrades stalwart Mervyn, completed her 20th consecutive Comrades in 10.51.38 and became the first woman to earn a double green number.

Carl Peatfield received his green number after a personal best of 7.00.51. A few months later, he came close to losing his life in an industrial accident. A colleague was overcome by cyanide fumes. Courageously, Carl went to the rescue, only to suffer the same fate. The colleague died, and Carl only regained consciousness after ten days in intensive care. He had lost 70 per cent of his vision and suffered severe brain damage.

With impaired coordination, he was unable to walk properly, yet he was determined to run. After all, he reasoned, it was running that had saved his life: 'Having done ten Comrades Marathons gave me an enormous reservoir of mental strength, not to mention physical stamina, and I sincerely believe that this is what brought me through my accident. Plus the fact that I was also super fit when it happened.'

His coordination problem meant that he was unable to run without falling over. Thanks to the ingenuity of a clubmate, Alf Paine, a way of overcoming this handicap was found. He would run strapped inside a harness with two friends, one on either side, helping him stay upright. Together they completed the 2002 Comrades Marathon in 10.55.21. Since then, running on his own, Carl has maintained a steady improvement in annual performance. His 2005 time was 9.38.01.

1999 COMRADES MARATHON RESULTS

1. Jaroslaw Janicki	5.30.11
2. Andrew Kelehe	5.32.42
3. Lucas Matlala	5.33.30
4. Alexei Volgin	5.35.00
5. Anatoliy Korepanov	5.38.04
6. Walter Nkosi	5.40.20
7. Joseph Ikaneng	5.41.08
8. Konstantin Santalov	5.41.36
9. Shaun Meiklejohn	5.44.07
10. Grigoriy Murzin	5.47.25

1999 COMRADES BOWL RESULTS

1. Birgit Lennartz	6.31.03
2. Grace de Oliveira	6.34.53
3. Marina Bychkova	6.36.34
4. Maria Venancio	6.40.18
5. Valentina Shatyayeva	6.45.07
6. Madeleen Otto	6.47.06
7. Berna Daly	6.48.13
8. Ina Sanders	6.56.20
9. Ann Chester	7.01.56
10. Charlotte Noble	7.02.04

2000 COMRADES MARATHON
THE MILLENNIUM RUN

Before thoughts could turn to this year's marathon, the human race had to survive one of the greatest deceptions in history, the millennium bug (with magic formula Y2K). At midnight on 31 December 1999, we were told, aircraft would fall out of the sky, digital alarm clocks would cease to work (whoopee!) and computer-related machines would malfunction. We all fell for it, didn't we? We bought or upgraded computer equipment and took out special insurance cover. We made sure that an old truth remained valid: prophets of doom generally have the most effective get-rich-quick schemes. And profits of doom were quite numerous as we entered the new era.

In the early part of 2000, members of the Comrades Marathon Association – who this year unamimously elected popular Alison West as their first female chair – proposed that this year's marathon would be a wonderful way of celebrating the dawn of the new millennium. They were rather ambitiously hoping to attract a field of 20 000, which would be a new record by some considerable margin. It would appear as if they underestimated their marketing skills and the lure of the great race. When entries closed, the total field numbered 24 505, of whom 23 901 actually turned up and registered. There is no doubt that an extended 12-hour cut-off and a friendly five-and-a-half-hour qualifier were partly responsible.

Special arrangements had to be made to accommodate such a huge entry. The traditional three-day Comrades Expo was moved from the Durban Exhibition Centre to the more prestigious International Convention Centre. In order to ensure a smooth getaway and avoid penalising slower runners unfairly, it was wisely decided to introduce compulsory seeding. All runners would be seeded according to their qualifying times, possibly adjusted in their favour in consideration of their 1998 and 1999 Comrades finishing times.

In addition to the seeding, a decision, supported by many athletes, was taken to deny access to the starting enclosure to spectators and supporters. The news was greeted with a tinge of sadness by those who had previously shared the excitement of the start with family members and well-wishers standing on the pavement. They had to understand that it had become logistically impossible to allow non-runners into an area that had become dangerously over-congested.

This year was also marked by commemorative medals. In many road races, medals and badges are awarded to those who finish successfully, but no other medal is as highly regarded and cherished as a Comrades medal. In fact, medals have been a feature of the race since 1921, when silver medals were presented to all official finishers and a special bronze one to L. E. W. Pearson, who arrived at the end 20 minutes after the cut-off.

Special commemorative medals have been struck on three occasions: in 1975, to mark the 50th running of the race; in 1988, in honour of the 150th birthday of the city of Pietermaritzburg; and in 2000, to celebrate the new millennium, as well as the 75th Comrades Marathon. With the exception of these special occasions, Comrades medals have retained their original dimensions and basic design since 1921.

In the first decade of the race, only silver medals were awarded. In 1931, gold medals, presented to the first six finishers, were introduced. In 1972, the awarding of gold medals was extended to the top ten runners, and a bronze medal was introduced for those who didn't make silver, whose time was between seven and a half and 11 hours. From 1980, owing to increased costs, 'gold' medals became silver medals plated with gold, and 'silver' medals were made of high-quality gilding material with silver plating.

Women, having been barred from strenuous athletic competition for most of the 20th century, were awarded bronze medals from their admission in 1975. From 1979, a silver medal was presented to the first woman. In 1983, it was upgraded to gold. From 1988, gold medals were awarded to the first three women, and from 1995 to the first five. Since 1998, gold medals have been given to the first ten female finishers, putting males and females on the same footing. In 1989, Comrades officials were on the point of having to make a difficult decision when Frith van der Merwe, who eventually finished 15th overall, appeared close to a men's top-ten time. She might have gone home with two gold medals.

A most welcome innovation was the introduction of the Bill Rowan medal in 2000. The finish venue is always at fever pitch as the crowd awaits the final gold, silver and bronze medallists, but between the silver and bronze cut-offs, there used to be something of a lull. Now the Bill Rowan medal is awarded to those who miss the silver, but do better than nine hours. It commemorates Bill Rowan's victory in the first race in 1921, in a time of 8.59. In 2003, when the cut-off was permanently extended to 12 hours, a copper Vic Clapham medal was introduced for those finishing in the final hour.

Possibly the most surprising aspect of this year's race was the remarkably smooth getaway of the massive field. Even those who started right at the back were soon under way. All agreed that the organisation was quite superb. As the runners started to move up the freeway on the longish climb to Tollgate, they were greeted by the local fire department with ladders extended above their fire engines and lights flashing. The festive atmosphere would prevail throughout the day.

All that was needed from the athletes was a South African victory. It didn't appear likely. Dimitri Grishine, winner of the two previous 'up' runs and current record holder, once again looked in top form. With him was his first lieutenant, Alexei Volgin, as well as a relative newcomer, 42-year-old Vladimir Kotov, born in Belarus but living in Poland. Kotov, a qualified veterinarian, had enjoyed an impressive running career. Fourth in the 1980 Moscow Olympic Marathon, he had completed 31 sub-2.20 standard marathons with six victories and a personal best of 2.10.58.

Three South Africans managed to keep pace with the flying Eastern Europeans through Drummond in 2.46 and over Inchanga. One of them, Butiki Jantjies, succumbed to sudden cramp after 60 kilometres and retired. The others, Walter Nkosi and Andrew Kelehe, gamely maintained the local challenge. Kelehe went through a 'bad patch' shortly before Camperdown, the graveyard stretch of the 'up' run. Nkosi, after dropping back temporarily, fought back and was right up with the visitors as they approached the foot of Little Pollys. This was proven Grishine territory, and it appeared likely that the Ukranian would go on to a hat-trick of 'up' victories.

In a race preview, Riël Hauman, a respected athlete, statistician, commentator and celebrated author of *Century of the Marathon*, gave his prediction. Acknowledging that Grishine would start as favourite, he listed his main rivals, naming foreigners Janicki, Volgin, Korepanov, Kashapov and Murzin, as well as South Africans Mattheus, Sinqe, Ackermann, Kelehe, Nkosi, Jan van Rooyen, Bester and Matlala.

Then, almost as an afterthought, this is what Hauman had to say about a dark horse:

'But watch out for Vladimir Kotov. The 42-year-old Belarussian, who has been living in Poland for ten years, has an unfinished Comrades under his belt and is determined to win the race. In 1980, Kotov was fourth in the Olympic Marathon in Moscow in the closest mass finish in the race up to that point.

'His scything run through the Two Oceans field on Easter Saturday failed to catch leader Joshua Peterson by eight seconds and the experienced Kotov will not make the same mistake again. Kotov showed that he still had tremendous speed in his legs at the end of the race, even after the battering they took on Ou Kaapse Weg, the biggest hill on the route. Yes, the Comrades is almost another marathon longer, but if he can reproduce the same form on Friday, he may well be the first master winner of the race since George Claassen in 1961.'

Perhaps Kotov read Hauman's comments. On the descent from Ashburton to Polly Shortts, he suddenly took off, leaving his stunned rivals in his wake. Grishine, the uphill master, stopped for a short while, overcome by a vomiting attack. It would not be his day. Volgin, the 'nearly' man of Comrades, was the only one to keep up any sort of challenge, cresting Polly Shortts just 17 seconds behind the leader.

The final stages had seasoned Comrades-watchers shaking their heads in disbelief. Having already run the equivalent of two exceptionally difficult standard marathons, Kotov completed the last five kilometres in an amazing 16.02. In doing so, he set a new 'up' record of 5.25.33, a time second only to Bruce Fordyce's 1986 'down' record of 5.24.07. In his only previous attempt at the Comrades, Kotov had retired from the 1999 'down' run after 58 kilometres. Questioned about his age, the new Comrades champion said, 'It is very important that I do not feel like a veteran. I feel great. Age is not on my mind.'

For the first time ever, no South African had finished in the top three. It was time for the locals to consider what was happening to their race. Donovan Wright, in fourth place, was the first South African. The next three places were taken by his compatriots Andrew Kelehe, Fusi Nhlapo and Walter Nkosi. It was up to this quartet to ensure that the host nation wouldn't just produce 'also-rans'.

Apart from Rae Bisschoff's surprise win in 1998, recent women's races had been dominated by visitors. Once again, South African hopes were pinned mainly on Frith van der Merwe. Although her last few Comrades attempts suggested that her best days had come and gone, she had enjoyed an impressive build-up. Much was also expected of local lady Grace de Oliveira after her second-place debut in 1999. Of the overseas runners, defending champion Birgit Lennartz had to be respected, while past winner Maria Bak, returned after serving a two-year ban for substance abuse, would also be hard to beat.

The overseas athletes were first to show. Novice Tatiana Volgina, wife of Alexei Volgin, took an early lead, which she held until halfway. Bak and Lennartz, running in close proximity, were next, with Elvira Kolpakova fourth and Van der Merwe fifth. At Drummond, Bak joined Volgina, who had had enough and retired soon after.

The German Bak started pulling away and soon enjoyed a commanding lead. Kolpakova tangled briefly with Lennartz before falling back. The two South Africans were going in opposite directions. Van der Merwe, no longer the fabulous Frith of 1989, started slipping back, while De Oliveira, a cautious starter, was having another good run and began picking off those who were ahead.

There was no doubting who would win. Bak led for the entire second half, coming home for a second victory in 6.15.35. Lennartz, without ever threatening, claimed a comfortable second place, while local heroine De Oliveira made it two podiums out of two starts with a popular third spot. Van der Merwe finished 11th, just out of the golds.

Post-race celebrations were somewhat muted when it was learnt that 32-year-old Ellisras runner Deon Swanepoel had collapsed along the way and died of multiple organ failure the following day. It was the third death in Comrades history. While non-runners are inclined to cite such rare instances as 'proof' of the dangers of long-distance running, the opposite is the reality.

Many runners have overcome severe physical and psychological problems through their association with the Comrades Marathon. Often they significantly extend both their lives and their productivity and enjoy greatly enhanced relationships with family, friends and colleagues. There is no shortage of inspirational accounts by former alcoholics, drug addicts and general misfits of how their lives radically changed for the better when they acquired the Comrades habit.

Quote of the day came from 69-year-old Clive Crawley. After finishing his 42nd Comrades, the most by anyone, he was asked on television, 'Why do you run?' He responded immediately, 'Because the more I run, the more beer I can drink!'

2000 COMRADES MARATHON RESULTS

1. Vladimir Kotov	5.25.33
2. Alexei Volgin	5.27.08
3. Dimitri Grishine	5.32.47
4. Donovan Wright	5.35.37
5. Andrew Kelehe	5.36.32
6. Fusi Nhlapo	5.37.46
7. Walter Nkosi	5.40.18
8. Don Wallace	5.42.49
9. Mikhail Kokorev	5.43.15
10. Anatoliy Korepanov	5.44.38

2000 COMRADES BOWL RESULTS

1. Maria Bak	6.15.35
2. Birgit Lennartz	6.33.55
3. Grace de Oliveira	6.38.45
4. Elvira Kolpakova	6.43.35
5. Valentina Shatyayeva	6.46.54
6. Marina Bychkova	6.47.29
7. Carol Mercer	6.49.00
8. Tanja Schaefer	6.51.57
9. René du Plessis	6.53.51
10. Madeleen Otto	6.57.42

17

LOCALS RESPOND, BUT VISITORS PREVAIL
(2001 to 2005)

The Comrades Marathon belongs to South Africa, or should do. This is the overwhelming view of those South Africans who have established a lasting relationship with the great race. Comrades represents all that is good about South Africa and South Africans. It reflects a rainbow nation of pioneers and heroes of all colours, creeds and backgrounds.

In the latter half of the 1990s, the country's greatest sporting event fell, to an uncomfortable extent, into the hands of foreigners. At first, this was, although disappointing, acceptable to a nation that believed in sporting idealism. It wasn't pleasant to lose, but, if the opposition was superior and deserved victory, then South Africans would have to accept defeat graciously.

At the same time, it was difficult to accept that visitors could beat us in the one arena in which we had considered ourselves invincible. Almost a century of achievement had given us our national pride. Then, an ugly thought occurred. 'Drug abuse' and 'blood-doping' were expressions that had become commonplace in endurance competitions throughout the sporting world. Surely not in Comrades! Yet a few Comrades runners had been found guilty of taking banned substances in the past. At first, such infringements were regarded as naive errors on the part of innocents. Suddenly, there was talk of cynical cheating, which had no place in Comrades culture. Were international competitors beginning their Comrades runs with an unfair advantage slipped into their bloodstreams?

With proper testing for blood-doping inaccessible in this part of the world, there was only one response available to South Africans. They simply had to produce their own heroes, winners who could overcome almost insurmountable odds. This is precisely what happened as Comrades entered the new millennium. Eight of the top ten finishers in the 2005 race ran as South Africans, including recent immigrant Vladimir Kotov. An ecstatic crowd welcomed them home.

2001 COMRADES MARATHON
ANDREW KELEHE WINS IT FOR SOUTH AFRICA

In the build-up to this year's race, two issues were highlighted: the lack of success by South Africans in recent years and the use of illicit performance-enhancing substances, the scourge of world sport.

During the 1980s, that heady decade when television encouraged South Africans to fall in love with the world's premier ultramarathon, it was generally accepted that this nation produced the finest long-distance runners. There was plenty of evidence for that.

Earlier in the century, Arthur Newton, Wally Hayward, Hardy Ballington and Jackie Mekler, apart from becoming serial Comrades winners, had travelled abroad and broken virtually every record that existed. Throughout the eighties, but with a vastly greater audience, Bruce Fordyce had done the same thing.

In the 1990s, something went wrong. An era of professionalism brought an increasing number of visitors to South Africa to challenge the best that the host nation could offer. To the dismay of locals, these outsiders, mainly from Eastern Europe, had a nasty habit of winning. To the further dismay of South Africans, the performances of these invaders were not greatly, if at all, superior to those of locals in previous decades. Disappointment among patriotic supporters had become all too frequent a feature of the event. What had happened to our runners? Where were those who should have taken over the mantle from our former greats? These were the questions being asked as the country's most prestigious race continued to be dominated by foreigners who understood little of the history and culture of Comrades.

Alleged drug use was the big talking point in the final week before the race in 2001. It was common cause among athletes that drug abuse had long been a factor in the sport of cycling and in major athletic meetings such as the Olympic Games. Until fairly recently, the Comrades Marathon had been regarded as probably the least likely event to be sullied by such unsporting and illegal practices. That all changed. In 1999, two runners who finished among the golds, Russian Viktor Zhdanov and South Africa's Rasta Mohlolo, tested positive for banned substances.

Under the headline 'Dark cloud hangs over big race' in the *Sunday Times* of 10 June, just six days before the race, Simnikiwe Xabanisa wrote:

'EPO (erythropoietin), the illegal drug which dramatically increases athletic performance, is believed to have invaded the Comrades Marathon to such an extent that many of the top athletes are suspected to be using it.

'On the eve of what should perhaps be the greatest ever Comrades due to the quality of the field assembling for Saturday's race, doping officials – and even race administrators – have revealed that they believe the race is under the cynical grip of athletes doped up on the drug.'

It seemed that the type of testing done at Comrades – urine testing, that is – revealed steroid use but not blood-doping, apparently the most serious method of cheating – even more than the illicit use of taxis! In 2001, there were only two laboratories in the world that could pick up EPO use.

Clearly, Comrades race administrators, clean competitors and medical officials were concerned that the noblest of all sporting events was being tarnished by those who were prepared to ignore local and international rules and regulations, as well as the culture of the sport, in order to obtain a measure of wealth and fame that they could not earn legitimately. It was also obvious to those close to the action that fingers were being pointed, not at South African runners, but at those from abroad. This could, of course, represent paranoia on the part of those who lacked the humility to acknowledge their own deficiencies, but there was a strong body of opinion that thought otherwise.

As is so often the case nowadays, the first half of this year's race was a cat-and-mouse tactical affair, making it just about impossible for bystanders to grasp precisely what was happening in the real battle for line honours. Approaching halfway, Nick Bester and Charl Mattheus were running in tandem, suggesting that this might be South Africa's day. Sadly, both Bester and Mattheus, after promising much, retired from the race.

Their departure increased the likelihood of another Eastern European triumph, although Fusi Nhlapo did go to the front on the long stretch from Hillcrest to Kloof. Well though he was running, Nhlapo lacked experience and appeared to be a temporary leader, and so it proved. The Russian Leonid Shvetsov had been running a canny race. When Nhlapo felt the pressure going into the final 20 kilometres, Shvetsov's patience paid off. It was now his turn to lead and he looked comfortable in the role. Danger was lurking, however. 'Up' run champion Vladimir Kotov was having his best 'down' run to date and looked ominous. There was also another South African who took over the responsibility of local challenger from Nhlapo. Andrew Kelehe, second in 1999, moved into the picture.

A huge crowd had gathered at one of the race's favourite vantage points, 45th Cutting, to witness a crucial part of the race, the second-last uphill. After this, only Tollgate lay ahead. 45th Cutting isn't quite as decisive as Polly Shortts in the 'up' run, but it comes close to being so. Whoever reaches the top first holds a distinct advantage. It was here that Bruce Fordyce overcame Bob de la Motte in one of their epic duels.

Strangely, despite the vast throng of spectators, nobody seemed to have a portable radio or TV set. Everyone, however, could tell that the leader was about to appear. The telltale helicopter was getting closer and closer. Necks were craned as all awaited the special moment. Looking down the hill, runners would have to negotiate a slight bend before coming into view. Lead vehicles announced that this was imminent.

Eventually, he appeared, too far away to be instantly recognised. Then, suddenly, the crowd erupted. There was something about him that served to identify him: he was black, which meant he was South African. The crowd, 90 per cent white, went wild with delight. One of our own was winning the Comrades Marathon. A statuesque blonde woman danced across the road, whooping with joy. It was the 1995 Rugby World Cup final all over again. South Africans were South Africans, and a South African had taken charge of the nation's greatest annual event. Andrew Kelehe led the Comrades Marathon with only about ten kilometres to go.

Then came the shock. Vladimir Kotov appeared. Kelehe, holding a fair lead, had moved strongly and rather quickly up the hill. Kotov was sprinting. Surely he would catch the South African if he could maintain his breakneck speed. He couldn't. In fact, despite finishing in the fast time of 5.27.22, he had to yield second place to erstwhile leader Leonid Shvetsov.

There was no stopping Andrew Kelehe. This was his day. Together with his coach, John Hamlett, he had planned his run meticulously and had carried out the plan to perfection. There was no last-minute hiccup. Although his pursuers kept up the pressure, he was more than a match for them, crossing the line in 5.25.52, just 1 minute 45 seconds outside Bruce Fordyce's phenomenal record.

After finishing, Kelehe revealed the human tragedy that had sustained him throughout the race. With his wife Kefilwe at his side, Kelehe told of the illness that had claimed the life of their 17-month-old daughter in February. Initially, he had decided to withdraw from the event. After much soul-searching, he made up his mind to run the race in his daughter's memory. Speaking of the complex emotions that he had experienced, he later said, 'The tears on June 16 (Comrades day) washed everything out. It washed out the wound that was my daughter's death.'

Maria Bak was outright favourite to win the women's race. It didn't happen, and she only finished in fourth place. Although she was obviously disappointed, her post-race comment is worth recalling: 'At Comrades, you meet the best in the world. You cannot expect to win every time.' Her acknowledgement of the status of Comrades echoed similar comments made by overseas visitors over the years.

South Africa's hopes lay with Frith van der Merwe and Grace de Oliveira. While locals continued to expect miracles from their favourite daughter, Van der Merwe was now clearly past her best. Grace de Oliveira, ever reliable, could be relied upon to delight her many supporters and possibly finish fastest of the South Africans, as she had done the previous two years.

The first half went according to expectations. Maria Bak and Elvira Kolpakova led the way as the runners moved into the second stage, Van der Merwe having retired. Grace de Oliveira, 14 minutes off the pace, had too much ground to make up. Bak's toughness and knowledge of the Comrades course would surely make the difference. Kolpakova, not quite as athletic as her famous opponent, would probably be found lacking in experience.

Predictions don't always work out in Comrades. It was Bak who faltered and Kolpakova who strode strongly ahead to take the title in a fast 6.13.54. Bak was so demoralised that, in the closing stages, she allowed herself to be overtaken by Deborah Mattheus (wife of Charl) and Marina Bychkova, who finished second and third, respectively. Kolpakova, interviewed after the race, told the crowd that her motivation had been similar to that of Kelehe. Her 23-year-old sister had lost her life to drugs, coincidentally just five days before the death of Kelehe's daughter. When she said, with obvious emotion, 'I ran for my sister today,' tears flowed for the second time in an hour.

This time, De Oliveira wasn't the first South African. In a frantic dash for the line, Carol Mercer pipped her by just five seconds to take sixth place. The pair were jointly interviewed by the SABC's Trevor Quirk. Asked when either of them might challenge the Eastern Europeans, Mercer was clearly in no mood for pulling punches: 'We have to. But we have to start on the same playing fields. Then we've got a chance, Trevor, and I think Grace will stand by what I am saying. I'm very happy to give my blood and time. They can test me any time. I'm sure Grace would do, too.'

De Oliveira nodded her head. Asked to comment, she was a little reticent, saying simply, 'It is a problem. We just don't know what's going on out there.' She added that she would be quite prepared to submit to blood testing. It was clear that the top South African women shared the concerns of the experts about the use of EPO to gain an unfair advantage.

2001 COMRADES MARATHON RESULTS

1. Andrew Kelehe	5.25.52
2. Leonid Shvetsov	5.26.29

3. Vladimir Kotov	5.27.22
4. Alexei Volgin	5.27.41
5. Fusi Nhlapo	5.30.38
6. Grigoriy Murzin	5.33.00
7. Dimitri Grishine	5.36.04
8. Sarel Ackermann	5.36.51
9. Walter Nkosi	5.38.16
10. Michael Mpotoane	5.38.43

2001 COMRADES BOWL RESULTS

1. Elvira Kolpakova	6.13.54
2. Deborah Mattheus	6.23.04
3. Marina Bychkova	6.24.21
4. Maria Bak	6.25.48
5. Maria Venancio	6.39.03
6. Carol Mercer	6.41.00
7. Grace de Oliveira	6.41.05
8. Reneé Scott	6.54.58
9. Valentina Shatyayeva	6.57.06
10. Madeleen Otto	7.01.15

2002 COMRADES MARATHON
KOTOV AGAIN

South Africans had been absolutely delighted to witness Andrew Kelehe's wonderful victory in 2001, the first local triumph since Charl Mattheus four years earlier. They were also well aware that the last time a South African had won an 'up' race was the 1992 success, following the controversial disqualification of the self-same Mattheus, of Jetman Msutu.

The old apartheid government had, in its paranoia, frightened voters with dire threats of a potential invasion and takeover by 'die rooi gevaar' (the red danger – that is, communism). This had never come close to materialising.

Nevertheless, a peaceful invasion by 'red' athletes had taken far too many treasures from the Comrades trophy cabinet to Eastern Europe, in the minds of the local ultramarathon community. Hopefully, Andrew Kelehe had initiated a turnaround.

A welcome innovation in recent years has been the Spirit of Comrades awards, presented to those who display, to an exceptional degree, those qualities that make up that indefinable but almost tangible ethos known as the Comrades spirit. This year, two awards were given to three people. The first award was made to Manie Kuhn and Tommy Malone, two rivals and friends whose friendship and rivalry had become revered in Comrades folklore.

The second award was presented anonymously to a woman of extra-ordinary courage, simply referred to by the nom de plume Catherine, a Johannesburg domestic worker who began running in 1997 and ran her first Comrades in 1998, but after dropping out of the 1999 Comrades with two kilometres to go having struggled with her health in the build-up to the race, she was then diagnosed with full-blown Aids. After initially withdrawing into a deep depression, she resolved to learn to live with Aids, rather than die from it. She began a course of antiretroviral medication and started running again. As Cheryl Winn of the Comrades Marathon Association wrote of the woman, 'she has had the courage to make the most of her life, and her personal struggle contains a message of hope and inspiration for others. She continues to train each morning at 5 a.m. She continues to take her medication. And since being diagnosed with full-blown Aids, she has completed two Comrades Marathons, and is planning to run again in 2002. There is a message of hope in this story.'

Hope is possibly the word that, more than any other, encapsulates the spirit of Comrades. It was hope that sustained the military comrades of Vic Clapham in the desert campaign during the First World War. Hope drove Clapham to establish his dream, the Comrades Marathon. Hope enabled South Africans to play leading roles, admired by all their allies, in defeating the threat of Adolf Hitler. Hope inspired Hector Pieterson and other youngsters to risk (and, in many cases, lose) their lives as they stood up against the hated apartheid government on 16 June 1976, annually remembered as Youth Day, the day of the Comrades Marathon.

This year's race posed a few intriguing questions. Was Andrew Kelehe's

2001 victory the breakthrough he needed to fulfil his true potential? Would he become South Africa's next multiple winner? Vladimir Kotov had set a new 'up' record of 5.25.33 in 2000. Was this a fluke? He was getting long in the tooth. Could he repeat his previous victory? Willie Mtolo, KwaZulu-Natal's champion, was also getting on in age. Thirteen years had passed since he had achieved his best place, runner-up in Sam Tshabalala's memorable victory in 1989. He was still around. Could he turn back the clock?

Kelehe's build-up was interesting. Bruce Fordyce, acknowledged as the person who best understands the requirements of becoming a Comrades winner, has often spoken of the subtle pitfalls facing a new champion determined to defend his crown. The natural approach of such a winner is to put in 10 per cent extra effort, 10 per cent extra dedication and 10 per cent extra discipline on the reasonable assumption that that will produce an even better performance.

It seldom works out that way. As Fordyce has emphasised, sticking to the method that has succeeded in the past is the most likely way to triumph in the future. The law of diminishing marginal returns has significant relevance in the ultra-demanding field of ultramarathon racing. Tinkering with a proven formula is more likely to lead to disappointment than enhanced performance.

The relationship between Kelehe and his charismatic coach John Hamlett has been rightly admired by Comrades followers over the years. Nevertheless, fears were expressed that they might have been overdoing things when Hamlett described his charge's preparation for the 2002 race:

'His training, both on the track and up the hills, has improved substantially on last year's. We've never taken preparation for the "up" run as seriously. Andrew's best "up" placing so far is a fourth place, but I really believe he can beat them all again this year.

'He's really lean and mean right now. To be honest, for his last "up" run, he was not as fit as he should have been and also a little overweight. I know Bruce [Fordyce] always says you should be a little overweight, but I think at the time it was too much for Andrew.'

Ray de Vries, manager of the internationally assembled Mr Price team, was also in confident mode when he discussed the chances of his key runner:

'Vladimir Kotov, the last "up" winner in 2000, has really timed his Comrades preparation to a T. He is not only producing some fast standard marathons, but also went through really testing ice-chamber therapy in Poland recently. He's going to be extremely hard to beat. He'll be fast and very fit on June 17.'

Very little was said or written about the race prospects of Willie Mtolo. It was, however, revealed that Mtolo, along with others, had committed himself to the 'Return of the Greathearts' programme ('Greatheart' being the nickname given to the first Comrades multi-winner, Arthur Newton). This was an initiative of Starfish, one of the four official race charities, which was dedicated to the cause of raising funds for children orphaned by Aids. That's publicity a Comrades hopeful should be happy to get.

Race day, 17 June, was a torrid occasion: midwinter, but the temperature exceeded 30°C at times. In such conditions, some runners would suffer, no matter how talented or well prepared. One of those who really battled was Bruce Fordyce, supposedly leading the charge for sub-nine-hour Bill Rowan medals. He finished in 9.48, an hour behind schedule, and commented wryly: 'It's a long, long way.'

Talking of Fordyce, perhaps Andrew Kelehe should have paid more attention to the nine-time champion's advice. Not overweight and definitely not undertrained, he at no time threatened to challenge for line honours. Nevertheless, a gold medal for ninth place in 5.46.32 is certainly a noteworthy performance.

Mtolo and Kotov, however, were on top form. In the vicinity of Camperdown, they 'dropped' their previous companions, Joseph Ikaneng and Oleg Kharitonov, and effectively made it a two-horse race. What followed, for a short while, was a television producer's dream. Kotov, head down and businesslike, was all determination. Mtolo, silky smooth and wonderfully athletic, seemed effortless. One would surge, then the other, as each sought to establish an advantage.

On Little Pollys, with about 12 kilometres left, Kotov made the decisive move. In their battle of mental strength, the little Belarussian proved stronger. For Mtolo, it was 1989 all over again. Conscious of his tendency to suffer from cramps in the closing stages, Mtolo gingerly kept going, tenaciously clinging to his second place. He even walked up Polly Shortts, a sensible decision, but one that only just succeeded. He took second place, just two seconds ahead of Spaniard Jorge Martinez, with a frantic crowd screaming him home.

The 45-year-old Kotov had firmly established his reputation as an 'up' run specialist. Although his winning time of 5.30.59 was over five minutes slower than the record he had set two years previously, it was, given the race-day conditions, a splendid effort. He was certainly a remarkable athlete. If he could secure just one 'down' victory, he would have to be recognised as one of the Comrades greats. Until then, it would have to be accepted that something was lacking in his curriculum vitae.

It was almost taken for granted that the women's race would be a competition for foreign athletes, and the list of entrants more or less confirmed this. Frith van der Merwe was no longer a contender. Gwen van Lingen, who was certainly not lacking in talent, was recovering from surgery, and was a non-starter. In a pre-race interview, international team manager Ray de Vries spoke of one of his favourites:

'Don't count out Maria Bak, who posted a 34-minute ten-kilometre time recently. There's still plenty of speed in those strong legs. Many may think that Bak's career is almost over, but she has experienced victory here and knows both the "up" and "down" runs very well. Course knowledge at Comrades is a very important factor.'

There was no doubting the ability of Bak. There was, however, huge doubt as to the extent to which she had increased her natural talent by taking performance-enhancing substances. She had, in fact, served a ban after testing positive for the illicit use of anabolic steroids. To many Comrades purists, the achievements of Maria Bak are regarded with a degree of scepticism and always will be.

Whatever doubts may have been felt, Maria Bak won the women's section of the 2002 Comrades Marathon ahead of Russians Natalia Volgina, second, and Marina Bychkova, third. Cape Town's Farwa Mentoor was the fastest South African, taking fourth place in 6.41.20. Grace de Oliveira (6.43.12) and Sarah Mahlangu (6.53.41) claimed sixth and seventh places for the host nation.

While questionable conduct was suspected to have influenced the achievements of some visitors, certain South Africans enhanced the integrity of the race by being true to the noble virtues that lie at the heart of Comrades. Nobody did this more eloquently than an Athletics North runner, Pat Boyall.

Boyall accompanied her good friend and fellow Athletics North club member Carry Patterson in their joint quest to complete the Comrades course in the regulation time. They almost made it. In fact, they seemed to have ensured joint triumph as they approached the end with time to spare. Entering the stadium, Patterson collapsed. She couldn't go on. Despite the encouragement of Boyall and excited prompting from the crowd, Patterson was clearly unable to continue. Recognising this, Boyall knew that she could leave her friend, jog to the finish line and claim her medal. Instead, she chose to forfeit her own ambition and remained with Patterson only to be disqualified by time. For her steadfast adherence to all that makes Comrades great, Pat Boyall became a worthy recipient of the Spirit of Comrades award.

2002 COMRADES MARATHON RESULTS

1. Vladimir Kotov	5.30.59
2. Willie Mtolo	5.33.35
3. Jorge Aubeso Martinez	5.33.37
4. Oleg Kharitonov	5.34.43
5. Sarel Ackermann	5.39.05
6. Albe Geldenhuys	5.39.45
7. Joseph Ikaneng	5.44.11
8. Don Wallace	5.44.19
9. Andrew Kelehe	5.46.32
10. Fusi Nhlapo	5.46.59

2002 COMRADES BOWL RESULTS

1. Maria Bak	6.14.21
2. Natalia Volgina	6.17.26
3. Marina Bychkova	6.24.23
4. Farwa Mentoor	6.41.20
5. Elvira Kolpakova	6.41.56
6. Grace de Oliveira	6.43.12
7. Sarah Mahlangu	6.53.41

8. Yelena Razdrogina	6.57.54
9. Marietjie Montgomery	6.59.24
10. Valentina Shatyayeva	7.02.41

2003 COMRADES MARATHON
FUSI AND ZEB
(A WIN FOR BOTH HEAD AND TAIL)

In the build-up to this year's race, an important announcement was made. Newly appointed chairman of the Comrades Marathon Association, Peter Proctor (who has two Comrades medals to his credit), announced that the overall cut-off time had been extended from 11 to 12 hours. In keeping with the change, the qualification for entry would be a five-hour standard marathon, a relaxation of the existing four and a half hours.

As with most changes in life, there were some who gave their wholehearted support to the new dispensation and others who felt that the race would suffer irreparable damage. As usual, the optimists were more realistic, but both sides could advance reasonable arguments.

One criticism that made no sense whatsoever was that the decision was a desperate attempt by organisers to resuscitate a dying event. Yes, it is true that long-distance races in various parts of the world have reported a decline in the number of entrants and that some claim that the worldwide explosion of road-running has peaked.

There may be some truth in the 'peaking' theory, but there is no doubt that special events such as the Boston Marathon, the London Marathon and our own Two Oceans and Comrades have far too much substance to be threatened by ephemeral trends. Nevertheless, cognisance has to be taken of cogent arguments. This is precisely what happened in respect of the time allowed for completion of the Comrades Marathon.

The first argument put forward was a telling one, that of tradition. Contrary to the beliefs of many ill-advised 'purists', the original cut-off was 12 hours, not 11. The 12-hour limit applied to the first seven races, the reduction to 11 hours coming in 1928. The second argument was the realisation, as strongly evidenced by Wally Hayward's 1988 and 1989 comeback, that ageing runners were often still able to complete the course, but were simply slower. In particular, as Hayward showed in 1988, qualifying for the race became more difficult for senior citizens than actually completing it.

The third argument for an extension to the existing cut-off was a medical one. In the great millennium run of the year 2000, the 12-hour cut-off was reintroduced for the occasion, in order to involve as many as possible in the celebration. Nobody expected a field of 24 000, yet that is what happened. Despite the huge entry, including many returning to the race after an absence of several years, the demands made on medical services were relatively slight. The explanation was understood to be that those who would have strained to make the old 11-hour limit were able to slow down, walk, take their time and arrive at the finish later, but in far healthier condition than if they had squeezed every last second out of their broken bodies.

The Comrades Marathon Association evidently agreed with these sentiments, and, in 2003, the official cut-off reverted to 12 hours, this time on a 'tentatively' permanent basis. This decision is unlikely to be changed in the foreseeable future.

Another decision made by the association this year was to appoint a chief executive officer. This was in keeping with modern trends, recognising that the Comrades Marathon, like other formerly amateur organisations, now had to operate in a professional environment. John van den Aardweg, a man of significant skill and experience in sports administration, and a Comrades medal winner himself, was chosen as the first CEO. Van den Aardweg emphasised that his role would be the progressive organisation of the business side of Comrades, leaving all other facets in the hands of the existing structure.

The official theme of the 2003 Comrades Marathon was summed up in the slogan 'Because we can'. It was well chosen and certainly touched the hearts and minds of those who had previously tried and failed, those who were trying for the first time and those who had personal obstacles to overcome along with those posed by the demanding course. The initiative rekindled the pioneering spirit, which was an essential component of the traditional Comrades ethos. As many an old-timer will confirm, every year is the first year whenever you run the Comrades Marathon.

In the souvenir brochure for the 2003 race, a Manchester United supporter presented a tribute to a Liverpool Football Club supporter running his 30th

Comrades in succession: Alan Robb, four-time winner of the great race, was being congratulated by his former arch-rival and long-time friend Bruce Fordyce. In his tribute, Fordyce enunciated his admiration for his great rival with obvious sincerity:

'At the moment, I am quite knowledgeable on the subject of the 1914–18 conflict (which led to the foundation of the Comrades Marathon) since my son Jonathan has been completing a school project on trench warfare. "Going over the top" was an expression that Jonathan asked me to explain. I told him that, at the blowing of a whistle, soldiers had to climb out of their trenches and charge at the enemy, often to almost certain death. Often a line of soldiers would link arms before they charged. Indeed, the skeletons of soldiers of the Lincolnshire Regiment were recently found by archeologists, their arms linked, dead a few paces after "going over the top".

'"Who would you go over the top with, Dad?", asked Jonathan. "Alan Robb" was the name that sprang almost immediately to mind. In a modern world full of cheating, corruption, laziness and cowardliness, Alan Robb is one of the few exceptions.'

In those few words honouring a man who was possibly his number one opponent, Bruce Fordyce arguably expressed the ethos and camaraderie of Comrades as eloquently as anyone has done.

The start of this year's race was relatively cautious, with no one seeming to favour a front-running strategy. To knowledgeable observers, this suggested the prospect of a fast time, as 'come from behind' tactics have generally proved the more reliable approach. In comfortably warm conditions, a group of Russians appeared to take control at about one-third distance.

On the formidable Inchanga, Denis Zhalybin, Edward Takhbatullin and Oleg Kharitonov led the red assault, with Walter Nkosi the only local willing to stay with them. Shortly before halfway, Nkosi startled the Russians by breaking away and claiming the R20 000 reward for being the first gold medallist to reach Drummond, thus showing them that South Africans valued money just as much as they did!

In the early stages of the second half, the front-runners looked well in control. Nkosi's halfway time of 2.45.30 was sensible, and there were no signs of undue damage having been suffered by first-half ambition. Nevertheless, the race had not been sewn up. There were others who had also started prudently. Fusi Nhlapo had won three consecutive gold medals, yet hadn't attracted too much media attention in the build-up as South Africans pinned their hopes on a repeat 'down' victory from Andrew Kelehe.

Nhlapo was not only a talented runner. He was also a highly intelligent strategist. He explained his tactics afterwards: 'I thought the breakaway group was too fast, but I couldn't catch them alone, so I waited for Sarel Ackerman and Willie Mtolo and then we worked together. I'm a good "down" runner, they're good on "ups", so we helped each other.'

They helped each other so well on the section from Gillits to Kloof that they were up with the leaders at the top of Field's Hill. Field's Hill is known as a destroyer of imprudent racers, so they descended gently, except for Nhlapo. Realising that downhill running was his forte, he threw caution to the wind and simply took off. His boldness worked, and he quickly built up a sizeable lead. The problem would be maintaining it as he moved into the painful final section.

After the race, Nhlapo disclosed that he had spoken to himself: 'I told myself that today was my day.' Having taken the lead, he felt more determined than exhausted after his audacious move. Victory was in his sights, and he had the inner strength to realise his dream. He crossed the line in 5.28.53, the ninth fastest Comrades to date. Kharitonov fought back to claim second prize in 5.31.42, just 13 seconds ahead of third-placed Joseph Molaba. KwaZulu-Natal's favourite hero, Willie Mtolo, again suffered leg cramps. After finishing eighth, he said, 'I think I realise now that the "down" run isn't for me.' Sadly, his many supporters have had to accept that a Comrades victory for Mtolo is unlikely.

Andrew Kelehe, on the other hand, finished in a strong fifth position, claiming his seventh successive gold medal. 'Up' run champion Vladimir Kotov, reduced at times to walking, even in the relatively early stages, owing to a painful hamstring injury, manfully continued and finished 22nd. Visitors from abroad have at times been criticised by locals for jetting in, claiming prize money and disappearing without showing any real acceptance of Comrades ideals or interest in Comrades camaraderie. Kotov was different. He exhibited true Comrades spirit and was much appreciated for that.

In the women's race, Hungarian Two Oceans champion Simona Staicu set off like a rocket and was first through halfway with a new record seemingly on the cards. Once again, first-half overambition led to second-half collapse, and she faded to eventually take tenth place plus the cash prize for being the first gold medallist to reach Drummond. The Russian doctor Tatyana Zhirkova was second at halfway. She was experiencing stomach problems, however, and was simply brushed aside when the twins, Elena and Olesya Nurgalieva, surged to the front.

From then on, there was no stopping the two sisters, who were simply irrepressible. Once in front, they employed their usual tactics, running side by side until one found the pace too hot. It was Olesya who cracked, leaving Elena in full control. The stadium crowd was astonished when Elena started walking before the end. Her explanation was a simple one: 'I thought I had already finished.' Olesya duly took second place, while Zhirkova managed to hang on to third place. She would fare somewhat more successfully in the 2005 'down' run. Maria Bak, fourth, won her seventh gold from seven starts.

The South African ladies were once again outclassed, with only Farwa Mentoor (eighth) and Yolande Maclean (ninth) in the top ten. Mentoor did, however, have the satisfaction of knowing that she was the second-fastest local in Comrades history. Only Frith van der Merwe, in 1989 (still the race record) and 1991, had run faster. It was a superb effort on her part, but South African women were not meeting the overseas challenge. Comrades followers could only hope that there was, perhaps, another Frith van der Merwe waiting in the wings.

These days, former serial winner Bruce Fordyce runs with less ambition than he did when he dominated Comrades throughout the 1980s. He prefers to enjoy the companionship of friends. One such buddy is television actor David Vlok of *Egoli* fame. The pair decided to run the 2003 race together. At the foot of Polly Shortts, Fordyce dropped back a little. They didn't see each other again until shortly before the finish. With about two kilometres left, Vlok, as befits a gentleman and sportsman of his stature, waited until Fordyce caught up with him. In the finest tradition of the great race, Vlok throttled back and helped the ageing ex-champion Fordyce to a comfortable finish.

Another act of unselfishness came from Hennie Loots, who accompanied his nephew Henk Meyer. Meyer had the mental ability of a four-year-old and consequently required the assistance of someone who could look after him. He got this from Loots, who spoke of their relationship:

'Henk is my sister's son. He got malaria when he was four, which affected half his brain. But we've noticed that, with the running, he's starting to improve. I've been doing this for ten years and it's worth the effort. It's rewarding to see the positive effect it has on him.' This was a tough Comrades for the pair, as Loots explained. 'With ten kilometres to go, he started to cry and said that he couldn't continue, but there's an inner strength in him that's unexplainable and he kept going.' Loots and Meyer successfully completed their 11th and seventh Comrades Marathons, respectively.

Undoubtedly the star of the 2003 Comrades Marathon was a remarkable man named Zeb Luhabe, born in Idutywa, Transkei, on 30 March 1927. At the age of 62, Zeb decided that his ambition in life was a successful Comrades Marathon finish. He tried valiantly on ten occasions but failed each time. In 2003, he realised that the extra hour gave him one last chance at the unlikely age of 76. He used up every ounce of strength in his body to finally finish in a time of 11.59.59, with one second to spare before the cut-off. The Founder's Trophy for the oldest finisher and the Geraldine Watson Trophy for the last finisher were both awarded to the most courageous finisher, Zeb Luhabe, a man who personified everything that Comrades holds dear.

2003 COMRADES MARATHON RESULTS

1. Fusi Nhlapo	5.28.53
2. Oleg Kharitonov	5.31.42
3. Joseph Molaba	5.31.55
4. Jorge Aubeso Martinez	5.32.32
5. Andrew Kelehe	5.35.18
6. Sarel Ackermann	5.35.52
7. Walter Nkosi	5.39.26
8. Willie Mtolo	5.41.30
9. Denis Zhalybin	5.41.39
10. Moses Lebakeng	5.42.31

2003 COMRADES BOWL RESULTS

1. Elena Nurgalieva	6.07.47
2. Olesya Nurgalieva	6.12.08
3. Tatyana Zhirkova	6.17.51

4. Maria Bak	6.18.33
5. Marina Bychkova	6.19.22
6. Alena Vinitskaya	6.22.48
7. Elvira Kolpakova	6.24.30
8. Farwa Mentoor	6.32.38
9. Yolande Maclean	6.44.40
10. Simona Staicu	6.54.49

2004 COMRADES MARATHON
VICTORY TO A CAPE TOWN RUSSIAN

As Comrades Marathon followers are aware, the race is run over a varying course with occasional changes in finishing venues, although the start tends to remain fairly constant, allowing for the fact that the race is run in alternating directions from year to year. Generally, a 'down' run takes place in an odd-numbered year and an 'up' run in an even-numbered year such as 2004. While Trivial Pursuit might say that the distance of the race is 89 or 90 kilometres, in reality it varies between approximately 86 and 93 kilometres.

The 2004 race witnessed the sixth different finishing venue for an 'up' run. The first 'up' run ever, in 1922, which featured Arthur Newton's first victory, ended at the Royal Showgrounds. Two years later, Alexandra Park took over, keeping its status until 1954. The 1956 race, known as the 'Arthur Newton Comrades Marathon', was enriched by the presence of both Newton and race founder Vic Clapham. In their honour, the finish reverted to the Royal Showgrounds, scene of Newton's triumph. From 1958 to 1975, the organising club, Collegians Harriers of Pietermaritzburg, hosted the 'up' finish. Jan Smuts Stadium, with its notorious ramp (hated and loved by runners who had to negotiate the steep, short entrance into the arena), provided the venue for the next 11 'up' finishes. In 2000 and 2002, Scottsville Racecourse was used. While effective in certain ways, it did not really highlight the unique spirit of a Comrades Marathon finish. Consequently, the 2004 event was scheduled to end at the Oval in Alexandra

Park, just past Jan Smuts Stadium (now Harry Gwala Park).

In an interview before this year's race, Comrades spokesperson Cheryl Winn discussed the disappointment felt by the organisers at the drop in entries from 13 100 in 2003 to 12 030 this year. Preferring to ignore the obvious excuse that 'up' runs historically draw lower fields than their 'down' counterparts, Winn chose to look within, in self-critical style. She recognised the need for new role models to replace the likes of Bruce Fordyce and Frith van der Merwe, and pinpointed the dilemma created by the professionals from abroad:

'We keep getting these Russian machines who don't live here. They just come out, win the race and go back home. They're not warm and fuzzy people you can relate to.' Many will be able to relate to that view.

Acknowledging that the cut-off time this year was 12 hours, as had been the case in 2000, she admitted: 'The numbers for novices and women have dropped. The "up" run is a tough race and beginners normally go for the "down" run.' Well known as a champion of transformation, Winn added, 'The biggest challenge is to make sure the race stays relevant to today's South Africa.'

A few days after the 2004 race, Andrew Unsworth wrote an article in the *Sunday Times* that aptly linked the great race with Cheryl Winn's concern, the great challenge still facing South Africans – that of transformation:

'It is one of the ironies of history that people fight and die in great struggles so that their children and grandchildren can live in freedom – but that freedom usually means a freedom from the past as well.

'The point was abundantly illustrated this week on Youth Day, which now coincides with the running of the Comrades Marathon.

'On Wednesday, many public speakers, and even more callers to radio chat shows, urged that the true meaning of June 16 should not be forgotten and that it should never become just another public holiday.

'Some expressed concern that today's youth, who were not even born in 1976 – you would have to be well over 30 to have any memory of the events – are often unaware of the significance of the day.

'They are, of course, right. June 16 is perhaps the most meaningful of our secular holidays, commemorating a defining moment in our national history and psyche.'

June 16 2004 witnessed the 79th running of the world's foremost ultramarathon. While Comrades enthusiasts were thrilled to see athletes from 30 different countries taking part, locals were hopeful that a South African would again triumph in the 'up' run. After all, Andrew Kelehe had won the 2001 and Fusi Nhlapo the 2003 'down' runs. It wasn't as if locals didn't have the ability. Patriotic competitiveness was starting to demand an end to the successful Russian invasion. This year's race would provide a surprising, but admirable, compromise in the men's section. As far as the women were concerned, nobody really expected anything except another dose of foreign domination, although Farwa Mentoor was cited as South Africa's biggest threat to the top three, while Grace de Oliveira would always be loved along the Comrades course.

They say that a good Comrades winner controls the race from first position, while a great Comrades runner controls the event from behind, dictating the progress and strategy of those ahead of him through his sheer ability, tactical acumen and knowledge of the course and of his companions. Vladimir Kotov was fast becoming known as a great Comrades athlete. Admittedly, he had yet to make a major impact on the 'down' run. 'So what?' you might ask, 'Just look at his "up" record.' Yes, that does count, we must acknowledge, but true Comrades greatness demands success in both directions.

Kotov had won the previous two 'up' runs, beating Dimitri Grishine's best effort of 5.26.25 in 1998 with a phenomenal record time of 5.25.33 in 2000, which he followed with another victory in 5.30.59 in 2002. He was chasing an 'up' hat-trick, a fact that made many question his lack of success in the 'down' run. This was perhaps a little unfair. There's no shame in being a specialist. Furthermore, he held the record for the 'up' Comrades, just about as tough an event as you'll find worldwide.

Nevertheless, South Africans, like any other nation, tend to favour their own. Willie Mtolo, a former New York Marathon winner, Two Oceans champion, winner of numerous events and local KwaZulu-Natal hero, carried the hopes of his countrymen. It wasn't difficult to support him. Aesthetically, Mtolo in long-distance running was about as pleasing on the eye as American Carl Lewis in the sprints.

The race went much as expected, with the majority of the favourites keeping close company. Defending 'up' champion Kotov was similar to Bruce Fordyce and Hoseah Tjale in one respect: watching him gave no clue of how he was feeling. Fordyce always looked relaxed, Tjale seemed to be labouring and Kotov appeared to be in pain. It was all a matter of style. Their own thoughts, their strengths, their weaknesses and their doubts were well hidden from all but themselves.

The first half suited Kotov perfectly, as did the start of the second half. Kotov was a master of uphill running in the final section of an ultramarathon. In this respect, he was similar to Bruce Fordyce. Tactical acumen would have suggested that someone should try to break the Kotov stranglehold, keep him guessing, make him think that someone else was posing a threat. For a brief while, around Cato Ridge, former Two Oceans champion Simon Mphulanyane put in something of a surge, but it was all too fleeting and to no avail. Willie Mtolo, Jaroslaw Janicki, Oleg Kharitonov (and, to a lesser extent, Joseph Ikaneng, Mluleki Nobanda and Mphulanyane) kept up the pressure on Kotov, but he appeared to have all the answers.

Mtolo, South Africa's great hope, faltered when it was feared he might do so, just as the race entered the closing stages. Kotov surged and surged again. Janicki dropped back, then Kharitonov. Then there was only one. Acknowledging his understanding of the tactical nuances of the race, Kotov said afterwards: 'I knew when Oleg was surging early on that I would win. I also knew that I was stronger on the hills than him, so, when we got to Little Pollys, I was confident.'

The popular Pole Jaroslaw (Jarek, for short) Janicki finished strongly to take second place from Kharitonov, while Mtolo delighted his many fans by manfully hanging on to fourth spot. The foreigners had triumphed again – or had they? Vladimir Kotov had his own ideas on that subject.

Kotov, who hailed from Belarus, had settled in South Africa and was both a proud Capetonian, running most weekend races there (with significant success), and a proud South African citizen. At the age of 46, he had become the oldest Comrades winner, just edging out the legendary Wally Hayward. He was also eligible to claim the prize of R65 000 for being the first South African finisher. In the spirit of Arthur Newton and in the best Comrades tradition, he declined the prize, enabling it to be awarded to South African-born Willie Mtolo. In making this remarkable gesture, Kotov showed that he was a true South African (albeit of short duration) and a worthy Comrades champion.

The women's race remained the property of visitors (immigration officials, please take note). In particular, the Nurgalieva twins, Elena and Olesya, continued to dominate. The pair were first through halfway at Drummond with another Russian, Marina Bychkova, third and South Africa's Farwa Mentoor fourth.

In the early part of the second half, the twins were relentless. Mentoor kept up the South African challenge and moved past Bychkova and Olesya Nurgalieva to temporarily occupy second position. In the closing stages, Bychkova fought back to claim second place from the Capetonian.

The race, however, belonged to Elena Nurgalieva. Her winning time of 6.11.15 beat the previous 'up' record of American Ann Trason by over two minutes. Third-placed Farwa Mentoor's time of 6.18.23 was over 14 minutes faster than the previous best 'up' time by a South African, set by Frith van der Merwe in 1986. Mentoor's performance highlighted both her status as arguably South Africa's greatest ever female ultra-distance runner and the gulf between South Africa's best and the world's best.

Australian Chris Horwood noted some of his impressions of participation in the 2004 Comrades Marathon:

'The Comrades website is one of the best I've encountered for any event and contains a wealth of information, including a very comprehensive training programme which is posted monthly by Don Oliver, the official Comrades coach who has compiled programmes specifically for this event for many years now. It's graded into three different levels to cater for the finish time you want to achieve, but if you follow Don's programme, you'll realise your goal.

'Included in the entry fee is a coach tour of the race route for all novices and this is an invaluable way of determining a race strategy as you get to see where all the hills, declines and flat sections are. The tour guides are all Comrades veterans and provide some invaluable insights as to what to expect on race day. For me, one of the highlights of the tour was a visit to the Ethembeni Training School for Physically Handicapped Children.

'With all the real issues those beautiful children have to deal with, they were more interested in making us feel welcome than in their own problems and burst into several songs to show us just that. All they wanted from you was a high five when you ran past them on race day while they were lined up along the road in front of their school. Someone decided to whip around the hat and within minutes we'd gathered several hundred dollars which we presented to one of the staff. Her gratitude and explanation that what we considered to be a modest amount would provide for, say, the services of a speech therapist for 12 months certainly hammered home just how lucky we are and how trivial most of our problems really are by comparison. It was a wonderful, humbling experience.

'The aid stations (51 in total) are the best of any run in which I've competed. The sheer volume of goods needed to stock them is amazing, not to mention the 4 000-plus volunteers required to man them. Water is offered in 150-millilitre sachets (there's 1 040 000 of them consumed on the day), and they are so much better than cups whose contents slop out all over you and create a real trip hazard when discarded in their thousands.'

And Horwood's feelings after finishing in 9:47:54?

'Six months and 1400 kilometres of intense training in conjunction with five years of progressive development had culminated in the achievement of a lifetime and an experience I will never forget. In the catching area behind the finish line, all I wanted to do was simply stand there and soak up the atmosphere of the moment while reflecting upon the enormity of what I had accomplished.

'If certain moments live forever, that one certainly will – a salt-encrusted, aching wreck, overcome with emotion … too buggered to cry tears of joy … too excited to move, just standing there smiling, taking it all in – wow!'

This visiting Australian probably put the wonder of our great event into context more eloquently than any local might have done. At the same time, his account allows South Africans to realise just how much visitors can contribute to the global realisation of the ideals of Vic Clapham's race. Hopefully, Chris Horwood will be back to repeat his 2004 experience.

COMRADES MARATHON OFFICIAL RESULTS 2004

1. Vladimir Kotov	5.31.22
2. Jaroslaw Janicki	5.34.17
3. Oleg Kharitonov	5.39.08
4. Willie Mtolo	5.39.56
5. Andrew Kelehe	5.42.34
6. Joseph Ikaneng	5.43.03

7. Hlonepha Mphulanyane   5.44.10
8. Jorge Aubeso Martinez   5.45.34
9. Johan Oosthuizen   5.46.07
10. Jacob Madima   5.48.31

COMRADES MARATHON BOWL 2004

1. Elena Nurgalieva   6.11.15
2. Marina Bychkova   6.14.13
3. Farwa Mentoor   6.18.23
4. Olesya Nurgalieva   6.20.32
5. Tatyana Zhirkova   6.28.02
6. Maria Bak   6.30.44
7. Yolande Maclean   6.45.40
8. Grace de Oliveira   6.46.59
9. Reneé Scott   6.56.28
10. Riana van Niekerk   7.12.23

2005 COMRADES MARATHON
SOUTH AFRICANS DOMINATE

The 80th running of South Africa's most prestigious annual event was anticipated with relish by all associated with the race. Senior members of the Comrades Marathon Association travelled around the country, putting on roadshow appeals to long-distance runners to acknowledge the special stature of the event, to support Comrades 2005 and, hopefully, to enter the milestone race.

Various sideshows were scheduled to mark the special occasion. Not all of them succeeded spectacularly. It was announced that 49-year-old Gary Paul would try to break the world record for continuous running on a treadmill over a period of 24 hours. By the time early arrivals visited the expo, a notice sadly recorded the fact that Paul had been advised to cease his attempt on medical grounds. We can only assume that medical advice was prudent, as post-race results recorded G. Paul's successful finish in a time of 10.51.18.

The entire Comrades community was saddened shortly before race day at news of the sudden death of 1967 champion Manie Kuhn. In his sole victory, Kuhn had pipped 1966 winner Tommy Malone by mere inches. The two became the best of friends and shared a tongue-in-cheek rivalry that became part of Comrades folklore. On hearing the news, Malone reminisced about his 1967 defeat:

'We were at a running club two days after the race. Manie broke down and cried when talking about the race. He felt he shouldn't have beaten me and was thinking about what I was going through. That's the sort of man he was.'

In the last five years of his life, Kuhn had endured more than his fair share of mishaps, surviving both a triple-bypass operation and a near-fatal shooting as his motor vehicle was hijacked. Like Malone, he remained an active roadside supporter of the great race that had brought fame to both. Malone spoke with obvious sorrow at the loss of his great friend:

'He was a fierce competitor on the road and in the pub. There was a lot of respect between us. We've had some great fun down the years. He'd come through so much: a heart bypass, being shot. He's going to be missed at Comrades. He was a big part of the race.'

Pre-race speculation focused on a number of issues, one being the patriotic desire for a South African winner. While visitors had enjoyed the majority of the spoils in the professional post-isolation period, their success had been largely confined, among men at any rate, to the 'up' race. The previous two 'down' runs had been won by South Africans Andrew Kelehe and Fusi Nhlapo. Locals were hopeful that either of the two, or perhaps another South African, might prevail.

In the women's race, where Rae Bisschoff had been the last South African to triumph in 1998, there seemed little likelihood of stemming the foreign tide. Capetonian Farwa Mentoor had shown remarkable consistency, being the first local finisher for the past few years, but she had yet to make the top three. Ever popular Grace de Oliveira did have a second and a third to her credit, but that was five years ago and times had improved since then.

As race day loomed nearer, the assurance was given that, should any runner fall foul of conditions and the arduous nature of the race, he or she would be in the safest hands possible. Dr Jeremy Boulter, head of the association's medical portfolio, also announced that the Sports Science Institute, under

Professor Tim Noakes, would be conducting a controlled investigation, in collaboration with the association's medical team, to ascertain the most favourable method of resuscitating a collapsed athlete.

Conditions for the 2005 Comrades Marathon reflected the best of Comrades hospitality. The start in Pietermaritzburg was cool, but not overly cold. As the day progressed, the temperature became pleasantly warm, without reaching the type of extreme heat that had been experienced ten years previously. Away from Comrades, temperatures did become heated in another way, when young supporters of Jacob Zuma used Youth Day celebrations to protest against President Thabo Mbeki's axing of Zuma as his deputy president.

The early kilometres of this year's Comrades echoed the relatively mild climatic conditions that prevailed on race day. The top runners, while mindful of the pot of gold that would reward a race record, were experienced enough to know that a gentle start was the prudent way to achieve one's sensible objective. Consequently, the main contenders were quite content to watch each other in the early stages and ignore the early morning 'television sprinters'.

One runner who was right up with the leaders, but wasn't really fancied, was Sipho Ngomane of Nelspruit. The fact that he wasn't favoured was rather strange, as Nick Bester later pointed out: 'This year Sipho has come second in the National Marathon Championships, a week later he ran a 2.13 standard marathon and, a week after that, he came second in the Two Oceans. That's not all. A couple of weeks later, he was third in the Longtom half-marathon in 62 minutes, and then he went on to win the coveted Jock of the Bushveld race in record time.'

Certainly, Ngomane timed the first half of his race to perfection. He reached Umlaas Road after 18 kilometres in 1.16.24 and went through Drummond in 2.48.14, almost two minutes faster than Fordyce's halfway time during his 1984 record-breaking run. Feeling good at this stage, he put in a surge on the ascent of Botha's Hill. Afterwards, he explained his reason for doing so: 'I realised the others were holding back, and there were so many of us that I decided to step up the pace.'

Brave words, indeed! The start of the second half is recognised as a time to position oneself sensibly, watch what one's opponents are doing and bide one's time for a late assault, if possible. Ngomane's assault came in the early stages of the second half, and it worked. He soon found himself in the lead. Once there, he realised that it was important to stretch his lead, and set about doing so.

At Kloof, as the race entered the endgame stage, Ngomane was comfortably ahead. He extended his advantage on the descent of Field's Hill and was approximately a kilometre ahead of second-placed Elias Mabane as he entered Pinetown. Behind Mabane were Claude Mashiywa, Sipho Maisela, Oleg Kharitonov, Andrew Kelehe, Jaroslaw Janicki, Emerson Kayana, Andrias Maseou and Zamile Gebashe. Eight of the top ten were South African. Hopes were high for a significant local triumph.

Such hopes were realised. Ngomane's strength didn't waver for a moment in the closing stages. While the order of the following pack was shuffled slightly on the approach to Kingsmead, the leader remained unperturbed. A large crowd gave an ecstatic welcome to Ngomane, who broke the tape in the very fast time of 5.27.11. The Russian Kharitonov, second, also beat the five-and-a-half-hour barrier, with 2001 winner Andrew Kelehe third. Vladimir Kotov, reigning 'up' run champion, came through the field to claim fourth spot. With Kotov now officially a Capetonian, eight of the top ten were South Africans, much to the joy of the excited spectators.

Ngomane's financial reward, over R1 million, was especially welcome as burglars had recently cleaned him out of house and home: 'When they came to my house and stole everything, even my shoes, it was very bad. It helped concentrate my mind and I trained a lot more.'

Asked to comment on his relative youth, the 23-year-old from Nelspruit said: 'Yes, I am very young to have won the race. But I took a chance and I am the champion. After halfway, I started to kick because the guy [Elias Mabane, ninth] running with me was too slow.'

The seemingly unstoppable Nurgalieva twins, Olesya and Elena, were firm favourites, along with defending champion Marina Bychkova, to fight out the ladies' race. Elena had won the previous 'down' in 2003, with Olesya second. From the start, the twins kept each other company, but they certainly weren't having things all their own way. Tatyana Zhirkova, third in 2003, was determined to improve on that performance. A medical doctor, she had given up her profession to become a full-time athlete. Her business-like running style suggested that she would not easily be overcome – and so it proved.

The twins did not dominate, and the lead changed hands on several occasions. Elvira Kolpakova looked a good bet at one stage, but wasn't able to sustain her challenge. Marina Bychkova also threatened. When the leaders entered Pinetown, however, it was clearly a race between Zhirkova and the two sisters. Elena was having difficulties, and her sister lost some time staying with her and encouraging her. It's impossible to say how much time she lost, but it wasn't crucial. On the day, Tatyana Zhirkova was simply too strong and won convincingly in 5.58.51, the third-fastest time in history after Frith van der Merwe's 5.54.43 in 1989 and American Ann Trason's 5.58.25 in 1997. Farwa Mentoor was once again the pick of the South Africans, taking fourth place in 6.19.21.

Among the old-timers Alan Robb completed his 32nd Comrades in succession, as always wearing his Liverpool hat and red socks with the sort of distinction that befits the wonderful club which he supports. His perennial rival, Bruce Fordyce of Manchester United allegiance, also managed a successful finish. The pair still compete in terms of green numbers. At present, Fordyce has earned seven (for his nine wins, 11 golds and 20 runs) to Robb's six (for his four wins, 12 golds and 30 runs). If Robb completes a 40th run, he will draw level, whereas Fordyce could pull ahead again with a 30th finish. Faced with the prospect of lifelong rivalry, Fordyce commented, 'My knees are twingeing at the horrendous thought of Alan going for 50 Comrades runs!'

As has become customary, Fordyce, after showering, changing and chatting with television interviewers, presented green numbers to those who had earned them this year. Robb, who also performs this duty regularly, joined his wife Merle and fellow past winners Tommy Malone and Jackie Mekler. With 20 minutes of the race left, the four of them drank a toast in memory of their beloved friend Manie Kuhn.

Then, with just ten minutes before the gun, these three great champions, along with Merle Robb, went outside to welcome the most important people of all, those who had managed to scrape a successful finish in the nick of time. The Comrades Marathon spirit remains, undiminished by time and lesser considerations.

2005 COMRADES MARATHON RESULTS

1. Sipho Ngomane   5.27.11
2. Oleg Kharitonov   5.29.16
3. Andrew Kelehe   5.31.45
4. Vladimir Kotov   5.34.00
5. Fusi Nhlapo   5.39.02
6. Rasta Mohloli   5.40.18
7. Johan Oosthuizen   5.40.58
8. Claude Moshiywa   5.42.23
9. Elias Mabane   5.46.21
10. Albe Geldenhuys   5.46.38

2005 COMRADES BOWL RESULTS

1. Tatyana Zhirkova   5.58.51
2. Olesya Nurgalieva   6.10.40
3. Elena Nurgalieva   6.12.19
4. Farwa Mentoor   6.19.21
5. Marina Bychkova   6.19.30
6. Marina Myshlianova   6.28.50
7. Elvira Kolpakova   6.34.45
8. Yolande Maclean   6.37.36
9. Tatyana Titova   6.43.17
10. Lindsay van Aswegen   7.04.34

18

THE MODERN ERA
(2006 to 2010)

Comrades, the ultimate human race, has reflected and influenced the reality of South African society for nearly a century. Its origin, the realisation of Vic Clapham's prophetic vision of an ongoing memorial to his fallen comrades in the First World War, retains its meaning after all these years.

When South Africa has struggled, so too has Comrades. The Great Depression of 1929 and the early 1930s almost led to the race's premature demise. South Africa survived those awful times. So did Comrades, with difficulty.

The evil of Adolf Hitler brought most of the world to a virtual standstill from 1939 to 1945. South Africa was no exception. The Second World War brought about the only gap in Comrades history: for five years, from 1941 to 1945, no races took place.

When hostilities ended, despair was everywhere. Returning soldiers were unfit, uneducated and ill-equipped to provide the upliftment that the nation required. Jobs were scarce and money even more so. Leadership was needed, but in short supply. Thanks to the enterprise and optimistic outlook of stalwarts Morris Alexander, Bert Bendzulla and 'Skilly' du Bois, the Comrades Marathon was revived. It would be a wild exaggeration to claim that Comrades led the country out of the doldrums, but it cannot be denied that the innate strength of the Comrades community mirrored the resilience of post-war South Africans.

Political issues have dominated the nation's first century, since Union in 1910. Comrades, only a decade younger, has not been immune to this reality. The race was built on an all-inclusive ethos. For much of its history, this culture was frustrated by a government that imposed an ethnic exclusivity on all facets of society. Comrades seethed uncomfortably under this subjection, but seemed powerless to confront it.

The 1980s saw a shift in understanding. International condemnation of apartheid was growing. Economic, cultural and sporting isolation could not be ignored. The demands of the oppressed were legitimate. Responsible leaders emerged. Frederik van Zyl Slabbert, a Comrades medallist and former leader of the political opposition, led a delegation of influential South Africans to Dakar in Senegal, where they met Thabo Mbeki and other prominent exiles. Bruce Fordyce and others wore black armbands in the famous Comrades demonstration of 1981. The Comrades message, while not entirely unanimous, was proclaimed.

When isolation ended in the early 1990s, concerned Comrades supporters feared that the race might be swamped by the focus on other sports. The entire sporting landscape changed virtually overnight. During isolation, government-sponsored media had focused on the rugby Currie Cup and the Comrades Marathon to an almost obsessive degree. Would such attention be withdrawn now that readmission had brought the country into modern globalism, featuring money, television, sponsorship and endorsements, and more and more money?

Comrades' response was to introduce prize money. The hope was that the lure of financial incentives might attract the best of international athletes and keep interest in the race alive. After almost 20 years, we can now ask: Has it worked? First of all, the popularity of Comrades continues, largely untouched by monetary considerations. What of the foreigners? This is a hotly debated issue. On one hand, there are those who maintain that progress is inevitable, involves money and should be welcomed. Others claim that virtually all top athletes from abroad are Russians or close neighbours, speak barely any English, fly in, win prize money and fly out again without contributing materially to the event that has enriched them.

What is the truth? There can be no doubt that much of the criticism is well founded. At the same time, there are notable exceptions. The delightful Nurgalieva twins have endeared themselves to the local community. Vladimir Kotov has settled in Cape Town. The popular Jaroslaw Janicki has declared his allegiance by wearing a bandana sporting the colours of the South African flag on race day. Most encouragingly, there has been a significant growth in the numbers of rank-and-file visitors from abroad, amateur runners eager to savour the unique spirit of the Comrades Marathon.

As ever in South Africa, political issues remain. Thankfully, the evil of apartheid has gone: the country is well rid of the 'Old South Africa'. But what of the 'New South Africa?' Is it the real solution to the nation's long-standing issues? Has it provided a happy environment in which the great race can continue, unencumbered by political pressure?

Only a naive dreamer would answer in the affirmative. The country is beset by violent crime. Corruption is rife, in politics and in the business world. Greedy sports administrators seek personal gain, showing little concern for the sporting bodies they purport to represent. The highly regrettable saga of Athletics South Africa has been exposed publicly.

Is 'doom and gloom' a realistic assessment of the state of this troubled nation? The strength of spirit of South Africans, demonstrated in the annals of the Comrades Marathon, suggests a far more optimistic outlook. The illegitimacy of the Old South Africa has been recognised and discarded. The frailties of the New South Africa are apparent. The potential of the true South Africa is yet to be realised.

The Comrades Marathon, in its almost 100 years, has exemplified the pioneering spirit of all South Africans: black, white, male, female, short, tall, fat, thin, fast and slow (in some cases, exceedingly slow). The race will continue to draw people from diverse backgrounds in its annual odyssey, a voyage of shared aspiration and mutual fulfilment. Surely, Vic Clapham's dream, rather than the selfishness of opportunistic politicians, indicates the true direction for all South Africans to follow.

2006 COMRADES MARATHON
A DAY OF REMEMBRANCE

During the 1980s, a well-known supporter of the race would often be seen at his favourite vantage point, in the shade of a tree near the top of Botha's Hill. The renowned writer Alan Paton, author of *Cry, the Beloved Country* and other masterpieces of South African literature, fully appreciated the lure of the great race as well as its particular place in the nation's psyche.

An outspoken critic of the former Nationalist government's apartheid policy, Paton attended the funeral in Pietermaritzburg of a young soldier who had died during the apartheid era. The funeral was held on Comrades day. Paton expressed the bittersweet emotions of the day in an article that was published in the *Natal Witness*:

'The church is already full when I get there although I am not late. The atmosphere of love and grief is palpable. I have to sit near the front, in fact very near the family. Therefore I have to watch – I cannot help watching – the grief of a young boy weeping for his soldier brother. It makes me weep also.

'The usual unanswerable questions are asked. Why so young? Why does God demand the life of one who has hardly begun? Has he been called away to some other service?

'We are counselled not to blame God, or the government, or the army, or the ones who killed him. This is life and one must accept it.

'Man that is born of woman has but a short time to live. He comes up and is cut down like a flower. He flees as it were a shadow and never continues in one stay.

'There is one question that is not asked aloud here, and that is for what did he die? But it is in the minds of many who have come to mourn for a young soldier and for those whom he has left behind. For what did he die?

'One is not supposed to ask these questions. The asking of them is supposed, in some queer way, to show that one does not love one's country. The asking of them is supposed to undermine morale and to sap the confidence that the cause is just …

'Inside this church there is nothing but love, but outside, even in the streets of this quiet city, there is hate. You don't just weep for the young soldier who is dead, and the younger brother who grieves. You weep also for your country.

'It's the Comrades Marathon today, one of the greatest sporting spectacles in the world. Everyone has come to watch, everyone is happy, everyone is gay. There are more black runners than ever before. As each one appears, a young black woman with great bobbing breasts joins the race and runs with him, laughing and ululating, an exhibition of pure and innocent joy. I suppose she is interfering with the race, but the other runners do not seem to mind …

'Is it all real? It seems real enough. People could not simulate this gaiety and joy. There are no stones here, no curses, only encouragements. Two faces of South Africa, the one full of hate, the other full of joy. Or should we say three faces, for there is one that is full of grief. Not just because a young soldier is dead, but because of this vision of what our country might be, and is not.'

In keeping with Paton's vision, the Comrades Marathon of 2006 reflected its microcosmic relationship with the country as a whole. Once again, the Comrades ethos of shared endeavour and optimism found itself in conflict with the various and complex forces that threaten to tear out the heart of the still youthful nation. As always, the magical day stood out as a beacon of hope in a country experiencing renewed polarisation at a time when reconciliation should have been nearing fulfilment and economic growth should have become a tribute to a nation fully committed to overcoming the travails of the past.

Sadly, violence is a word that creeps into most South African conversations nowadays. It comes in various forms, one of them being the horrific slaughter taking place on the nation's roads, as the Comrades community experienced in 2006. Runners are acutely aware of the dangers of their proximity to motor vehicles and their extreme vulnerability should there be a collision between a fragile human being and a solid motorised object. Such calamities have occurred before and they will no doubt happen again.

Members of the Bedfordview Athletic Club suffered a terrible tragedy in March. In training for this year's Comrades Marathon, they split up into two groups as they set off for a run. According to newspaper reports, some of them were 'knocked down by a speeding motorist'. Richard Albrecht and Joe Mendoza (father of a five-year-old boy and husband of a pregnant wife,

Dina) were killed. Two other club members, Dr Wayne Korras and Karl Quinn, spent weeks in hospital recovering from horrendous injuries. Club chairman Alberto Riccardi arranged a memorial run for the athletes just four days after the event.

Criminal violence has assumed pandemic proportions in South Africa. The Comrades Marathon is not immune, as evidenced the day before this year's event. For the past seven or eight years, Dianne Hofland has been a regular presence at the charity stands, promoting the Sports Trust, Amabeadibeadi and other worthy causes with great enthusiasm. Her 15-year-old son Ryan, recently returned from America, was approaching the Comrades Expo when he was accosted by a youth and warned that nine armed men were behind him, ready to shoot if he ran or screamed. He was relieved of his watch, cellphone and money. Three years previously, Dianne's handbag had been stolen at the Amabeadibeadi stand. My own son, Christopher, then 13 years old, was mugged outside the Comrades Expo in 1988.

Politics once again reared its divisive head in 2006. The Comrades Marathon was inaugurated as a memorial to South Africans who had sacrificed their lives in the First World War. In later years, those who had succumbed during the Second World War, the Korean War and the discredited Angolan campaign would also be remembered. Particular honour would be accorded to the brave Sowetan youths who lost their lives protesting against the iniquities of apartheid education on 16 June 1976, a day now commemorated as Youth Day and an occasion that the Comrades Marathon respectfully included in its own special remembrance.

Between the 2005 and 2006 marathons, it became apparent that a vociferous political faction felt that Youth Day was their day, a holy day that belonged exclusively to the so-called 'previously disadvantaged' people of South Africa, one that could not be shared with the country as a whole. The intensity of their feeling was palpable, so much so that one could only empathise with their devotion to their cause in the light of previous injustices. At the same time, the exclusivity of their stand had to be regarded as questionable in a country trying to come to terms with transformation in a spirit of reconciliation.

Less than two weeks after the running of the 2006 marathon, the president of Athletics South Africa, Leonard Chuene, announced that future Comrades Marathons would be run on Sundays. According to Chuene, the

2007 race would take place on Sunday, 17 June, the 2008 event on 15 June and that of 2009 on 14 June.

On the same day that the dates were announced, Dr Frederik van Zyl Slabbert spoke at the launch of a report entitled 'The revival of racial classification in post-apartheid South Africa' and said, 'If you make yourself hostage to a racist past, you can bank on a racist future.'

A sad but inevitable event cast something of a shadow over the 2006 Comrades Marathon. Indestructible Wally Hayward, who ran (and won) his first Comrades in 1930 at the age of 21 and his final Comrades 59 years later in 1989, died in March at the age of 97. To many, he epitomised what Comrades was all about. The only unbeaten multiple champion, with five victories from 1930 to 1954, he came out of retirement shortly before his 80th birthday and surrendered his perfect record in order to proclaim the fact that old age can be met with dignity and strength.

Another of the great stalwarts of the past, Nick Raubenheimer, also departed after a long battle with a debilitating illness that never stopped him making his annual pilgrimage to Comrades. Raubenheimer was one of the elite runners of his day, whose best effort was third place in 1958. Yet he is best remembered for other things. As a lecturer at Technikon Natal, he translated Norrie Williamson's *Everyone's Guide to Distance Running* into Zulu, a language he spoke fluently. He was one of the leaders in establishing a place for blind runners.

In keeping with recent custom, visitors to the Comrades Expo on the eve of the race were entertained by a variety of stage performers. Most notable were the Zulu dancers and choir from the Ethembeni School for the Physically Disabled and Visually Impaired, who have enjoyed a special symbiotic relationship with Comrades for many years. On race day, they would as ever line the side of the road and exchange greetings with runners, some of whom would be benefactors of the school. Folk singer Duncan Eriksson's performance featured a song he had composed about the event.

The weather on the eve of Comrades was cold, windy and unpleasant. Race day, as usual, provided near-perfect conditions with clear skies, a light north-west wind and a maximum temperature of 22°C. Runners would be assisted by 4 000 volunteers at 50 refreshment stations along the 86.775-kilometre route. Provisions for the athletes included 200 water troughs, 500 trestle tables, 420 000 plastic drinking bottles, 25 000 litres of water and 480 pockets of oranges.

As the huge throng of just under 12 000 congregated at the start, the variety of their vests and shorts was colourful testimony to the ever-broadening appeal of Comrades. There were those from abroad who would enjoy special recognition from spectators along the way. There were those whose apparel identified charities that they were supporting. There were those, six in number, who were attempting their 30th Comrades. There were 71 running their 20th and 476 'going for green' – that is, trying to finish their tenth race, whose yellow numbers clearly identified them. Of the local clubs, Rand Athletic Club boasted the most entrants (345), followed by Chatsworth (206) and the Gauteng North Club Irene (179).

Would a South African end the dominance of the Eastern Europeans in the 'up' run? This was the fervent hope of many of the locals who struggled to understand why the visitors would regularly prevail in the 'ups' yet fail in the 'downs'. It soon became apparent that home athletes had appropriate aspirations. At Cowies Hill, 15 kilometres into the race, leader Fanie Matshipa was followed by Tshepo Masebi, Petros Sosibo, Frans Chauke, Sipho Ngomane, Doctor Mtsweni, Charles Tjiane, Peterson Khumalo, Jabulani Nxumalo and White Modisenyane. The top ten were all South African. Frans Chauke was highly regarded as a legitimate challenger and Sipho Ngomane was the defending champion.

At Drummond, the halfway mark, South Africans seemed to be in control of proceedings. Matshipa still led from Chauke and Ngomane. More than ten minutes behind, a determined and experienced trio were biding their time. 'Up' run record holder Vladimir Kotov, 1999 'down' champion Jaroslaw Janicki and Oleg Kharitonov looked ominous as they powered their way up Inchanga. Ironically, the experience of the European trio over the Comrades course gave them a distinct advantage over their local opponents.

As is customary, various contenders moved into challenging positions in the early stages of the second half. Shortly before Cato Ridge, 2003 winner Fusi Nhlapo joined the lead group. At the two-thirds mark, Frans Chauke led, with the consistent Andrew Kelehe now in tenth position. Jaroslaw Janicki (ninth) was the only foreigner in the top ten. Vladimir Kotov (now a South African) and the local novice Brian Zondi were keeping him company.

Chauke's lead came to an end on the subtle climb to Camperdown. On the undulating stretch from Camperdown to the highest point at Lion Park, the endgame started to take shape. Now there were just four in contention: Kotov, Kharitonov, Janicki and Zondi. On the descent to the chicken farm, with the pace hotting up, Kotov dropped back. Now there were only three.

With 16 kilometres to go, the trio raced shoulder to shoulder. Janicki, perhaps trying to elicit local support, wore a cap sporting the colours of the South African flag. Zondi was wearing black gloves while Kharitonov, world record holder over 100 miles, wore a solitary white glove on his left hand and a kerchief on his head. With 11 kilometres to go, Brian Zondi, after waving to the crowd, put in a surge and broke clear of his rivals. Had he made his move too soon? We would soon know.

Janicki, who had looked strongest of all for most of the second half, was unable to respond and fell back. With Kotov over two minutes behind, it was now a two-horse race between the experienced Russian Kharitonov and his brave South African rival Brian Zondi. Kharitonov soon moved up to the shoulder of the local novice. Together, they approached the most formidable obstacle in ultra-distance running, Polly Shortts.

On the steep ascent, the Russian dug deep into his reservoir of strength and experience and inched ahead. The gap grew wider and gradually became decisive. Kharitonov had the bit between his teeth. He had come close before. Nobody would stop him now. When he crested Polly Shortts, victory was assured. Kharitonov's time of 5.35.16 was not one of the fastest on record, but it certainly made amends for second place in 2003, third in 2004 and another second in 5.29.15 in the 'down' run of 2005.

For South Africans, Brian Zondi was the hero of the day. While some might have felt that his breakaway attempt on Little Pollys was premature and possibly the reason for his not having won the race, he could point to the fact that he had beaten everyone other than Kharitonov in his first attempt at the great race. He acknowledged that he had drawn inspiration from Tim Noakes's monumental book *Lore of Running*. Rather surprisingly, he spoke of his wife's doubts about his training programme and added, 'I told her that I couldn't do the training and still pay attention to her.'

The women's event was as predictable as everyone had expected it to be. Elena Nurgalieva displayed scant regard for the Comrades virtue of caution when she sprinted through Drummond to beat Tatyana Zhirkova to the bonus prize on offer at halfway. The effort didn't sap her strength, and her win broke the 'up' record for the second consecutive time in 6.09.23.

In addition to bonus prizes, Nurgalieva was reported to have earned R1.25 million in prize money and incentives from her major sponsors, Mr Price, and her shoe sponsors. It was an extremely lucrative return for someone whose rather unathletic looks were described by *Sunday Times* writer Simnikiwe Xabanisa as 'roly-poly'.

South African women were, for whatever reason, once again eclipsed by the visitors, who took the first five places. Farwa Mentoor, as usual, claimed top position among the locals, with Yolande Maclean in seventh place. Grace de Oliveira delighted her many supporters with yet another top-ten finish.

This year's event was graced by the participation of one of the legends of marathon running in the USA. Ambrose (Amby) Burfoot, winner of the 1968 Boston Marathon, expressed his undiluted excitement at being back and the Comrades community was equally delighted to welcome him again.

Burfoot, the executive editor of *Runner's World* magazine in the USA, had previously visited South Africa in 1993 for the launch of the local edition of *Runner's World*. Quite naturally, the occasion was arranged to coincide with the 1993 Comrades Marathon, and a then 46-year-old Burfoot, well past his athletic prime, had achieved a bronze-medal finish in 9.50.49.

The Comrades bug had well and truly caught this legendary American superstar, as he recalled in 2006: 'I always knew that I hadn't truly run Comrades until I also did the "up" race, so I was thrilled when *Runner's World* told me I could run and write about this year's race. I even talked my brother and brother-in-law into coming with me.'

While neither of his close relatives managed to finish the race in time, Burfoot did, in 11.05.03. Afterwards, he paid a tribute to Comrades that was so sincere that he opened the minds of even the most dedicated of local devotees:

'I have had the chance to run Comrades twice. I have gone "down" and "up". I am not a "Green" and never will be one, but I have completed my own cycle of Comrades runs. I believe Comrades is the world's greatest foot race. In my home, we have displayed only three running medals: a Boston Marathon winner's medal, a Comrades bronze medal and a Comrades Vic Clapham medal. Those three are the great landmark races of my running career.'

In the VIP enclosure, 1966 champion Tommy Malone was happily following events when his cellphone rang. Immediately, his whole demeanour changed. He had just received word that his daughter, Amanda Harvey, had 12 kilometres to go. Malone assured everyone around him that he had absolute faith in Amanda, but his furrowed brow showed all the anxiety of a troubled parent. He needn't have worried. Amanda arrived safely in 10.38.00 and Tommy proudly announced that she had achieved 'negative splits' – that is, her second half had been faster than the first. Asked to comment on her day, she said, 'I must have said 80 Hail Marys out there.' She was wearing her famous father's old number, 62.

The competitive nature of sport invites interested followers to rank top athletes according to their ability and performances. The Comrades Marathon is no exception. Who are the true Comrades greats? Who is the greatest Comrades runner of all? Thankfully, such questions are for bar-room enthusiasts rather than historians. Nevertheless, they do get asked, and a reluctant response is sometimes required.

Most Comrades aficionados regard the five-time-or-more winners Arthur Newton, Hardy Ballington, Wally Hayward, Jackie Mekler and Bruce Fordyce as being in the very top echelon, and would add four-time champion Alan Robb and female superstar Frith van der Merwe to their shortlist. Traditionally, the debate ends up in a shoot-out between Wally Hayward and Bruce Fordyce.

In 2006, it became apparent that a new name had to be considered, that of Andrew Kelehe. In 1996, Kelehe ran his debut Comrades, finishing 30th in a time of 5.58.29. It was the start of an 11-year sequence of sub-six-hour times, an unprecedented record. In 1997, Kelehe came fifth in 5.33.24. It was the first of ten consecutive gold medal finishes, another unprecedented record. Although he has only one victory to his credit, his winning time of 5.25.52 in 2001, given the course distance, reflected an average running speed that has not been bettered.

Who, then, can rightly be regarded as the greatest of all Comrades champions? It is one of those fascinating sporting questions that can never be authoritatively answered. It can certainly be argued that Bruce Fordyce's nine wins out of nine starts, his reign of over a quarter of a century as a Comrades record holder and his long-standing world record over 50 miles place him in a category of his own. At the same time, it has to be acknowledged that other greats such as Newton, Mekler, Hayward, Ballington, Robb, Van der Merwe and now Kelehe faced their own challenges successfully under differing circumstances. It's an extremely subjective issue. May the debate continue.

Shortly after the firing of a pistol signalled the end of the race, the traditional Sunset Ceremony took place. While a youthful choir produced a stirring rendition of the national anthem, Comrades greats Tommy Malone, Jackie Mekler and Mick Winn stood to attention. Immediately afterwards, the trio drank a special toast to Wally Hayward, Nick Raubenheimer and other members of the Comrades family who had crossed the ultimate finish line in the preceding 12 months. The Comrades spirit remained fully intact.

2006 COMRADES MARATHON RESULTS

1. Oleg Kharitonov	5.35.19
2. Brian Zondi	5.37.32
3. Vladimir Kotov	5.40.56
4. Grigoriy Murzin	5.41.26
5. Fusi Nhlapo	5.41.43
6. Jaroslaw Janicki	5.42.06
7. Andrew Kelehe	5.44.20
8. Mncedisi Mkhize	5.44.28
9. Frans Chauke	5.46.01
10. Leboka Noto	5.47.29

2006 COMRADES BOWL RESULTS

1. Elena Nurgalieva	6.09.24
2. Marina Bychkova	6.12.58
3. Tatyana Zhirkova	6.27.21
4. Maria Bak	6.31.07
5. Marina Myshlianova	6.38.51
6. Farwa Mentoor	6.41.32
7. Yolande Maclean	6.47.03

8. Riana van Niekerk	7.04.37
9. Madeleen Otto	7.17.08
10. Grace de Oliveira	7.24.11

2007 COMRADES MARATHON

When Vic Clapham initiated the Comrades Marathon over 80 years previously, he faced many challenges, and overcame them all, one by one. Obtaining permission from the League of Comrades to stage his dream event presented probably the most serious obstacle of all. Maintaining the event with minimal participants in the early days posed enormous problems for the imperturbable Clapham. With great fortitude and ingenuity, he made light of such travails and kept his baby alive and kicking.

Clapham's successors faced further threats to the survival of the race. The Great Depression of the early 1930s, the Second World War and the need to revive the event after wartime all stretched the resourcefulness of Comrades organisers. Fortunately, the inherent strength of the annual happening and the dedication of those entrusted with its survival ensured that it continued to take place.

Then came the golden years. The worldwide running explosion, the long-awaited arrival of television in South Africa, the Bruce Fordyce era and a growing awareness that ordinary mortals were capable of completing ultramarathons changed mindsets. Numerous boys and girls next door were out on the road before dawn, training for running races of ever-increasing distance. Comrades grew exponentially, reaching its zenith in 2000 when a field of over 20 000 took part in the millennium run.

The main responsibility of the Comrades Marathon Association was providing the support structures required to keep up with the demands of a race that would feature increasing numbers of local participants and a rapid escalation of overseas competitors. The future of the race was assured, so marketing the event would be unnecessary and futile, surely? Well, that's the way things appeared on the surface, but the reality was rather different.

As all involved in the management of South African sport would have to agree, whatever their own personal views, politics has always been a significant factor. This is hardly surprising. Political interference in sport, limiting meaningful participation to the white minority, was a feature of the apartheid era. Nelson Mandela, aware of the importance of the nation's sporting culture, wisely and successfully utilised this phenomenon in bringing about the euphoric unification that took place in 1994 and 1995, uniting South Africans of diverse backgrounds through the happy and healthy medium of sporting competition.

Since those heady day, politicians have endeavoured to use sport as a means of achieving their own ends: sometimes noble, sometimes factional, often selfish. 'Transformation' is the political buzzword, and it is a much misunderstood term. There can be no denying that true transformation – providing opportunities and facilities previously denied to the majority of the population – is one of the country's most pressing needs. At the same time, a distorted conception of transformation, designed to promote the self-seeking aspirations of administrators unconcerned with the needs of the public at large, has become a debilitating reality affecting the potential growth of virtually all of the nation's sporting codes.

Comrades Marathon followers initially shared a tacit understanding that political considerations would pass them by. After all, Comrades, right from day one, had been a totally apolitical institution. Indeed, the so-called New South Africa was entirely in line with the tradition of inclusivity that lay at the heart of Comrades culture. Surely, Comrades would be immune from political interference.

This would prove to be an incorrect assumption. Indeed, it is not unreasonable to suspect that the race's pre-eminent status made it a likely target for political opportunists: so-called 'athletics administrators' and others. This was the reality facing the Comrades Marathon Association in the build-up to the 2007 event.

The announcement, shortly after the 2006 race, that Comrades would no longer take place on Youth Day, 16 June, but on the nearest Sunday to that date, was not well received by the Comrades faithful. The Comrades community, while comprising the most diverse spread of people imaginable, has, at its heart, a solid core of mature and principled individuals sharing traditional values. Holding a sporting event on a Sunday doesn't pose too much of a problem for any other than the most puritanical. But when the event starts at 5.30 a.m. and finishes at 5.30 p.m., thus making it virtually impossible for those taking part to attend church services, then it becomes a more serious matter. When it became apparent that the change had been brought about by the ANC Youth League, a political organisation, resentment grew among runners. Such resentment played a telling role in the reduced number of entrants for the 2007 race. It also, very unfortunately, led many South Africans to reject the solemn remembrance of those courageous youngsters who had perished in 1976, a commemoration that had become a regular part of the traditional Comrades closing ceremony.

The problems continued as race day approached. 'Comrades vs Comrades' was the bold headline of the *Weekend Witness* on the very eve of the race. The Congress of South African Trade Unions, the nation's umbrella trade-union federation, had let it be known that striking public servants intended to disrupt the event in order to attract publicity and greater awareness of their grievances in their ongoing dispute with the government. On the day before the event, it would be normal for the chairman of the Comrades Marathon Association to be seen visiting members of his organising team and checking that all the preparations were in order. But Dave Dixon was nowhere to be seen. He was embroiled in lengthy negotiations with trade unionists. Knowing that the orderly holding of the race was under threat, an association official defiantly commented, 'Let them try and stop over 10 000 people running Comrades. They'll soon find out!'

Fortunately, Dixon's efforts prevailed. Just as fortunately, those who wished to disrupt the event failed to turn up. This was fortuitous for them. On 7 October, some three and a half months after Comrades day, the organisers of the Chicago Marathon cancelled their race in midstream due to extreme heat. At the time, approximately 4 000 of the 36 000 starters were still on the road, and police and fire department workers were unable to bring runners to a halt. It would take a superhuman effort to stop long-distance athletes from fulfilling the dream that had dominated their lives for months.

The 2007 Comrades Marathon went ahead as scheduled. Planning, as usual, was comprehensive and involved numerous organisations and individuals. The race had certainly inspired loyalty over the years, and loyalty had been provided by runners, organisers, sponsors, supporters (they were not just spectators) and helpers. This year's field would be particularly well served. Over 50 rescue vehicles would be on hand to provide transport to the finish for those unable to meet the challenge. Somewhat more optimistically, 50 refreshment tables (strategically stationed and equipped with water, cola, energy drinks, cream soda, oranges, bananas, chocolates, petroleum jelly, heat rubs and lashings of encouragement) would endeavour to make the challenge a little more attainable.

Whatever the misgivings about the annual 'foreign invasion' of professional athletes, there can be no doubt that the growing influx of less competitive visitors, drawn to Comrades by the reports of their compatriots, has introduced a most welcome international diversity. In 2007, 41 countries were represented. The United Kingdom, with 57 runners, provided the biggest contingent, closely followed by Brazil (49), the United States of America (48), Australia (47) and Zimbabwe (42). Other participating nations were the Philippines, Israel, Malaysia, Northern Ireland, Scotland, Trinidad and Tobago, and Guadeloupe.

As the Comrades faithful gathered to prepare for their annual pilgrimage, one notable personality was missing. On 12 September 2006, two-time winner and former record holder Lindsay Weight had died suddenly at the young age of 44. Shortly before her death, Lindsay had successfully completed an ultramarathon. Fellow runners were dumbfounded. An autopsy, while confirming that she had died of natural causes, was unable to pinpoint the exact cause.

Dr Lindsay Weight's legacy is multi-faceted. At the age of 21, she won her first Comrades Marathon in a record-breaking 6.46.35. Her athletic performances are legendary. Yet it is her post-running contribution that will be best remembered. As researcher, journalist, author and commentator, Lindsay passed on her knowledge, understanding and love of long-distance running to countless newcomers to the sport, particularly women. Her oft-quoted remark, 'Running connects me to the soul of the universe', was in the hearts and minds of her many friends who took part in a gentle jog along one of her favourite Table Mountain routes in celebration of her life just days after the funeral.

There were, of course, other members of the Comrades community whose lives had come to an end in the past 12 months. As always, there were some who dedicated their special day to some such friend. Record holder for the 'down' run, Bruce Fordyce, was one whose 2007 race was run in memory of someone who had been close to him. His great buddy, Thami Ngubane, a double green-number holder with 18 silver medals to his credit, had died in his early forties less than a fortnight before the race. Mindful of Thami's encouragement for fellow runners throughout his Comrades career, Fordyce ran the 2007 Comrades with Thami Ngubane as his spiritual partner.

While tradition ensures that established routine remains an essential feature of the day, a couple of innovations were introduced this year. In deference to those whose Sunday observance had been compromised by the change in date, an interdenominational church service was scheduled to take place in Pietermaritzburg about an hour before the gun. With about 15 minutes to go, a Zulu praise singer provided encouragement to the athletes. Although some felt that this led to a delayed and slightly truncated rendition of *Chariots of Fire*, international visitors were delighted to savour a special African experience.

In cool but not overly cold weather, the field left the Pietermaritzburg City Hall and set out in their individual attempts to achieve over 11 000 separate but equally meaningful goals. Meteorologists promised favourable conditions, and close to half a million onlookers were already assembling, determined to urge runners forward in their quest for glory.

Would a South African prevail? This was a hope expressed by many locals. Brian Zondi's gallant efforts in 2006 had fired the imagination of his compatriots. Could he step up a gear and bring the Comrades crown back home? Noting that the three most recent 'down' runs had been won by South Africans Andrew Kelehe, Fusi Nhlapo and Sipho Ngomane, journalist Iqbal Khan confidently stated that the 'smart money was on Zondi'. In furthering his prediction, he quoted Zondi's manager, 1991 Comrades winner Nick Bester:

'The man is dedicated, disciplined and a determined athlete. He surprised everyone with his outstanding run last year. And now he wants to go a step further to preserve the South African tradition – winning the race to make it four out of four for the locals. He's got what it takes to win the race. He's put in the hard work and he will reap the benefits and do South Africa proud.'

Zondi was equally confident as he enunciated prior to race day: 'Everything has gone perfectly for me. Apart from the normal little jabs of pain, which are nothing serious and part of the life of a long-distance athlete, I have had no injuries or illnesses at all.'

Seasoned Comrades followers were concerned that he might be about to become yet another runner who would make the mistake of trying to convert a good run into a great one by overdoing his preparation the following year.

Television commentator Norrie Williamson, in typically forthright fashion, stated emphatically beforehand that 2001 runner-up Leonid Shvetsov would claim the Comrades crown ahead of up-run champion Oleg Kharitonov. According to Williamson, Brian Zondi, Fusi Nhlapo and Mncedisi Mkhize would be relegated to a battle for first of the locals. Others disagreed. Rhyn Swanepoel, CEO of Harmony KwaZulu-Natal, which was sponsoring several runners, predicted a win for Oleg Kharitonov, with Sipho Ngomane and Grigoriy Murzin occupying the minor podium positions. Cuan Walker of Mr Price (with similar vested interests) plumped for Fusi Nhlapo ahead of Claude Moshiywa and Kharitonov. Former Comrades CEO and ex-winner Cheryl Winn, ever the patriotic optimist, opted for Zondi, with Frans Chauke and Kharitonov as his main threats.

On the road, two things were clear. The temperature was encouragingly cool and the initial pace was frighteningly hot. This was not a morning for 'television rabbits' grabbing early morning attention. All attention was drawn to the hectic, although deceptively smooth, speed of true race contenders determined to establish early supremacy.

Leonid Shvetsov, Norrie Williamson's favourite, was a man on a mission. Not for him the tried-and-trusted strategy of a conservative first half followed by a late well-timed challenge for line honours. Before the start, he had decided that victory was not enough. A new course record, valued at approximately R2 million, was his goal. For him to fail, he would have to collapse en route or be beaten by a superior opponent. He wasn't prepared to entertain the possibility of any such eventuality.

In the early stages, Fusi Nhlapo, Sipho Ngomane and Grigoriy Murzin provided what could only be described as token resistance. By halfway, Shvetsov had firmly stamped his authority on proceedings. A medical doctor by profession, he clinically set about attacking Bruce Fordyce's 21-year-old record, the longest-standing in Comrades history. At one stage, television commentators predicted that the record would be lowered by over five minutes. When he crested Cowies Hill, the last of the Big Five, any thoughts of a late challenge had evaporated. Now he could cruise to a new record time, and this was precisely what he did.

A large crowd welcomed the triumphant Russian as he entered the stadium, powerfully completed the mandatory semi-circuit of Kingsmead and breasted the tape in a phenomenal time of 5.20.49. He had produced a performance that defied all previous understanding. As he came to a halt, his legs momentarily wobbled and he looked rather tottery. Then the realisation of his achievement hit him. He jumped up and down with hands held high and acknowledged the cheers of the ecstatic spectators. His immediate post-race comments emphasised his superiority over his rivals: 'I'm very pleased with the run. I felt very good over pretty much the whole distance. It was my pace. It was my comfortable pace. I guess it was too fast for the others. That's why they faded back.'

Bruce Fordyce was no longer a holder of the record for either the 'up' or the 'down' run. For many, this was difficult to digest. Since his first victory in 1981, Fordyce had held at least one of the records over a period of 26 years. He had set fastest times on no fewer than five occasions. His 'down' record, now consigned to history, had stood for 21 years, another record. There was a tinge of sadness in the air as a new champion was heralded and possibly the greatest of them all left centre stage. (Shvetsov's achievement was later tainted by allegations in 2010 – made by certain international athletes – associating him with banned performance-enhancing substances.)

One person who showed no overt sign of sorrow at the 'changing of the guard' was Fordyce himself. He had long realised that holding a record was a temporary circumstance and was clearly delighted that the new record holder was articulate in English, having lived in the United States for a few years, and showed a keen appreciation of Comrades culture. Fordyce boldly predicted, 'Leonid Shvetsov will wear the Comrades crown with distinction for several years.'

Shvetsov was equally gracious in his moment of triumph. Recognising Fordyce's unique place in history, he said to him, 'Bruce, you are still the Comrades king.' Somewhat impishly he added, 'Perhaps we should form a new club, one for all those Comrades runners who have finished in less time than 5 hours 25 minutes.' Thus far, they would be the only ones to qualify. A warm friendship between the fastest finisher yet and the most comprehensive champion of all was clearly emerging.

The women's race was rather disappointing. It turned out to be yet another Nurgalieva procession. The Russian twins were overwhelming pre-race favourites. As expected, they dominated the race and at no stage looked threatened by anyone but each other. South African hopes had been pinned on Riana van Niekerk, the form lady who had posted wins in the 'Om die Dam' and Loskop ultramarathons. Sadly, a throat infection, possibly brought on by too much racing, put paid to her chances. It was left to the tried-and-tested trio of Farwa Mentoor, Yolande Maclean and Grace de Oliveira to keep the host nation's flag flying. They didn't disappoint, despite being well off the winner's pace. Mentoor was once again the first South African, Maclean claimed her fifth gold medal and the ever-popular De Oliveira delighted the home supporters with her tenth place. Olesya Nurgalieva, second in the previous two 'down' races, turned the tables on her sibling Elena to record victory by just 29 seconds. Two Oceans champion Madina Biktagirova, also of Russia, came third. South Africans were left wondering when the next Frith van der Merwe would emerge. A consolation was the realisation that Frith's 1989 record of 5.54.43 remained intact.

Every Comrades Marathon produces uplifting accounts of those who have overcome severe obstacles in order to achieve their goals. This year was no exception. A special newcomer was English visitor Richard Whitehead, who had been born with legs that reached from hip to knee and stopped there. Prosthetic lower limbs had enabled him to complete marathons and even the 56-kilometre Two Oceans. Doubters questioned the advisability of attempting the ultimate running challenge. His finishing time of 9.54.27 echoed the message tattooed on his right arm: 'Cometh the hour, cometh the man.'

In 1974, Johnny Demas was the victim of a vicious gang attack that left him unconscious for 45 days and blind for life. Eleven years later, he met Denis Tabakin, founder of the Jardine Joggers, and was persuaded that blind runners, accompanied by 'pilots', were capable of running long distances. In 1988, assisted by Richard Shakenovsky, Demas completed his first Comrades in 10 hours 29 minutes. Ever since, he had been an inspiration to sighted runners. In 2007, at the age of 56, Johnny Demas completed his 20th consecutive Comrades in 9.53.53.

Stacey Barbaglia's story was somewhat different. A non-running mother of two, she, like many others, enjoyed an extremely sociable vacation in Plettenberg Bay in December 2006. The jollification included a charity ten-kilometre jog and a party on 29 December. On each occasion, she bumped into a fellow reveller by the name of Bruce Fordyce, who planted a rather challenging seed in her mind. An adventurer by nature, she accepted the bait and later described her experience: 'It is and was my most gruelling challenge and the hardest thing I have ever done. The longest day of my life, in horrible pain, but against which all others pale in comparison. Injured and unable to keep up after 20 kilometres, I hobbled, limped, walked, ran and crawled to the finish – the most exhilarating, heart-wrenching blood, sweat and tear-drenched moment I have experienced!' Her time: 11.43.23.

Business executive Rob Taylor was another novice, inspired by Bruce Fordyce and David Vlok, who eloquently recounted his race-day emotions: 'I was anaesthetised, the adventure had entered its final stages. I was in the dragon's den with nowhere to hide. *Chariots of Fire*, the cockcrow, the lights and the throng lifted me and carried me through the start. There are no words to describe the next nine hours and 48 minutes. I had entered another world. The scenery, the ululating crowd, the pain, the famous landmarks conspired to produce an amazing spiritual experience. I tried not to cry when we crossed the finish, but that was impossible. I had completed the greatest adventure of my life in the presence of my friends, who were now my Comrades.'

Since 1921, only five deaths had been recorded during Comrades Marathons, but this year's race produced a double tragedy. Thirty-four-year-old Michael Gordon entered the stadium shortly before the bronze medal cut-off. He collapsed on the field and was carried across the line by fellow runners. Attempts to resuscitate him failed. By a strange quirk of fate, 48-year-old Willem Malapi was seen to be in distress just a few hundred metres behind Gordon. He died in hospital a few hours later. Both will be remembered respectfully as fallen Comrades in the truest and oldest tradition of the race.

The 2007 Comrades Marathon was one of the most dramatic of all. The date change, the threat of a disrupted start and loss of life tore at the heart of the country's most treasured annual sporting occasion. Superb performances, highlighted by Leonid Shvetsov's record-breaking run, underlined the athletic stature of the event. Inspirational accounts of triumph over adversity proclaimed the awesome capacity of the human spirit. Clearly, the inherent strength of Comrades would continue to overcome all obstacles and enrich the lives of those fortunate enough to be drawn into its spell.

Rob Taylor emphasised how profoundly he had been affected:

'Comrades has, more than any other institution, bridged the social and economic divide and built trust between cultures, thereby building social capital, which is essential to what our country currently needs so badly in order to overcome the problems of poverty and crime. The race has done more than give me new-found confidence and a deep sense of humility. In fact, it has shaped me, crystallising a clear understanding that community and service will be part of whatever I do next in my life.'

2007 COMRADES MARATHON RESULTS

1. Leonid Shvetsov   05:20:41
2. Grigoriy Murzin   05:30:12
3. Mncedisi Mkhize   05:32:50
4. Fusi Nhlapo   05:33:48
5. Leboka Noto   05:35:27
6. Oleg Kharitonov   05:39:54
7. Stephen Muzhingi   05:40:11
8. Sipho Ngomane   05:45:21
9. Lucas Nonyana   05:47:32
10. Godfrey Sesenyamotse   05:48:18

2007 COMRADES BOWL RESULTS

1. Olesya Nurgalieva   06:10:03
2. Elena Nurgalieva   06:10:32
3. Madina Biktigirova   06:21:55
4. Farwa Mentoor   06:24:30
5. Marina Myshlyanova   06:25:18
6. Alena Vinitskaya   06:28:43
7. Yolande Maclean   06:29:47
8. Maria Bak   06:33:48
9. Adinda Kruger   06:38:31
10. Grace de Oliveira   06:57:29

2008 COMRADES MARATHON
SHVETSOV'S RECORD-BREAKING DOUBLE

Tragedy had marred the 2007 race. A repeat would be unthinkable. The Comrades Marathon Association was understandably determined to avoid any possibility of this happening. Very sensibly, the Association invoked a standard regulation of the International Amateur Athletics Federation. In doing so, it incurred the wrath of purists who felt that the very essence of the race, the legendary camaraderie, was being undermined.

The rule, well publicised in the media, was explained to runners in the official brochure by Comrades medical convenor Dr Jeremy Boulter:

'As the name and the origin and ethos imply, it is a personal battle to finish, and the support and encouragement of one's fellow runners is an intimate part of the race. However this could, and has, led to runners being helped and carried when they should have stopped running and sought medical help. From this year forward, any runner who is unable to move forward under his/her own power, (ie is being carried by other runners) will be prevented from continuing and medical attention will be called for, and that runner's race will be over!'

It was also made clear that runners who were seen to carry stricken companions in the finish area would risk disqualification. Most athletes found the change both reasonable and acceptable.

One runner who would not participate this year was politician Hansie Louw, then leader of the African Christian Democratic Party in the Western Cape, who linked the 2007 loss of life with Comrades' move to Sundays: 'Last year, two athletes died during or after Comrades. Was this a message from above? How many athletes will run with this type of threat?' Calling for a boycott of the event, Louw added, 'For me and many other Christians, it is now a final farewell. May Comrades soon be dead and buried! Christ will live forever!'

As one of the previous year's casualties was a member of the Jewish faith, many regarded Louw's comments as deplorably insensitive. The thousands of Christians who took part this year effectively denounced his remarks as decidedly unchristian.

During 2007, three special people received Spirit of Comrades awards:

Comrades great, Alan Robb, proudly wearing the
hat of the great Liverpool Football Club

Vladimir Kotov and Elena Nurgalieva: winners in 2004

Leon van Wyk humbly embraces the spirit of Comrades

Amanda Harvey with her illustrious father, Tommy Malone

Pat Boyle receives the 2003 Spirit of Comrades Award from Barry Varty

Record holder Leonid Shvetsov in full flight

Clive Crawley and Kenny Craig finished their 40th runs in 1998

Popular Pole, Jaroslaw Janicki wins in 1999

Zeb Luhabe in the nick of time in 2003

Comrades chairman, Dave Dixon
with 2001 winner, Andrew Kelehe

Grace de Oliveira: darling
of the home crowd

1999 champion, Birgit Lennartz

2005 champion, Sipho Ngomane, aged 24

The tactical battle in the final stages

Canadian Comrades ambassador, Andrea Moritz,
dressed for training in the Canadian cold

The indomitable Nurgalieva twins

Stephen Muzhingi wins the 2010 Comrades Marathon

road-running enthusiast and organiser Val Wilkinson, Comrades veteran and road-running institution Paul Selby, and British double amputee Richard Whitehead, who completed the 2007 Comrades on prosthetic legs in under ten hours.

Over 11 000 runners entered the 2008 Comrades Marathon. Some didn't make it to the start. Some starters didn't make it to the finish. Few would have been aware of the achievements of those honoured with Spirit of Comrades awards. Those who lined up at the start would have their own tales to tell at the end of the day. Many would exhibit their own brand of heroism, discovering levels of courage that far surpassed the previously perceived limits of their potential.

Conditions were favourable. The early morning temperature in Durban was a comfortable 11°C. A sunny day was forecast with a light north-east wind and a maximum temperature of 27°C. The meteorologists were spot on. If ever there was a time to make an assault on the record, this was the day. An ambitious Russian named Shvetsov shared these thoughts.

After years of foreign domination, South Africans yearned for a local winner. Would this be the year? Brian Zondi had shown such promise in the previous 'up' run. Had he learned from that experience? Would he be the one? Or would another unknown emulate Zondi's 2006 effort and perhaps even surpass it?

The early portents seemed favourable. The first ten athletes to crest Cowies Hill were all South Africans, but that wasn't unusual. Over the years, numerous local no-hopers had shown an appetite for television exposure. Could a potential winner be lurking in their midst?

Early pace-setter Professor Mollen led the race up and over Field's Hill. Mollen's age of 22 was perhaps an indication that Professor was his name and not an academic title. Perhaps fortuitously, a similar observation could be made about third-placed Prodigal Khumalo.

On the flattish section between Kloof and Hillcrest, pre-race favourite Leonid Shvetsov eased into the top ten. Significantly taller than the stereotype uphill specialist, his blue vest and dark shorts made him even more conspicuous, as did his strong running style. He appeared to have inherited the Fordyce-like knack of dictating proceedings from behind. Not too far behind Shvetsov, 'up' run record holder Vladimir Kotov was handily placed.

At the foot of Botha's Hill, Prodigal Khumalo took the lead from Mollen, who started walking when the Shvetsov group passed him near Kearsney College. The pattern of the race was unfolding as the main contenders moved into challenging positions. On the descent to Drummond, Charles Tjiane first joined and then passed Khumalo to take the outright lead. Tjiane was first through halfway, followed by Khumalo and Shvetsov. Frans Chauke was eighth, with 1999 winner Jaroslaw Janicki tenth.

Inchanga maintained its reputation as a source of heartache to pacesetters. Although Tjiane crested the fearsome hill in first place, he walked a few steps at the top and again shortly after. His resolve was broken. On Harrison Flats after 3 hours 12 minutes, Shvetsov broke away from his erstwhile companions and surged past Tjiane. Mabule Raphotle managed to join him, but only for a while. On one of the subtle uphills of Harrison Flats, Shvetsov surged again. With approximately 30 kilometres to go, the race was effectively over.

Shvetsov was confident that victory was assured. His thoughts presumably turned to other matters: the record and the proverbial pot of gold that would ensue. First place was worth R220 000 in prize money. With bonuses, a new record would boost his earnings to virtually R2 million. Conditions were ideal. The sky was clear, the temperature comfortable and the wind barely perceptible. The forecasters were right. Shvetsov was feeling strong and looked full of running. Frequent glances at his watch were clear indicators of his intentions.

At Camperdown, Shvetsov was 2.22 ahead of second man Janicki. Despite the leader's apparent composure, he later acknowledged that he had gone through a bad patch at this stage: 'I began to have difficulties with my knees on the hills around the 63-kilometre, 65-kilometre mark, but before that, everything was OK. It wasn't anything too serious, just a slight twinge, but all the same it was like a message to me to watch out.'

At the foot of Polly Shortts, Shvetsov was told that he was on record pace. He already knew this. Looking strong and relaxed, he powered his way up the hill. At the top, he looked in total control. He wasn't quite sure, as he later explained: 'At the top of Pollys, with around eight kilometres to go, I knew I would have to step up the pace again if I was to break the record, so I tried to make up for lost time on the downhills to the finish.'

His doubts were soon erased. A large crowd gave him a standing ovation as he sped around the track and crossed the line in 5.24.26, 47 seconds inside Vladimir Kotov's seven-year-old record. Shvetsov became the first runner since Bruce Fordyce to record consecutive victories. After crossing the line, he collapsed and lay prone for a while. He later explained this in terms familiar to South Africans: 'It was more out of relief that my legs gave way. After such a long, hard race, it was great just to be able to let go, like after crossing the Kalahari Desert and reaching for a cold beer!'

Sporting his familiar cap in the colours of the South African flag, the popular Pole Jaroslaw Janicki claimed second place, finishing almost 14 minutes behind Shvetsov. Zimbabwean Stephen Muzhingi sprinted to the line to come third. His strong finish caused observers to question how much he had in reserve. He would provide the answer 12 months later. The defending 'up' run champion Oleg Kharitonov came fourth, Vladimir Kotov was eighth and evergreen Willie Mtolo took the final gold medal to the delight of local supporters.

A Russian victor in the women's race was regarded as an inevitability. In fact, pre-race speculation suggested that the winner's surname could already be engraved on the trophy. The only question was which of the Nurgalieva twins, Elena or Olesya, would be the first to finish. A South African victory was simply unthinkable.

The sisters soon made their intentions clear, taking a joint lead virtually from the start. Then disaster almost struck. Shortly before Westville, Elena tripped and fell, gashing her left knee. A makeshift dressing was applied and she continued without losing too much time. At the foot of Cowies Hill, the twins were still in front, followed by fellow Russians Tatyana Zhirkova and Marina Bychkova. Of the South Africans, Farwa Mentoor, Grace de Oliveira and Riana van Niekerk were well placed.

Before Hillcrest, the dressing came off Elena's leg and she looked somewhat uncomfortable. The strong running Zhirkova joined the twins and seemed their most likely threat. Then, just before Botha's Hill, Elena fell again. Her race was now in real jeopardy. On the descent to Drummond, Zhirkova moved ahead. The Nurgalievas seemed content to follow a few paces behind, probably assessing the damage to Elena's knee. They appeared satisfied and led Zhirkova through halfway.

For much of the second half, the trio fought a cat-and-mouse battle. On the descent of Inchanga, Olesya dropped back. Zhirkova took advantage of Elena's sisterly concern and again moved to the front, but not for long. The lead kept changing hands. They were together at Camperdown with 24 kilometres to go. Shortly afterwards, the twins surged. This time, the move was decisive.

Although Elena had looked in trouble at times after her two tumbles, she proved the stronger of the sisters and claimed her fourth victory in 6.14.36. After the race, she spoke of her ordeal:

'There was a lot of blood running down my leg, but the injury did not sit in my mind. I quickly forgot the pain. Everything worked out perfectly in the end, so I suppose you can now call me the queen of the "up" run.'

Olesya, the reigning 'up' champion, finished 1 minute 15 seconds behind her sister, with Zhirkova third in 6.17.45. Fourth-placed Marina Myshlanova was over 13 minutes behind Zhirkova, a clear indication of the dominance of the leading threesome. Riana van Niekerk (sixth) was the leading South African. Farwa Mentoor (eighth) was followed by Lesley Train and Carol Mercer.

Shvetsov wasn't the only athlete to set a record. Dave Rogers, a 65-year-old Westville runner, took 11 hours 9 minutes and 3 seconds to register his 43rd successful finish and take over Clive Crawley's mantle as Comrades' most prolific medal-winner. A talented sportsman, Rogers was once chosen to represent his province at hockey. He declined the offer, as it would have clashed with Comrades. In 1976, he came third in a time of 5 hours 52 minutes. Durbanville's Riël Hugo joined the elite group who have completed 40 runs with an 11:51:57 finish.

The Stella Running Club had good cause to celebrate this year's race. A total of 91 members entered, four of them aiming for their 20th finish. All four, Arthur Zimmerman, Shane Hinchliffe, Pat Freeman and Roger Bailey, achieved their goal with over an hour to spare. Pat Freeman, the only woman, was first home and first recipient of the coveted double green.

Charities continued to be an integral part of the event. In addition to the official charities, various individuals used the occasion to raise funds for worthy causes. One such runner was Capetonian Peter Walsh, who ran for the benefit of burn survivors, highlighting a growing problem in South

African society, with a particular focus on children.

People are drawn to running for a variety of reasons. Xolani Mthembu, a security guard from Northdale, explained his motivation: 'I wanted to start participating in sport so that I would not be attracted to the life of drugs and sitting around on street corners waiting to commit crime. Running helped me get away from that.' A time of 6:57:44 suggested that running did rather more than just keep him out of mischief.

2008 COMRADES MARATHON RESULTS

1. Leonid Shvetsov	5.24.47
2. Jaroslaw Janicki	5.38.29
3. Stephen Muzhingi	5.39.40
4. Oleg Kharitonov	5.42.03
5. Grigoriy Murzin	5.43.07
6. Harmans Mokgadi	5.47.10
7. Mncedisi Mkhize	5.48.18
8. Vladimir Kotov	5.48.42
9. Johan Oosthuizen	5.50.52
10. Willie Mtolo	5.53.36

2008 COMRADES BOWL RESULTS

1 Elena Nurgalieva	6.14.37
2. Olesya Nurgalieva	6.15.52
3. Tatyana Zhirkova	6.17.45
4. Marina Myshlianova	6.30.49
5. Marina Bychkova	6.38.01
6. Riana van Niekerk	6.43.31
7. Maria Bak	6.53.32
8. Farwa Mentoor	6.59.40
9. Lesley Train	7.02.08
10. Carol Mercer	7.09.37

2009 COMRADES MARATHON
AT LAST, JOY FOR THE HOME CROWD

After his record-breaking run in the 2008 Comrades Marathon, Russian Leonid Shvetsov paid tribute to the man who had set more records than any other in the long history of the race: 'It was Fordyce himself who gave me the best advice the day before the race. He told me to first go for the win, then worry about the record if I was in a position to go for it – and that's exactly how it panned out.' This year, Shvetsov may have ruefully reminded himself of these words as he reflected on an unexpected disappointment.

Race day was set for Sunday, 24 May 2009. It was also announced that the 2010 event would take place on Sunday, 30 May. Association football (or soccer) was responsible for the change of dates. The FIFA Confederations Cup was scheduled for 14 to 26 June 2009, while the big one, the FIFA World Cup, would take place in South Africa from 11 June to 11 July 2010. Comrades Marathon Association chairman Dave Dixon explained the necessity for Comrades to defer to the football: 'We simply cannot hold the Comrades during June as we normally do. It will be impossible to obtain essential resources. The SAPS and traffic authorities will be fully occupied, attending to thousands of visitors, while most of the country's broadcast facilities will be tied up in the coverage of football matches.'

In a regular feature called 'Where are they now?', the *Sunday Times* of 17 May focused on Hoseah 'Hoss' Tjale, fondly remembered by Comrades followers for his superb athleticism, uniquely laboured running style and tongue-in-cheek brand of humour. Tjale now lived in a squatter camp near Tembisa with his student son Ramila. His wife Tshwane was working in Kuruman. Since 1993, he had been employed as a messenger for an entertainment company based in Langlaagte, Johannesburg.

Tjale was one of the first black runners to challenge seriously for line honours. His popularity was such that many hoped he would be the first black winner, but this was not to be, largely because his career coincided with that of Bruce Fordyce, with whom he shared a few close-fought battles. He spoke warmly of his former rival: 'We were later to become very good friends. Bruce has a very good heart and he has done so much for me even after we retired. The competition between us was so tough that I remember one day I told him I was not running any more. He said that he was also not going to run because without me there was no competition. We decided to run and he beat me again.'

On a few occasions, Tjale had led the race, only to be overtaken by Fordyce in the closing stages. Fordyce would start slowly and invariably make his way through the field. He was known to shake the hand of the leader he had hunted down. This became know as the 'kiss of death' handshake. There was much speculation as to what he said at the time. Tjale finally revealed the truth: 'He would say, "Don't give up. We are almost there and only have ten kilometres to go." Then he was gone.' Clearly 'Hoss' hadn't lost his impish sense of fun.

The Comrades Expo provides a special annual experience. It's a place where runners register, meet other runners, carbo-load and generally soak up the atmosphere. It's also a venue where old-timers get together, reminisce and pass on snippets of wisdom to novices. There are special facilities for green-number holders and international visitors. Bruce Hargreaves, Australian ambassador for Comrades, described the expo as 'excellent – not as big as Boston's, but bigger than London and definitely bigger than any in Australia'.

There are stage performances, stalls, giants on stilts and clowns to entertain the kids. There are cars to be won at the charity stands and medical personnel eager to take samples of your blood. Physiotherapists are on hand to prepare athletes' legs for the ordeal ahead and jovial bartenders to remind runners of the anticipated joy of after-action gratification. The Comrades Shop offers a wide range of memorabilia.

Every year, visitors are drawn to the magnificent picture gallery, which displays the history of the race in photographs, newspaper cuttings and other attractions. This year, I was at the gallery, chatting to Comrades veteran Barry Varty, the man responsible for the exhibition, when we were approached by a Canadian runner. She introduced herself as Andrea Moritz and told us that she had come to South Africa on her own in order to run Comrades. Impressed by her courage, we asked what had prompted her visit. 'The Comrades Marathon is legendary in Canada,' was her reply. Naturally, our Comrades (and South African) hearts filled with pride. We gave her some local advice and wished her a successful day.

Pre-race comment focused on one man, Leonid Shvetsov. He had won the previous two races, an 'up' and a 'down'. On both occasions, he had set records and finished well ahead of his opposition. He was a true Comrades all-rounder without any apparent weakness. There was no one in this year's field who looked likely to trouble him. The 1999 'down' champion, Jaroslaw Janicki, was back, along with Grigoriy Murzin and Oleg Kharitonov. They were top-class athletes, but Shvetsov had proven his superiority over them. Among the South Africans, Lucas Nonyana, Fusi Nhlapo, Sipho Ngomane and Mncedisi Mkhize warranted attention, but seemed unlikely to threaten the tall Russian. Zimbabwean Stephen Muzhingi's strong third place last year looked promising, but his hard-run Two Oceans and Chatsworth victory in April appeared to rule him out.

Conditions were ideal. As usual, Pietermaritzburg was cool, but not as cold as is sometimes the case. It was noticeable that a few went to the start clad only in their running gear, without the warm extras that are usually discarded along the way. Early indications suggested that another Shvetsov tour de force was unfolding. Wearing the distinctive green of the Nedbank club, the Russian was maintaining the same pace that had dominated proceedings two years previously. He went through halfway in second place, about four minutes behind Charles Tjiane.

By the top of Botha's Hill, Shvetsov had cut Tjiane's lead to three minutes. Tjiane was running the race of his life and Shvetsov sensed this. Instead of sticking to his pre-race schedule, he set about hauling in the surprise leader. Was this a mistake that would cost him victory? It may well have been. Tjiane was dictating the tempo and Shvetsov allowed himself to be sucked into his rival's game plan.

At Kloof, after 3 hours 45 minutes on the road, Tjiane at last showed signs of faltering. He dropped his arms a few times and slowed visibly. Then he stopped for a call of nature. That cost him time. He walked a few steps at a feeding station. That cost him further time. Field's Hill came at the right moment. He resumed a normal stride for about a kilometre. Then the ordeal seemed to hit him. He grimaced and walked a few steps. He looked a beaten man.

Tjiane led the race into Pinetown, but his challenge was clearly over. With just over 20 kilometres to go, Shvetsov took the lead. Briefly, Tjiane defiantly came back and ran alongside Shvetsov for about 100 metres.

He couldn't keep up and again walked, now resigned to defeat. During this battle for the lead, third-placed Zimbabwean Stephen Muzhingi kept a watching brief. On the ascent of Cowies, he passed Tjiane to take over second spot. Onlookers wondered if the forlorn Tjiane would manage to claim one of the gold medals on offer.

At the top of Cowies, Muzhingi was less than a minute behind Shvetsov. After Westville, Muzhingi swiftly whittled down the lead from a tired-looking Russian, worn out by his tussle with Tjiane and in no shape to resist the assault of a stronger and fresher man. Shortly before the climb up to 45th Cutting, Muzhingi surged past Shvetsov and immediately put in a determined effort in order to establish a significant lead.

Although a Zimbabwean, Muzhingi, running in the colours of the relatively new Formula One Bluff Club, had been living in Durban North. He was now in familiar territory and looked unstoppable. The Durban crowd was eager to welcome a local winner. Fortunately, the renowned attention to detail of the Comrades organisers ensured that a barrier separated him from wildly enthusiastic supporters on the approximately three-kilometre final stretch from the freeway to Kingsmead. To the delight of the stadium crowd, Muzhingi crossed the line in 5.23.26, the second fastest time yet.

Afterwards, Muzhingi provided a glimpse of his dedication when he revealed that his strict training regimen had prevented him from attending the birth of his son in Zimbabwe six weeks previously: 'It was hard for me to accept that I could not go home and be there for my wife and to see my child because I had to prepare for the race. I am still shocked that I won because I knew that I had to do this for my son and that winning the race would change my life. I pushed myself to pass the other runners on the road and cross the finishing line first so I can meet my son and return home a proud man.'

The vanquished Shvetsov graciously acclaimed the new champion, 'I do take my hat off to the winner, who ran such a great race.' He also acknowledged the role played by third-placed Tjiane: 'I have no problems in settling for second place on a day when the warmer weather played a part, but I must pay tribute to the guy [Tjiane] who set it up, especially after running from after the halfway mark. That I believe frightened the top runners – me, too – and that's when everything started going wrong.'

In *The Witness* of 22 May, two days prior to the race, Norrie Williamson wrote the following: 'Farwa Mentoor, the perennial winner of the first South African finisher in the Comrades Marathon, doesn't hide the fact that she intends reclaiming her crown in Sunday's down run Comrades Marathon.'

This made disturbing reading for local supporters. The clear implication was that South Africa's most successful female runner in recent years did not consider herself a contender for line honours. Victory, it seems, had been conceded to the overseas contingent before race day. This was despite the fact that none of the visitors had remotely threatened Frith van der Merwe's 'down' record set in 1989.

Did the top Russians merely have to turn up in order to claim the lion's share of the spoils? If so, the Nurgalieva twins certainly obliged, taking the lead virtually from the start. That's where they stayed, all the way to the finish. At no stage did any South African come close to mounting a serious challenge. In fact, the only athlete to come near the sisters was fellow Russian Tatyana Zhirkova, and she was comfortably dealt with, as the victorious Olesya explained:

'Approximately 15 kilometres from the finish, our seconds told us that the next lady [Zhirkova] was more than six minutes behind us. Elena and I spoke to each other and decided that we could afford to run comfortably with such a big lead. But about three kilometres later, we were told that our lead was down to only three minutes. As I was feeling stronger than Elena, I moved ahead and managed to stay clear until the finish.'

Elena duly took second spot ahead of Zhirkova and Marina Myshlanova, another Russian. Farwa Mentoor achieved her ambition and was the first South African home in fifth place. She was followed by Lesley Train, whose joyful jig across the line delighted the crowd. Afterwards, Mentoor commented: 'I was very tired at the time and dehydrated. That's why after the race, I was very dizzy. It's difficult to win against the Russian twins because they train at an extremely high altitude.' Whatever happened, one might ask, to South Africa's well-documented Highveld advantage?

Dr Wayne Korras was one of the group of Bedfordview runners involved in the terrible accident in 2006 described earlier in this book, in which two colleagues were killed. Wayne survived, but only just, regaining consciousness after 28 days. His injuries were so severe that he could not resume his profession as a medical doctor, but his spirit enabled him to return to the ultimate physical challenge. He completed the 2009 Comrades Marathon in the amazing time of 7.51.39. He summed up his relationship with the event: 'Comrades is my story and my life has been about it. The beauty of Comrades is that it strips you to the core and only you know the answers.'

2009 COMRADES MARATHON RESULTS

1. Stephen Muzhingi	5.23.27
2. Leonid Shvetsov	5.33.10
3. Charles Tjiane	5.34.21
4. Fusi Nhlapo	5.36.17
5. Lucas Nonyana	5.39.29
6. Mncedisi Mkhize	5.41.14
7. Bongmusa Mthembu	5.41.52
8. Peter Molapo	5.42.25
9. Bethuel Netshifhefhe	5.43.35
10. Harmans Mokgadi	5.44.49

2009 COMRADES BOWL RESULTS

1. Olesya Nurgalieva	6.12.12
2. Elena Nurgalieva	6.13.14
3. Tatyana Zhirkova	6.15.03
4. Marina Myshlianova	6.30.42
5. Farwa Mentoor	6.45.33
6. Lesley Train	7.01.07
7. Marina Bychkova	7.03.24
8. Lindsay van Aswegan	7.08.55
9. Belinda Waghorn	7.09.36
10. Kashmira Parbhoo	7.16.13

2010 COMRADES MARATHON
THE 85TH EVENT IN WORLD CUP YEAR

The enduring success of the Comrades Marathon can be attributed to various factors. Foremost among them is the simple fact that the event has remained true to the motivating spirit of its founder, Vic Clapham. For this, the organisers deserve full credit.

From time to time, individuals imbued with the unique ethos of the great race have emerged and imprinted their own particular influence on the Comrades community. One such person is a modest, self-effacing and therefore little-known beacon of the Comrades spirit. Leon van Wyk does not seek recognition, but the Comrades Marathon Association overruled him and presented him with a Gold Fields Spirit of Comrades Award on 23 October 2009. Holder of 36 Comrades medals himself, Leon had made a practice of sending commemorative clocks to distinguished Comrades runners and organisers, at his own initiative and expense, with citations of their achievements. Additionally, he had once even stepped in to subsidise the manufacture of Comrades medals when the race organisers were facing financial difficulties.

Leon's dislike for the limelight is well known to those closest to him. He would have taken consolation from knowing that his brief encounter with centre stage was shared with two other worthy members of the Comrades community. Cancer survivor Ann Margolin became the first woman to complete 25 Comrades Marathons and also holds the women's record for the most consecutive Two Oceans finishes. She overcame serious surgery (on more than one occasion) in order to continue her Comrades career. The third recipient was Josaya Moima, a fitness trainer who is rapidly approaching green-number status. He is devoted to the task of providing young people with the same athletic opportunities that have enriched his life. In 2006, he founded the Ndlovu Road Runners Athletics Club. Membership already exceeds 2 000 and Josaya is hoping to increase the club's annual Comrades contingent.

All families suffer losses from time to time. The Comrades family is no ordinary one. It boasts many members yet enjoys a special intimacy among all of its members, even between those who have never met. In the build-up to the 2010 race, a few significant members of this exclusive (yet intrinsically inclusive) family made their final departure.

Allison West had served on the CMA executive for 19 years and remains its only female chairperson. Dave Spence was best known to Western Cape runners, although his influence spread throughout the country. He was an accomplished coach whose expertise stretched from sprints (including national record holder Johan Rossouw) to ultramarathons. In latter years, he was known as the 'Old Mutual Two Oceans Virtual Coach'. George Koertzen was a fun person – a delightful companion, always humorous and optimistic. At the same time, he was a serious and dedicated supporter of the sport. George was an integral part of the Gauteng road-running community. He was only 52.

Comrades runner and Western Province rugby player Frederik van Zyl Slabbert ('Van' to his friends) was an exceptional man. A gifted academic, he was persuaded to enter politics, became leader of the opposition and enjoyed significant popularity as a charismatic and intellectual speaker. He startled the nation by walking out of Parliament on 6 February 1986, declaring the legislative body 'irrelevant'. The following year, he infuriated President P. W. Botha by leading a delegation of mainly Afrikaans-speaking intelligentsia to Dakar in Senegal to engage in talks with the banned ANC. Slabbert was ahead of his time and became a highly controversial figure. Hindsight enables us to acknowledge that this Celtic Harriers runner played a pioneering role in the political process that would provide the country with real hope and international respectability.

Slabbert would have been dismayed to learn of the sad demise of the superb Lesotho athlete Gabashane Vincent Rakabaele. Early in 2010, word spread around the road-running community to the effect that Rakabaele had died the previous year. Everyone was shocked. How could the death of the great man pass unnoticed for so long? Then the news worsened. He hadn't died in 2009. His grave had been found in 2009. In fact, Rakabaele had died in 2003.

The year of 1976 will always be associated with Rakabaele. Although apartheid still ruled the land, its iron grip was loosening and people of colour were able to compete officially in major road races at last. In a breathtaking climax, Rakabaele just managed to pip Alan Robb by six seconds to win the 1976 Two Oceans Marathon in a record time of 3.18.05. It was the first ultramarathon victory by a black runner. A few weeks later, he became Comrades' first black gold medallist. An enigmatic individual, Rakabaele was as likely to pulverise all opposition, as he did once again in the 1979 Two Oceans, as he was to fail to arrive at the start.

A familiar sight in the 1970s was that of Rakabaele tucked in behind his great rival, Alan Robb. A stunned Robb expressed his sadness when he poignantly commented: 'Everybody just assumed he'd gone back to Lesotho. It's what happened to a lot of good black runners from those years, guys like Johannes Thobejane. I don't know why, but they all seemed to disappear and no one kept in touch.'

While some Comrades stalwarts have left, others have remained, including a few from early days. In late April, I enjoyed the privilege of meeting my predecessor as Comrades historian, Morris Alexander, now 91 years old, along with his charming wife Huibrecht (Huibie). I was accompanied by Don Oliver, a well-known coach and inspirational speaker, and Jonathan Basckin, professional photographer, internationally acclaimed architect and entrepreneur of note. It was a special occasion. Morris, recovering from a bout of pneumonia that had hospitalised him for a while, demonstrated his Comrades spirit and strength by moving furniture around to accommodate his guests. His mind remains exceptionally sharp, and he recounted wonderful stories of the early days. He made it clear that he still spends Comrades day glued to his television set.

Clockmaker Leon van Wyk was significantly instrumental in tracing Morris and other great names from the past. Morris appears to be the only surviving Comrades runner from before the Second World War. Who, then, is the oldest living winner? That distinction belongs to George Claassen, winner of the 1961 'down' run. Claassen, now 93 years old, lives with his son Danie on the western outskirts of Cape Town. Another son, Wynand, is a green-number holder who captained the Springboks on their 'demo' tour to New Zealand in 1981.

One other question remains. Who is the oldest person alive who has successfully completed the Comrades Marathon? A lot of effort went into this investigation. The result surprised a close relative with very strong connections. Tom Wallet, now 94 years old and living in Australia, ran one Comrades Marathon. In 1955, he completed the 'down' run, in the colours of Durban Athletic Club, in 10.04.24. His nephew, Mike Bath, is the recently retired curator of the Comrades Museum.

Could any major sporting event in South Africa take place without some political interference? It would appear unlikely. Thankfully, Athletics South Africa had become so discredited that it was, to all intents and purposes, quite irrelevant. Nevertheless, a public spat between administrator Ray Mali and champion marathon runner Hendrick Ramaala did capture headlines just weeks before the 2010 race. Fortunately, Comrades was away from, and decidedly above, such distasteful diversions.

One thing Comrades could not avoid, and did not want to avoid, was football. This was World Cup year, and Comrades embraced the occasion with wholehearted enthusiasm. The Comrades Marathon Association offered a special carrot to prospective entrants: a special race medal commemorating the 85th running of the Comrades and the holding of the FIFA World Cup in South Africa. The association also announced that the 2010 race would be another 'down' run, meaning that there would be two such runs in succession.

The Comrades Marathon Association caught the mood of the country perfectly and runners responded. Over 20 000 entries were received. Bruce Fordyce, as eloquent a speaker as South African sport has produced, was commissioned by South African Breweries to give a series of talks aimed at inspiring the nation to embrace the 2010 FIFA World Cup. Fordyce, in collaboration with writer Gus Silber, entertained his audiences with his own brand of humour while promoting the combination of football and Comrades.

Just 11 days before the World Cup was due to kick off, a massive crowd of runners assembled outside Pietermaritzburg's stately city hall. Their target was to reach Kingsmead Stadium in Durban within the time allotted to them and in accordance with their own pre-set plans. The weather was perfect. Everything was in their favour.

It can arguably be claimed that no previous field of ultra-athletes had ever been pampered to the same extent as the 2010 Comrades runners. The logistics were staggering. No fewer than 46 refreshment stations were positioned en route. Each station was manned by, on average, 75 workers. Running is thirsty work: in order to assuage thirst, 1 000 000 plastic bottles, 1 900 000 water sachets, 600 000 energy sachets, 105 000 litres of cola and 72 litres of cream soda were available. For the hungry, there were 6 000 kilograms of potatoes and 650 kilograms of biscuits. It's no wonder that the entry was so large. It was a party all the way. Well, not quite – there was a fair amount of work to be done.

The final entry comprised 17 972 male and 5 553 female athletes. It was a rather mature field, with average ages of 42 for the males and 40 for the females. Forty-three countries were represented, as against the 32 contesting the World Cup. Among the runners were 15 actors, 360 television personalities, nine taxi drivers (hopefully, this was their day off), 68 psychologists, five politicians, five judges, 12 game rangers, 381 doctors, nine authors and one Manchester United supporter.

As ever, the start was impeccably organised and the massive gathering gradually wound its way through the dark of Pietermaritzburg as it commenced its long journey to the sea. The national anthem, Shosholoza and *Chariots of Fire* had punctuated the build-up to the start. Polly Shortts brought a reminder of the dual celebration. Vuvuzelas trumpeted another type of culture that the world would soon get to know.

Gilbert Mutandiro claimed an early, but short-lived, lead. Among the lead group after ten kilometres were Professor Mollen and Teacher Motendo. Despite their names, they had a lot to learn about race tactics. At the Dardanelles turn-off after 1.07.30, it was clear that last year's front-runner, Charles Tjiane, had again thrown down the gauntlet. Would history repeat itself?

Novice Wellington Chidodo led the way through Camperdown. It was noticeable that many, although not all, of the leaders selfishly discarded their tops on the road with no concern for those behind as the day began to warm. Fortunately, feeding station attendants cleared the way. At Cato Ridge, Michael Ngaseke, another novice, was second with Samuel Pazanga third. Tjiane was sixth at this stage.

Chidodo was still ahead after 45 kilometres, but this soon changed. Tjiane swept past and led the field past Alverstone Tower. Thenceforth, the race became virtually a repeat of the previous year, except for the absence of Leonid Shvetsov. On the ascent to Botha's Hill Village, Tjiane was nine minutes ahead of the chasing pack: a quartet comprising Claude Mashiywa, Bethuel Netshifhefhe, Fanie Matshipa and defending champion Stephen Muzhingi. Tjiane's lead should have been decisive, but his pace was suicidal.

Tjiane walked just before Kearsney College, a sure sign that his race was over. With about 27 kilometres to go, Mashiywa and Matshipa passed Tjiane, with Muzhingi a few hundred metres adrift. Mashiywa dropped Matshipa and powered down Field's Hill. As he had done the previous year, Muzhingi paced his race to perfection. In Pinetown, he went on the attack. On the steep ascent of Cowies, he took the lead. By Westville, the race was over. Stephen Muzhingi recorded his second straight victory in 5.29.01. This time, his wife Erina and 13-month-old son Methan were at the finish to greet him.

Ludwick Mamabolo came second. Third place provided an unwanted and hugely disappointing setback. Sergio Motsoeneng was the third runner to cross the line. Television commentators and sports writers were overjoyed and glowingly praised him for having overcome his past shame. In 1999, he had been disqualified after cheating by surreptitiously running in relay with his brother Arnold. Now, or so it seemed at first, he had wiped the slate clean. His comments after this year's race seemed humble and apologetic:

'It's been a long time now and I have come through a tough time in life. I'd rather not talk about it as it's in the past. I know I should not have done that. I was a young man then and, when the idea was thrown at me, I went with the flow. It's now history. I'm a family man now and I'm a grown man at 33. I realise that one makes mistakes in life. I came through a tough five-year period of suspension and want to look ahead. I knew this would crop up again when I got close to winning the race. It has come back to haunt me but I appeal to all to leave it at that. It's really the past. It's finished and I look ahead all the time.'

Motsoeneng's contrition was convincing and quite heart-rending. Then came the results of the post-race drug testing, with the chilling announcement: 'Sergio Motsoeneng, the third-placed finisher at this year's Comrades Marathon, has been disqualified after failing a doping test – 11 years after he was disqualified for cheating.'

While the men's race had shown marked similarities to that of the previous year, the women's event was virtually a carbon copy of 2009. The Nurgalieva twins, Elena and Olesya, were simply in a class of their own. At the Dardanelles turn-off, they enjoyed a lead of three minutes. At halfway, they were 14 minutes ahead of their compatriot Marina Myshlianova. At one stage, there was speculation about a possible assault on Frith van der Merwe's long-standing record of 5.54.23. It was not to be. Elena's winning time of 6.13.04 was just a second ahead of that of Olesya, with third-placed Myshlianova 13 minutes behind.

Elena's post-race comment was almost as predictable as the race itself: 'Today I was the stronger one, so I won. We were very fast in the first half but someone told us we had more than a ten-minute lead, so we slowed down a bit.' Ever-reliable Farwa Mentoor was the first South African, but over 25 minutes behind the winner. Locals continue to ask, 'Where is Frith's successor?'

The 2010 Comrades Marathon was a huge success and yet another feather in the cap of the Comrades Marathon Association. Over the years, Comrades has demonstrated its special value to the nation. Numerous obstacles have been overcome, and Comrades stands out as a beacon of positivity embracing all communities in the Rainbow Nation.

Internationally, Comrades has long been regarded as the world's premier ultramarathon. Official recognition came after the 2010 event, when it was announced that the successful finish of 14 343 runners had been accepted as a Guinness World Record. As the event has expanded, Comrades Marathon ambassadors have been appointed in various countries. By 2010, there were 12 such ambassadors: Mark Bloomfield (USA), Bruce Hargreaves (Australia), Marie Barreau (France), Nato Amaral (Brazil), Sandy Kondo (Japan), Amit Sheth (India), Andrea Moritz (Canada), Klaus Neumann (Germany), Hans Koeleman (Netherlands), Don Mellor (Scotland), Christian Madsen (Scandinavia) and David Marsh (United Kingdom). Brazil's Nato Amaral completed his ninth Comrades in 2010 while on honeymoon, and promised to return and earn his green number in 2011.

Of course, there are those whose experience isn't quite as easy as that of others. This year's 'fall guy' was a popular television actor by the name of David Vlok. His erstwhile friend Bruce Fordyce recounted Vlok's 2010 tale of woe:

'David was in Durban to celebrate what should have been an extremely proud occasion; the running of his 20th Comrades and the award of a coveted double green number. He spent the night before the race at Durban's famous Elangeni Hotel. He knew he would have to wake especially early to join dozens of others for the long bus ride to the start at the Pietermaritzburg City Hall the next morning. But he wasn't concerned. The general hustle and bustle of runners waking up all over the hotel would ensure that he woke well in time.

'David woke to the sound of his phone ringing. He had to get out of bed to sleepily answer it. It was his girlfriend Candice phoning. "My darling," she said, "I know that you are in the bus driving to Pietermaritzburg now, and I wanted to wish you luck and to remind you, Shnookums, that I'll be thinking of you all day."

'In a millionth of a nanosecond David was wide awake as a giant surge of superheated adrenalin surged through his veins. It was 4:45 am and he wasn't on any bus. The race was due to start in 45 minutes, and he was standing naked in his hotel room 90 kilometres from the Comrades start line on the most important racing morning of his life. David screamed down the phone to a poor night-duty clerk at reception, "I don't care about the cost, get me a hotel car now and get me to Pietermaritzburg."

'Things began to get worse. There was no car available to drive him to the start. Cowering behind the counter the terrified receptionist explained apologetically, "All our cars are driving to Pietermaritzburg taking runners to the start of the Comrades, sir." David sprinted out into the street and to his immense relief found a sleeping taxi driver slumped over the steering wheel of a wreck of a taxi. Banging on the side window he woke the slumbering driver and demanded, "How much to drive me to Pietermaritzburg … now?" "R800!"

'The wreck of a taxi lurched into gear and trundled off towards a very distant Pietermaritzburg. Even though it was a wreck and had no lights, neither to see by nor to read the instrument panel, David began to calm down. It would be all right, he reasoned. He would be late, but not desperately late. But David's nightmare was about to get much worse.

'A pink glow tinged the horizon as the taxi rattled its painstaking way towards Pietermaritzburg. Suddenly the rattle became a shaking, then a spluttering and then the taxi shuddered to a halt. It had run out of petrol. David was going to be running a lot further than he had anticipated that day. Grabbing an empty can he sprinted the two kilometres to the petrol station they had just recently passed. Then he sprinted back with the fuel. At last Pietermaritzburg hove into view.

'David began his second hard run of the day, another two-and-a-half-kilometre sprint to the start line. He had to get there to run over the special mat to ensure that his race chip recorded that he had started. But as he arrived at the start line, the Comrades officials had just finished rolling up the mat. A young lady spectator offered to take his photograph as David stood under the start banner. Her photograph recorded that he was starting half an hour late. As he set off on his journey to Durban and in pursuit of the 20 000 runners ahead of him, an official leapt into the road. "David Vlok," he shouted officiously, "I am disqualifying you for a late start."

'The few remaining spectators begged the official to allow him to run and urged David to go. He set off with the official pursuing him, still shouting that he was disqualified. Despairingly, as he ran down the road to Durban, David turned to the official and said, "Listen, mate, I'm running to Durban. Are you going to chase me all the way there?" The official abandoned his pursuit and David set off in the dark.

'And then finally David Vlok's luck changed and his nightmare began to end. A lone traffic officer spied him wandering lost and alone and gave him a police escort until he had caught the tail end of the Comrades field. Accompanied by a flashing blue light and wailing siren for nearly an hour, David almost experienced the thrilling sensation of leading the Comrades marathon. In reality he was stone last for all that time.

'His Comrades ended 11 hours and 13 minutes after the official starting gun, so he probably ran the race in about 10.40. As he finished Comrades, officials were there to greet him, hand him a medal and, inform him that he was indeed an official finisher. Later it was an honour and privilege for me to be asked to present him with his double green permanent number, 2575, for successfully completing his 20th Comrades. It will forever be remembered as one of the most memorable runs in the history of the race. I've been chuckling about it ever since.'

The contribution of Bruce Fordyce inspires a familiar debate, a question that Comrades followers love to discuss. Who is the greatest Comrades runner of all? With the centenary of the first race a mere decade away, perhaps it is time to address the issue objectively.

What are the criteria that one should consider? Obviously, only champions can be considered. Multiple winners have a significant advantage, as do record-breakers. Consistency over a number of years must count. Outright speed versus longevity is a matter of contention. After 90 years, one would imagine that certain athletes have produced startling and/or regular performances that lay claim to special recognition.

Comrades statistics reveal several significant contenders. There are the major multiple winners: Arthur Newton, Hardy Ballington, Wally Hayward, Jackie Mekler, Alan Robb and Bruce Fordyce. Andrew Kelehe has set an unparalleled record of ten straight golds. The Nurgalieva twins have utterly dominated the women's race in recent years. Alan Robb's 1978 down record of 5.29.14 remains an awesome example of power running. Frith van der Merwe's 5.54.43 in 1989 puts her in a class of her own. Leonid Shvetsov's consecutive record-breaking runs in 2007 and 2008 put him at the top of the current leaderboard, although allegations of doping from as early as 1996, published in *Runner's World* in the USA in December 2010, raise serious questions about his achievements.

When all claims have been considered and analysed, two individuals stand supreme. Wally Hayward won the 1930 race at the age of 21. After a break of two decades, he returned and achieved four victories in the 1950s, including the first sub-six-hour run. Almost miraculously, he came back again and beat half the field a few weeks before his 80th birthday.

Bruce Fordyce dominated Comrades in the 1980s, winning nine times from nine starts. The second-highest victory tally is five. Fordyce broke the record on five occasions. His record of 5.24.07 for the 'down' run, set in 1986, remained intact for over 20 years, longer than any other.

Hayward maintained that Fordyce was the greatest Comrades champion of all. Fordyce is adamant that the accolade belongs to Hayward. Who can argue with these two super-athletes? In our recent discussion, Morris Alexander and I were unable to separate the pair. It seems logical to acknowledge Fordyce and Hayward jointly as Comrades' greatest ever champions.

Well, maybe Frith?

2010 COMRADES MARATHON RESULTS

1. Stephen Muzhingi   5.29.01
2. Ludwick Mamabolo   5.35.29
3. Bongmusa Mthembu   5.37.49
4. Fanie Matshipa   5.39.53
5. Fusi Nhlapo   5.40.26

6. Claude Moshiywa	5.43.04
7. Petros Sosibo	5.45.58
8. Peter Molapo	5.46.19
9. Leboka Noto	5.48.45
10. Peter Muthubi	5.49.10

2010 COMRADES BOWL RESULTS

1. Elena Nurgalieva	6.13.04
2. Olesya Nurgalieva	6.13.05
3. Marina Myshlianova	6.26.03
4. Kami Semick	6.32.55
5. Farwa Mentoor	6.38.41
6. Lizzy Hawker	6.39.43
7. Irina Vishnevskaya	6.44.27
8. Lindsay van Aswegen	6.46.52
9. Adinda Kruger	6.51.15
10. Anna Pichtova	6.51.34

SOURCES

Alexander, Morris: *The Comrades Marathon Story, 3rd Edition*: Delta Books, Johannesburg. 1985

Cameron-Dow, John: *Bruce Fordyce Comrades King*: Guide Book Publications, Johannesburg. 2001

Cameron-Dow, John: *A Newspaper History of South Africa*: Don Nelson Publishers, Cape Town. 2007

Cameron-Dow, John: *The Two Oceans Marathon Story, 2nd Edition*: Don Nelson Publishers, Cape Town. 1997

Cottrell, Tom: *Comrades Marathon Highlights and Heroes*: Jonathan Ball Publishers (Pty) Ltd and Guide Book Publications, Johannesburg. 2000

Cottrell, Tom: *Comrades Marathon Yearbook*: Southern Book Publishers (Pty) Ltd, Johannesburg. 1998

Fordyce, Bruce and Renssen, Mariëlle: *Marathon Runner's Handbook*: Struik Publishers, Cape Town. 2002

Fordyce, Bruce: *Run the Comrades*: Delta Books, Johannesburg. 1996

Greyvenstein, Chris: *Springbok Rugby: An Illustrated History*: Sable Media (Ltd), Cape Town. 1995

Hauman, Riël: *Century of the Marathon*: Human & Rousseau (Pty) Ltd, Cape Town. 1996

Hayward, Wally – compiled by Jamieson, W. M. (Bill): *Just Call Me Wally*: Penprint, Durban. 1999

Noakes, Tim: *Lore of Running, 4th Edition*: Oxford University Press, Cape Town. 2001

Reader's Digest: *Illustrated History of South Africa: The Real Story, 3rd Edition*: Reader's Digest, Cape Town. 1994

Sunday Times: A Century of Sundays: Zebra Press, Cape Town. 2006

Sunday Times: The Miracle of A Freed Nation: Don Nelson Publishers, Cape Town. 1994

COMRADES MARATHON TROPHY WINNERS

Men Positions One to Three

Year	The Comrades Marathon First Place Trophy		The Anderson Trophy Second Place		The T C McCullagh Trophy Third Place	
1921	Bill Rowan	08:59:00	Harry Phillips	09:40:00	John Annan	10:10:00
1922	Arthur Newton	08:40:00	Harry Phillips	09:09:00	Bill Rowan	09:13:00
1923	Arthur Newton	06:56:07	Lukas Nel	07:48:24	Butcher Purcell	08:17:03
1924	Arthur Newton	06:58:22	Percy Shackleford	08:13:00	Charles Strassburg	08:48:23
1925	Arthur Newton	06:24:45	Harry Phillips	07:05:30	Percy Shackleford	07:17:22
1926	Harry Phillips	06:57:46	Arthur Newton	07:02:00	Ron Sutton	08:09:00
1927	Arthur Newton	06:40:56	Frank Sutton	07:15:55	Winston Sutton	07:52:06
1928	Frank Sutton	07:49:07	Ron Sutton	07:57:17	Felix Henricksen	08:19:12
1929	Darrell Dale	07:52:01	Fred Wallace	08:10:17	Albert Marie	08:17:31
1930	Wally Hayward	07:27:26	Phil Masterton-Smith	07:28:03	Frank Munnery	07:39:30
1931	Phil Masterton-Smith	07:16:30	Noel Burree	07:16:32	Wessel Strydom	07:32:20
1932	William Savage	07:41:58	Lionel Knight	07:50:54	Bill Cochrane	07:57:46
1933	Hardy Ballington	06:50:37	Bill Cochrane	07:11:21	Lionel Knight	07:16:00
1934	Hardy Ballington	07:09:03	Bill Cochrane	07:24:41	Ivor Luke	07:44:39
1935	Bill Cochrane	06:30:05	Hardy Ballington	06:31:56	Johnny Coleman	06:55:20
1936	Hardy Ballington	06:46:14	Arthur Reeve	07:50:53	Liege Boulle	07:51:08
1937	Johnny Coleman	06:23:11	Allen Boyce	06:40:19	Fred Wallace	06:41:47
1938	Hardy Ballington	06:32:26	Allen Boyce	07:03:05	Fred Morrison	07:38:57
1939	Johnny Coleman	06:22:05	Allen Boyce	06:26:34	John Ballington	07:28:01
1940	Allen Boyce	06:39:23	Dymock Parr	08:29:51	Gordon Morrison	08:55:21
1946	Bill Cochrane	07:02:40	Dymock Parr	08:00:27	Bill Rufus	08:27:06
1947	Hardy Ballington	06:41:05	Reg Allison	07:23:30	Eddie Hofmeyr	07:42:17
1948	William Savage	07:13:52	Reg Allison	07:35:55	George Burdett	07:42:06
1949	Reg Allison	06:23:21	John Ballington	06:52:54	Allan Ferguson	07:02:52
1950	Wally Hayward	06:46:25	Reg Allison	06:59:35	Trevor Allen	07:32:37
1951	Wally Hayward	06:14:08	Reg Allison	06:38:40	Trevor Allen	07:00:15
1952	Trevor Allen	07:00:02	Don Spencer	07:06:17	Gerald Walsh	07:07:23
1953	Wally Hayward	05:52:30	Sid Luyt	06:05:08	Trevor Allen	06:28:15
1954	Wally Hayward	06:12:55	Trevor Allen	06:45:14	Gerald Walsh	06:58:38
1955	Gerald Walsh	06:06:32	Frans Mare	06:18:34	Trevor Allen	06:24:13
1956	Gerald Walsh	06:33:35	Allen Boyce	07:12:08	Mercer Davies	07:14:10
1957	Mercer Davies	06:13:55	Gerald Walsh	06:26:33	Frans Mare	06:46:15
1958	Jackie Mekler	06:26:26	Andy Greening	07:11:49	Nick Raubenheimer	07:23:40

1959	Trevor Allen	06:28:11	Gerald Walsh	06:33:33	Jackie Mekler	06:35:52
1960	Jackie Mekler	05:56:32	Gerald Walsh	06:31:07	George Claassen	06:37:07
1961	George Claassen	06:07:07	Frikkie Steyn	06:09:05	Trevor Allen	06:22:49
1962	John Smith	05:57:05	Jackie Mekler	06:04:04	Don Turner	06:07:08
1963	Jackie Mekler	05:51:20	Pieter De Villiers	05:58:45	Fritz Madel	06:08:05
1964	Jackie Mekler	06:09:54	Manie Kuhn	06:19:37	Charlie Chase	06:36:19
1965	Bernard Gomersall	05:51:09	Jackie Mekler	05:56:19	Manie Kuhn	06:04:24
1966	Tommy Malone	06:14:07	Manie Kuhn	06:31:46	Fritz Madel	06:33:45
1967	Manie Kuhn	05:54:10	Tommy Malone	05:54:11	Gordon Baker	06:02:32
1968	Jackie Mekler	06:01:11	Manie Kuhn	06:03:54	Gordon Baker	06:11:33
1969	Dave Bagshaw	05:45:35	Dave Box	05:57:57	Jackie Mekler	06:01:30
1970	Dave Bagshaw	05:51:27	Dave Box	05:58:07	Twerrie Rencken	06:10:11
1971	Dave Bagshaw	05:47:06	Dave Levick	05:48:53	Gordon Baker	05:57:26
1972	Mick Orton	05:48:57	Dave Bagshaw	05:53:54	Dave Box	05:59:59
1973	Dave Levick	05:39:09	Gordon Baker	05:42:53	John Mc Brearty	05:46:18
1974	Derek Preiss	06:02:49	Koos Sutherland	06:04:25	Alan Robb	06:06:45
1975	Derek Preiss	05:53:00	Gordon Shaw	06:03:15	Koos Sutherland	06:06:40
1976	Alan Robb	05:40:43	Cavin Woodward	05:49:00	Dave Rogers	05:52:00
1977	Alan Robb	05:47:00	Steve Atkins	05:57:00	Dave Wright	05:58:00
1978	Alan Robb	05:29:14	Dave Wright	05:48:00	Anton De Koning	05:49:00
1979	Piet Vorster	05:45:02	Johnny Halberstadt	05:50:30	Bruce Fordyce	05:51:15
1980	Alan Robb	05:38:25	Bruce Fordyce	05:40:31	Malcolm Ball	05:40:45
1981	Bruce Fordyce	05:37:28	Johnny Halberstadt	05:46:00	Tony Abbott	05:52:41
1982	Bruce Fordyce	05:34:22	Alan Robb	05:41:26	Graeme Fraser	05:41:55
1983	Bruce Fordyce	05:30:12	Gordon Shaw	05:45:48	Graeme Fraser	05:46:20
1984	Bruce Fordyce	05:27:18	Bob De La Motte	05:30:59	Chris Reyneke	05:34:39
1985	Bruce Fordyce	05:37:01	Hoseah Tjale	05:42:40	Derrick Tivers	05:53:53
1986	Bruce Fordyce	05:24:07	Bob De La Motte	05:26:12	Hoseah Tjale	05:29:02
1987	Bruce Fordyce	05:37:01	Bob De La Motte	05:43:38	Hoseah Tjale	05:44:42
1988	Bruce Fordyce	05:27:42	Mark Page	05:38:28	Nick Bester	05:39:00
1989	Samuel Tshabalala	05:35:51	Willie Mtolo	05:39:59	Jean-Marc Bellocq	05:42:28
1990	Bruce Fordyce	05:40:25	Hoseah Tjale	05:45:19	Meshack Radebe	05:45:40
1991	Nick Bester	05:40:53	Shaun Meiklejohn	05:43:55	Colin Thomas	05:45:13
1992	Jetman Mosotho	05:46:11	Mark Page	05:48:58	Shaun Meiklejohn	05:49:37
1993	Charly Doll	05:39:41	Theophilus Rafiri	05:42:16	Mahlala Mohloli	05:42:41
1994	Alberto Salazar	05:38:39	Nick Bester	05:42:52	Mahlala Mohloli	05:43:15
1995	Shaun Meiklejohn	05:34:02	Charl Mattheus	05:35:01	Alexei Volgin	05:40:38
1996	Dmitri Grishine	05:29:33	Nick Bester	05:30:48	Alexei Volgin	05:32:21
1997	Charl Mattheus	05:28:37	Nick Bester	05:30:41	Jaroslaw Janicki	05:32:50

1998	Dmitri Grishine	05:26:25	Charl Mattheus	05:31:32	Alexei Volgin	05:33:57
1999	Jaroslaw Janicki	05:30:11	Andrew Kelehe	05:32:42	Lucas Matlala	05:33:30
2000	Vladimir Kotov	05:25:33	Alexei Volgin	05:27:07	Dmitri Grishine	05:32:47
2001	Andrew Kelehe	05:25:51	Leonid Shvetsov	05:26:28	Vladimir Kotov	05:27:21
2002	Vladimir Kotov	05:30:59	Willie Mtolo	05:33:35	Jorge Aubeso Martinez	05:33:37
2003	Fusi Nhlapo	05:28:52	Oleg Kharitonov	05:31:41	Joseph Molaba	05:31:54
2004	Vladimir Kotov	05:31:22	Jaroslaw Janicki	05:34:17	Oleg Kharitonov	05:39:08
2005	Sipho Ngomane	05:27:10	Oleg Kharitonov	05:29:15	Andrew Kelehe	05:31:44
2006	Oleg Kharitonov	05:35:19	Brian Zondi	05:37:32	Vladmir Kotov	05:40:56
2007	Leonid Shvetsov	05:20:41	Grigory Murzin	05:30:12	Mncedisi Mkhize	05:32:50
2008	Leonid Shvetsov	05:24:47	Jaroslaw Janicki	05:38:29	Stephen Muzhingi	05:39:40
2009	Stephen Muzhingi	05:23:27	Leonid Shvetsov	05:33:10	Charles Tjiane	05:34:21
2010	Stephen Muzhingi	05:29:01	Ludwick Mamabolo	05:35:29	Bongmusa Mthembu	05:37:49

Women Positions One to Three

Year	The Comrades Bowl First Place		The City of Pietermaritzburg Trophy Second Place		The City of Durban Trophy Third Place	
1976	Lettie Van Zyl	09:05:00	Alet Ten Tusscher	09:35:00	Lynn Oberholzer	09:53:00
1977	Lettie Van Zyl	08.58.00	Thea Claassen	09:18:00	Marie-Jeanne Duyvejonck-Dick	09:51:00
1978	Lettie Van Zyl	08:25:00	Sue Wagner	08:43:00	Joan Clark	08:53:00
1979	Jan Mallen	08:22:41	Moira Hornby	08:29:10	Lettie Van Zyl	08:32:55
1980	Isavel Roche-Kelly	07:18:00	Cheryl Winn	07:22:00	Ralie Smit	07:50:00
1981	Isavel Roche-Kelly	06:44:35	Cheryl Winn	07:21:55	Ralie Smit	07:46:34
1982	Cheryl Winn	07:04:59	Lise Warren	07:52:26	Ralie Smit	08:01:16
1983	Lindsay Weight	07:12:56	Jenny Wilson	07:23:45	Gail Ingram	07:27:00
1984	Lindsay Weight	06:46:35	Priscilla Carlisle	07:15:32	Gail Ingram	07:15:51
1985	Helen Lucre	06:53:24	Lindsay Weight	07:01:23	Priscilla Carlisle	07:24:07
1986	Helen Lucre	06:55:01	Ralie Smit	07:07:40	Lettie Greeff	07:14:49
1987	Helen Lucre	06:48:42	Lindsay Weight	06:58:44	Ralie Smit	07:01:13
1988	Frith Van Der Merwe	06:32:56	Lettie Greeff	07:04:00	Helen Lucre	07:07:50
1989	Frith Van Der Merwe	05:54:43	Valerie Bleazard	06:56:08	Naidene Harrison	07:00:09
1990	Naidene Harrison	07:02:00	Annette Schoeman	07:07:35	Diana Terreblanche	07:09:42
1991	Frith Van Der Merwe	06:08:19	Heleen Reece	06:54:17	Tilda Tearle	06:55:01

1992	Frances Van Blerk	06:51:05	Tilda Tearle	07:07:44	Susan Deetlefs	07:11:25
1993	Tilda Tearle	06:55:07	Rae Bisschoff	07:00:30	Berna Daly	07:03:32
1994	Valentina Liakhova	06:41:23	Valentina Shatyayeva	06:45:49	Martha Vass	06:51:04
1995	Maria Bak	06:22:45	Helene Joubert	06:34:04	Valentina Shatyayeva	06:42:21
1996	Ann Trason	06:13:23	Maria Bak	06:24:08	Valentina Shatyayeva	06:30:33
1997	Ann Trason	05:58:25	Maria Bak	06:00:28	Valentina Liakhova	06:22:59
1998	Rae Bisschoff	06:38:57	Valentina Liakhova	06:39:16	Valentina Shatyayeva	06:44:13
1999	Birgit Lennartz	06:31:03	Grace De Oliveira	06:34:53	Marina Bychkova	06:36:34
2000	Maria Bak	06:15:35	Birgit Lennartz	06:33:54	Grace De Oliveira	06:38:44
2001	Elvira Kolpakova	06:13:53	Deborah Mattheus	06:23:04	Marina Bychkova	06:24:20
2002	Maria Bak	06:14:21	Natalia Volgina	06:17:26	Marina Bychkova	06:24:23
2003	Elena Nurgalieva	06:07:46	Olesya Nurgalieva	06:12:07	Tatyana Zhirkova	06:17:50
2004	Elena Nurgalieva	06:11:15	Marina Bychkova	06:14:13	Farwa Mentoor	06:18:23
2005	Tatyana Zhirkova	05:58:50	Olesya Nurgalieva	06:10:39	Elena Nurgalieva	06:12:18
2006	Elena Nurgalieva	06:09:24	Marina Bychkova	06:12:58	Tatyana Zhirkova	06:27:21
2007	Olesya Nurgalieva	06:10:03	Elena Nurgalieva	06:10:32	Madina Biktigirova	06:21:55
2008	Elena Nurgalieva	06:14:37	Olesya Nurgalieva	06:15:52	Tatyana Zhirkova	06:17:45
2009	Olesya Nurgalieva	06:12:12	Elena Nurgalieva	06:13:14	Tatyana Zhirkova	06:15:03
2010	Elena Nurgalieva	06:13:04	Olesya Nurgalieva	06:13:05	Marina Myslyanova	06:26:03

Hardy Ballington Trophy: Awarded to the first novice finisher

Year	Name	Time	Overall Pos.
1938	Fred Morrison	07:38:57	3
1939	Willie Amron	08:22:59	8
1940	Gordon Morrison	08:55:21	3
1946	Reg Allison	08:55:35	5
1947	Eddie Hofmeyer	07:42:17	3
1948	George Burdett	07:42:06	3
1949	Fritz Von Hell	07:31:12	6
1950	Brian Danckwerts	08:20:40	8
1951	Arthur Hampton	07:20:13	5
1952	Jackie Mekler	07:45:03	7
1953	Syd Luyt	06:05:08	2
1954	Jackie Goldie	08:06:14	8
1955	David Dodds	06:25:15	4
1956	Trig Wang	08:47:43	14
1957	Clive Crawley	08:02:30	15
1958	Denis Stephenson	07:36:08	6
1959	Trevor Haynes	06:49:22	6
1960	George Claassen	06:34:07	3
1961	Tim Blankley	07:21:04	11
1962	John Smith	05:57:05	1
1963	Pieter de Villiers	05:58:45	2
1964	Frank Pearce	06:49:31	5
1965	Bernard Gomersall	05:51:09	1
1966	Tommy Malone	06:14:07	1
1967	Gordon Baker	06:02:32	3
1968	Bob Orchard	07:02:40	19
1969	Dave Bagshaw	05:45:35	1
1970	Dave Levick	06:34:12	8
1971	Donald Carter-Brown	06:21:13	16
1972	Mick Orton	05:48:57	1
1973	John Mcbrearty	05:46:18	3
1974	Alan Robb	06:06:45	3
1975	Dewald Steyn	06:26:00	16
1976	Cavin Woodward	05:49:19	2
1977	Kassim Isman	06:24:00	15
1978	Trompie Strydom	05:54:14	5
1979	Johnny Halberstadt	05:50:30	2
1980	Tammy Bilibana	05:56:49	9
1981	Danny Biggs	05:54:08	5
1982	Brian Dinkleman	06:20:36	30
1983	Malcolm Don-Wauchope	06:25:04	45
1984	Kevin Shaw	05:51:56	10
1985	Siphiwe Gqele	06:04:40	12
1986	Stephen Seema	05:54:34	13
1987	Joshiah Sangweni	06:05:22	16
1988	Mark Page	05:38:28	2
1989	Jean-Marc Bellocq	05:42:28	3
1990	Meshack Radebe	05:45:40	3
1991	Simon Tshabalala	05:53:17	9
1992	Zephania Ndaba	05:54:08	9
1993	Charly Doll	05:39:41	1
1994	Alberto Salazar	05:38:39	1
1995	Alexei Volgin	05:40:38	3
1996	Dmitri Grishine	05:29:33	1
1997	Zithulele Sinqe	05:33:18	4
1998	Ogor Tyupin	05:35:23	4
1999	Grigoriy Murzin	05:47:25	10
2000	Fusi Nhlapo	05:37:46	5
2001	Leonid Shvetson	05:26:28	2
2002	Jorge Aubeso Martinez	05:33:37	3
2003	Denis Zhalybin	05:41:38	9
2004	Hlonepha Mphulanyane	05:44:10	7
2005	Sipho Maisela	05:53:03	16
2006	Brian Zondi	05:37:32	2
2007	Peter Muthubi	06:07:56	32
2008	Melikhaya Sithuba	05:57:38	12
2009	Bethuel Netshifhefhe	05:43:35	9
2010	Ludwick Mamabolo	05:35:29	2

Founders Trophy: Awarded to the oldest finisher

Year	Name	Age	Time
1954	Wally Hayward	46	06:12:55
1955	Liege Boulle	46	07:26:47
1956	Ian Jardine	54	09:57:31
1957	Ian Jardine	55	09:08:03
1958	Ian Jardine	56	09:53:35

1959	Archie Archibald	53	08:33:36
1960	Ian Jardine	58	09:22:34
1961	Ian Jardine	59	08:52:19
1962	Ian Jardine	60	09:59:25
1963	Ian Jardine	61	09:00:55
1964	Ian Jardine	62	09:32:11
1965	Ian Jardine	63	08:38:40
1966	Ian Jardine	64	09:56:10
1967	Ian Jardine	65	09:30:18
1968	Ian Jardine	66	09:52:33
1969	Ian Jardine	67	09:30:16
1970	Vernon Jones	61	10:25:00
1971	Vernon Jones	62	10:41:56
1972	Vernon Jones	63	10:40:30
1973	Vernon Jones	64	10:35:00
1974	Liege Boulle	65	09:27:00
1975	Frank Hargraves	63	09:45:00
1976	Frank Hargraves	64	09:14:00
1977	Harry Curwen	64	10:46:00
1978	Harry Curwen	65	10:42:00
1979	Liege Boulle	70	10:01:49
1980	Liege Boulle	71	10:10:00
1981	Liege Boulle	72	10:12:37
1982	Liege Boulle	73	10:07:59
1983	Liege Boulle	74	10:34:38
1984	Doug Horton	69	10:15:26
1985	Gottieb Brommke	70	10:39:21
1986	Doug Horton	71	10:47:44
1987	Cliff Taylor	72	10:34:18
1988	Wally Hayward	79	09:44:15
1989	Wally Hayward	80	10:58:02
1990	Jeremiah Mnisi	74	10:02:01
1991	Ivan Coll	71	10:26:11
1992	Ivan Coll	72	10:47:22
1993	Jeremiah Mnisi	77	10:56:09
1994	Allan Ferguson	73	09:56:52
1995	Allan Ferguson	73	10:16:57
1996	Derrick Page	69	10:44:57
1997	Gert Koen	71	10:50:18
1998	Max Jones	71	10:39:42
1999	Max Jones	72	10:49:30
2000	Lucas Nel	76	11:55:40
2001	Hans Stucki	71	10:40:23
2002	Terence Kelly	73	10:53:43
2003	Zeb Luhabe	76	11:59:59
2004	Hans Stucki	74	11:15:36
2005	Ossie Kurten	74	11:50:00
2006	Ossie Kurten	75	11:49:58
2007	Martin Coetzee	75	10:58:17
2008	Norman Alderton	73	11:52:30
2009	Martin Coetzee	77	11:28:08
2010	Caspar Greeff	75	11:40:13

Gunga Din Trophy: Awarded to the winning open men's team

1931	Maritzburg United
1932	Albion Harriers
1933	Durban Athletic Club
1934	DLI & Umbilo & Cong (Tie)
1935	Durban Athletic Club
1936	Durban Athletic Club
1937	Maritzburg Harriers
1938	Durban Athletic Club
1939	Durban Athletic Club
1940	Durban Athletic Club
1947	Germiston Callies Harriers
1948	Germiston Callies Harriers
1949	Germiston Callies Harriers
1950	Collegians Harriers
1951	Collegians Harriers
1952	Durban Athletic Club
1953	Durban Athletic Club
1954	Durban Athletic Club
1955	Germiston Callies Harriers
1956	Durban Athletic Club
1957	Durban Athletic Club
1958	Durban Athletic Club
1959	Durban Athletic Club
1960	Germiston Callies Harriers
1961	Durban Athletic Club
1962	Durban Athletic Club
1963	Savages Athletic Club
1964	Durban Athletic Club

1965	Savages Athletic Club
1966	Savages Athletic Club
1967	Savages Athletic Club
1968	Savages Athletic Club
1969	Savages Athletic Club
1970	Savages Athletic Club
1971	Savages Athletic Club
1972	Tipton Harriers (Eng)
1973	Savages Athletic Club
1974	Germiston Callies Harriers
1975	Westville Athletic Club
1976	Westville Athletic Club
1977	Westville Athletic Club
1978	Germiston Callies Harriers
1979	Germiston Callies Harriers
1980	Germiston Callies Harriers
1981	Hillcrest Villages
1982	Hillcrest Villages
1983	Hillcrest Villages
1984	Rand Athletic Club
1985	Rand Athletic Club
1986	Rand Athletic Club
1987	Rand Athletic Club
1988	Rand Athletic Club
1989	Magnolia Road Runners
1990	Rand Athletic Club
1991	Spectrum Athletic Club
1992	Rand Athletic Club
1993	Rand Athletic Club
1994	University of Pretoria
1995	Gengold Harriers
1996	Gengold Harriers
1997	Voltaren Tuks
1998	Rentmeester R/Gel Athletic Club
1999	Liberty Life CG
2000	Liberty Life CG
2001	Liberty Life AC
2002	Harmony Gold GN
2003	Liberty Nike Athletic Club CG
2004	Harmony Gold GN

2005	Liberty Nike Athletic Club GN
2006	Liberty Nike Athletic Club GN
2007	Mr Price Running Club CG
2008	Mr Price Running Club CG
2009	Mr Price Running Club CG
2010	Mr Price Running Club CG

Arthur Newton Shield: Awarded to the second open men's team

1960	Durban Athletic Club
1961	Germiston Callies Harriers
1962	Savages Athletic Club
1963	Germiston Callies Harriers
1964	Germiston Callies Harriers
1965	Germiston Callies Harriers
1966	Germiston Callies Harriers
1967	Collegians Harriers
1968	Germiston Callies Harriers
1969	Germiston Callies Harriers
1970	Collegians Harriers
1971	Wits Athletic Club
1972	Savages Athletic Club
1973	Collegians Harriers
1974	Westville Athletic Club
1975	Savages Athletic Club
1976	Savages Athletic Club
1977	Collegians Harriers
1978	Durban Athletic Club
1979	Collegians Harriers
1980	Collegians Harriers
1981	Germiston Callies Harriers
1982	Germiston Callies Harriers
1983	Rand Athletic Club
1984	Germiston Callies Harriers
1985	Hillcrest Villagers
1986	Germiston Callies Harriers
1987	Magnolia Road Runners
1988	Magnolia Road Runners
1989	Hillcrest Villagers
1990	Rocky Road Runners
1991	Magnolia Road Runners

1992	Sasol Marathon Club
1993	Gengold Harriers
1994	Rocky Road Runners
1995	FITT 2000
1996	Liberty Life CG
1997	Liberty Life Athletic Club
1998	Voltaren Tuks
1999	Voltaren Tuks
2000	Rentmeester F&M GN
2001	Harmony Gold Athletic Club
2002	Liberty Nike CG
2003	Harmony Gold Athletic Club
2004	Liberty Nike athletic club GN
2005	Harmony Gold MPL
2006	Mr Price Running Club CG
2007	Harmony AC GN
2008	Nedbank Running Club CG
2009	Nedbank Running Club GN
2010	Mr Price Running Club KZN

Vic Clapham Memorial: Awarded to the winning men's veteran team

1979	Germiston Callies Harriers
1980	Collegians Harriers
1981	Germiston Callies Harriers
1982	Germiston Callies Harriers
1983	Pretoria Marathon Club
1984	Rand Athletic Club
1985	Rand Athletic Club
1986	Rand Athletic Club
1987	Rand Athletic Club
1988	Yellowwood Park
1989	Durban Athletic Club
1990	Forresters
1991	Spectrum Athletic Club
1992	Magnolia Road Runners
1993	Magnolia Road Runners
1994	Rand Athletic Club
1995	Stella Athletic Club
1996	Rand Athletic Club
1997	Rand Athletic Club
1998	Gengold Evander

1999	Liberty Life CG
2000	Liberty Life CG
2001	Rand Athletic Club
2002	Harmony Gold GN
2003	Liberty Nike Athletic Club CG
2004	Harmony Gold Athletic Club GN
2005	Harmony Gold Athletic Club GN
2006	Harmony Gold Athletic Club GN
2007	Harmony AC GN
2008	Rocky Road Runners
2009	Nedbank Running Club GN
2010	Mr Price Running Club KZN

CMA Shield: Awarded to the winning open women's team

1984	Savages Athletic Club
1985	Rand Athletic Club
1986	Rand Athletic Club
1987	Savages Athletic Club
1988	Savages Athletic Club
1989	Savages Athletic Club
1990	Rand Athletic Club
1991	Rocky Road Runners
1992	Savages Athletic Club
1993	Rand Athletic Club
1994	Rand Athletic Club
1995	Rand Athletic Club
1996	Mr Price Savages
1997	Rand Athletic Club
1998	Liberty Life GN
1999	Liberty Life GN
2000	University of Pretoria
2001	Mr Price KZN
2002	Harmony Gold GN
2003	Harmony Gold AC
2004	Harmony Gold GN
2005	Harmony Gold GN
2006	Liberty Nike Athletic Club GN
2007	Harmony AC GN
2008	Collegians Harriers
2009	Nedbank Running Club GN
2010	Nedbank Running Club GN

South African Legion Trophy: Awarded to the first veteran men

1990	JP Halberstadt	05:59:30
1991	A Lemos	05:54:46
1992	D Mponye	06:07:28
1993	D Holtzhausen	05:52:29
1994	P Camenzind	05:43:47
1995	C Matomane	06:02:28
1996	B Van Staden	06:03:02
1997	P Camenzind	05:34:47
1998	J Burger	05:51:06
1999	A Korepanov	05:38:05
2000	Vladimir Kotov	05:26:33
2001	Vladimir Kotov	05:27:21
2002	Vladimir Kotov	05:30:59
2003	Mohlala Mohloli	05:46:47
2004	Vladimir Kotov	05:31:22
2005	Andrew Kelehe	05:31:44
2006	Vladimir Kotov	05:40:56
2007	Mohlala Mohloli	05:57:56
2008	Jaroslaw Janicki	05:38:29
2009	Leonid Shvetsov	05:33:10
2010	Petros Sosibo	05:45:58

South African Legion Shield: Awarded to the first veteran women

1998	R Bisschoff	06:38:57
1999	I Sanders	06:56:20
2000	Maria Bak	06:15:35
2001	Deborah Mattheus	06:23:04
2002	Maria Bak	06:14:21
2003	Maria Bak	06:18:32
2004	Grace De Oliveria	06:46:59
2005	Grace De Oliveira	07:05:54
2006	Maria Bak	06:31:01
2007	Madina Biktigirova	06:21:55
2008	Marina Myshlyanova	06:30:49
2009	Marina Myshlyanova	06:30:42
2010	Marina Myshlyanova	06:26:03

75th Anniversary Trophy: Awarded to the winning women's veteran team

2000	University of Pretoria
2001	Durbanville Athletic Club
2002	Durbanville Athletic Club
2003	Westville Athletic Club
2004	Harmony Gold Athletic Club GN
2005	Harmony Gold Athletic Club GN
2006	Harmony Gold Athletic Club GN
2007	Westville Athletic Club
2008	Westville Athletic Club
2009	Westville Athletic Club
2010	Nedbank Running Club GN

Premiers Trophy: Awarded to the first KwaZulu-Natal man & women

Year	Men	Time
2005	Nkosi Dladla	5:52:16
2006	Mncedisi Mkhize	5:44:28
2007	Mncedisi Mkhize	05:32:50
2008	Mncedisi Mkhize	05:48:18
2009	Mncedisi Mkhize	05:41:14
2010	Bongmusa Mthembu	05:37:49

Year	Women	Time
2005	Grace De Oliveira	07:05:55
2006	Grace De Oliveira	07:24:11
2007	Grace De Oliveira	06:57:29
2008	Carol Mercer	07:09:37
2009	Kerry Koen	07:18:51
2010	Melanie van Rooyen	07:01:54